BEYOND THE EUROMAIDAN

BEYOND THE EUROMAIDAN

Comparative Perspectives on Advancing Reform in Ukraine

Edited by HENRY E. HALE
and ROBERT W. ORTTUNG

STANFORD UNIVERSITY PRESS

Stanford California

Stanford University Press
Stanford, California

Library of Congress Cataloging-in-Publication Data
Names: Hale, Henry E., editor. | Orttung, Robert W., editor.
Title: Beyond the Euromaidan : comparative perspectives on advancing
    reform in Ukraine / edited by Henry E. Hale and Robert W. Orttung.
Description: Stanford, California : Stanford University Press, 2016. |
    Includes bibliographical references and index.
Identifiers: LCCN 2016011056 (print) | LCCN 2016012449 (ebook) |
    ISBN 9780804798457 (cloth : alk. paper) | ISBN 9781503600102
Subjects: LCSH: Ukraine—Politics and government—1991– |
    Comparative government.
Classification: LCC JN6635 .B49 2016 (print) | LCC JN6635 (ebook) |
    DDC 320.9477—dc23
LC record available at http://lccn.loc.gov/2016011056

Printed in the United States of America on acid-free, archival-quality
paper. Typeset at Stanford University Press in 10/14 Minion.

Contents

List of Figures and Tables

Figures

Tables

Preface

HENRY E. HALE AND ROBERT ORTTUNG

Why has Ukraine failed to undertake the reforms necessary to become an economically developed democracy after nearly a quarter-century of independence? An analogous question could be asked of many countries that have spent long decades wallowing in corruption and political fecklessness despite great initial hopes for a brighter future. At the same time, the world does provide some success stories, countries that have managed to do a lot despite challenging starting conditions. What, then, separates the successes from the failures, and what lessons might this hold out for Ukraine and countries like it? The present volume takes up these questions, with its distinctive approach being to combine the advantages of comparative analysis with deep country knowledge by bringing a "dream team" of leading specialists on Ukraine together with leading experts on the comparative experience with reform globally.

This approach begins by identifying six areas of reform on which to focus. While we might have decided to address very specific topics, such as how to reform concrete institutions like the military or a particular ministry, we chose instead to train our attention on more fundamental challenges that Ukraine (and countries like it) must meet in order for reforms of any specific organs to have hope of succeeding.

The first such fundamental challenge is Ukraine's divided society, which some might label challenges related to political culture. Research has found that persistent political cleavages centered on identity and history have consistently structured not only electoral competition, but also political conflict and even violent insurgency. Opposition from one part of the country has regularly thwarted attempts at reform made by leaders of other parts of the country, with the thwarting coming either by election or by revolution. Ukraine is not alone in facing such problems, as many countries must deal with divides in identity and collective memory, ranging from Spain to Germany to Bangladesh. But some, notably Spain, have also experienced significant success in overcoming major cleavages en route to successful growth and democracy. Comparative analysis, then, can shed light on the potential and constraints facing Ukraine in handling this issue.

The second major challenge we address is the corruption that is so pervasive in Ukrainian society, both reflecting the weakness of and undermining the rule of law. While its exact origins are disputed, what is clear is that Ukrainian leaders' repeated proclamations of a "war on corruption" have produced little benefit. Perhaps even more disturbing is that during the years when Ukraine has experienced its most democratic forms of government, there is strong evidence that corruption actually *increased* rather than decreased (see Popova's chapter in this volume). Ukraine's problem with corruption, then, does not boil down to authoritarianism or any specific leader. Instead, it represents a deeply embedded social equilibrium that has proven extremely stubborn. And so long as this social equilibrium is not broken, it is hard to see how Ukraine can ever hope to establish a true democracy (where rights cannot be sold off to the highest bidder) or even a developed market economy (which depends on a rule of law capable of lending confidence to investors and those who would make the deals necessary for production). Clearly, Ukraine is not the only corrupt country in the world, being firmly in the company of countries like Russia, Venezuela, and Uganda. But just as clearly, there are some countries that have made real progress in battling it, such as Singapore or (to some extent) Georgia. Comparative analysis can help us analyze the factors conducive for success in fighting corruption, helping explain Ukraine's plight while suggesting a productive pathway for its future.

The third broad reform challenge we identify is the basic formal law on which Ukraine's most important political institutions are founded, the constitution. When a country becomes independent or democratizes for the first time, one of the first choices it must make is for a constitution that will determine what political institutions exist and the specific powers with which each is endowed. Bad choices can lead to bad outcomes. In Ukraine, one problem has been that outside advisors have tended to assume that constitutions will work in the post-Soviet world in essentially the same way they work in Western countries like France or the United States. Another problem has been that Ukrainian leaders themselves have all too well understood that this is not the case, and have manipulated the constitution in ways that look just fine to Westerners on paper but that in fact have laid the groundwork for authoritarian trends in Ukrainian reality. These, too, are problems not unique to Ukraine, as anyone familiar with cases ranging from postcolonial Nigeria to today's Russia can attest. But just as certainly, some countries that resemble Ukraine in important ways have managed to find constitutions that help them make the best of bad situations, even in the postcommunist world, such as Macedonia or Mongolia. A comparative understanding can assist us in identifying the most promising features of the constitutional success stories that might transfer to Ukraine.

A fourth crucial challenge facing Ukraine is to reform its judicial system, putting in place a system that produces courts and judges capable of impartially and competently adjudicating the disputes that inevitably arise in any complex society, underpinning the rule of law. This has been a major problem for Ukraine. During the Soviet period, courts and judges existed, but they were tightly subordinated to Communist Party authority and had autonomy to rule justly in only a limited realm of cases that were considered politically nonsensitive. The system for educating judges produced cadres who would work well within such a system. When Communist Party rule broke down, new judges did not simply appear to take over from the old. In most cases the old judicial authorities remained in place, or at best were reshuffled somewhat. Again, Ukraine is not unique in facing such a situation. Running a court and knowing the law (not to mention having a body of good law to know!) requires training and experience, and any country emerging from dictatorship cannot hope to develop it overnight. Many countries have thus continued to face problems of judicial nonindependence, as in Romania. But as in the other areas of reform discussed so far, one can also point to relative success stories, such as the Czech Republic. Comparative study makes it possible to highlight factors that have driven success in reforming the judiciary, while identifying some potential lessons for Ukraine.

The fifth challenge is the fundamental question of how to deal with concentrations of wealth and power that today dominate much of Ukrainian politics. This is the problem of "oligarchs" (super-rich and politically connected business owners), mafias, and informal "clans" that can create de facto monopolies in certain sectors of both economy and polity, subverting both market and democratic competition. Some, following the great sociologist Max Weber, would call this the problem of *patrimonialism* (Fisun and Polishuk 2012), a situation in which private wealth accumulation and state management are inseparably intertwined. This problem is also not unique to Ukraine, as students of countries ranging from Turkey to China will recognize. At the same time, some countries have managed to achieve enduring and dynamic economic growth despite such phenomena (as in China), and of course many countries have greatly tamed the power of such "chieftains," including the United States with its "robber barons" of old and its infamous patrons of Tammany Hall. Comparative analysis, then, can shed light on what separates the success stories from the failures, helping us understand why Ukraine has been bogged down in the latter category and what escape paths might open up for it in the future.

The final reform challenge on which this volume focuses concerns the economy more generally. Despite receiving a great deal of advice from some of the world's most prominent economists and successful managers of other countries' economies, Ukraine's parliament and government have consistently failed to provide a framework capable of truly kick-starting Ukraine's floundering economy after the collapse of the 1990s. Indeed, even before the economic problems brought on by the 2014 war, its economy per capita was *still* lower than it had been prior to the USSR's demise. But here, too, Ukraine is not alone, being far from the only country to have experienced difficulties in economic reform. Moldova, Pakistan, and Haiti are just a few examples from across the globe. At the same time, however, other countries have succeeded in turning the economic corner, generating sustained economic growth after a substantial period of decline. Poland is one such success story. Outside the postcommunist world, the "Asian tigers" stand out. It will by now come as no surprise for the reader that we think comparative analysis can help us understand why some countries succeed while other states fail, with lessons for Ukraine emerging in the process.

Our strategy for addressing these six challenges was to invite some of the best Ukraine experts we could think of and put them in the same room as some of the best comparative specialists on these issues, asking each to consider both the specific and comparative problems with an eye to coming up with solutions. We think that we have found just such a group, and we physically brought them together twice in the process of producing this volume, thanks to George Washington University's Elliott School of International Affairs (and particularly the SOAR Initiative), its Office of the Vice President for Research, and its Petrach Program on Ukraine in the Institute for European, Russian, and Eurasian Studies (IERES). First, we gathered the authors in Washington in June 2013 for a brainstorming session to hash out a larger agenda and some common ideas, charging them with producing a draft chapter for a next conference in Kyiv in December 2013, where we would invite a range of leading policy-makers and experts based in Ukraine for their feedback on the project. We did not insist strictly that the "comparativists" avoid discussion of Ukraine, or that the "Ukraine specialists" focus myopically on Ukraine. Indeed, some of our comparativists know a great deal about Ukraine, and some of our Ukraine specialists are themselves outstanding comparativists who know a lot about many other parts of the world. But we did require that the focus of each type of chapter be different; for each reform area, we wanted one chapter that concentrated primarily on evidence from Ukraine and one that concentrated primarily on evidence from other countries.

Of course, back in 2012–13 when the project was first launched, we did not anticipate the dramatic events that would unfold between the June and December 2013 "authors' summits." Indeed, in November 2013, the Euromaidan protests erupted onto the globe's political scene, with tens and even hundreds of thousands of citizens pouring into the streets initially to protest President Viktor Yanukovych's decision to delay signing an Association Agreement with the European Union. As the mobilization continued, the central demands shifted to calls for deposing Yanukovych himself, especially after his police attempted to disperse the protesters by force, ultimately producing more than a hundred fatalities in the streets of Kyiv.

The authors' workshop in Kyiv thus turned out to be a remarkable experience. During the morning and daytime we intensively discussed Ukraine's problems in comparative perspective and what might be done, and in the evenings and whatever other time could be found, we had the chance to visit the protests themselves, including not only the Euromaidan rallies but also the encampments of the "anti-maidan" forces. This field research afforded the authors with the opportunity to talk with protesters themselves to hear what they thought about Ukraine's reforms, listening to views of both the ordinary citizens who had turned out as well as the leaders of the movement. Indeed, thanks to some well-placed colleagues such as Oleksiy Haran of the Kyiv Mohyla Academy, we were even joined at the workshop itself by many figures who went on to play leading roles both in the revolution and in the postrevolution leadership of the country, some of whom commented directly on some of the papers. This experience, of course, produced no unity of viewpoints. Members of our authorial collective have often had rather heated debates with each other over whether the Euromaidan movement was making the right choices both before and after the revolution itself. But what it did clearly produce was a depth of insight that we think now reflects a major and unanticipated strength of the book before you.

One of the best decisions we made in preparing the volume was to invite a leading scholar of both Ukraine and reform more generally to join the discussion and, carefully listening to everyone at both meetings, to produce a chapter on the challenges of reform that would help develop some theoretical propositions that resonate both with Ukraine's experience and with what we know from the comparative studies presented here. That scholar is Paul D'Anieri, who presents his argument and introduces the scholars who are part of the team and their contributions in Chapter 1. His chapter situates this volume in the broader comparative literature on reform and the literature on Ukraine, a task we decided not to duplicate in this preface. As the editors of the volume, we return to D'Anieri's ideas and offer up our own set of conclusions and practical recommendations in the book's final chapter. We hope they will be useful not only for scholars who care about Ukraine or the general problem of reform in newly independent or newly democratic countries but also for Ukrainians themselves, now struggling to rebuild a country rent by revolution, invasion, and war.

PART I

Introduction

1   Establishing Ukraine's Fourth Republic: Reform after Revolution

Paul D'Anieri

The Ukrainian state is being founded anew. When Viktor Yanukovych fled Kyiv in February 2014, the constitutional order was disrupted and in important respects the state ceased to function. In Kyiv, the state did not control the monopoly on the legitimate use of force that is the sine qua non of the modern state. The state was also redefined territorially with the seizure of Crimea and parts of the Donbas by Russia. In important respects, then, we can think of the period since early 2014 as the founding of Ukraine's "fourth republic."

It is remarkable that Ukraine can already be on its fourth republic, but such is the case, if we consider the number of times since 1991 that a new constitutional order (not merely a new constitution) was adopted. In 1991, Ukraine's first republic formed with independence from the Soviet Union. In 1996, the second was formed when a new post-Soviet constitution was finally adopted. The third began in 2004, when street protests forced a major revision of the constitutional distribution of powers between the president and prime minister. That order was undermined by Viktor Yanukovych after 2010, and the collapse of his regime brought Ukraine again to a point of fundamental discontinuity. Fear for Ukraine's future mixes with hope that the country is finally going to build a "normal" "European" state, as envisioned by the protesters who pushed Yanukovych from power, and the possibility that Ukraine would succeed seems to have so worried Russia that it has done a great deal to undermine the chances of success.

Russia's intervention has raised the stakes for reform in Ukraine. At stake now is not only whether Ukraine will have democracy, a functioning state, and a market economy, but whether it will be independent and mostly whole, or whether it will be further dismembered. Ukraine's success in reforming itself to create a prosperous democracy tied to Europe is now seen as the best and perhaps the only defense against further predation by Russia.

For more than two decades, Ukraine has staggered forward without making the reforms that are widely viewed as necessary. Many of the same problems that have existed since 1991 remain, and the fact that Ukraine is on its fourth constitutional order in twenty-five years leads us to wonder if enduring change is possible. Once again, Ukraine faces both the opportunity to remake itself and the fear that somehow old patterns will persist. Can Ukraine reform?

This book, rather than lamenting Ukraine's past performance, seeks to glean from that experience lessons that can now be applied. Reform, in this context as in others, has two overlapping meanings. The broad meaning of reform is that of coherent policy change for the better. A narrower meaning is that of the elimination of some defect in institutions, policies, or outcomes. Both meanings apply here: corruption is a defect which many people in Ukraine and outside seek to eliminate. Democracy, rule of law, and economic growth are positive goods of which people seek more.

Therefore the chapters in this book focus on two questions: Why has there not been more reform in Ukraine? And what can be done to promote or facilitate reform? We approach these questions through a two-pronged approach. On each of the six issues addressed, a chapter that focuses primarily on Ukraine is paired with a chapter that examines Ukraine in light of comparative experience. Thus the questions are approached from two distinct vantage points, one "inside" and one "outside" Ukraine. Identifying which facets of the problem are unique to Ukraine and which are not helps to identify the kinds of strategies that might help overcome the barriers to reform. Ultimately the goal is to identify pathways to positive change.

At least on the surface, the problem with reform in Ukraine is not disagreement about goals. While political infighting in Ukraine is endemic, there is a great deal of consensus on many of the country's problems and objectives. Economic growth has been slow and volatile. After twenty-two years of transition, Ukrainian GDP was still smaller in 2013 than it had been in 1991. In 2009 Ukraine experienced a drop of 15 percent in GDP, and this indicator fell nearly 7 percent in 2014. Corruption is rampant, earning Ukraine a ranking of 142 out of 175 countries on Transparency International's Corruption Perceptions Index in 2014. Life expectancy is low, and Ukraine scores poorly on a range of quality of life, public health, and comparative happiness measures. Moreover, Ukraine is not subject to the typical left-right cleavage. The leading political parties and politicians all present themselves as pragmatists and centrists; debate over the relative roles of government and market is largely absent. Nor is there significant disagreement that Ukraine should be a democratic country. Even corruption is not a partisan issue. Consensus on these goals makes the inability to accomplish them even more puzzling.

Of course, Ukraine's politicians are divided, Russia exerts influence as a powerful and interventionist neighbor, the legacies of the Soviet Union hamper the country today both socially and economically, and internal regional divisions color politics and impede the formation of a consensus. Pointing to those obvious problems, however, does not explain the lack of reform in two important senses. First, other countries have had the same challenges—or worse—and managed to address them. Second, analytically, this large array of possible causes points to the need to identify their relative importance. Which are fundamental obstacles to reform and which are not?

Why Does Reform Fail?

The question of why reform does not occur has been asked for decades about many countries. A range of answers is available, stemming from various theoretical approaches and historical cases, and the contributors to this volume apply many of them. A central premise of this volume is that comparative experience is highly relevant for understanding the obstacles to reform in Ukraine and the potential to overcome them.

A substantial literature in the rational choice vein shows how the pursuit by rational actors of private goals undermines or blocks the achievement of widely desired reform. In this view, the determinants of macrolevel outcomes are found in microlevel incentives. Prominent among this work is Joel Hellman's (1998) concept of a "partial reform equilibrium." Hellman argues that a partially reformed economy provides enormous rent-seeking opportunities for well-placed elites, and that once reform reaches a murky land between the command economy and the market, actors who benefit from this arrangement will seek to obstruct further reform. Because these actors have profited from partial reform, they have the most resources with which to pursue their goals. Thus an equilibrium is reached in which those enriched and empowered by partial reform work to maintain it. In this volume, this kind of approach is demonstrated by Serhiy Kudelia, who argues that Ukrainian political elites benefit hugely from corruption, and therefore have a powerful incentive to keep it going, even as they initiate various "anticorruption" programs.

Another immense literature focuses on institutional design, and whereas much of the rational choice literature focuses on incentive-based barriers to reform (for example, collective action problems), the institutional design literature focuses on solutions. The common thread is the assumption that actors are rational. The goal of institutional design is to create institutions that align the private interests of actors with the public good. This literature gains weight from the presumed role of the U.S. Constitution in channeling behavior in the United States, as elaborated in the Federalist Papers and much subsequent analysis of U.S. institutions, such as rules of procedure in the Congress. Among the first orders of business in constructing postcommunist politics was the writing of new constitutions. These constitutions, as well as electoral laws and other rules, have been repeatedly altered, in Ukraine and elsewhere, in the belief that better rules would lead to better results and would constrain actors from doing things that are viewed as nondemocratic or simply corrupt. In particular, the design of legislatures and executive-legislative relations is seen as essential in determining whether disagreements are resolved peacefully or not (Ostrow 2000).

In this volume, several authors emphasize the role of formal institutions. Henry Hale, for example, focuses on the constitutional division of authority between the president and the prime minister, finding that in the patronal politics that characterize many of the postcommunist states, unified executives with strong presidential powers tend to bolster autocracy.

The institutional design approach begs the question of why institutions were designed badly in the first place. Daniel Beers asks whether institutions are best thought of as cause or effect. It may be that "bad" institutional design is not the result of poor engineering, but rather of good engineering intended to serve someone's interest. As Smith and Remington (2001, 3–4) stress, actors have multiple goals in designing institutions, and good government may not top the list. Certain institutions may serve the overall public interest poorly while privileging some actors, and those privileged actors will defend those institutions. To the extent that institutional design is the problem, resolving it is nearly always more complicated than just identifying a more optimal solution. It requires amassing sufficient power to defeat defenders of prevailing practice.

The historical institutionalist school of thought also focuses on the effects of formal and informal institutions, but has a different understanding of where institutions come from. They are not simply "designed" but rather emerge during particular historical circumstances and then endure after the circumstances that led to their creation have passed (North 1990, Acemoglu and Robinson 2012). Scholars of post-Soviet Ukraine have tended to assume that the collapse of Soviet power led to a fundamental historical discontinuity, but Pauline Jones Luong, writing about Central Asia, showed how "the persistence of old formulas produced new institutions" (2002, 3), and Valerie Bunce (1999) showed how the shift from coercion to economic incentives to maintain control in the late Soviet period undermined state power. Taras Kuzio's chapter applies a similar approach, showing how the economic, industrial, and social practices that emerged in the late Soviet period contributed to the rise of the post-Soviet Party of Regions.

Several approaches to reform go beyond the focus on the state itself to examine the relationship between the state and society. The seminal work in this line of argument was Samuel Huntington's *Political Order in Changing Societies* (1968), in which Huntington traced the downfall of many new democracies to the inability of new, weak states to manage the demands placed by liberated and increasingly well organized societal actors. In a similar vein, Joel Migdal (1988) identified the problem in many African states as one of "strong societies and weak states." Several actors have applied this approach to Ukraine. Almost from the time of independence, Alexander Motyl (1993) argued that Ukraine could not build a functioning democracy unless it first constructed a functioning state. Motyl's argument was in stark contrast to prevailing thinking, which saw the state as a source of unwanted interference in society and the market. An in-depth study of institutions in Ukraine identified a wide range of deficiencies (Kuzio, Kravchuk, and D'Anieri 1999). In the present book, Maria Popova's chapter on the politicization of the judiciary touches on this view, showing how the judicial organs are often thoroughly penetrated by special interests.

A different take on state-society relations sees the shortcomings not in a weak state, but in a weak civil society, which is unable to bend the state to the needs of the mass of citizens, leaving the state controlled by a small number of self-serving elites. This view also has a rich history, emerging from Almond and Verba's classic study of *The Civic Culture*. Robert Putnam's (1993) work on "social capital" followed a similar line of thinking and had a significant impact on the study of democratization and on democracy promotion programs. In Ukraine, social capital and the civic culture were assumed to be moribund prior to the Orange Revolution, and then were assumed to be powerful in its aftermath. A book edited by D'Anieri (2007b) explored why civil society seemed to lose its influence in Ukraine so quickly after the Orange Revolution. In this volume, society is the focus of analysis for Shevel's study of historical memory, Lucan Way's study of regional divisions, and Kuzio's understanding of why the Party of Regions came to dominate and then collapse.

Modernization theory emerged in the 1960s as a way of explaining why some postcolonial societies changed more quickly than others, and found the answer in the durability of traditional social structures, including patterns of authority. While the theory has fallen out of favor, concepts central to it have endured. Thus the role of traditional authority structures such as clans and patrimonial networks has received extensive attention, especially in research on Central Asia but also in Ukraine. Fisun's chapter, which looks extensively at the patrimonial nature of authority, is a case in point, and similar ideas are evident in Way's discussion of clans and Hale's account of patronal presidentialism.

The issue of national identity has perhaps received more scholarly attention than any other in the study of Ukraine (Barrington and Herron 2004; Birch 2000; Darden 2008). A central question asked in this literature is whether Ukraine's regional, linguistic, and ethnic divisions impede reform. While some have seen this pluralism as a bulwark against autocracy (D'Anieri 2007a, Pop-Eleches and Robertson 2014), the prevailing (and not necessarily contradictory) view is that such pluralism undermines reform (Kubicek 1999). This argument shows up in Shevel's examination of the politics of memory and in Way's examination of regional divisions. Deep societal divisions may impede the formation of the strong state needed to implement significant reforms. This is especially true when there are active secessionist movements supported from abroad.

More recently, the success of democracy promotion in postcommunist Europe and around the world has led to a literature on the role of external support in promoting reform (Bunce and Wolchik 2006; Jacoby 2006; Levitsky and Way 2006; Beissinger 2007; Levitsky and Way 2010; Pop-Eleches 2008). This literature then expanded to include the ways that international and transnational support has been significant in the revolutions that have overthrown autocrats, first in the "colored revolutions" of the post-Soviet states and then in the Arab spring.

The European Union has been a beacon for postcommunist states pragmatically and symbolically. Pragmatically, the European Union provided access to the world's largest single market. Symbolically, membership in the EU attests to a state's "European" status, including a bundle of positive attributions, including being "modern," "Western," and democratic. It also conveys separateness from Russia and Eurasia. This beacon is sufficiently powerful that it reverses the typical relationship between nationalism and supranational organizations: whereas nationalism in many countries correlates with antipathy to strong supranationalism, nationalists in many postcommunist countries saw EU membership as strengthening national identity (Abdelal 2001).

The perceived need to embrace reform to gain EU membership helped consolidate public opinion and motivate leaders. EU financial aid eased the pain of transition and EU technical assistance facilitated successful implementation (Vachudova 2005). The important role played by the EU elsewhere in eastern Europe helps explain why so many people, both inside and outside Ukraine, placed such high hopes on the Association Agreement that was due to be signed in Vilnius in November 2013. Closer links to the EU are sometimes viewed as a panacea, and while such views are unrealistic, an EU commitment would likely bolster the political will needed to undertake painful reforms.

This brief survey of literature on reform yields two conclusions. First, Ukraine is not immune from the conceptual chaos that characterizes the broader study of economic and political development. Second, the lack of reform in Ukraine seems in many respects to be overdetermined. The literature reviewed implies that whatever one hypothesizes to limit reform, Ukraine has it.

Learning from Success

While the premise of the volume is that Ukraine has fallen short in many respects of its reform, the record is not entirely negative. Such a conclusion is important not only for perspective but also to realize that there is significant variation in the outcome of reform projects in Ukraine. While many fail—or are never attempted—there are several notable successes that, by showing what is possible, highlight the shortcomings in other areas. What can be learned from these successes? What led to success in these areas? Was it something in the nature of those issues, or was there something about the tactics or approach used that explains the different outcomes?

A short list of successes would include the following reforms:

Establishment of sovereignty in 1991–92, in which Ukrainian state institutions were disentangled from those of the Soviet Union and Russia, or created from scratch

Basic market reforms after 1991, including:
Liberalizing prices and international trade
Privatization and private sector development
Market institutions and hard budget constraints
Ethnic relations in 1990–91, notably developing a civic definition of the
    nation and giving citizenship to all residents of Ukraine
Denuclearization (1994)
Macroeconomic stabilization and the introduction of the hryvnya in 1996,
    and the subsequent stability of the hryvnya
Constitutional reform following the Orange Revolution to weaken the
    presidency (subsequently reversed, then reinstated).

What did all of these successes have in common? We might tentatively identify two factors. First, in each case there was a looming crisis that needed to be averted (Pop-Eleches 2008). In other words, the normal Ukrainian deferral of reform was seen to be untenable. Second, in each case the international arena provided powerful positive impetus toward reform in three overlapping ways. Each of the reforms helped Ukraine to become more "European" in the sense that the changes brought Ukraine more into line with prevailing European norms. This may have helped build the case. Both the EU and the United States applied pressure, with the U.S. being especially influential in the case of nuclear weapons. Finally, in almost every case, international actors provided financial support to help accomplish the reform in question, whether that meant bilateral aid from the United States in support of denuclearization or loans from the IMF to underwrite the introduction of the stable hryvnya. However, to the extent this superficial account of commonalities holds, it does not mean that these factors contain a recipe for reform, because we could identify other cases in which these factors did not lead to reform—such as the decision not to sign the EU Association Agreement in 2013. Therefore, a more nuanced analysis of specific issues and cases is necessary to trace the sources of meaningful policy change.

Despite these successes, Ukraine appears stubbornly immune to many efforts at reform. Particularly glaring is that when a huge window of opportunity opened for Ukraine after the Orange Revolution, the country and its elites somehow managed not to step through it. Thus, looking beyond Ukraine at comparable cases is essential to our understanding of what is possible and how. Examining countries that have managed to pursue reform despite similar constraints to Ukraine helps broaden our sense of what is possible and what works. That is what the individual chapters in the book endeavor to provide.

Assessing the Prospects

After twenty-five years of unfulfilled potential, is it naive to believe that significant progress is possible? Cross-national comparison will provide some potential answers. What are the historical cases we see of successful transitions out of Ukraine-like situations? What drove those successes? For example, Hale's work identifies examples of successful democracy emerging in patronal systems. Key questions in these cases include those of structure and agency: what structural conditions make significant reform possible, or even inevitable? What kinds of action by what kind of agents need to be taken?

We tend to prefer explanations focused on agency, because they are particularly well suited to producing policy prescriptions. To the extent that reform depends on structural factors, such as the emergence of a middle class, a unified nation, or a favorable international environment, success may be more a case of waiting for propitious conditions to emerge. If reform is a matter of particular actions by actors, we can specify who should do what, and try to get them to do it. Ultimately, any policy prescription assumes that choices by actors can have at least some impact.

Who are the crucial agents? The literature reviewed above provides three potential foci. One is the state itself. In this view, we should focus on actions that the state—including the parliament and executive branch—can take to change policies and improve outcomes. Potential changes range from the microlevel laws, policies, and institutional arrangements to changes in the constitution. At this level, we see two different kinds of barriers. The first is that of the partial-reform equilibrium: in many cases, those in power may not have much incentive to alter the institutions that got them there, and that in many cases are helping to enrich them. The second problem is that of division within the government. Indeed, many would dispute the notion that the state is *an* actor.

Ukraine has not been able to address both these problems simultaneously. For much of the 1990s, the basic problem in Ukraine appeared to be that divisions within the state were the main barrier to reform. The president, parliament, and prime minister all competed for preeminence, and the parliament itself was fragmented. Immobility was the result. When Leonid Kuchma concentrated power in the presidential administration after 1999, government division was reduced, but the partial reform equilibrium was strengthened. Concentration of power led not to reform but to autocracy and corruption. Conversely, when the status quo established by Kuchma was undermined in the

Orange Revolution, and the path to reform was opened, institutional conflict between president and prime minister re-emerged, as did increased instability within a parliament without a reliable majority.

It is not clear that there is some necessary relationship in which concentration of power causes autocracy and corruption, rather than reform, but so far that has been the tendency in Ukraine. This correlation points to a tension that has been apparent in the literature at least since the 1960s. One of the objections to Huntington's work is that, by arguing for the necessity of a strong state, Huntington appeared to be excusing autocracy. Autocrats in a variety of settings have justified their rule on the basis that it paves the way for needed reforms, though autocracy is much more likely to facilitate corruption than reform. An essential question for Ukraine is whether it can have government that is both democratic and effective.

A related question is that of sequencing—does Ukraine need to develop an effective state before it develops a democratic state (Bunce 1995)? Similarly, does corruption need to be tackled in order for democracy to thrive?; does reducing corruption depend on a more independent judiciary?; and does reform require a better reception from the EU?; or in each case is it the other way around? Claus Offe (1991) argued that postcommunist transition was complicated by the fact that a "triple-transition" had to take place, including democratization, marketization, and state-building. Ukraine, Kuzio argued, faced an even more complicated "quadruple transition," because it also needed to build a nation (2001). Motyl (1993) and Linz and Stepan (1996) were among those who argued that state-building was a prerequisite for these other transitions. However debatable that may be in theory, in early 2014 it became an urgent issue in Ukraine, as the state apparatus collapsed around Yanukovych and an interim government scrambled to re-establish order.

The inability of the state reliably to drive reform leads reform advocates to shift attention to other actors. The next place to look is civil society. Civil society in Ukraine showed its muscle in 2004 when it helped to drive the Orange Revolution and again in 2013–14 with the Euromaidan. While it has been periodically successful in threatening the government through street demonstrations, it has been much less successful in creating a steady, long-term pressure for reform (D'Anieri 2010). We do not see the dense network of social institutions that Putnam sees as the essential fabric of civil society. Yanukovych was elected in 2010 in what was widely acknowledged as the freest election in Ukrainian history. The clear implication is that the citizenry of Ukraine are motivated by a variety of issues in addition to, or apart from, reform. If civil society is to drive reform, a first step would be for citizens to reward at the polls those politicians and parties who advocate reform and deliver. In Ukraine, as elsewhere, what counts as reform to some observers or participants appears to others as an unacceptable injury to their interests. Reform of pensions, gas prices, and various subsidies are examples.

A central issue, therefore, in assessing the prospects for reform, is recognizing the extent to which the current set of arrangements constitutes an equilibrium. We tend to assume that reform will make everyone better off, but in many cases, even if reform increases overall efficiency or welfare, some actors are worse off after reform than before. To the extent those actors have the ability to do so, they can be expected to oppose reform. The notion of "partial reform equilibrium" focuses on powerful actors, such as oligarchs, who block reform, but here we are talking about average citizens who wish to keep particular entitlements. Even at the bottom of society, supporting reform requires some confidence that change will lead to the benefits promised by reformers. The experience of the past two decades does not inspire trust in the promises made by reformers. In sum, then, there are powerful political obstacles to reform in Ukraine, both among elites and among citizens.

If the state cannot drive reform, and civil society struggles to force it to do so, then external actors might have to play a role. Particularly for Ukraine, lying as it does on the edge of the European Union, external actors can provide crucial support for reform. The experience of the region to its west, where the support of Europe has played a powerful role, provides an example of what is possible, and repeatedly since 1991, reformers inside Ukraine as well as outside observers have implored Western governments to do more to bolster reform and reformers in Ukraine. As noted above, most of the significant reforms in Ukraine since independence have been boosted by some sort of external support, whether in the form of pressure, encouragement, technical assistance, or financial support. While external support appears to have played a significant role in many cases, it is less clear exactly how such support succeeds or what methods work best. Thus the literature on "democracy promotion" contains a strand that is highly skeptical both about goals and methods. Similarly, the literature on economic development shows wide disagreement about what works and an increasingly prominent vein is highly skeptical of the benefits of international development support (Easterly 2006).

Moreover, in contrast to the some of the more successful postcommunist states, Ukraine has in Russia an international influence that is opposed both to reform and to Western influence in Ukraine. Democracy promotion is countered by autocracy promotion (Levitsky and Way 2010; Silitski 2010), and there are international efforts to foil other kinds of reform, in large part because "reform" in its broad sense is often viewed as correlated with democracy and with geopolitical orientation (D'Anieri 2014). Ukraine's geopolitically pivotal position between East and West is, therefore, an important dimension of the reform puzzle. Russia, concerned both about geopolitics and the domestic challenge that a democratic Ukraine would set for itself, apparently perceives an interest in seeing reform in Ukraine fail. Europe apparently perceives a much weaker interest in Ukraine's success, and in any event it may be easier to spoil reform than to promote it.

Overall, then, the question of the structural prerequisites for reform—and by extension the room available for reform—remains open. The problem of voluntarism, the assumption that actors have more control over outcomes than they actually do, came up repeatedly in discussions among the chapter authors. While advocates of reform need to be realistic about the barriers to reform and chances for success, pessimism can become a self-fulfilling prophecy. It is hard to know where to strike the balance between realism and idealism.

Topics

The volume addresses six issue areas, pairing a chapter focused on Ukraine with one putting Ukraine in comparative perspective. Lucan Way and Oxana Shevel focus on identity issues. Shevel takes up the theme of historical memory as a central component of Ukrainian identity. Conceptions of history have become pivotal in understanding what it means to be Ukrainian, and in particular the nature of the relationship between Ukraine and Russia. Shevel seeks to explain why these issues have become so polarized and what paths might be open to handling the politics of memory in a way that is less divisive. She sees potential in the fact that a significant minority of survey respondents favor a pluralism in which individuals are free to maintain different interpretations of historical events. This pluralism, if it can be maintained, will be crucial in the coming years.

Whereas Shevel draws inspiration from the Spanish experience of dealing with the past, Way examines regional aspects of Ukrainian identity by comparing it with similar phenomena in Bangladesh, Albania, and Kyrgyzstan. He points out that in each of these cases, regionalism makes it difficult to consolidate democratic government and carry out reforms. However, regionalism also undermines efforts by authoritarian leaders to consolidate their power because it helps opposition to mobilize. As regionalism becomes less pronounced in Ukraine following the Russian annexation of Crimea and the fighting in the Donbas, the key challenge is to promote reform without excluding groups central to Ukraine's democratic future. One promising reform would reverse the strongest curbs on Soviet era symbolism, and some form of decentralization might also help.

Ukraine's pervasive corruption is the subject of chapters by Serhiy Kudelia and Daphne Athanasouli. Kudelia takes an institutional approach to understanding corruption in Ukraine, arguing that as Ukraine's institutional model has changed, patterns of corruption have changed along with it. Despite Ukraine's turbulent post-Soviet evolution, neither the fact of corruption nor the extent of it has changed dramatically. This continuity he attributes to permissive conditions, in terms of weak institutionalization, and to powerful incentives for actors to engage in venality. His analysis is troubling in that it shows that political competition, the goal of democratization, tends to spur corruption on the part of leaders.

Athanasouli compares corruption in Ukraine to that in Georgia, Kazakhstan, Poland, Romania, and Russia using the World Bank's Worldwide Governance Indicators and then examines the firm level, using the Business Environment and Enterprise Performance Survey. She shows that Ukraine's problems are quite similar to those elsewhere in the region, and confirms that corruption in Ukraine rivals that in Russia and Kazakhstan. Nevertheless, she points to policies like improving the use of e-government techniques and the role of a free media as potentially helping to ensure that anticorruption efforts are fully implemented in the future.

The biggest formal institutional issue is the constitution. From independence until the present, debate has persisted about what form of constitutional arrangements Ukraine should have. The primary question has been about the relative prerogatives of the president, the prime minister, and the parliament. Oleksandr Fisun and Henry Hale both look at the problem of "patronal presidentialism" in Ukraine. Fisun focuses on the repeated renegotiation of constitutional arrangements as the political power of patronal presidents rises and falls. In this view, constitutions are effects more than causes. He then considers the various contextual shortcomings that undercut any constitutional arrangement in Ukraine. These include penetration of the government by powerful rent-seekers, the absence of a balanced tax base, and the weakness of the Weberian state. Hale looks at patronal presidentialism across the postcommunist space, and concludes that where patronalism prevails, divided-executive constitutions are more conducive to democracy than those with strong presidencies. In this sense, Ukraine moved forward in 2004, backward when those constitutional changes were subsequently overturned, and forward again when the 2004 constitution was restored in 2014. However, as Hale points out, constitutional provisions are not all-determining. Whether divided executives are effective at promoting other kinds of reform, such as market reforms, is unclear.

Maria Popova and Daniel Beers look at the administration of justice in Ukraine. Scholars and practitioners alike recognize that many other aspects of reform, including economic reform and democratization, depend in large part on a functioning judicial system. Popova's findings on politicized prosecution in Ukraine are sobering. Looking at a series of cases from 2001 to 2010, she determines that under the Yanukovych administration, political prosecution became a more effective means to sideline one's rivals. While this might be explained in terms of Yanukovych's greater enmity to democracy, Popova hypothesizes that a process of authoritarian learning is at work, in that Yanukovych and others have learned over time how to use the prosecution process more effectively. This highlights that not all actors are interested in reform; and that policy innovation can be for the worse as well as the better. Beers looks at the experience of judicial reform across the postcommunist cases, and gleans several lessons. Among the most important is that "institutional solutions have important limitations" as drivers of the reform process. Not only do informal practices sometimes negate the effects of institutional reforms, but when they do, the entire concept of judicial reform is undermined by cynicism.

Moreover, highly autonomous courts can be as hazardous as dependent ones, because they can become targets of politicians jealous of their authority. This comparative evidence indicates that simply seeking to increase the autonomy of Ukrainian courts may be insufficient. Rather, what is more important—and more elusive—is broad political support for an independent judiciary. Beers finds two important sources of meaningful reform. First, the European Union has played a widely acknowledged role in judicial reform in the postcommunist region. More surprisingly, Beers finds a strong positive role for low-level actors—individuals and firms that turn to the courts to resolve disputes and court employees committed to improvement. Politicians and parties, in contrast, appear in Beers's study to be as much a part of the problem as the solution.

Oligarchic groups are at the heart both of corruption and politics in Ukraine, and their stature has risen since the early post-Soviet years. In contrast to many other scholars, Taras Kuzio shows how the corruption, shadow economy, and organized crime that plague Ukraine today emerged in the late Soviet period and then took advantage of the collapse of the Soviet Union. Through a detailed analysis of oligarchs' roles in a wide range of enterprises, he shows empirically how corruption works at the microlevel. He also shows why the foundations of the Donetsk group in organized crime networks prepared it to outcompete the Dnipropetrovsk oligarchs for power in post-Soviet Ukraine. Kuzio's chapter leaves it clear that the current patterns of "nonreform" that we see in Ukraine are deeply entrenched and resistant to change. While the 2014 revolution opened space for reform, many actors are striving to take advantage of the current turmoil to gain control over economic assets.

Georgi Derluguian helps to explain why Ukraine wound up with this oligarch problem in the first place, identifying the cause as Ukraine's peripheral position in the world economy and the failure of its elites to cooperate for a larger good during the critical moment of the USSR's collapse. Here a comparison with China proves useful. Derluguian argues that China succeeded because its relatively simple state allowed its leaders to work together to orient the country toward the needs of the global economy, while the complexity of Soviet institutions (including its division into multiple federal units) made such cooperation much more challenging. After the USSR collapsed, various "violent entrepreneurs" were able to take advantage of the resulting chaos to their own advantage, becoming oligarchs or state-based predators that have vested individual interests in subverting reforms, as Kuzio's detailed analysis makes clear.

The specific issue of economic reform is addressed by Alexander Pivovarsky and by Alexander Libman and Anastassia Obydenkova. Pivovarsky points out that Ukraine succeeded in making basic market reforms by reducing the state's role in the economy, but he sees these as necessary but not sufficient conditions for a well-functioning economy. Ukraine, he finds, lacks necessary "market enhancing" institutions that are needed to make markets effective, including rule of law, competition policies, and market institutions specific to particular economic sectors. Libman and Obydenkova set out inductively to identify the countries whose economies are most similar to Ukraine's using a hierarchical cluster analysis of indicators of the microlevel institutions, such as obtaining permits, registering property, and enforcing contracts. This analysis indicates that in terms of formal institutions, Ukraine performs like a country of southeastern Europe, while in informal terms, it looks more like the other post-Soviet states. While the formal institutional environment in Ukraine has improved, perceptions of the business climate have worsened. This highlights the disconnect between formal institutions and informal practices. They stress that government cannot directly change informal practices—it can only change formal rules or personnel.

The conclusion, by Henry Hale and Robert Orttung, lays out an action agenda. As the preceding chapters make clear, laying out a plan that is realistic, rather than simply wishful thinking, is a challenge.

Conclusion

Across all these chapters we see three central questions emerge that vex discussions of reform in Ukraine. First, who will lead the way? Second, how will any official changes overcome the powerful informal practices that seem so often to negate or resist reform efforts in Ukraine and in many other countries in the region and around the world? Third, how does the need to concentrate political power sufficiently to overcome resistance to reform fit with the goals of democratic reform? Put this way, the agenda looks ominous, but one of the key benefits we get from looking at Ukraine in comparative perspective is the ability to see how other similar countries have overcome many of the same obstacles. In 2013–14, Ukraine again confronted a movement in the streets demanding a fundamental reordering of politics in the country. That is one indicator that the prevailing arrangements are not such a well-entrenched equilibrium that they cannot be disrupted. For Ukraine, however, it has proven easier to overturn an existing set of institutions than to build the kind of government and economy that many people believe is necessary and attainable, as the chapters' treatments of the post-2014 period well demonstrate.

PART II

Identity-memory Divide

2

No Way Out?
Post-Soviet Ukraine's Memory Wars
in Comparative Perspective

OXANA SHEVEL

It is not surprising that coming to terms with the recent and more distant past has proven to be a challenging task for political elites and citizens in independent Ukraine. The young state has a complex history, defined in part by a prior lack of statehood and regions that were at various times divided by state borders and even battle lines.

Mutually exclusive interpretations describing a plethora of historical events and time periods have been articulated in Ukraine and embraced by competing political actors and different segments of the public. There are competing "memory regimes" (the term will be defined below) on a host of events, personalities, organizations, and historical periods spanning Ukrainian history: from the heritage of Kievan Rus, through the question of Cossack Hetman Ivan Mazepa's "loyalty" or "treason" during czarist rule, to the "indigenousness" versus "imposition" of Soviet rule.

The Soviet period is particularly rich in events and personalities to disagree about. Was the 1932–33 killer famine that decimated Ukraine a crime of the Soviet regime against the Ukrainian nation? Or was the Holodomor, as Ukrainians call it, a class-based crime without a national dimension? Or was it not even a man-made crime at all, but a tragedy caused only by bad weather and the resulting poor harvest? What constitutes loyalty and treason to the motherland in the Soviet period, in particular during World War II? Were those who fought for the Soviet Union heroes and those who opposed Soviet rule, such as the Organization of Ukrainian Nationalists (OUN) and its armed wing, the Ukrainian Insurgent Army (UPA), traitors? Or, by contrast, were these

Ukrainian nationalist fighters true heroes because they fought for Ukrainian state independence?

At the same time, not everything about Ukraine's past is contested and politicized. As Portnov notes, figures of Ukrainian history who had already gained official sanction in the Soviet period remain broadly accepted throughout Ukraine. Among them are literary and cultural figures, such as Taras Shevchenko, Ivan Franko, and Lesia Ukrainka, and political figures such as Bohdan Khmelnytsky. In the post-Soviet period, only Mykhailo Hrushevskyi was able to join this list of consensus historical figures (Portnov 2010, 98–99).

Divided memory of the past poses a problem at several levels. Because collective memory and collective national identity are closely related, a nation's collective memory can be considered "a historical dimension of national identity" (Kulyk 2013, 64), and conflicts over memory can undermine the creation of a common national identity. Conversely, the politics of historical memory is ultimately about the construction of a cohesive national identity (Torbakov 2011), which in turn directly impinges on the "stateness" problem (Linz and Stepan 1996) and the viability and stability of a democratic statehood that necessitates a historical narrative underpinning and validating it. That said, a common national identity can be created in a society divided by memory of past conflicts. As the Spanish example to be discussed below shows, a common national identity can be built on foundations other than a common historical memory. Ukraine, however, so far lacks the kind of alternative basis for national unity that proved successful in Spain—namely, success in establishing democracy and integrating into European political and economic institutions.

In addition to complicating the construction of a common national identity, conflicts over memory can also hamper democratic politics. In the context of memory conflicts, political actors are tempted to politicize and instrumentalize sensitive differences, which in turn centers electoral politics on emotional and stubborn conflict over past wrongs and rights, heroes and villains, us and them, rather than on more pragmatic issues and ills, such as the scope and content of socioeconomic reforms, state institutions, rule of law, and corruption. Political competition becomes more antagonistic as well. There is little motivation to engage with opponents in constructive debates aimed at advancing reforms because rivals can simply be delegitimized as "other," their views not worthy of consideration.

As for the prospects for reforms—in the sense of systematic positive change in institutions, policies, and practices (D'Anieri, this volume)—the question is whether in Ukraine disagreements over historical memory can be resolved in ways that reduce conflict and advance democracy. I will analyze the politics of memory and assess the likelihood of reforms by situating the Ukrainian case within a comparative context empirically and theoretically. Empirically, I will use Spain as an illustrative example of how political elites in a society divided by conflicting memories of the recent past can develop a set of legal and institutional measures to allow different parts of the society to debate and disagree over the past without these disagreements undermining democratic governance. I will then consider the prospects for this democratization of memory politics in Ukraine. Theoretically, prospects for reforms in Ukraine will be examined through the lens of a theory of memory politics developed by Jan Kubik and Michael Bernhard (Kubik and Bernhard 2014).

The chapter will argue that reforms in Ukraine could hypothetically be achieved through one of the three mechanisms. One would be for the Ukrainian political elites to propose more pluralistic and less exclusionary narratives of the historical past. In terms of Kubik and Bernhard's typology, key political elites would need to start acting like *mnemonic pluralists* rather than *mnemonic warriors*. The chapter will discuss why Ukrainian political elites did not act in this manner after 1991, and why, following the annexation of Crimea by Russia and the ongoing separatist conflict in the Donbas, it remains unlikely that mnemonic pluralists will emerge in the near future. However, the territorial crisis now affecting Ukraine inadvertently opens new possibilities for reforms that have not existed previously—the emergence of *mnemonic abnegators* and of a *unified* memory regime within the territory of Ukraine that remains under central government control.

The second possible reform mechanism is the European orientation and the goal of eventual membership in the EU. Orientation toward Europe mandates certain approaches to history, and offers institutional and legal mechanisms aimed at fostering pluralistic memory politics. Specifically, reforms in Ukraine could be achieved through the implementation of European approaches to history teaching reflected in the 2001 Council of Europe recommendation "On History Teaching in Twenty-first-century Europe," which advocates developing "a pluralist and tolerant concept of history teaching" and "the promotion of fundamental values, such as tolerance, mutual understanding, human rights and democracy."[1] As will be shown below, this path was explored but not realized during Yushchenko's tenure, abandoned by Yanukovych, and, following the fall of the Yanukovych regime, so far has not been taken up by the new government, despite its proclaimed European orientation. In fact, the "decommunization laws" adopted in April 2015 contain provisions that explicitly ban and even criminalize public expression of certain opinions on the historical past. Nevertheless, if and when Ukrainian political elites were to embrace the European approach and principles contained in the European instruments for confronting disagreements about history, the blueprint for reforms developed by Ukrainian historians in 2010 could become a pathway for reforms.

Finally, the third possible reform pathway toward a less conflictual memory regime in Ukraine originates in society. As this chapter will show through the example of perhaps the most divisive historical memory battle in Ukraine—over the way to remember the OUN and the UPA—a substantial part of Ukrainian society is *ambivalent* and does not firmly embrace any of the main competing historical narratives. If not for the current territorial conflict over Crimea and the Donbas region, this popular ambivalence could have served as a basis for the emergence of a more pluralistic memory regime over the long term, even in the absence of elite actors advocating such a regime at the official level. However, violence during the Euromaidan protests and Russian aggression after the fall of Yanukovych changed the attitudes of Ukrainians, in particular causing substantial parts of the South and even the East to shift toward a more pro-Ukrainian position, and the Center to move even closer to the West in its attitudes. This attitudinal "catching up with western Ukraine" (Zhurzhenko 2014) in regions of Ukraine that used to hold Russia-friendly attitudes was, ironically, spurred by Russia's actions aimed at keeping Ukraine in Russia's orbit. However, as the polling data to be presented in this chapter will show, ambivalent attitudes have not totally disappeared in Ukraine, and the South may now become the new Center, showing less categorical attitudes than either the Center-West or the reduced East. Therefore popular attitudinal ambivalence could still potentially serve as a basis for building a democratic memory regime and pluralistic memory politics.

Theoretical and Comparative Lens on the Politics of Memory Reforms in Ukraine

The politics of memory theory proposed by Kubik and Bernhard in a recent book (Kubik and Bernhard 2014) marks an important advance, since up until now the politics of memory as a separate field of inquiry, particularly in political science, has been weak on systematic theorizing. To address this lacuna, Kubik and Bernhard propose a generalizeable theory that defines different types of *mnemonic actors* and the types of *memory regimes* that emerge as a result of interaction among the actors. A memory regime is defined as an "organized way of remembering a specific issue, event, or process . . . at a given moment or period," and becomes official when its "formulation and propagation involves the intensive participation of state institutions and/or political society" (Kubik and Bernhard 2014, 16). Actors, such as political parties, seek to influence the content of official memory regimes "to construct a vision of the past that they assume will generate the most effective legitimation for their efforts to gain or hold power" (Kubik and Bernhard 2014, 9).

Kubik and Bernhard identify four ideal types of mnemonic actors: *mnemonic warriors,* who believe that they hold the one correct vision of history and that alternative visions of the past need to be delegitimized or destroyed; *mnemonic pluralists,* who accept that there are multiple visions of the past and that the others are entitled to their visions; *mnemonic abnegators,* who are uninterested in and avoid memory politics—either because the country has one broadly unified and broadly shared vision of the past, or because the abnegator actors strive to avoid participating in cultural and memory wars; and *mnemonic prospectives,* who oppose any form of thinking founded on the celebration of the past, since they "believe that they have solved the riddle of history and thus have the key to a better future" (Kubik and Bernhard 2014, 14). As the authors note, with a possible exception of "extreme warriors," who are "reflexively dogmatic," the same political actors do not have to behave the same way as mnemonic actors at all times, and can change position based on their calculations of political benefits or the salience of a given historical issue or event (Kubik and Bernhard 2014, 17). At a particular moment in time, however, different constellations of mnemonic actors interact to produce different *memory regimes.* If at least one mnemonic warrior (or, rare in the postcommunist region, mnemonic prospective) is present, the type of memory regime that emerges is *fractured* and *contested.* For the memory regime to be democratic, actors involved in shaping these regimes need to behave as mnemonic pluralists (or mnemonic abnegators). When at least one mnemonic pluralist is present and there are no mnemonic warriors, the type of memory regime that emerges is *pillarized*—a memory regime in which actors differ in their interpretation of the past, but toleration of differences of opinion allows competing visions of the past to coexist peacefully.

Kubik and Bernhard's theory provides a useful lens through which to address prospects of reforms in the area of memory politics in Ukraine. For Ukraine, a reform would be the formation of a pillarized memory regime whereby different interpretations of the past peacefully coexist. A pillarized regime was also the essence of Spain's approach to memory politics (Shevel 2011a). Spain is a relevant comparison with Ukraine in terms of the problem of divisive memories of the past and prospects for reforms in this issue area. In Ukraine, one of the most highly charged issues in contemporary memory wars is the legacy of World War II, and in particular the "OUN-UPA" problem. During the Soviet period, the OUN and the UPA were unambiguously presented as traitors to the Soviet motherland, but in independent Ukraine the question arose of whether they should continue to be regarded as such, or should they, by contrast, be considered heroes who fought for an independent Ukrainian state—even though they fought for it against the Soviet forces? Since Ukrainians fought in both the Soviet Army and in the UPA, the debate is real, raw, and easily politicizable. Spaniards also fought against each other in recent history, during the Spanish Civil War (1936–39). Under the subsequent Francoist dictatorship (1939–75), the dominant historical narrative was that Franco's coup and subsequent Francoist victory in the civil war saved the country from the chaos and destruction of the republican period. The villains were thus "godless" republicans, communists, anarchists, and other leftists. The heroes were God and Spain-loving Francoists. When Spain embarked on its transition to democracy following Franco's death in November 1975, it faced the dilemma of re-evaluating the past regime's designation of "heroes" and "villains." The way the Spanish state dealt with this dilemma is instructive.

The transition to democracy was initiated by the pro-Franco reformers who had to find a compromise with the moderates in the opposition to move forward with democratic reforms, given that the extreme right and left would have preferred some form of violent confrontation to prevent the establishment of a liberal democracy. A central element of this compromise was the informal *pacto del olvido*, or pact of forgetting, which was instituted during the transition by the post-Franco reformers and the democratic anti-Franco opposition and remained in place until several years ago. The two sides agreed to "forget" past political excesses, including the mass killings of the civil war and the repression of the Francoist era, in order to avoid a repetition of bloody civil conflict (Aguilar 2001; Aguilar Fernández 2002; Encarnación 2008; Faber 2005; Keene 2007). The pact aided the process of institutional democratization in Spain—and by doing so has challenged transitional justice theories that see successful democratization conditioned on reckoning with a painful historical past (Encarnación 2008, 435–36). In Spain, because the elites agreed not to reckon with their painful historical past, they were able to agree on a variety of measures that allowed for the launching of a successful democratization process.

However, while drawing a curtain over the past in the name of national reconciliation, the pact left the historical narrative created under Franco relatively undisturbed, and by doing so suppressed the memory of the republican side (Aguilar 2001; Faber 2005; Davis 2008; Valls-Montes 2007). Only in 2004 did the 36th Congress of the Spanish Socialist Party (PSOE) include in its electoral platform the recovery of Spain's historical memory as a means of addressing the injustices of the past committed against fellow socialists (Encarnación 2008, 441). Upon entering office after the March 2004 election, the socialist government made the recovery of Spain's historical memory a legislative priority, arguing that the democratic transition was marked by "much agreement and little memory" (Encarnación 2008, 452). The government appointed an interministerial commission to study the situation of the victims of the civil war and Francoism, and after more than two years the commission presented to the Spanish legislature the recommendations that eventually became the basis of the Law of Historical Memory approved on October 31, 2007.

The law was a compromise rather than a victory for one side, and both the right and the left criticized it. The right accused the socialists of rewriting history (Keene 2007), while the left and international rights groups criticized the law for not going far enough in undoing past injustice—in particular because the law did not automatically nullify sentences handed down under the dictatorship, nor did it invalidate the amnesty declared during the transition which made it virtually impossible for anyone ever to be prosecuted for past blood crimes (Encarnación 2008).[2] But this was precisely the point of the law—to "privilege historical reconstruction over accountability" (Encarnación 2008) or "truth rather than justice" (Davis 2008, 879). If the *pacto del olvido* allowed the official historical narrative created under Franco to remain relatively undisturbed, the 2007 memory law redressed this imbalance, but—crucially—explicitly prohibited the state from designating any single version of memory as correct for the nation as a whole.

The law recognized the right of each individual or group to remember the past in its own way; put emphasis on the rights of the victims; and refrained from glorifying any side of the conflict. As for the role of the government, the law saw it enabling "the recuperation of personal and family memory" and the search for "knowledge of our history and the promotion of democratic memory," which, as one scholar put it, is "presumably a public sphere open to competing 'memories'" (Boyd 2008, 146). The Spanish memory law therefore had two dimensions. The first was political and was manifested in the law's departure from the previously dominant historical narrative that was formed in the Francoist period by acknowledging the victims of Francoism and restoring "the image of the Second Republic as a forerunner to Spain's modern democracy" (Encarnación 2008, 458). The second dimension of the law, which can be termed democratic, is equally, if not more, important. The memory law refrained from glorifying any one side of the past conflict and from designating any one version of memory as the correct one for the nation as a whole. Instead, the law explicitly acknowledged the multiplicity of historical memories held by individuals, families, and groups, the legitimacy of these memories, and the state's commitment to giving space to these memories in the public domain. Because there is no broad consensus in Spain on what exactly is to be remembered, scholars of Spain expect the collective memory of the past to remain contested "for many years to come, maybe forever" (Encarnación 2008, 459). The political elites nevertheless were able to institutionalize a reconciliation or, in Kubik and Bernhard's terms, to create a pillarized memory regime by acting like mnemonic pluralists.

The Spanish case is not identical to Ukraine's, and some elements of the Spanish solution do not apply in Ukraine. For one, the repetition of the "pact of forgetting"—postponing confrontations over divisive historical issues until democratization and economic stability are achieved—is not possible at this point in Ukrainian history, nor was it possible at the time of transition from the Soviet rule. Because the birth of independent Ukraine followed Gorbachev's perestroika and glasnost reforms, questions of historical memory came out in the open, and the politics of memory had already become politicized in the late Soviet period. This debate could not be silenced in the new Ukrainian state in which political elites on the right and the left routinely instrumentalized identity politics for electoral gains. That said, a Spanish-like solution to the conflictual politics of memory—specifically, institutionalization of a pillarized memory regime with the government promoting "democratic memory," which is to say, committing to creating a public space where open debate over contested historical issues can take place—remains hypothetically possible in Ukraine. The following discussion will consider the likelihood of this happening and what specific reforms would need to take place.

Prospects for Reforms in Ukraine

Political Elites as Mnemonic Warriors before
and after the Euromaidan

Throughout two and a half decades of independence, the official memory field in Ukraine has been fractured and contentious, to use Kubik and Bernhard's terminology. Key elite mnemonic actors in post-Soviet Ukraine comprised two sets of mnemonic warriors (communist and nationalist) who have been striving to establish a unified memory field wherein their view of the past will be hegemonic, and a power-holding center that has occasionally preferred strategic abnegation but has frequently acted also as a mnemonic warrior siding with either the left or the right. A pillarized memory field, where different visions of the past can coexist and where political elites act as mnemonic pluralists, did not materialize in Ukraine prior to the tectonic political shift brought on in 2014 by the Euromaidan protests, the overthrow of President Yanukovych, and the subsequent territorial conflict with Russia over annexed Crimea and the separatist insurgency in the Donbas. Nor has such a reform occurred in the post-Yanukovych era. However, even though a pillarized memory regime remains elusive, obstacles to the emergence of such a regime now are different.

Prior to the Euromaidan, political competition in Ukraine played out within the threefold division of the political spectrum that emerged in the late Soviet period. This division has been extensively described in many studies (Kuzio 1998; Kulyk 1999; Riabchuk 2012; Rodgers 2008; Wilson 2000). None of the three main groups of political actors—the national-democratic and nationalist right who favored a pro-Western foreign policy, market reforms, and saw Ukrainian history as a continuous "national liberation struggle" from foreign, in particular Russian, domination; the unreformed communists and their allies who rejected market capitalism, opposed Western-oriented foreign policy, and continued to embrace the Soviet-era conception of Russians, Ukrainians, and Belarusians as "brotherly peoples" and three "branches" of the same nation; or the ideologically amorphous and opportunistic political "center" dominated by former party apparatchiks and the new business and regional elites—acted as mnemonic pluralists, because each saw the benefits of exploiting identity divisions, including disagreements over history, and capitalized on the regional dimension of these divisions during elections. Electorally, neither warring side in the identity/memory conflict could dominate, and the course of "memory wars" ran in parallel with election cycles. Attempts to institutionalize one "true" version of the historical past in state policies were made, most notably by President Yushchenko between 2005 and 2010, when multiple unsuccessful attempts to pass legislation on formal recognition of the OUN and UPA fighters were undertaken, and two controversial leaders of these organizations, Stepan Bandera and Roman Shukhevych, were designated as heroes by presidential decrees (Amar, Balyns'kyi, and Hrytsak 2011). During 2010–13 under Yanukovych the pendulum of memory politics swung in the other direction, and the pro-Russian/neo-Soviet narrative of the past, in particular of the World War II and 1932–33 Holodomor, was promoted at the official level.[3] However, such attempts by the ruling elites to clearly privilege one of the conflicting historical narratives received pushback from the opposing elite and segments of society (Brudny and Finkel 2011; Osipian and Osipian 2012). The stand on identity and memory issues was a contributing, though not the only, factor that cost Yushchenko his second term in office, and cost Yanukovych his presidency and forced him to flee Ukraine.

The post-Yanukovych government has not engaged in mnemonic pluralism. Instead, in April 2015 the parliament passed, and the president subsequently signed, a package of laws that became known as the "decommunization laws."[4] The laws have drawn much criticism from scholars, intellectuals, and rights groups for criminalizing debate and making it a punishable offense to engage in vaguely defined "propaganda" of communist or Nazi regimes, "public denial of the criminal nature" of these regimes, "falsification of the history" of World War II, or "public display of disrespectful attitudes" to the people defined as fighters for Ukraine's independence, including members of the OUN and the UPA.[5]

The political context in which these laws were adopted was very different from the environment in which pro-Yushchenko forces tried to legislate similar measures in 2005–9. Following the annexation of Crimea by Russia and Russian support for the separatists in eastern Ukraine, political fault lines in Ukraine shifted in two important ways: first, the most pro-Russian electorate was excluded from participating in the electoral process as a result of the territorial annexation of Crimea and ongoing armed insurgency in the Donbas; second, public opinion in eastern and especially southern Ukraine became less pro-Russian. This shift is manifested most clearly in the sharply reduced support for membership in the Russia-led Customs Union, as shown by a February 2015 Kyiv International Institute of Sociology (KIIS) poll.[6] Nationwide, support for membership in the Customs Union fell from 35 percent in February 2013 to just 12 percent in February 2015. Not only in the western and central but also in the southern (although not eastern) regions, opponents of the Customs Union outnumbered supporters (33 to 12 percent in the South). Positive attitudes toward Russia also declined sharply in Ukraine after the annexation of Crimea—nationwide from 88 percent in September 2013 to 34 percent in February 2015, including all regions and even the East (from 96 to 55 percent).[7] As a result of these changes, through the summer of 2015 there was no substantial backlash against the decommunization laws, and political elites opposed to the decommunization drive, such as the Opposition Bloc, have not capitalized on their stand against these laws.[8]

In terms of prospects for reforms, two possible future scenarios can be outlined. One possibility is that, as the problems of Crimea and the Donbas insurgency linger, the shift in popular attitudes that took place in the wake of the Euromaidan will continue, with southern and eastern regions continuing to move in their attitudes away from pro-Russian/Soviet memory paradigms. If this attitudinal shift continues, in terms of Kubik and Bernhard's typology, Ukraine (without Crimea and the separatist-controlled part of Donbas) might eventually move closer to having a unified memory regime (predicated on an agreement regarding the interpretation of the past and thus largely free of mnemonic conflicts). Political actors would then be in a better position to serve as mnemonic abnegators who stay away from memory politics, because, in the presence of a broadly shared version of the past, not much is gained from efforts to create and propagate an alternative perspective.

Such a unified memory regime is by no means a certain future for Ukraine, however, since regional divisions are still evident, albeit in an evolved and reduced form. For example, according to a December 2015 to January 2016 poll by the Democratic Initiatives Foundation, attitudes to the formation of the OUN and the UPA remain one of the two issues (the other being the 2004 Orange Revolution) that continue to divide Ukraine into two large parts, with the Center-West having an overall positive attitude to these phenomena and the South-East overall negative.[9] Further, conflicts over memory in Ukraine are not a purely domestic matter, but are also influenced by actions and rhetoric coming from Russia, which can be expected to try to keep memory wars alive. However, without the electorate of Crimea and Donbas reintegrated into the Ukrainian electoral process, it is unlikely that the proponents of the pro-Russian memory narrative can gain enough electoral power to shape the content of state policies as they did during Yanukovych's tenure. The adherents of what is referred to as Ukrainian patriotic discourse can therefore be expected to remain in a position to shape state policies for the foreseeable future, even if regional divisions over memory and identity issues persist. It remains to be seen whether these elites, who have declared their pro-European and democratic orientation, will at some point follow their Spanish counterparts and start acting as mnemonic pluralists, or if they will persist in trying to legislate one "correct" vision of the past while benefiting from the fact that the numerically shrunken opposition is unable to mount an effective challenge. The amendments to the decommunization laws promised by President Poroshenko when he signed the laws to address their shortcomings "with regard to free speech and academic research" will be the first indicator of what path the currently ruling elites in Ukraine are willing to take.[10]

Europeanization as a Driver:
The European Approach to History Teaching

As noted above, orientation toward Europe and European values can advance reforms in Ukraine if Ukraine adopts European approaches to dealing with its divisive historical past. The Spanish solution—official recognition and state aid in the expression of "individual and family memories" and the promotion of "democratic memory" through a public sphere open to competing memories—is the essence of a European solution. So far the Ukrainian political class has not embraced this approach to history for reasons discussed above. However, if political actors willing to embrace this approach emerge, they can benefit from an already prepared "how-to" guide. This guide is a concept for a new textbook and new approach to history teaching developed by a group of Ukrainian historians during the Yushchenko presidency.

From 2007 through 2009, twelve professional historians from different regions of Ukraine working under the auspices of the Ukrainian Institute of National Memory held a series of meetings in which they reviewed the history textbooks used to teach history in school grades seven through twelve, and proposed a radically new concept for a basic history textbook. The proposed approach fits very closely with the general spirit and recommendations of the 2001 Council of Europe's "On History Teaching in Twenty-first-century Europe." According to Natalia Iakovenko, the head of the working group and the leading Ukrainian historian of the early modern period, all existing textbooks depict the Ukrainian society of the past "in anachronistic categories—as an ethnic, linguistic, and confessional whole with shared goals and common ideals" that is collectively engaged in constant "liberation struggles" (Iakoveno 2008, 114). Iakovenko and her colleagues identified many problems with this self-image, but for the goal of fostering national unity, the key problem is that this self-image simply does not resonate with the contemporary Ukrainian students (and, one might add, adult citizens). The disconnect is not because the Russian/Soviet "Slavic unity" narrative is somehow more convincing or historically accurate, for it suffers from the same methodological and epistemological pitfall of seeing the nation as an organic whole with shared goals and common ideas. The nonacceptance of the collective self-image presented in the Ukrainian textbooks stems from the fact that contemporary students who live in a socially complex patchwork society of overlapping interests, small communities, and multiple identities cannot relate to "an internally contradictory and too outdated socio-cultural image of the Ukrainian society," as presented in the textbooks, and therefore this image "does not evoke feelings of emotional connectedness and is perceived instead as a 'remote,' 'not ours' or even 'untrue' history" (Iakoveno 2008, 114). The historians concluded that to present a version of historical memory that can form the basis of national unity, the textbook needs to approach history not through the prism of historic ethnic nations but through the prism of individuals and groups inhabiting the territory of today's states. Instead of presenting the nation as an organic entity that formed at the dawn of time and persisted through history "in a unidirectional and uninterrupted manner towards a pre-determined goal" (Ukrains'kyi instytut natsional'noi pamiati 2009, 11), the textbook would "treat social life of all communities on Ukrainian territories . . . as an inseparable part of Ukrainian history" (ibid.) and would focus "on explaining the motives and mechanisms of behavior of different segments of Ukrainian society in different historical situations" (Mudryi 2008, 39).

Engaging in what Iakovenko called "a maximum detailization (*multyplikatsia*) of the society" (Iakoveno 2008, 115–16) and focusing history teaching on the illumination of the motivations and mechanisms of actions by different groups in society, would de facto be pursuing the Spanish solution to the problem of divisive historical memory. The goal of history teaching—and of state policies—would be to introduce the actors involved in a particular historical event, give full information about the interests, motivations, constraints, and decision-making mechanisms underlying the choices they made, while letting the students—and the citizens—decide whether they want to approve of these choices. This conception of history teaching would be in line with the principles reflected in the 2001 Council of Europe recommendations as well, and as such can be considered a European approach.

Given that narrating history not through the prism of historical ethnic nations but through the prism of individuals and groups inhabiting the territory of today's states would effectively deconstruct both the "Soviet" and the "national" approaches to the country's past, it is interesting to note that the project was undertaken under the auspices of the state-funded Institute of National Memory during the tenure of President Yushchenko, who personally embraced a much different view of Ukraine's past.[11] Yushchenko departed from office before the historians finished their work in March 2010, and under Yanukovych the commission, in the words of its head, Iakovenko, "died a quiet death."[12] Even though the historians' textbook initiative collapsed under Yanukovych's tenure, other efforts toward the same goal continued. In January 2011, for example, a group of twenty-eight historians from different regions of Ukraine launched a civic movement to promote historical reconciliation based on European democratic principles in the field of history teaching.[13]

The likelihood of the post-Yanukovych government adopting the Iakovenko group approach to dealing with conflictual historical memories so far seems low. The decommunization laws took essentially the opposite approach, legislating one correct way to remember the Soviet past in particular, and outlawing public expressions of alternative views. According to public statements made by the proponents of the decommunization laws, rejection of the mnemonic fundamentals associated with the Soviet era is nothing less than a security issue. In the words of the deputy director of the Institute of National Memory Volodymyr Tilishchak, "[W]here there are no monuments [to Lenin and Soviet party leaders], there is no war today. Where this tradition, this mythology, this hatred that was propagated by communist propaganda is alive—this is where we see war, confrontation, and deaths."[14] Under an optimistic scenario, at some future point the political environment may change enough for the Ukrainian political elites to stop interpreting memories of the Soviet past as a security issue. Such a shift could happen, for example, if a substantial political change occurs in Russia, with the post-Putin government withdrawing support for separatists in the Donbas, the conflict over Crimea somehow gets resolved, and Russia itself democratizes. It may also happen if the Ukrainian economy is revived, political and economic corruption is noticeably reduced, and the Donbas problem becomes a "stable" frozen conflict, so much so that it does not impede the move by the rest of Ukraine toward

Europe. If and when the Ukrainian political class stops interpreting memory politics in security terms and becomes ready to allow and facilitate open public discussions of the past, the blueprint for history teaching developed by the Iakovenko group could be used as a ready road map for both historical reconciliation and the Europeanization of history teaching.

Society as the Driver, or Societal Ambivalence as a Possible Driver of Reforms

Since to date no political elite group in Ukraine has acted as mnemonic pluralists, the formation of a pillarized memory field remains a tall order. However, elite mnemonic offerings are only one of the components of a memory regime. Another component is the societal response to these offerings, and looking at how the Ukrainian public has been responding to the elite mnemonic offerings gives some hope for the prospects of reforms. Prospects for societally driven reforms in the field of memory politics are in particular augmented by the fact that Ukraine is not divided into two monolithic opposing camps—a Russian-speaking pro-Russian East and a Ukrainian-speaking pro-Western West—but that there exist more ambiguous identities in the large geographic center of the country, and that fractured and multilayered identities exist within each of the stereotypical "East" and "West" camps. The East-West divide is a real, important, and persistent feature of the country (Arel 2006; Katchanovski 2006), but the fractured and multilayered local, regional, and borderline identities that exist within each of the two camps lead many scholars to caution against oversimplifying the importance of this divide (Hrytsak 2004; Portnov 2010; Richardson 2004; Zakharchenko 2013).[15] Furthermore, even if the East and the West have strong and often opposite opinions on a variety of issues, there is also a sizable center of the country that is distinguished from both the East and the West by its ambivalent attitudes—a fact that is still underanalyzed by scholarship on Ukraine. Differently put, on virtually any hot-button contentious issue, a trifold rather than a twofold division has existed in Ukraine, with the extreme West and East of the country holding for the most part opposite opinions, while the numerically large and strategically important center of the country remained ambivalent on many issues, including historical memory and the Soviet past.

One good illustration of this trifold rather than bifold division in society and of the ambiguity in attitudes in the geographical center is evident on the question of support for granting the UPA fighters the status of participants in the national-liberation struggle. The "correct" way to remember the UPA, a nationalist anti-Soviet resistance movement, may be the single most contested issue in memory politics in postindependence Ukraine. The narratives on the "OUN-UPA" issue advanced by the political elites do not give Ukrainians a choice other than "heroes and freedom fighters" or "traitors and murderers" when it comes to remembering these groups. This either/or focus has been the case both before and after the Euromaidan, with the latest legislative measure being the law "On the Legal Status and Honoring of Fighters for Ukraine's Independence in the 20th Century," one of the "decommunization laws" adopted in April 2015, which makes it a punishable offense to publicly display "disrespectful attitudes" to the people defined as fighters for Ukraine's independence. At the same time, even on this arguably most divisive historical issue, there appears to be some room for compromise in society.

Thus a December 2007 poll by the Democratic Initiatives Foundation asking Ukrainians if they support granting the UPA fighters the status of participants in the national-liberation struggle predictably showed that the East and the West sharply disagreed on the matter: in the western regions, 77 percent supported the idea, while in Donetsk and Crimea, just 13 percent did.[16] The Center, however, was not nearly as polarized. Voters in central Ukraine were equally divided, with 38 percent opposing recognition and 38 percent supporting it partly or fully.

The poll allowed respondents the options not only of expressing support for or opposition to the UPA veteran status but also of answering "difficult to say" or "I support recognition [of UPA fighters as veterans] as long as the government does not impose its view on the citizens and everyone can decide whether or not to honor UPA fighters." Nationwide, these two responses gathered 18 percent and 16 percent, respectively, which can be interpreted to mean that more than one-third of the population was (in 2007) potentially open to a compromise solution to the "OUN-UPA problem" and accepted the existence and the legitimacy of different memories of the OUN and the UPA. Central Ukraine again stood out as the region most open to a memory compromise, given that it had the largest share of undecided (25 percent, compared with 18 percent in Ukraine as a whole).

In the year following the Euromaidan uprising, the geographic center attitudinally moved closer to the West, as can be seen from the polls on European integration and attitudes to Russia cited above. However, attitudinal ambivalence has not entirely disappeared, and it is the South and the South-East that may now be becoming the new "Center," showing fewer categorical attitudes than the West and the East. As long as a substantial part of the population remains ambivalent about the contested historical past (rather than siding firmly with one or another camp of mnemonic warriors), this state of popular mnemonic ambivalence will continue to offer possibilities for the emergence of a pillar-ized memory regime. On remembering World War II in particular, it is not unrealistic to suggest that a broad segment of Ukrainian society may accept a Spanish-like solution to the OUN-UPA problem. This solution would have two pillars: first, explicit condemnation of any and all blood crimes against noncombatants, no matter under what banners—Soviet or nationalist—these actions were carried out, and, second, the state-embraced toleration of differ-ent memories of World War II and its participants, and a commitment to fa-cilitating open public debate instead of seeking to advance one narrative as the officially sanctioned "correct" version of history.

Pursuing this two-pillar policy would involve some changes to the existing laws. If the official position were to include explicit condemnation of all blood crimes against civilians, the law on the legal status of fighters for Ukraine's independence would need to be amended to exclude from status those who committed blood crimes against civilian populations. This would exclude from legal recognition some members of the OUN and the UPA, as well as the lead-ers of these organizations, given crimes against Jewish, Polish, and Ukrainian civilians that were committed by members of these organizations and sanc-tioned by the leadership (Marples 2007; Snyder 2010; Shkandrij 2015). At the same time, the 1993 law "On the Status of War Veterans and Guarantees of Their Social Protection," which honors those who fought on the Soviet side during World War II, would also need to be amended. The veterans law cur-rently confers the status of veterans and combatants on all members of Soviet armed formations, including the security and interior ministry troops, and does not exempt from status and state benefits either formations or individuals guilty of murder and brutalization of the civilian population in the process of establishing Soviet rule in Ukraine. At the same time, the 1993 law recognizes as veterans and combatants only those members of the UPA who did not fight the Soviet regime after 1944, and "who did not commit crimes against peace and humanity" (Article 4, Part 16). There is thus both an ideological standard (one needed to have fought for, and not fought against, the Soviet state to be legally recognized as a veteran), and a double moral standard (committing crimes against humanity excludes from status only members of the UPA but not members of the pro-Soviet armed formations). Thus neither the 1993 vet-

OXANA SHEVEL

erans law nor the 2015 independence fighters law squares well with European principles and the Spanish model where the state unequivocally condemns all violence against civilians.

Conclusion

This chapter has argued that reforms in the sphere of memory politics would constitute the creation of a public space in which competing narratives of the past can be freely voiced, and where the state sees its role not in the promotion of any version of the past as existentially correct and thus mandatory for inculcation in the society, but instead in fostering open debate and recognizing the multiplicity and validity of individual and collective memories of the past. The chapter suggested that there are three hypothetical pathways by which this reform might be achieved in Ukraine. The first pathway would be for the Ukrainian political class to start acting as mnemonic pluralists rather than mnemonic warriors: articulate narratives of the past that are less exclusionary, recognize the legitimacy of competing narratives, and seek societal compromise by identifying points of overlap among competing narratives. So far the track record of the Ukrainian political class in this regard is essentially absent—including among the current pro-Western ruling elites who came to power after the victory of the Euromaidan. The profound transformation of attitudes that took place in some of the formerly pro-Russian regions in parts of the East and especially in the South of the country following the Russian annexation of Crimea and the separatist conflict in the Donbas region opens the door to another pathway for future reforms—a unified memory regime emerging on the government-controlled territories, with the political class becoming mnemonic abnegators as historical memory ceases to be a hot-button political issue.

The second possible pathway for reforms is what I called Europeanization. Under this pathway Ukraine would embrace, as part and parcel of its turn toward Europe, European approaches and instruments to dealing with divided historical memory. As discussed in this chapter, by 2010 a group of Ukrainian historians had already developed a new conception of teaching history informed by European principles that current or future governments can choose to implement. As of this writing, the post-Euromaidan government has not chosen this reform path.

The third possible reform pathway originates in society rather than in the

Ukrainian political class. A reform-enabling feature of the Ukrainian society is the fact that there is a substantial part of Ukrainian society—concentrated in the geographical center of the country before the Euromaidan, and now possibly in the South—that remains ambivalent in its attitudes rather than firmly embracing one of the main competing historical narratives. This popular ambivalence could become the basis for the formation of a more democratic memory regime, although this alternative still requires political elites becoming mnemonic abnegators who seek to gain and maintain political power by exploiting issues other than historical memory.

Notes

1.   Council of Europe, Committee of Ministers, "Recommendation Rec(2001)15 of the Committee of Ministers to Member States on History Teaching in Twenty-first-century Europe," adopted by the Committee of Ministers on October 31, 2001, at the 771st meeting of the Ministers' Deputies. See https://wcd.coe.int/ViewDoc.jsp?id=234237.

2.   V. Burnett, "Bill in Spanish Parliament Aims to End 'Amnesia' about Civil War Victims," *New York Times*, October 28, 2007.

3.   Kateryna Kapliuk, "Perepysana istoriia Ukrainy. Versiia epokhy Dmytra Tabachnyka," *Ukrains'ka pravda*, August 28, 2010. Accessed July 15, 2012. See http://www. pravda.com.ua/articles/2010/08/26/5332444/.

4.   These are Law No. 2538-1, "On the Legal Status and Honoring of Fighters for Ukraine's Independence in the 20th Century"; Law No. 2558, "On Condemning the Communist and National Socialist (Nazi) Totalitarian Regimes and Prohibiting Propaganda of Their Symbols"; Law No. 2539, "On Remembering the Victory over Nazism in the Second World War"; and Law No. 2540, "On Access to the Archives of Repressive Bodies of the Communist Totalitarian Regime from 1917–1991."

5.   Halya Coynash, "Decommunization Laws: Deeply Divisive and Destined for Strasboug," *Krytyka*, May 2015. Accessed July 9, 2015. See http://krytyka.com/en/solutions/opinions/decommunization-laws-deeply-divisive-and-destined-strasbourg; Dronova and Stadniy, "Dekomunizatsiini zakony. Propozytsia pravok," *Krytyka*, May 2015. Accessed July 9, 2015. See http://krytyka.com/ua/solutions/opinions/dekomunizatsiyni-zakony-propozytsiya-pravok; John-Paul Himka, "Legislating Historical Truth: Ukraine's Laws of 9 April 2015," *Ab Imperio*, April 21, 2015. Accessed July 9, 2015. See http://net.abimperio.net/node/3442; David Marples, "Open Letter from Scholars and Experts on Ukraine Re. the So-Called 'Anti-communist Law,'" *Krytyka*, May 2015. Accessed July 9, 2015. See http://krytyka.com/en/articles/open-letter-scholars-and-experts-ukraine-re-so-called-anti-communist-law; OSCE, "New Laws in Ukraine Potential Threat to Free Expression and Free Media, OSCE Representative Says," May 18, 2015. Ac-

cessed August 2, 2015. See http://www.osce.org/fom/158581; Andrij Portnov, "On Decommunization, Identity, and Legislating History, from a Slightly Different Angle," *Krytyka*, May 2015. Accessed July 9, 2015. See http://krytyka.com/en/solutions/opinions/decommunization-identity-and-legislating-history-slightly-different-angle; Oxana Shevel, "'De-communization Laws' Need to Be Amended to Conform to European Standards," *Vox Ukraine*, May 14, 2015. Accessed July 2, 2015. See http://voxukraine.org/2015/05/07/de-communization-laws-need-to-be-amended-to-conform-to-european-standards/.

6. Kyiv International Institute of Sociology, "Geopolitychni orientatsii hromadian Ukrainy: stale i minlyve ostannikh rokiv (liutyi 2012-liutyi 2015)," March 18, 2015. Accessed July 9, 2015. See http://www.kiis.com.ua/?lang=ukr&cat=reports&id=507&page=1.

7. *Ukrains'ka pravda*, "Ukraintsi rizko zminyly svoiu dumku pro rosiian," May 21, 2015. Accessed July 9, 2015. See http://www.pravda.com.ua/news/2015/05/21/7068635/.

8. In July 2015, the Opposition Bloc polled at 4.1 percent, less than the 9.3 percent it had received in the October 2014 elections. *Ukrains'ka pravda*, "BPP and Bat'kivshchyna vyhraly b vybory v Radu," July 20, 2015. Accessed August 7, 2015. See http://www.pravda.com.ua/news/2015/07/20/7075094/.

9. Democratic Initiatives Foundation, "Shcho objednuie ta rozjednuie ukraintsiv," December 24 , 2014–January 15, 2015. Accessed July 9, 2015. See http://dif.org.ua/ua/publications/press-relizy/sho-obednue-ta-rozednue-ukrainciv.htm.

10. "Hlava derzhavy pidpysav zakony pro dekomunizatsiyu," May 15, 2015. See http://www.president.gov.ua/news/glava-derzhavi-pidpisav-zakoni-pro-dekomunizaciyu-35325.

11. Although, as I have discussed elsewhere, the initiative came from historians rather than from the state, and the approval of the historians' final proposal by Yushchenko's government was also not certain (Shevel 2011a, 157–64, esp. fn. 96).

12. Iakovenko, as quoted in Hanna Trehub, "Natalia Iakovenko: "V Ukraini dilalane "sovetskaia vlast'" a radians'ka vlada," *Ukrains'ka pravda*, June 12, 2011. See http://www.istpravda.com.ua/articles/4edaa6d60e8d0/.

13. *Ukrains'ka pravda*, "28 ukraiins'kykh istorykiv zaiavliaiut', shcho "ne viddadut'" mynule i maibutnie Ukrainy v ruky politykiv," January 24, 2011. Accessed September 20, 2013. See http://www.istpravda.com.ua/short/2011/01/24/17727/.

14. July 5, 2015, interview on Hromadske Radio. See https://soundcloud.com/hromadske-radio/5a-6.

15. Tatiana Zhurzhenko, "The Myth of Two Ukraines," *Eurozine*, September 17, 2002. Accessed September 20, 2013. See http://www.eurozine.com/articles/2002-09-17-zhurzhenko-en.html.

16. "Use men'she ukraintsiv opyraiut'sia statusu voiakam OUN-UPA," *Ukrains'ka pravda*, January 17, 2008. Accessed September 3, 2009. See http://www.pravda.com.ua/articles/2008/01/17/3351003/.

3   Democracy and Governance in
                        Divided Societies

                         Lucan A. Way

Few topics have received as much attention in Ukraine as the sources and impact of the country's national and regional divide—particularly in the aftermath of the 2014 crisis and Russia's invasion. Yet, with very few exceptions, such
studies have focused exclusively on Ukraine—with no reference to other divided societies.[1] This chapter seeks to understand the impact of Ukraine's divide
on democracy and reform through an analysis of other divided societies in
transition. The experience of these other cases suggests that Ukraine may face a
dilemma: national divisions may simultaneously promote dynamic and (semi)
democratic political competition while at the same time undermining both reform and the development of stable, well-functioning democratic institutions.[2]
In turn, greater national unity that emerged following Russian aggression in
2014 has created greater possibilities for reform—but also new potential sources of autocratic behavior.

     Albania, Bangladesh, Kenya, Kyrgyzstan, Moldova, and Ukraine were all rel-
atively poor countries,[3] without significant natural resources, that underwent
transitions from fully authoritarian to democratic or competitive authoritarian
rule in the early 1990s. These countries were also *divided societies* in which there
are relatively evenly matched and politically significant divisions in national
identity along ethnic, regional, cultural, or other lines (Way 2015).[4] By "evenly
matched," I mean that the primary identity groups have adequate support to
gain power at the national level by themselves or as an equal partner in an alliance with other groups.[5]

     A comparison of these countries' post–Cold War trajectories reveals a key
dilemma facing many divided societies that lack strong democratic prerequisites: national divisions often promote dynamic political competition but

undermine governance as well as the development of stable democratic institutions. On the one hand, national divisions have provided oppositions with critical mobilizational tools that have made it much harder for any side to monopolize political control. On the other, such divisions have also undermined governance and democratic consolidation by fostering stalemate and in many cases violence between groups. While it may be possible to reduce the political effects of this division, such efforts may also facilitate authoritarian state building efforts.

Russia's invasion of Ukraine fundamentally altered the dynamics of national identity, democracy, and reform. On the one hand, Putin's aggressive behavior unified the country and transformed nationalism into a key potential source of reform. At the same time, the country's existential crisis has created newly salient justifications for crackdown on dissent.

National Divisions, Democracy, and Governance

Divisions over national identity have almost universally been considered dangerous for both governance and democracy (Dahl 1971, 205–23; Lijphart 1977, 1, 17–18; D'Anieri 1999/2000, 139–78). Discussions have focused on the ways in which divisions promote instability and violence and undermine democracy (Lijphart 1977, 1; Suny 1999/2000, 176). Such conflicts can make it nearly impossible for competing groups to agree on reform or even on which institutions are "legitimate." They undermine the development of stable and consensual rules of the game. Indeed, a glance at divided societies around the globe suggests that such fears are well founded. Violent national conflict in Albania in 1996–97, Bangladesh in the mid-1990s and 2000s, Kenya in the late 1990s and 2007, and Kyrgyzstan in 2010 suggests the ways in which national divisions may undermine the ability of countries to function peacefully and to agree on any kind of serious reform. Such divisions threatened the territorial integrity of Ukraine in early 2014.

Such divisions make it harder to rally the population around reform objectives. In countries such as Japan, South Korea, and Taiwan, nationalism was a powerful force for reform and economic development in the 1950s and 1960s. In these countries, elites used nationalism and threats to national survival to convince domestic actors of the need for painful changes to the economic and social structure. By contrast, it is much harder to use nationalism to motivate reform in the absence of a strong and unified sense of national identity.

At the same time, the impact of national divisions is not uniformly negative. While divisions in Albania, Bangladesh, Kenya, Kyrgyzstan, Moldova, and Ukraine have arguably facilitated conflict and undermined governance, they have also promoted political competition and made it harder for autocrats to monopolize political control. In the absence of other constraints on authoritarianism—including a well-institutionalized civil society and a strong rule of law—such divisions between relatively equal groups have made it harder (albeit certainly not impossible) for any single group either to impose certain policy priorities or to monopolize political control. Such divisions have helped opposition to mobilize support—both at the ballot box and on the streets—in the face of significant harassment and uneven access to media and other resources.

Identity divisions have bolstered opposition forces by allowing them to tap into networks of highly motivated activists and voters. Ethnic or national identities are powerful tools for social mobilization because of their ability to arouse intense emotion (Rothschild 1981, 60; Barany 2002, 282; Berezin 2001, 86; Beissinger 2002, 79). Heightened emotion in turn motivates individual activism by shaping the conception of gains and losses involved in political activity and helps to explain a willingness to engage in high-risk behavior (Aminzade and McAdam 2001, 17, 31). All of this makes ethnicity and nationalism a particularly effective way for opposition to mobilize support where it is otherwise sidelined and faces significant harassment. By tapping into national identity, opposition has been able to attract committed activists and sacrifice that is often necessary to create a regime crisis.

National identities have been an important means of mobilizing both demonstrators and voters over to the side of the opposition. Divisions often form the basis of enduring cleavage structures that facilitate opposition's ability to garner electoral support even in an unfriendly media environment (Lipset and Rokkan 1990 [1967], 138). Such divisions have also stimulated protest. Thus, Mark Beissinger's (2002, 76) in-depth investigation of protest in the USSR shows that nationalism played a significant role in stimulating demonstrations against Soviet rule in the Gorbachev period.

The mobilizational power of such identities helps explain their persistence. National identity appeals have frequently been the easiest and most efficient means for politicians to attract reliable voter support and help leaders to tap into highly motivated activist networks. Politicians have found it costly to ignore such appeals. As a result, national identity often dominates politics—*even* when individuals across the divide share many values and policy priorities.

National divisions are likely to facilitate competition only where each of the main competing groups has the potential (either by itself or in coalition with others) to gain national power. By contrast, divisions would seem likely to undermine competition in cases in which one or more of the competing identity groups is too small or isolated to gain national power—as in countries plagued by national separatist movements (for example, Chechens in Russia) or those that are host to vulnerable minorities (such as Coptic Christians in Egypt). Such divisions are likely to assist autocrats in monopolizing control by allowing them split opposition.

It is important to stress that national divisions are obviously not the only ones that facilitate opposition mobilization. A range of other phenomena—robustly institutionalized civil society, powerful labor organizations—constrain autocrats and facilitate opposition mobilization (Howard 2003; LeBas 2011; Levitsky and Way 2010). My point is that in the many countries where opposition lacks such resources or constraints, identity divisions are often critical for mobilizing political opposition.

In sum, national divisions between relatively evenly matched groups have both facilitated competition and undermined governance by hampering efforts of competing groups to monopolize political control. Such divisions have often resulted in dynamic, disorderly, and often very dysfunctional political competition. Below, I provide an overview of the dynamics of national divisions in Bangladesh, Albania, and Kyrgyzstan. These cases exhibit different types of national identity divisions. Yet they all show how splits may both undermine governance and democratic consolidation but also help opposition forces to tap into powerful mobilizational appeals that allow them to overcome incumbent abuse. In turn, increased national unity has created both new impetus for reform but also new threats to democracy.

Bangladesh

Despite their obvious differences,[6] Bangladesh and Ukraine share a number of important similarities. Both countries emerged out of dictatorship in 1991 but remained competitive authoritarian throughout most of the post–Cold War period. (Both countries had similar Freedom House and Polity scores after the Cold War.)[7] Further, economic oligarchs have infiltrated electoral politics in both countries (Ahmed 2011). In addition, as in Ukraine, leaders from all ends of the political spectrum have demonstrated a willingness to use antidemocratic measures when in power.

But the most striking similarity between the two cases lies in the dynamics of national identity. Former colonies, both Bangladesh and Ukraine witnessed the emergence of potent divisions in national identity that reflected diverging interpretations of their colonial heritage. As in Ukraine, this division generated a powerful and persistent electoral cleavage that undermined efforts by either side to monopolize political control while at the same time engendering profound stalemate and dysfunction—thereby inhibiting democratic consolidation and governance.

Following the end of British control over India in 1947, today's Bangladesh (East Pakistan) was joined with today's Pakistan (West Pakistan) to create a single Muslim state separated by a thousand miles—creating a kind of sandwich with India in the middle. While they shared the same religion, East and West Pakistan possessed distinct ethnic and linguistic cultures: West Pakistan was dominated by an Urdu-speaking elite; East Pakistan was overwhelmingly populated by ethnic Bengalis, who also represented a significant (Hindu) ethnic minority in neighboring India. Tensions rapidly emerged. While Bengalis accounted for a greater share of the population in Pakistan, the political and military elite mostly came from West Pakistan and refused to recognize the Bengali language as coequal with Urdu. Many in East Pakistan perceived West Pakistan as a colonial power in their region. In the 1960s, East Pakistani Bengalis mobilized behind the nationalist Awami [People's] League (AL), led by Sheikh Mujibur Rahman, to demand independence from West Pakistan. The AL justified independence on the basis of ethnic and linguistic differences between the two Muslim territories. After a short and violent civil war, Bangladesh won independence in 1971 with significant military support from India.

Despite the overwhelming dominance of ethnic Bengalis in newly independent Bangladesh, divisions rapidly emerged between two competing versions of Bangladeshi national identity: on the one hand, the AL viewed Bangladesh primarily in *ethnic* terms and thus allied with India. On the other hand, the Bangladesh National Party (BNP), created by former members of the Pakistani military in the late 1970s, viewed Bangladesh primarily in *religious* terms and thus allied with Pakistan (Moshin 2013, 332).

Just as in Ukraine, the main national divisions following the transition from authoritarian rule in 1991 centered around "conflicting interpretations of the country's history and purpose" (Sobhan 2013, 303). Thus politics continued to be dominated by the split between the AL and BNP—a split that went to "the very heart of the state itself, the national vision and definition of the country (Milam 2007, 157). Identity based appeals have since played a central role in elections. Thus, the Awami League has sought to take religious references out of the constitution and ban religiously based parties, and it has repeatedly attacked the BNP as being "anti-Liberation" (referring to the war of independence against Pakistan in 1971) (Schaffer 2002, 78). By contrast, the BNP has sought to promote the role of Islam in politics and has routinely "played the anti-Indian card" (Milam 2007, 157; also Kochanek 1997, 139).

This division has both promoted dynamic political competition and gravely undermined governance and democratic consolidation in Bangladesh. First, the division between the two political forces has thwarted efforts by either side to monopolize political control. Partly as a result of passions surrounding this identity divide, each party possesses "large core groups of traditional supporters" (Schaffer 2002, 79). In the four elections since 1991, each party has garnered support of at least a third of the electorate—with the rest of the electoral support divided among smaller groups. À la Lipset and Rokkan (1990 [1967]), the cleavage between pro-Indian ethnic and anti-Indian religious identities created a potent basis for a relatively stable two-party system.

Simultaneously, in a context in which all major political forces have readily engaged in antidemocratic behavior, identity-based mobilization has been key to hampering efforts by either side to monopolize political control. In elections in February 1996, for example, "massive vote rigging" and a boycott by the opposition AL resulted in an overwhelming victory by the BNP (Kochanek 1997, 137). The AL responded with an enormous *hartal* (general strike) that brought the "entire country to a standstill" (Kochanek 1997, 137). In the wake of months of economic and political paralysis brought about by 175 days of political disturbances led by the AL, the BNP backed down and agreed to neutral administration of repeat elections that brought the Awami League to power in June of that year (Kochanek 1997, 139). As a result of the split in identity, however, opposition to the new AL regime remained strong: the BNP retained a significant presence as the "largest and strongest opposition party" in parliament with nearly 40 percent of seats (Kochanek 1997, 141). In 2001, it won power again in the face of "political violence and intimidation."[8] Again in 2006, a political crisis was precipitated when the BNP sought to manipulate the electoral roles. In the midst of widespread violence by both parties and threats by the AL to boycott the election scheduled for early 2007, the army declared martial law. After ruling for nearly two years, the military, in the face of massive unrest and pressure from donors, agreed to step down and hold elections, which were held in December 2008. The AL won the elections convincingly and took power.

These events highlight a central dilemma facing divided societies such as Bangladesh. On the one hand, the identity-based conflict has severely undermined governance and the consolidation of democratic institutions. As a result of sharp polarization between the two sides, fed both by identity polarization and personalistic rivalries, each side regularly refused to recognize the electoral victories of the other, and boycotted parliament. This divide created a "toxic political culture" (Milam 2007, 157) and reduced governance "to a shambles" (Alamgir 2009, 51). On the other hand, this polarization and the powerful mobilizational capacity possessed by both sides has made it nearly impossible for one or the other side to monopolize political control.

In an ideal world, of course, it would be preferable to have both national unity and democracy. Yet, in a country with as weak institutions as Bangladesh, it is not obvious that opposition would be able to mobilize against autocratic rule in the absence of such an identity divide. "Deep seated" cleavages over national identity have arguably been a central force behind opposition mobilization and the persistence of two-party competition.

Albania

Albania's democratic prospects in the early 1990s were clearly bleak. One of the poorest and most isolated countries in Europe, Albania lacked virtually any civil society or democratic tradition. Under longtime ruler Enver Hoxha (1944–85), Albania had been one of the most closed and repressive communist regimes in the world. Yet, since the end of the Cold War, Albania has witnessed four electoral transitions between two relatively stable parties. As in Bangladesh, the emergence of dynamic political competition in Albania can be traced in part to divisions in national identity. This long-standing cleavage has nonetheless played an important role in promoting polarization and weak governance.

Since at least the early twentieth century, residents in northern and southern Albania have spoken different dialects of Albanian and have been separated by perceived cultural differences.[9] The Ghegs, who traditionally occupied the northern, more mountainous regions, have been considered poorer and more isolated than the Tosks in the South. While the Ghegs apparently dominated under King Zog (1928–39), the communists found most of their support among Tosks in the South. Enver Hoxha and "nearly all top Communist leaders" came from the South (Peters 1975, 283). Hoxha "widened the gulf between the Ghegs and Tosks": 60 to 80 percent of the Communist Party and a stunning 90 percent of high-level military officers were from the South (Vickers 2006, 294, 164; Daci 1998, 35, 41).

In turn, the transition from communist rule in 1990–92 was brought about by protests against the regime, which centered in the North (Szajkowski 1994, 2). The main opposition Democratic Party, based in the North, was founded by Sali Berisha, a former Communist Party official from that region. After defeating the (formerly communist) Socialist Party in elections in 1992, Berisha sought to redress the perceived regional imbalances in power. Thus Berisha quickly slashed military spending and purged up to two-thirds of the military officer corps—a move that was partly seen as an attempt to bring northerners into the Albanian state (Biberaj 1998, 324, 152–53; Daci 1998, 41; Vickers and Pettifer 2000, 217). Berisha "purged the state apparatus of hostile Tosks, replacing them with partisan northerners" (Gardner, Schaffer, and Kobtzeff 2000, 107).

In the 1990s and 2000s, the (formerly communist) Socialist Party with its base of support in the South and the Democratic Party, based in the North, formed the foundation for a quite stable two party system (Szajkowski 1994). Each party was able to rely on relatively consistent support in "its" region.[10] As in Bangladesh, this cleavage has made it hard for either side to sideline the other completely. Thus, neither party has received less than a quarter of the vote in any election since 1991, and each party has averaged about the same share of the vote over the post–Cold War period.

And as in Bangladesh and Ukraine, identity-based mobilization has undermined efforts to monopolize political control by one side or the other. Thus, protesters in the North helped to bring down the communist regime in 1991–92. In 1997, regional identity again played a role in overthrowing the democrats. Thus, following the collapse of a major countrywide pyramid scheme in late 1996, riots began in the South and moved North (Vickers and Pettifer 2000). In part because Berisha had weakened the state several years earlier by firing large numbers of northern military officers, he was unable to control the situation in the South, where the main leader of the Socialist Party was spontaneously released from prison (Gross 1998). Berisha was forced to call early elections in 1997, which were won by the socialists. Since that time, Albania witnessed two turnovers: the democrats replaced the socialists in 2005 but were ousted by the socialists in 2013.

But as in Bangladesh, divided identity has also contributed to a breakdown of governance in Albania. As in Bangladesh, "polarization" has "plagued Albanian politics" since the transition from authoritarianism.[11] For example, the Democrats boycotted the legislature for much of the late 1990s and early 2000s and, ignoring pleas by the OSCE, refused to take part in negotiations over a new constitution. In 2002 the EU was forced to intervene to force the two parties to cooperate in the election of a (largely figurehead) president of parliament. In the 2000s, politics suffered from perpetual "political gridlock."[12] Thus, regional divisions have hardly led to the creation of a stable democratic system. Yet, given Albania's underdevelopment, recent legacy of Stalinist-type rule, and lack of strong institutions, it is not obvious that opposition in the absence of identity divisions would have the capacity to mobilize against authoritarian rule.

Kyrgyzstan

National identity divisions have also shaped politics in Kyrgyzstan—albeit to a lesser extent. While arguably less ideologically polarized than in Albania, Bangladesh, or Ukraine, divisions have provided a central cleavage separating incumbent and opposition forces and periodically facilitated opposition mobilization against incumbent efforts to monopolize political control. Splits between northern[13] and southern[14] Kyrgyzstan have widely been viewed as a "key" divide in Kyrgyz politics (Anderson 1999, 39; Huskey 1997, 243–44, 248). In contrast to Albania, Bangladesh, and Ukraine, however, such divisions have not represented competing ideologies or cultural/geopolitical perspectives. Instead, these splits have mostly echoed particularistic "clan" networks (Collins 2009; Radnitz 2010). In the post-Soviet era, "clans remained far more powerful political actors than any of the new parties" (Anderson 1999, 39).

To an important extent, political contestation in Kyrgyzstan has reflected regional tensions. Thus, upon his appointment as leader of the Kyrgyz Communist Party in 1985, Absamat Masaliev displaced existing northern networks with personnel from the South (Collins 2009, 116). Subsequently in 1990, support for Askar Akaev's bid for the presidency came in part from groups in northern Kyrgyzstan who had been displaced by Masaliev (Collins 2009, 121, 126). Akaev in turn consolidated control in the mid-1990s by appointing northerners from his own clan as leaders of southern regions (Collins 2009, 244; Huskey 1997, 274).

Such efforts to impose regional power on the whole country created a backlash in the South, which became "the core of opposition to Akaev" (Collins 2009, 179). As Radnitz (2010) demonstrates, clientelism played a central role in the mobilization of opposition to Akaev's rule in the 2000s. In 2002, the arrest of a popular opposition deputy, Azimbek Beknazarov, sparked protests throughout southern Kyrgyzstan by those who had been "excluded from power" (Collins

2009, 248; Radnitz 2010, ch. 5).[15] Then in 2005 losers in parliamentary elections began protests in southern Kyrgyzstan that eventually resulted in the overthrow of Akaev (Hale 2011, 590). On March 18, 2005, protesters seized the regional government in Jalal-Abad in southern Kyrgyzstan and, within a week, had taken over about half of the country. Much of this protest was spearheaded by politicians in the South who successfully activated their "subversive clientelist ties" (Radnitz 2010, 140–43, 156–61). Finally, on March 24, Akaev abandoned power as about ten thousand rallied in the capital and stormed the government headquarters—forcing Akaev to flee the country and eventually resign.

Following Akaev's ouster, Kurmanbek Bakiyev from southern Kyrgyzstan won election as president. However, in April 2010, Bakiyev was ousted in a coup that ultimately resulted in the election of Almazbek Atambayev from northern Kyrgyzstan. Bakiyev in turn fled to his stronghold in the South before fleeing to Kazakhstan.

Thus, like the other countries discussed in this chapter, national political competition partly reflected regional divisions in national identity. While the nature of the regional divisions in Kyrgyzstan differed in important respects from those in Albania, Bangladesh, and Ukraine, (Radnitz 2010, 134–35), the case of Kyrgyzstan highlights that the same factors that facilitate political competition may also undermine reform and governance.

Finally, we see a similar dilemma in other divided societies after the Cold War. Moldova, for example, emerged from the Soviet collapse with a society starkly divided between a Russophile East and Romanophile West. These tensions have contributed to stalemate and a short-lived civil war in the East in 1991–92. Yet, polarization between Russophile and Romanophile forces has also contributed to the emergence of dynamic political competition. Indeed, opposition overturned incumbent power four times—in 1990, 1996, 2001, and 2009—by mobilizing either pro-Romanian/Moldovan or Russophile sentiment. Similarly, ethnic divisions in Kenya—in particular between Kikuyu, Kalenjin, and Luo ethnic groups—facilitated both ethnic violence in the late 1990s and 2007 but *also* opposition mobilization to the autocratic incumbent, Daniel arap Moi, in the 1990s and early 2000s (Way 2012).

Divided Society, Governance, and Democracy in Ukraine

These brief case studies of divided societies in transition suggest that the same passion and intransigence that thwarts reform efforts and the establishment of stable democratic institutions may *also* facilitate pluralism by motivating opposition in the voting booth and on the streets. While identity conflicts have certainly not been the only source of pluralism,[16] they have given opposition critical access to a reliable base of voter support as well as networks of passionate activists willing to take enormous risks to challenge autocratic rule. As evidenced by the 2014 crisis, this dilemma is also central to Ukrainian politics.

As numerous scholars have long noted, Ukraine is a highly regionalized country. Until 2014, the country could be divided into three regions—West, Center, and East—that reflect historical and ethnolinguistic differences. First, eastern/southern Ukraine,[17] merged into Russia before the nineteenth century, has been the region most closely tied to Russia, is dominated by Russophones, and has traditionally exhibited a relatively underdeveloped sense of Ukrainian identity. By contrast, western Ukraine, populated by Ukrainian speaking ethnic Ukrainians, is dominated by provinces that only became part of the USSR/Russia after World War II. In particular, Austrian rule over Galicia (Ivano Frankiivsk, L'viv, Ternopil) generated a robust Ukrainian nationalism that has persisted for generations. While surveys have suggested relatively equal levels of support for democracy, there are striking differences in foreign policy attitudes—including support for NATO, the EU, and Russia (Katchanovski 2006, 113–14). Finally, central Ukraine lacks the history of intense nationalism found in much of western Ukraine but consists of a greater number of Ukrainophones than in eastern and southern Ukraine (Barrington and Herron 2004, 58).

For the first twenty years of independence, this divide arguably undermined Ukrainian governance and efforts at reform. In 1993, anti-Russian policies by Kravchuk contributed to a strike wave in eastern Ukraine as polarization between Ukrainophiles from the West and pro-Russian forces in the East threatened the stability of the country. Kravchuk essentially used divisions and Ukrainian state-building as a way of avoiding more in-depth economic reform. Then in the late 1990s under Kuchma, pro-Russian communists based in eastern Ukraine blocked efforts at economic reform. Tensions between East and West arguably contributed to violence in 2014. Such divisions also hampered Ukraine's integration into the EU. Thus, while enthusiasm for Europe was strong in Kyiv, Ukraine as a whole was clearly divided on this question (Figure 3.1).

At the same time, this divide critically boosted political competition during the first quarter-century of Ukraine's independence. Thus, in the wake of the failed Soviet coup of 1991, Kravchuk took advantage of widespread anticom-

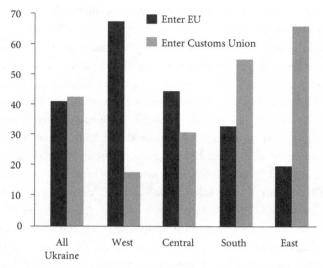

FIG. 3.1: Support for EU vs. Customs Union prior to the 2014 Crisis. Source: Kyiv International Institute of Sociology. The poll was conducted November 9–20, 2013.

munism to push for Ukrainian independence. However, his efforts to promote Ukrainian autonomy from Russia—together with a collapsing economy—antagonized forces in the East (D'Anieri 1999). In the wake of a wave of strikes in eastern Ukraine against Kravchuk, the president lost power to his former prime minister, Leonid Kuchma. Given the fact that Kuchma had had extraordinary power as prime minister during the worst of the Ukrainian economic crisis in 1993, Kuchma might have been considered as culpable for Ukrainian economic problems as Kravchuk. Yet he was able to distance himself from the crisis by supporting closer ties to Russia and defeated Kravchuk in 1994. Thus, while economic issues were clearly important in the 1994 presidential election, they were largely interpreted through the frame of identity (Wilson 2000, 193).

In the twenty-first century, regional identity was critical to the ousting of the same autocrat—Viktor Yanukovych—*twice*. In both 2004 and 2013/14, a combination of provocative pro-Russian actions and authoritarian abuse stoked regional tensions that contributed to large-scale demonstrations that forced regime collapse. First in 2004, Yanukovych was picked as the successor to Kuchma. A close partisan of the highly pro-Russian Donetsk region, Yanukovych ran on a stridently Russophile platform—inviting Russian president Vladimir Putin to campaign on his behalf. Then on November 21, Yanukovych engaged in extensive fraud in order to beat former prime minister Victor Yushchenko. In response, Ukraine witnessed an explosion of protest in Kyiv and across western Ukraine. In fact, although the biggest demonstrations took place in the capital, Kyivans accounted for a significantly lesser share of pro-Yushchenko demonstrators (14 percent) than did residents of nationalist Galicia (36 percent).[18] Western Ukrainians also provided a larger share of protesters than did residents of central Ukraine (Way 2011, 147). Similarly, Mark Beissinger (2013, 590) cites "overwhelming evidence that identity trumped ideology (and nearly everything else) in defining who participated in the revolution."

While the 1994 and 2004 crises avoided violence and resulted in negotiated transfers of power, the crisis in 2014 led to violent confrontations and a unilateral seizure of power—events much more in line with Bangladesh, Albania, and Kyrgyzstan, discussed above. The Ukrainian crisis began when Yanukovych decided against signing the European Association agreement. His sudden about-face stimulated massive demonstrations in central and western Ukraine that lasted for three months. As in 2004, western Ukrainians accounted for a significant share of protesters. While initially about half of the protesters in Kyiv were from the capital, western Ukrainians (representing 20 percent of the population) accounted for about half of the protesters in Kyiv by late January.[19] Across the country, a disproportionate share of protests were concentrated in western Ukraine.[20] According to one survey, 53 percent of western Ukrainians participated in the protests, as compared with 17 percent of central Ukrainians and 2–4 percent of southern and eastern Ukrainians.[21]

At the same time, Yanukovych's control over western and parts of central Ukraine began to break down—as provincial administrative offices and police and security headquarters throughout western and parts of central Ukraine were seized by protesters. Such defections were fatal for the regime because they greatly increased the challenge of putting down the rebellion. While the regime could have possibly cleared the square in Kyiv, it did not have sufficient capacity to regain control over the West—a fact that likely encouraged defection of key supporters from Yanukovych and convinced him to flee on February 21.

In sum, splits in national identity have constrained autocrats in Ukraine by fostering opposition mobilization both on the streets and at the ballot box. Such division has hardly fostered stable democratic institutions. (The constitutional structure in Ukraine has been radically revised three times since the mid-1990s.) Yet this divide has made it easier for opposition to tap into a highly passionate base of support willing to take significant risks that are often necessary to undermine incumbent autocratic control. Thus, in each of the four turnovers in Ukraine since independence, opposition succeeded in part by mobilizing either Russophile (1994, 2010) or Ukrainophile (2004, 2013/14) sentiment.

It is worth emphasizing that the political effects of the East/West divide are not immutable or predetermined. Indeed, the degree of regional electoral polarization varied over different elections: it was higher in presidential elections in 1994, 2004, and 2010, but somewhat lower in 1991 and 1999. Simultaneously, in contrast to the eastern and western electorates, Ukrainian leaders (Kuchma and Tymoshenko in particular) showed a remarkable flexibility in crossing the national divide—switching sides and actively seeking alliances with the other side.

However, the popular salience of identity issues in eastern and western Ukraine made it costly for Ukrainian leaders to ignore East/West divisions. In the first twenty years of Ukrainian independence, national appeals provided a relatively inexpensive way for politicians to garner public support. Thus, almost all successful politicians in Ukraine have relied on strong regional bases of support. In addition, the strongest parties in Ukraine (the national democratic *Rukh*, the communists, the Party of Regions) had clear regional foundations. This fact further increased the costs of creating an "all Ukrainian" movement encompassing both East and West before 2014.

The political salience of such divisions also explains why even rapacious politicians who do not care about identity have often evoked it. Thus, Party of Regions officials told U.S. officials privately that they had to "talk about NATO membership and Russian language" in order to win parliamentary elections,[22] and worried that if the party ceased to advocate for Russian issues, it would "sink into oblivion."[23] In addition, Tymoshenko in 2002 adopted Ukrainophile symbols to increase her appeal and move beyond her oligarchic past (Way 2015).

Overall, then, Ukraine's "pluralism by default"—driven to an important extent by the regional divide—has hardly been ideal. Most significantly, such pluralism impeded European integration and undermined both reform as well as the development of stable, democratic institutions. Clearly, the most preferable alternative would be the creation of a majority pro-European Ukrainian identity. Yet, such a prospect seemed highly uncertain at best in early 2014.

Ukrainian Identity and Prospects for Reform after the Crisis

The 2014 crisis and Russia's invasion of Crimea and Donbas radically altered the dynamics of national identity in Ukraine. First, the crisis created a much more unified Ukraine. The exit of Crimea and Donbas resulted in the departure of a highly Russophile 20 percent of Ukraine's electorate. War with Russia also made it substantially harder for politicians to mobilize Russophile support. The pro-Russian population in 2014 was demoralized, weakly organized, and substantially smaller. Indeed, presidential and parliamentary electoral results in 2014 reflected far less significant regional divisions than in the past—in part because many in the East refrained from voting. In May 2014, Poroshenko won every single province in Ukraine—although he received a somewhat lower share of the vote in the East.

Next, the crisis created a much greater consensus around European integration. Before the crisis, most polls suggested that the country was essentially split on Europe. While different polls show varying levels of support for European integration, most showed around 40 to 45 percent support for European integration as compared with about 30 to 40 percent support for the Customs Union.[24] Polls by the Razumkov Centre in 2012 indicated that very few in Ukraine saw European integration as an idea that could unite Ukraine.[25] However, Putin's aggression significantly increased support for Europe to about 50 to 55 percent. By contrast, support for the Customs Union declined dramatically to about 10 to 20 percent.[26] In eastern Ukraine, support for Russian integration declined by half—from about 60–70 percent in late 2013 to 30 percent in 2015.[27] Thus, nationalism and fears for national survival would now appear to be critical forces for change.

Yet changes in identity also seem likely to create new opportunities to undermine pluralism. The combination of war and a more unified Ukrainian identity allowed leaders to exploit nationalism to unite the population around a common threat, discourage opposition, and justify repression. Poroshenko used the conflict to threaten the imposition of martial law in early 2015.[28] War with Russia also made it harder for Russophile forces to mount a serious bid for power within Ukraine.

Indeed, while the central problem until 2014 was how to overcome Russophile opposition to European integration, the dilemma now is to prevent the complete disengagement of pro-Russian forces. One mechanism of engagement is decentralization. Throughout 2014 and 2015, peace negotiations included promises for special rights for communities in the Donbas.[29] At the same time, federalism was intensely unpopular among Ukrainophiles and was widely seen as a backdoor means for Russia to control Ukraine. Thus Putin's proposals would have essentially made it impossible for Ukraine to join European institutions without the support of representatives in the East. For many in the Ukrainian elite, federalism was seen as a means for Putin to revive the Soviet Union.[30] At the same time, given eastern Ukraine's distrust of Kyiv and the country's weak rule of law, it is not clear formal guarantees of autonomy will mollify forces in the East.

Finally, Russophile engagement can be encouraged by limiting attempts to remove Soviet era symbols or to dictate pro-Ukrainian interpretations of history. The fall of Yanukovych led to a surge of efforts to eliminate the symbolic vestiges of Soviet rule—including Lenin statues and Soviet era place names. In April 2015, the Rada passed a series of "anticommunist laws" banning Soviet symbols and outlawing the denigration of pro-Ukrainian groups—including the Organization of Ukrainian Nationalists, who were responsible for the killing of Poles during World War II (see Shevel chapter in this volume). Such measures seem likely to further alienate eastern Ukrainians whose support is critical for the country's territorial integrity. For example, there was wide discussion of the need to rename the "Dnipropetrovsk" region in the East, changing its Soviet-era name. Yet a plurality of the region view the Soviet era positively.[31] Renaming would seem unlikely to encourage engagement of this critical population.

In sum, historical divisions in Ukraine have had contradictory consequences—ones found in other divided societies. Such divisions undermined reform and severely complicated governance—but also bolstered opposition and guaranteed a certain level of pluralism. In today's more united Ukraine, a key challenge is to use the power of nationalism to promote reform without excluding groups central to the country's future as an inclusive, democratic state.

Notes

1. For an important exception, see Shevel (2011a).
2. See Paul D'Anieri's chapter in this volume for a discussion of reform.
3. All were lower-middle or low-income countries as coded by the World Bank in 1995.
4. National identity is defined as the conception of community that forms the basis or justification of claims for statehood.
5. This definition excludes national divisions involving separatist minorities that do not seek national power (for example, Abkhaz in Georgia, Chechens in Russia). This definition also does not refer to countries with minorities (such as Coptic Christians in Egypt) that are widely considered to be too small ever to gain national power.

6. Ukraine has a different culture than does Bangladesh. In addition, it is wealthier, more economically developed, urban, and has a significantly greater rate of literacy. World Bank, World Development Indicators. See http://data.worldbank.org/data-catalog/world-development-indicators.

7. Ukraine's average Freedom House score (1992–2012) is 6.6; Bangladesh's (1991–2012) is 7.05; Ukraine's average Polity (1992–2011) is 6.4; Bangladesh (1991–2011) is 5.4.

8. See "Bangladesh," in Freedom House, *Freedom in the World: 2002*, www.Freedomhouse.org.

9. At the same time, these cultural/regional differences do not appear to be as salient as are divisions in Bangladesh or Ukraine Thus there is not as much ideological content to the division as in Bangladesh and Ukraine. In addition, while the North and South exhibit different levels of support for the different parties, these differences are not as stark as in Ukraine (or the United States); thus the standard deviation of regional support in the most recent Albanian election in 2011 was 9.4—as compared with 27 in Ukraine in 2010.

10. For example, in 2009 the socialists garnered more votes in each of the six southern provinces, while the Democratic Party garnered majorities in each of the five northern provinces (results from Wikipedia).

11. Fabian Schmidt, "Row over Albanian Election Commission," *RFE/RL Reports,* January 14, 2000.

12. "Albania's 2013 Parliamentary Elections: Political Prospects and Democratic Challenges," *Dielli Online,* May 7, 2013.

13. Naryn, Talas, Chui, Issyj-Kul oblasts.

14. Jalalabad, Osh oblasts.

15. International Crisis Group, "Kyrgyzstan's Political Crisis: An Exit Strategy," August 20, 2002. http://www.crisisgroup.org/en/regions/asia/central-asia/kyrgyzstan/037-kyrgyzstans-political-crisis-an-exit-strategy.aspx·

16. In particular, identity divisions seem to matter more in conditions in which authoritarian party and state institutions are relatively weak. See Way (2012, 2015).

17. This combines what others call East (Dnipropetrovsk, Donetsk, Kharkiv, Luhansk, and Zapporizhe) and South (Crimea, Kherson, Mykolaiv, Odesa).

18. Results of a survey conducted in mid-December 2004 by the Kyiv International Institute of Sociology.

19. "Vid Maidanu-taboru do Maidanu-sichi: shcho zminylos'ia?" Fond Demokratichni Initsiatyvy. See http://dif.org.ua/ua/events/vid-ma-zminilosj.htm.

20. "Statystyka protestnykh podii Maidanu: uchasnyky, heohrafiia, nasyl'stvo." See http://www.cedos.org.ua.

21. "Richnytsia Maidanu—opytuvannia hromads'koii ta ekspertnoii dumky." See http://www.dif.org.ua.

22. See the American embassy cable, "Ukraine: Regions Focuses on Campaign;

Puts Aside Internal Differences," September 28, 2007. See https://wikileaks.org/plusd/cables/07KYIV2481_a.html·

23. "Georgii Kriuchkov: Esli Ianukovich zabudet pro russkii iazyk, Partiia Regionov uidet v nebytie," *IA Regnum*, September 11, 2006.

24. See kiis.com.ua; razumkov.gov.ua.

25. Thus, Razumkov Centre polls between 2005 and 2012 showed that between 26 and 36 percent saw European integration as a uniting idea (razumkov.gov.ua).

26. See http://www.kiis.com.ua/?lang=ukr&cat=reports&id=530&page=1. "Ukraiintsi bil'she ne vvazhaiut' vidnosyny z Rosieiu priorytetnymy, a pidtrymka MS vpala do 12%," *UNIAN.* See http://www.unian.ua/society/1070610-opituvannya-sered-ukrajintsiv-zrostae-pidtrimka-proevropeyskogo-kursu-krajini.html.

27. See http://www.kiis.com.ua/?lang=ukr&cat=reports&id=530&page=1. "Ukraiintsi bil'she ne vvazhaiut' vidnosyny z Rosieiu priorytetnymy, a pidtrymka MS vpala do 12%," *UNIAN.* See http://www.unian.ua/society/1070610-opituvannya-sered-ukrajintsiv-zrostae-pidtrimka-proevropeyskogo-kursu-krajini.html.

28. "Poroshenko Will Impose Martial Law if Cease-fire Fails," *Kyiv Post*, February 14, 2015.

29. "A Complex of Measures to Fulfill the Minsk Agreements," *Kyiv Post*, February 12, 2015.

30. "Putin vystupaet za federalizatsiiu Ukrainy," *Zerkalo nedeli*, November 17, 2014.

31. "Shcho ob'ednue ta roz'ednue ukraiintsiv-opytuvannia hromads'koii dumky Ukraiiny." See http://dif.org.ua/en/polls/2015a/sho-obednue-ta-rozednue-.htm. The poll results combine Dnipropetrovsk and Zaporizhzha.

PART III

Corruption

4

Corruption in Ukraine: Perpetuum Mobile or the Endplay of Post-Soviet Elites?

Serhiy Kudelia

Numerous cross-national studies examining the spread of corruption picture an overwhelmingly gray world, with countries differing only in terms of their various shades. While the developed countries in Europe, North America, and parts of Asia have moved toward the lighter side, becoming less severely affected by this scourge, post-Soviet states remain mired in the darkest part of the corruption spectrum. These comparisons, however, obscure crucial differences in the drivers and patterns of corruption around the world. While any politician might feel tempted by a lucrative funding offer or a chance to enjoy a luxurious lifestyle, some are more likely to pursue these opportunities with impunity, while others risk both political and legal consequences. Take, for example, former Virginia governor Robert McDonnell, who was convicted of accepting excessive gifts from a private businessman, or former French president Jacques Chirac, who used public funds to pay his party allies. Despite the relatively modest level of their corrupt acts, they were both exposed and investigated by state agencies. By contrast, it took a mass uprising to dispossess former Ukraine president Viktor Yanukovych of a lavish mansion acquired for an artificially low price with the assistance of allied businessmen.[1] While the attributes and practices of grand corruption may be similar across the world, its volume and legal consequences for corrupt officials are qualitatively different.

This chapter examines the changes in the patterns of corrupt practices in Ukraine over the last two decades and identifies specific mechanisms that allowed grand corruption to proliferate and flourish despite a whole array of anticorruption initiatives.

It focuses primarily on grand corruption involving public officials in different state institutions or government agencies who abuse the powers of their offices in order to acquire personal wealth or gain exclusive access to financial resources. While petty corruption, such as bribing in educational or medical institutions, has been similarly widespread, grand corruption has been most harmful to the functioning of Ukraine's economic and political system.

This chapter links changes in the patterns of grand corruption to the evolution of the country's institutional setup and demonstrates how changes in the distribution of formal powers made grand corruption both better structured and more large-scale. It starts with an overview of the general corruption levels in Ukraine and the types of anticorruption measures adopted by the Ukrainian authorities so far. It then reviews different theoretical explanations accounting for the failure of anticorruption policies and growth in grand corruption over the last two decades. The third part of the chapter will use a theoretical institutional framework to distinguish between three types of corrupt patterns prevalent in Ukraine in different periods and analyze each of these patterns chronologically. In the conclusion, I offer three broad anticorruption policy recommendations that follow from the analytical approach used in this chapter.

Corruption in Ukraine: Perceptions, Policies, and Outcomes

Based on purely formal criteria, the anticorruption efforts of the Ukrainian authorities have been extensive. More than thirty presidential decrees and government resolutions combined with a dozen legislative acts adopted over the last two decades have targeted all types of corrupt practices. The first major piece of legislation—the Law on Combating Corruption—was adopted in 1995 and detailed ways to control and punish corruption offenses for a relatively broad range of public officials.[2] Numerous other legislative acts have been adopted since then to address those issues that the first law failed to deal with, particularly measures to prevent corruption and expanding both the definition of corrupt actions and the types of persons liable for them.[3] In addition, each of Ukraine's previous presidents issued his own official concept paper on combating corruption. These documents, however, proved to be paper tigers, all roar and no bite. Not only did they remain largely unimplemented, but, in addition, the sheer volume of grand corruption under each of the successive presidents has only increased.

The poor anticorruption record of Ukraine's first four presidents stemmed

from similar root problems. First, each anticorruption drive was excessively centralized and bureaucratized, with the presidents usually setting up and chairing
various types of groups composed of executive agencies that supposedly had to
help them coordinate their policies. In reality, the high-level meetings of these
commissions amounted to a mere publicity stunt for the presidents to demonstrate their commitment to fighting corruption. Without the mechanism and
resources for continuous oversight of policy implementation and lacking even
a semblance of independence, these groups became "smokescreens for action"
(Rouso and Steves 2006, 253). Second, each of the four presidents resisted creating a genuinely independent agency with a broad mandate to investigate all
types of corrupt activities. At least four different state institutions—Interior
Ministry, Tax Administration, Security Service, and Prosecutor General—had
the formal authority to conduct investigations into corruption-related crimes
with numerous other smaller agencies created within the executive for the purpose of oversight. The result was an overlap in their functions and politicization of their activities, which has only contributed to the overall inefficiency
and selectivity of anticorruption measures. Third, numerous and often contradictory legal instruments to prosecute corruption contained in administrative
and criminal codes and separate legislative acts created a confusing legal environment that further weakened their enforcement and created more opportunities for selectivity in their application. As a result, many progressive measures,
such as extending liability for corruption to legal entities or enhancing access to
public information, became largely meaningless. Fourth, and most important,
all key elite actors and public officials have been benefiting from the lack of
strong legal constraints over corrupt practices, which created a self-enforcing
equilibrium encouraging high-level corruption to continue unabated. As the
first Group of States against Corruption (GRECO) report noted in 2007, while
Ukrainian public officials recognize the need to change the current state of
affairs, "[I]t appears politically difficult to establish a structure to effectively coordinate and consistently monitor the necessary reforms."[4] Six years later, GRE-
CO's review similarly concluded that "numerous and sometimes contradictory
measures have been taken, but have rarely been pursued to reach meaningful results."[5] Momentum for substantive change, hence, depends primarily on
pressure from external actors, such as civil society groups or the international
community.

The failure of the Ukrainian authorities to rein in corruption has been
clearly recorded in the indices of major international organizations and public

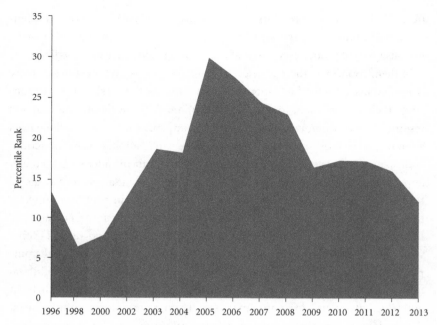

Fig. 4.1: Control of Corruption in Ukraine, 1996–2013. Source: World Bank's Country Data Report for Ukraine, World Wide Governance Indicators, 1996–2013. See http://info.worldbank.org/governance/wgi/c226.pdf.

opinion surveys. The Corruption Perception Index of Transparency International (TI) and the Control of Corruption Index of the World Bank (WB) show a consistently high level of perceived corruption in Ukraine. The WB placed Ukraine in the bottom twentieth percentile of states with the weakest control over public sector corruption for most of the last decade. Despite some notable improvements in 2005–6, the index had regressed below its 1996 level by 2013 (see Figure 4.1).

Corroborating this data, TI ranked Ukraine among the 35 countries (out of more than 170) with the highest level of perceived corruption for most of the same period. According to the 2013 TI report, Ukraine had the highest perceived level of public sector corruption in Europe with a score equal to that of the Central African Republic, Nigeria and Papua New Guinea.[6] Public opinion surveys show that about two-thirds of the society consistently characterized the level of corruption in Ukraine as "high" (37.9 percent in 2004 and 32.7 percent in 2009) or "very high" (32 percent in 2004 and 46.4 percent in 2009).[7] Grand corruption has also been continuously ranked among the most severe problems for the country by more than 90 percent of the public.[8] By October 2013, a month before the start of the Euromaidan protests, 85 percent of Ukrainians expressed dissatisfaction with President Yanykovych's policies to eradicate corruption.[9]

One clear indicator of the Ukrainian authorities' failure to curb corrupt practices has been the absence of any top-level public officials convicted of corruption.[10] For example, among the four officials charged with taking the biggest bribes in 2013, two were attorneys representing the state in bankruptcy cases, while the other two worked in village councils.[11] Bribe-related cases also typically involved relatively small sums. The biggest bribe registered in Ukraine in 2012 was the $350,000 demanded in Kyiv's Pedagogical Academy, while the average amount for the top ten highest bribes that year was $20,000.[12] These cases were a minuscule part of the high-level corruption in Yanukovych's government exposed following his ouster from power.

What Accounts for Grand Corruption?

Explanations accounting for high-level corruption in developing states generally focus on personalities (greed), institutions (opportunity structure), or political calculus (strategy). Greed-based explanations emphasize the insatiable appetites of political leaders, bureaucrats, and businessmen pursuing personal material wealth at the public expense. Institutional explanations, by contrast, put the actors' cost and benefit calculations at the center of the analysis. One set of explanations focuses on norms guiding public behavior in post-Soviet states (Cheloukhine and King 2007). It stresses the normative continuities with the Soviet era and argues that the implicit public acceptance of corrupt practices disables the mechanism of social sanctions that could have deterred higher-level corruption. Polling results consistently indicate tacit public approval of corruption in Ukraine on all levels. In a survey conducted in Ukraine in 2007, 2009, and 2011, about half of the respondents argued that corruption was either always or sometimes justified, with the younger respondents (from eighteen to forty-four) being far more likely to justify corrupt acts.[13] In a 2013 survey, two-thirds of the respondents (67 percent) acknowledged volunteering an unofficial payment for the provision of services.[14]

Another set of institutional explanations looks at state capacity and points to the weakness of law enforcement or other institutions of accountability as the key reason for the spread of corruption (Holmes 1997; Karklins 2005). Other studies assess the impact of different institutional designs, particularly the type of executive-legislative relations, the electoral rules, and the degree of decentralization (Kunicovà 2006). Despite substantial disagreement about the effects of plurality or proportional representation electoral systems and federalism, most institutional accounts agree that presidentialism is strongly correlated with higher level of grand corruption. At the same time, as Treisman points out, this statistically strong relationship becomes insignificant when controlling for Catholicism, which he explains by the effect of corrupt presidential regimes in South America (Treisman 2007, 235).

The third set of explanations approaches grand corruption as a strategy used by political leaders to maintain power. The selectorate theory has gained prominence for offering a formal model that explicates the rationale behind the purposeful decision of political leaders to promote grand corruption among their supporters (Bueno de Mesquita et al. 2003). It looks at the incentives for corruption that arise with changes in the size of the winning coalitions relative to the size of the selectorate. A leader who relies on a small group of supporters to remain in office will prefer to distribute more private goods targeting his allies than public goods benefiting society as a whole. This strategy leads to the most egregious abuses of power for the sake of ensuring the loyalty of key political actors, but may also turn bad governance into good politics (Mesquita and Smith 2011). Another strategic view of graft, developed from a case study of Ukraine during Leonid Kuchma's presidency, argues that it serves to strengthen informal hierarchy within the state bureaucracy by allowing principals to threaten their agents with sanctions in case of disobedience (Darden 2008). By this logic, corruption reinforces elite compliance by giving rulers an additional coercive power to blackmail their subordinates rather than just buy their loyalty. In both cases, graft is expected to strengthen the state and the existing political regime.

My argument complements the strategic approach to corruption, but views it as elites' response to a particular institutional environment that sets the ground rules for corrupt patterns. A weakly institutionalized political system with an unclear distribution of formal powers among state agencies and poor enforcement of laws leads to chaotic horizontal corruption with free access to corrupt opportunities. By contrast, a political system organized in a vertical manner around a political leader with broad discretionary powers produces a patronal form of corruption, which requires strict sanction from above (Hale 2011). It is driven primarily by the patron's political interest in maintaining a broad and loyal clientelistic network. Finally, a political system may include several elite cliques organized as political parties competing for access to different decision-making centers. In this case, corruption is a response to the party leaders' need to gain or maintain comparative advantage over their opponents or, at least, remain competitive in the political process. Revenues from corruption help to build party organizations, maintain public presence, acquire useful allies, and wage election campaigns. This type of corruption combines both horizontal elements, with party cartels engaging in corruption independently of each other, and vertical elements in relations between patrons and clients within party cliques. As James Scott argued in the study of corrupt patterns in Thailand forty years ago, such corruption does not result from the random greed of public officials or political leaders, but rather becomes a "consequence of a narrowly elitist political order that encourages clique conflict over the spoils of office" (Scott 1972, 41).

The Evolution of Corruption Patterns in Ukraine

The patterns of corruption in Ukraine have closely followed changes in the institutional structure of the state. In the first years following Ukraine's independence in 1991, the weakness of state control over the economy and the lack of oversight and accountability produced an atomized free-for-all form of corruption characterized by uncoordinated predation and disorganized rent-seeking on all levels of the state. This period ended with the adoption of the 1996 Constitution, which privileged the president over all other institutional actors. The newly acquired extensive powers allowed the president not only to become the ultimate arbiter in the fight over spoils but also to channel corruption to specific political purposes. Ukraine's shift to a parliamentary-presidential system in 2006, accompanied by the introduction of a proportional representation election law, elevated the role of political parties in the political process. Their new prominence led to the transformation of elite cliques into party machines, which played an increasingly central role in the distribution of patronage and rent-seeking opportunities (Kudelia and Kuzio 2015). Ukraine's return to a superpresidential system in 2010 produced a partial revival of "patronal corruption," marked by the rise of the president's family as one of the key beneficiaries of the government's policies. At the same time, party cartels maintained their significance as centers of accumulation and redistribution of corrupt rents by competing political elites. They again took center stage once the "patronal" presidency was dismantled in February 2014.

Atomized Corruption (1991–96)

After the Soviet breakup, Ukraine emerged as a financially impoverished state with a factionalized political elite, rapacious entrepreneurial class, and weak civil society (Way 2005). This situation created a favorable environment in which political and business actors, guided primarily by short-term interests of quick wealth accumulation, could prey on the state without limits. As Ukrainian billionaire Dmytro Firtash recounted his experience in the early 1990s, in order to obtain any government permit, he first needed to win permission from the appropriate "businessman" working with the particular official in charge of issuing permits.[15] In reality, many of these "businessmen" proved to be organized crime members. The state bureaucracy across all levels of government thus played the central role during this reign of free-for-all corruption (Aslund 2009; Havrylyshyn 2000). The prime exhibit from this period was acting prime minister Yuhym Zviahilsky (1993–94), who was later prosecuted for embezzling $25 million worth of state-owned aviation fuel, which was then sold abroad with the proceeds deposited to his offshore account. Others, like then governor of Dnipropetvsk oblast Pavlo Lazarenko, established partnerships with local businessmen and provided them with rent-seeking opportunities in return for a percentage of their monthly revenues (Leshchenko 2013, 158). By various estimates, rents generated in Ukraine during the first two years following independence equaled the country's annual GDP at the time (Aslund 2009, 56).

The multitude of actors involved in corrupt dealings with the state maintained their access to spoils largely through personal ties and a commitment to share acquired wealth. The system of grand corruption, however, was decentralized and devoid of unified political purpose. Its consequences were the near bankruptcy of the Ukrainian state and the dispersion of wealth across different elite networks. The abysmal performance of the Ukrainian economy prevented incumbent president Leonid Kravchuk from winning re-election in June 1994. His successor—Leonid Kuchma—quickly concentrated all executive power in his hands, leading to a change in the prevailing pattern of corruption in Ukraine.

Patronal Corruption (1996–2004)

The adoption of a presidentialist constitution in July 1996 gave rise to a hierarchical system of patronage and rent distribution in which the president wielded the ultimate authority (Hale 2011). By appointing his loyalists to key government agencies Kuchma could single-handedly influence the provision of state funds, set conditions for privatizing state firms or issue trade quotas for specific private companies. This power, in turn, expanded his clientelistic base and allowed him to redistribute assets and other economic benefits to a select few business clans, which quickly emerged as the largest oligarchic groups in Ukraine. The story of Pryvat Group's privatization of Ukraine's largest oil company, Ukrnafta, and iron ore mining company, KZhRK, illustrates the patterns of "patronal corruption" characteristic of that period. According to a court deposition by Pryvat Group owners Ihor Kolomoiskiy and Gennadiy Bogolyubov, Victor Pinchuk (Kuchma's son-in-law and the owner of a major industrial holding company) approached them in 2002 and offered to assist with privatizing Ukraine's largest oil and gas company Ukrnafta using his influence with the president. In return he asked for an option to later purchase a portion of the shares issued by the companies that would come to own it.[16] In addition, Kolomoiskiy and Bogolyubov had to contribute at least $5 million in monthly payments to Kuchma's campaign fund for the upcoming presidential election in 2004. Although Kuchma ultimately decided not to stand for a third term, they ended up paying $100 million in campaign contributions. In his own lawsuit, Pinchuk also claims that he asked the two Pryvat owners to privatize the Ukrainian iron ore mining company KZhRK on his behalf for a 10 percent commission and deposited $130 million to their bank to close the deal.[17] Pinchuk's de facto ownership of the asset was clear from the fact that his representatives were appointed to chair the management body of the company right after its privatization in September 2004 and acted on his behalf until Kuchma lost power in early 2005. As Kolomoiskiy explained in his court deposition, they had to recognize Pinchuk's shadow ownership of their asset because they were concerned that Kuchma would pressure them otherwise.[18]

In addition to cultivating loyal business clans, Kuchma also developed clientelistic relationships with subordinate officials who had direct access to cash flows to the state budget and capable of diverting them for his political purposes. The most telling is the example of Ihor Bakai, a prominent gas trader in the mid-1990s, who unexpectedly became the chairman of the state oil and gas monopoly Naftogaz in February 1998. According to the recordings of conversations between Kuchma and then head of the Tax Administration, Mykola Azarov, Bakai had to divert up to $250 million for the president's re-election campaign, but in reality contributed only $66 million out of at least $184 million he had made on illegal transactions charged to Naftogaz's account (Koshiw

2013, 105–6). Despite the cheating of his client, Kuchma later appointed Bakai to head the department in charge of handling the state property controlled by the presidential administration. This episode demonstrates that the principal-agent bargain under Kuchma allowed for violating some financial obligations to the patron as long as the agent remained loyal politically.

Similarly, as the case of former prime minister Pavlo Lazarenko showed, political disloyalty rather than egregious corruption was the real reason for prosecution. Lazarenko defrauded the state budget of more than $200 million in the period from 1993 to 1997 through gas trading and other schemes. President Kuchma did not interfere with Lazarenko's activities as long as he remained loyal to his patron, but his permissive attitude changed once it became clear that the prime minister intended to use the funds to finance his own presidential bid. Kuchma fired Lazarenko in July 1997 and opened criminal cases against him after his party, "Hromada," gained representation in the parliament and went into opposition to Kuchma. Under pressure from the authorities, Lazarenko had to flee to Switzerland and then to the United States, where he was immediately arrested on money-laundering charges in February 1999. Most of his clientelistic network, however, survived under the new patronage of his erstwhile client Yulia Tymoshenko, who now shifted her loyalties to Kuchma and supported his re-election campaign (Koshiw 2013, 29–30). In mid-1999 she also created her own political party—"Bat'kivshchyna" (Fatherland)—which became a new shelter for Lazarenko's former associates. Along with another party created around that time—Party of Regions—it would come to dominate the Ukrainian political scene for most of the next decade. Both of these parties evolved into large "party cartels" that would soon represent a new stage in the evolution of corruption patterns in Ukraine (Katz and Mair 2009).

"Party Cartel" Corruption (2005–)

In the first postindependence decade, political parties in Ukraine remained highly rudimentary and resembled Russia's "politicized financial-industrial groups" (Hale 2005b). Most of them served as mere instruments of lobbying or gaining access to lucrative government positions. They were, in effect, formalized clientelistic networks created around minor patrons and embedded in a larger power pyramid. Their quick rise and demise, hence, followed the fortunes of their powerful oligarchic chiefs. In the early 2000s a new type of political organization emerged in Ukraine with oligarchs no longer playing a decisive role. While contributing financial resources to beefing up the organizational muscles, they shared control with, or even followed the lead of, charismatic politicians or influential government administrators with access to state funds. They also operated as umbrella organizations for smaller political parties eager to collude to acquire influence and access to funds. Two main examples of these political groups in the early 2000s were the Party of Regions led by former Donetsk oblast governor Viktor Yanukovych and Our Ukraine, led by former prime minister Viktor Yushchenko. The rise of the third group— Bloc of Yulia Tymoshenko, based on "Bat'kivshchyna"—only intensified competition for scarce resources and government positions. Rather than serving as temporary vehicles for quick enrichment, they attracted long-term investments meant to offer their members a promise of continued political and financial rewards. They sought to divide the electoral market between themselves with Our Ukraine and Bat'kivshyna vying for the control of western and central Ukraine, while Party of Regions monopolized most of the Southeast (Kudelia and Kuzio 2015).

A set of institutional changes adopted in 2004 accelerated the transformation of the pattern of corruption in Ukraine from one centered on patronal pyramids to one built around party cartels. The redistribution of formal powers from the president meant that there was no longer a unified and cohesive patronal system that could regulate and control corrupt practices. The parliamentary majority coalition consisting of party factions now gained power to form most of the government, while the prime minister acquired crucial powers to decide on the distribution of economic rewards. At the same time, the shift to a party-list voting system in parliamentary and local council elections elevated the role of political parties and made access to party leadership indispensable for receiving patronage and rents.

When Yanukovych's Party of Regions won the 2006 parliamentary election and formed a new government, key cabinet positions went directly or indirectly to the party funders—Rinat Akhmetov, Andriy Kliuev, and Dmytro Firtash. Similarly, following an early parliamentary election in September 2007, a new majority coalition emerged with Tymoshenko's donors—Serhiy Buriak, Vitaliy Haiduk, and Tariel Vasadze—taking important positions in the new government.

Party cartels have proven to be far more efficient than the ad hoc funding coalitions of the late 1990s for three main reasons. First, they allow for better monitoring and less waste in the use of financial resources. When running for re-election in 1999, Kuchma relied on several self-contained campaign funds linked to different oligarchic groups. This made it nearly impossible to track and control their actual contributions to his campaign. By centralizing funds in party cartels, political elites ensure better oversight by party officials and fewer losses related to internal malfeasance. Allegiance to a political machine is also used as a signaling mechanism. It helps to minimize losses associated with opportunistic corruption by politically unaffiliated officials who reap personal benefits without sharing with the party.

Second, party cartels allowed their leaders to sustain permanent political contestation, which is particularly important given how competitive Ukraine's political process is. A year after winning his re-election campaign, Kuchma faced the worst political crisis of his presidency but had few organizational resources with which to respond to a growing popular movement against him. Eventually he managed to cobble together another ad hoc support coalition, drawing on some of the earlier funders, but he lost momentum to the opposition. Party cartels allow for the continuous accumulation of funds and, hence, a quick reaction to any political challenges to their leaders. They also help to conduct preemptive campaigns in order to neutralize emerging threats.

Finally, party cartels serve as a reassurance mechanism to funders concerned with the durability of the politicians' commitments. A lack of party ties allows political leaders to renege on initial promises unilaterally and without major costs. Kuchma excluded several of his backers from his inner circle and bypassed others in the distribution of government jobs after his re-election. Membership in party cartels, by contrast, ensures funders representation in the parliament, the executive branch, or local councils and continuous access to the party's elite circle (often formalized in the parties' political councils). The notorious practice of party leaders to offer positions on the parties' electoral lists in exchange for campaign contributions, which became widespread in the early 2000s, has been one of the most effective ways for them to continuously raise funds.

Apart from collecting business contributions, party cartels also absorb a share of corruption rent obtained at different levels of public bureaucracy. While earlier the centralization of government worked to the benefit of top government officials, now the system of party patronage allows the ruling cartel to control key positions on all bureaucratic levels. Hence, bureaucratic rent gets redistributed not only to satisfy the needs of greedy officials but also to maintain party operations. In addition to the usual party activities, such as organizational maintenance, political campaigns, and media publicity, party cartels often adopt shadowy tactics like the use of "charities" in different regions to establish clientelistic relations with voters, the cooptation of strategic allies, and even the creation of fake candidates and parties to run against their opponents (Wilson 2005).

The operation of party cartels thrives on legislative loopholes that allow for unlimited contributions with minimal oversight and accountability. According to GRECO's 2011 evaluation report, Ukrainian laws permit cash and noncash donations to political parties from domestic physical and legal persons with no fixed maximum value thresholds.[19] At the same time, the legal requirements regarding public disclosure of the parties' annual budgets are minimal. The law requires public release of only a total income and expense statement, offering no detailed information on the sources of income and itemized breakdown of expenditures. Parties are not required to submit these financial statements to state bodies, but only publish them in the national press. The law also precludes differentiating between various types of donations, such as regular membership fees or larger one-time contributions. This limits the possibility for exercising any public control over the parties' financial activities and assessing the extent of their dependence on private donors.

The law also privileges political parties as a source of funding in election campaigns. It stipulates that a particular candidate running in a national or local election can receive unlimited amounts of money from a political party, while individual donations to an election fund are restricted and legal entities are barred from making donations to individual candidates. Moreover, donations from political parties allow the giver to remain anonymous, while anonymous donations to independent candidates are prohibited. According to the legal reporting requirements, only a payment date, order, and value of the donation must be specified.[20] This lax legal environment, in effect, turns political parties into clearing houses for large donations intended for a particular candidate. Given that there are currently no spending limits in parliamentary elections, it also advantages party-backed candidates by offering them unrestricted access to financial resources from party coffers. Large party contributions thus become a legitimate way for businessmen not only to buy influence but also impose their own clients on party leaders as potential candidates to take parliamentary or governmental seats and then act on their behalf.

Even the existing feeble checks over party funding have been enforced only weakly. Oversight over election campaign funding is the prerogative of the central and territorial election commissions, but there have been no cases of financial inspections carried out by any of these commissions.[21] As a result, there have been no political parties sanctioned for violating the financial regulations or election funding laws. Even if financial violations were detected, however, the maximum possible sanction is a warning to a political party with no individual liability or further legal implications.

Despite Ukraine's return to a consolidated executive system in 2010, the patterns of corruption in the country changed only partially. The re-established patronal pyramid once again became an important mechanism of wealth maximization, now benefiting the president's family and his primary business donors (Akhmetov and Firtash) (Kudelia 2014). The reinstatement of a hierarchical power pyramid revived coercive subordination of other clientelistic networks to a single patron. However, competing party cartels remained important actors in the system of corrupt dealings in Ukraine. Party of Regions subjugated the parliament and exercised control over the regions. It accumulated more power than any of Ukraine's political parties before it. Still, the opposition parties, often funded by the oligarchs close to Yanukovych, retained substantial representation in the parliament and majorities in local councils in western Ukraine. The parliamentary election in 2012 was held under a mixed system, maintaining party leaders' full control over the composition of the party lists and privileging wealthy donors. Hence, while the names of some opposition parties changed after 2002, they functioned by the same logic. Each of the prominent opposition leaders—Vitaliy Klitschko, Arseniy Yatsenyuk, Oleh Tyahnybok—received funds from major businessmen, offering them in return parliamentary seats or an opportunity to hedge their risks in case Yanukovych fell. The favorable coverage of the Euromaidan protests by major oligarch-controlled media (owned by Pinchuk, Kolomoiskiy, Firtash, and even Akhmetov) was an indirect sign that some oligarchs had turned their backs on the incumbent president.[22]

While Yanukovych's ultimate ouster presented a unique opportunity for cracking down on grand corruption, post-Euromaidan authorities proved as reluctant to end the informal practices or prosecute high-level graft as their predecessors had been.[23] As a result, despite Ukraine's adoption of anticorruption legislation in line with the demands of international organizations, the prospects of its consistent enforcement remain uncertain.[24] The analysis presented in this chapter suggests three key priorities for the campaign to eradicate Ukraine's notorious corruption at the top.

Fighting Grand Corruption

Major political parties remain the locus of graft in Ukraine. President Petro Poroshenko's party "Solidarnist'" (Solidarity) is run by his business partners and associates of the infamous former mayor of Kyiv, Leonid Chernovets'kyi. In the run-up to the October 2015 local elections, it absorbed Klitschko's UDAR to limit political competition. Other major parties—such as Yatsenyuk's People's Front, Yulia Tymoshenko's Bat'kivshchyna, Oleh Liashko's Radical Party, and Andriy Sadovyi's Samopomich—function as personalized political machines engaged in quid pro quos with the government and sustained through arcane dealings with oligarchic donors. The first step in dismantling Ukraine's party cartels will be breaking the exclusive powers of party leaders over the selection of candidates for national and local races. This would require a shift to an election system that allows voters to rank political candidates and supersede the authority of political leaders in deciding who should represent them. It would also require instituting a ban on informal funding of political parties and their election campaigns. It should include restrictions on the amount of individual donations, full transparency requirements on the sources of party funding, identities of donors, and strict reporting rules on campaign spending. Parties should be required to submit annual reports on their incomes, expenditures, and assets, available for public review. A new independent auditing agency would review parties' financial and election reports and investigate their correspondence to the parties' actual spending levels. Major irregularities should result in criminal rather than administrative responsibility for party officials. Finally, Ukraine should introduce public funding for political parties based on clear eligibility criteria and fair allocation formulas that would promote a diverse multiparty system. On October 8, 2015, the Ukrainian parliament adopted a set of legislative amendments (Law 731-VIII) that established stricter controls over party financing and specified criteria for parties eligible to receve public funding. While these changes represent a major step toward greater party transparency and minimizing graft, they still have important deficiencies. The new provisions establish an unusually high cap on annual donations (approximately $22,000 for citizens and $45,000 for legal entities), preserve loopholes allowing for indirect campaign contributions via third parties, prevent a newly established anticorruption agency from monitoring the financing of election campaigns, and offer weak sanctions for violation of the new laws.[25] Empowering voters vis-à-vis party leaders and instituting further restrictions on political donations, along with stronger enforcement of the financing rules, should grad-ually erode the corrupt nexus between private interests and political parties.

The second priority should be strengthening the prosecutorial capacity of state agencies charged with fighting corruption. Ukraine's prosecutor generals have been traditionally appointed based on their personal political loyalty and limited in their selection of targets by the president's dismissal powers. The experience of a diverse set of highly corrupt states, from Romania to Brazil, shows that the success of anticorruption drives depends on public prosecutors who can investigate and take to court top officials from the government and state corporations. Such high-level prosecutions would require granting broad autonomous powers to a special group of anticorruption prosecutors selected by a coalition of actors and shielded from political influence by a guaranteed tenure. Only an explicit renunciation of the informal immunity currently en-joyed by the political class could prevent any future intervention into the in-ner workings of the prosecutorial office. While there should be an oversight mechanism to prevent the possible corruption of the prosecutors, the priority should still be on ensuring the immunity and wide discretionary powers of the prosecutors. It is also important for the prosecutorial agency to establish a high degree of decentralization so that lower-level prosecutors can take the lead in their investigations.

The third priority area is establishing a depoliticized and impersonal civ-il service. Political and business elites would be severely constrained in their ability to collude if they face a professional civil service that could resist their demands for rents. The criteria for appointments and promotions within the civil service, particularly for top positions, should therefore be clearly stated and require multiple veto points within the system. The level of petty corrup-tion would also decrease, since civil servants at all levels would not be appoint-ed to extort businessmen and collect bribes for their patrons. Not surprising-ly, the civil service remains one of the least reformed areas of the Ukrainian state. According to the 2013 GRECO evaluation report, public administration reform has suffered continuous setbacks since the mid-2000s, with no progress achieved under the last two presidents.[26] Granted, it took decades for West-ern states to transition from a civil service based on political patronage to one based on a meritocratic and impersonal system of recruitment and promotion (Fukuyama 2013). Moreover, democracy may often hinder the creation of in-dependent public administration by encouraging competing political parties to gain greater political influence and power through clientelistic strategies

(Shefter 1993). Still, without a substantive civil service reform aimed at privileging qualifications and performance over political loyalty, Ukraine would not be able to achieve a lasting decline in all types of corruption.

The adoption of institutional changes could have a major effect on limiting the volume of grand corruption only if they are accompanied by the simultaneous public commitment of political actors to clean up the government (Warner 2001).[27] The negative equilibrium that reinforces corrupt activities is based on converging expectations about the continued prevalence of informal rules. Changing these expectations and, hence, the very dynamics of their interaction, is a protracted and difficult process given the path-dependent nature of any long-lasting institutions. The first step showing Ukraine's new commitment to anticorruption reform was the establishment of a special independent agency—the Anti-Corruption Bureau—authorized to monitor and investigate corruption-related offenses among public officials and political leaders. However, it can acquire public credibility only if it displays the capacity to bring high-level officials to justice irrespective of their political affiliations. The leverage of civil society organizations, proreform interest groups, and independent media has also increased following the 2013–14 revolution. Ultimately, however, progress in anticorruption reforms depends on the cooperation and compliance of political elites. One of the lessons from Yanukovych's rule is that egregious corruption can become self-defeating in the long term. However, the Euromaidan experience also shows that large-scale popular mobilization may selectively punish individual corruption, but it cannot dismantle the broader incentive structure of informal exchange that made it possible. Unless the country's current leaders can properly assess the personal risks of continuing the status quo and take action to change it, Ukraine will experience not only continuing corruption but also more popular discontent and further political turmoil.

Notes

1. Maria Danilova, "Secrecy Surrounds Ukrainian President's Home," Associated Press, October 24, 2012. Accessed January 8, 2014. See http://bigstory.ap.org/article/secrecy-surrounds-ukrainian-presidents-home.

2. "Zakon Ukrainy 'Pro borot'bu z koruptsieyu,'" Verkhovna Rada Ukrainy, October 5, 1995. Accessed December 23, 2013. See http://zakon4.rada.gov.ua/laws/show/356/95-%D0%B2%D1%80.

3. "Zakon Ukrainy 'Pro zasady zapobihannya i protydii koruptsii,'" Vidomosti

Verkhovnoi Rady Ukrainy, No. 40, 2011, p. 404. Accessed December 24, 2013. See http://zakon4.rada.gov.ua/laws/show/3206-17.

4. "Evaluation Report on Ukraine," Adopted by GRECO at 32nd Plenary Meeting, March 19–23, 2007, p. 9.

5. GRECO, March 2013, "Third Addendum to the Compliance Report on Ukraine," GRECO Secretariat/Council of Europe, May 24, 2013, p. 18: https://www.coe.int/t/dghl/monitoring/greco/evaluations/round2/GrecoRC1&2(2009)1_ThirdAdd_Ukraine_EN.pdf.

6. "Ukraine: The People Speak Out," Transparency International, December 10, 2013. Accessed December 24, 2013. See http://www.transparency.org/news/feature/ukraine_the_people_speak_out.

7. "Zvit za rezul'tatamy doslidzhennya Koruptsiya ta koruptsiyni ryzyky v derzhavnyh administratyvnyh organah: gromadska dumka naselennia Ukrainy, pidpryemtsiv, ekspertiv," *Democratic Initiatives Foundation*, May 2009. Accessed June 20, 2013. See http://www.minjust.gov.ua/21891.

8. *Corruption in Ukraine: Comparative Analysis of National Surveys: 2007—2009, 2011* (Kyiv, 2011), p. 17. Accessed December 25, 2013. See http://uniter.org.ua/data/block/corruption_in_ukraine_2007–2009_2011_engl.pdf.

9. *IFES Public Opinion in Ukraine 2013: Key Findings* (Washington, DC: IFES, December 2013), p. 3. Accessed December 25, 2013. See http: //www.ifes.org/Content/Publications/Press-Release/2013/2013-Public-Opinion-Survey-in-Ukraine.aspx.

10. The only exception could be Vasyl' Volha, a former head of the state commission for regulating financial services, who was convicted to a five-year jail term in 2012 for accepting a bribe worth $500.000. However, he was never a member of the ruling Party of Regions.

11. "Top-5 naibil'shyh habariv v 2013 rotsi," October 19, 2013. Accessed December 25, 2013. See http://www.acrc.org.ua/ua/news-and-events/news/all/top-5-najbilshix-xabariv-v-2013-roczi.html.

12. Oksana Khmeliovs'ka, "Top-10 naibil'shyh habariv za mynulyi rik," *Tyzhden.ua*, May 10, 2013. Accessed June 20, 2013. See http://tyzhden.ua/News/79227.

13. *Corruption in Ukraine*, p. 20.

14. "Tsynichni ukraintsi dobrovil'no dayut' habari," *Antykoruptsiynyi Portal*, September 20, 2013. Accessed December 26, 2013. See http://www.acrc.org.ua/ua/news-and-events/news/all/czinichni-ukrayinczi-dobrovilno-dayut-xabari-i-ne-xochut-borotisya-z-korupczieyu.html.

15. "Ukraine: Firtash Makes His Case to the USG," U.S. Embassy Kyiv, December 10, 2008. See http://wikileaks.org/cable/2008/12/08KYIV2414.html.

16. Viktor Pinchuk and Gennadiy Bogolyubov, Igor Kolomoisky, *Defense of the First Defendant*, High Court of Justice Queen's Bench Division Commercial Court, Folio 354, September 30, 2013. Accessed March 31, 2016. See http://johnhelmer.net/wp-content/up-

loads/2013/10/Pinchuk-Defence-of-the-First-Defendant.pdf.

17. Viktor Pinchuk and Gennadiy Bogolyubov, Igor Kolomoisky, *Particulars of Claim*. Accessed December 26, 2013. See http://johnhelmer.net/wp-content/uploads/2013/10/Pinchuk-2013-03-12-KZhRK-Particulars-of-Claim-Final.pdf.

18. Viktor Pinchuk and Gennadiy Bogolyubov, Igor Kolomoisky, *Defense of the Second Defendant*, High Court of Justice Queen's Bench Division Commercial Court, Folio 354, Claim No. 2013. See http://johnhelmer.net/wp-content/uploads/2013/10/Pinchuk-Defence-of-the-Second-Defendant.pdf.

19. *Evaluation Report on Ukraine Transparency of Party Funding (Theme II)*, Third Evaluation Round, GRECO, October 21, 2011, Section 33. Accessed December 26, 2013. See http://www.coe.int/t/dghl/monitoring/greco/evaluations/round3/GrecoEval3(2011)1_Ukraine_Two_EN.pdf.

20. *Evaluation Report on Ukraine Transparency*, Section 45.

21. *Evaluation Report on Ukraine Transparency*, Sections 60 and 62.

22. "Euromaidan and Oligarchs," *The Insider*, December 10, 2013. See http://www.theinsider.ua/politics/52a61fcd3ea9d/.

23. David Herszenhorn, "In Ukraine, Corruption Concerns Linger a Year after the Revolution," *New York Times*, May 17, 2015. See http://www.nytimes.com/2015/05/18/world/europe/in-ukraine-corruption-concerns-linger-a-year-after-a-revolution.html?_r=0.

24. "Joint First and Second Evaluation Round. Fifth Addendum to the Compliance Report on Ukraine," Adopted by GRECO's 68th Plenary Meeting, June 15–19, 2015, http://www.coe.int/t/dghl/monitoring/greco/evaluations/round2/GrecoRC1&2(2009)1_FifthAdd_Ukraine_EN.pdf.

25. For a review of these laws, see GRECO Secretariat/Council of Europe, "Second Compliance Report on Ukraine, Third Evaluation Round," December 14, 2015, available at https://www.coe.int/t/dghl/monitoring/greco/evaluations/round3/GrecoRC3(2015)22_Second_Ukraine_EN.pdf.

26. *Third Addendum to the Compliance Report on Ukraine*, GRECO, March 18–22, 2013, p. 13, https://www.coe.int/t/dghl/monitoring/greco/evaluations/round2/GrecoRC1&2(2009)1_ThirdAdd_Ukraine_EN.pdf.

27. Postwar France offers a precedent of such public rejection of corrupt practices by major political parties.

5   Corruption in Ukraine in Comparative Perspective

DAPHNE ATHANASOULI

Since 1989 the countries of central Europe have generally developed more successfully than the countries of south-eastern Europe, whereas the economic performance of Ukraine, Russia, and the other countries of the Commonwealth of Independent States (CIS) has lagged behind virtually all their counterparts farther west.[1] One of the biggest factors holding back CIS countries has been corruption. In states like Ukraine, partial reforms reinforced insiders, giving rise to interest groups that extracted benefits from the volatile environment and blocked the implementation of comprehensive reform packages that would provide access to information and resources for the whole population. Despite public recognition that corruption is a problem, little has been done to reduce it. The "formal" aspects of anticorruption reform often have been adopted, but exist mainly on paper, their implementation limited in practice. In 2013, corruption in Ukraine was among the highest in the former Soviet Union (FSU), below only the Central Asian countries of Uzbekistan, Kyrgyzstan, Turkmenistan, and Tajikistan, according to the World Bank's control of corruption indicator (World Bank 2014), whereas Transparency International in 2014 ranked Ukraine in 142nd place among 175 countries.[2] Anticorruption efforts to date in Ukraine (and many other countries) tend to suffer from unclear guidelines, contradictory measures and laws, the lack of independent anticorruption agencies, and significant delays in implementation. Ukraine seems to remain stuck in a partial reform state, where institutional problems hinder transparency and obstruct the implementation of any anticorruption reform agenda.

A more drastic approach, similar to the one followed in Georgia to tackle petty corruption, might help. However, some cross-country differences should be considered when evaluating the various policies and their relative successes.

This chapter shows that corruption hinders private sector development though two main channels related to the external business environment and the internal structure of the firm. In the external environment, corruption may decrease competition. The number of competitors drops in industries where some firms are actively seeking to influence laws and regulations affecting their business, through bribery and other gifts to public officials. Individual firms may enjoy benefits and special favors from public officials who implement regulations and may block specific measures of regulatory packages and increase entry barriers for other firms in the sector. These practices and the unlawful favor-for-favors relationship between the state and some firms deter competition, obstruct restructuring, and create inefficiencies that prevent private sector development. Even inefficient firms with poor corporate governance may remain in business and obstruct the entry, survival, or expansion of new firms, if their "connections" are the right ones.

Corruption is also expected to weaken private sector development through its impact on the internal structure of the firm (Athanasouli and Goujard, 2015). Initially, firms may adapt their structures according to the institutions and corruption, which can lead to inefficiencies. Corruption may incentivize managers to engage in activities that are not directly productive, such as winning over public officials through unofficial payments or gifts in exchange for various services. Through these additional operational costs, corruption can cause a distortion of the firm's resources and activities away from efficiency. Such influences can obstruct the development of effective firm strategies, incentives for firm restructuring, and employee empowerment.

Following the above pattern, this chapter examines the channels through which corruption affects the business environment by investigating three aspects of corruption: the rent-seeking behavior of firms, the perception of corruption as a barrier in doing business, and the differential impact of regulatory capture on different firms based on their size and origin, examining both de novo firms and privatized, previously state-owned firms.

Finally, the chapter highlights the linkages between corruption and overall institutional and governance quality. The development of the institutional framework can affect corruption through two main channels: accountability and property rights. Progress in these institutions could lead to higher transparency and lower corruption by reducing information costs. The accountability of politicians influences their incentives to respect their electoral mandates (Treisman 2000; Fan, Lin, and Treisman 2009). Ferraz and Finan (2008, 2011) demonstrate that disclosing information on corrupt activities significantly decreases corruption, and that this effect is magnified when local media can expose the information about corrupt practices. Property rights, contract institutions, and their enforcement are the second channel though which the institutional setting can affect corruption levels. The institutional setting can limit the scope for bribery and deviation from agreed contracts, and may also decrease the costs of contract enforcement by facilitating the monitoring of firms, households, and civil servants. It is expected that the development of these institutional factors will play a substantial role in the global anticorruption effort.

The chapter is organized as follows. The first section describes the evolution of corruption. The second section lays out the main findings of the analysis on the severity of corruption and regulatory capture for different firms. The third section conducts a comparative analysis of the institutional environment and progress in governance, and determines the most significant factors for improving governance and advancing corruption reform in Ukraine. The conclusion proposes some policy recommendations based on the findings.

Magnitude of Corruption over Time

Corruption is generally defined as "the abuse of public power for private gain" (Cuervo-Cazurra 2006) and can also be defined as "an arrangement that involves an exchange between two parties (the 'demander' and the 'supplier'), which: a) has an influence on the allocation of resources either immediately or in the future, and b) involves the use or abuse of public or collective responsibility for private ends" (Kwok and Tadesse 2006). Corruption should not only be examined as the interaction of the state with firms, but also as the exertion of influence from firms to public officials (Hellman and Kaufmann 2001). The following subsections discuss different dimensions along which the magnitude of corruption can be measured and discusses trends, comparing Ukraine with other countries.

Institutional Environment and Governance in Ukraine

With a weakly governed institutional framework, wide discretionary power among public officials leads them to select projects based on their ability to extract rents. Consequently, corruption and rent seeking become integral parts of economic governance and more difficult to tackle (Ngo 2008).

The World Bank has developed a composite index, the Worldwide Governance Indicators (WGI), which includes a measure of the extent to which public power is perceived to be exercised for private gain, covering both petty and grand corruption (Kaufmann, Kraay, and Mastruzzi 2010). Figure 5.1 shows this control of corruption indicator for Ukraine, five other transition countries that are geographically close to Ukraine but that differ widely in transition process (Georgia, Kazakhstan, Poland, Romania, and Russia), and three EU countries (Greece, Spain, and Germany). The indicator ranges from approximately -2.5 (weak) to 2.5 (strong) governance performance. Although Georgia has made clear strides toward transparency and in 2012 surpassed average levels in the control of corruption, Russia and Ukraine (followed by Kazakhstan) show the weakest control of corruption and no sign of steady improvements. Romania, which joined the European Union in 2007, has lower corruption levels but remains below average in its control of corruption. The stronger performers are Germany and Spain, with both countries being in the European Union and the Eurozone. Poland has also maintained above-average levels in control of corruption and shows a gradual progress toward transparency since 2005. However, another country of southern Europe, Greece, also a member of the EU and the Eurozone, shows severe deterioration in the control of corruption, dropping below-average levels in 2010. The perception of anticorruption progress seems to have deteriorated from 2009 in the southern European countries, particularly Greece, as a result of the 2008 debt crisis. Overall, we see wide variation in the perception of corruption levels, particularly in the two contradictory cases of Greece and Georgia. These different stories indicate that corruption is subject to change and underline the importance of policies in anticorruption reforms.

Figure 5.2 shows that in Russia and Ukraine the control of corruption indicator follows the same pattern, but with Ukraine lagging behind Russia by about two years. This is a clear indication of the strong similarities in the institutional environment between the two countries, and it is not observed in any other country comparable to Ukraine.

The high corruption levels in Ukraine are associated with weaker government effectiveness and regulatory quality. Based on the Worldwide Governance Indicators, changes in the control of corruption in Ukraine are positively correlated with government effectiveness, regulatory quality, and the rule of law, as Table 5.1 shows. Additionally, the high frequency of corruption in public services is associated with weaker government effectiveness, and reflects a lower quality of public services and civil service, along with a possible dependence on political pressures. Rent-seeking and regulatory capture are associated with lower regulatory quality, which reflects the perceptions of the government's ability to formulate and implement sound policies and regulations that sup-

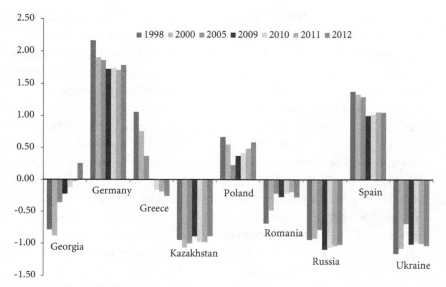

FIG. 5.1: Control of Corruption for Comparator Countries. Source: World Bank, Worldwide Governance Indicators, 2013.

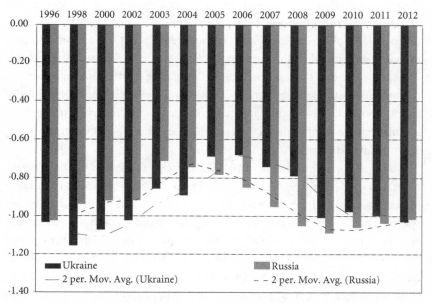

FIG. 5.2: Control of Corruption Comparing Russia and Ukraine. Source: World Bank, Worldwide Governance Indicators, 2013.

TABLE 5.1: Standardized Covariance Matrix of WGI Indicators for Ukraine, 1996–2012

	Government Effectiveness	Regulatory Quality	Rule of Law	Control of Corruption
Government Effectiveness	1.000	0.369	0.228	0.537
Regulatory Quality		1.000	0.205	0.528
Rule of Law			1.000	0.497
Control of Corruption				1.000

SOURCE: *World Bank, Worldwide Governance Indicators, 2013.*

port the development of the private sector. Finally corruption in courts is associated with the rule of law, as contracts may not be enforced, rights may not be properly protected, agents may not abide by the rules, and there may be a low trust in (and low quality of) contract enforcement.

Firms' Experience of Corruption

To gain more understanding about the changes in different forms of corruption, Figure 5.3 investigates firms' experience of corruption using large surveys of firms conducted by the European Bank for Reconstruction and Development (EBRD) and the World Bank in 1999, 2005, and 2009. The questions included in the Business Environment and Enterprise Performance Survey (BEEPS) are designed to elicit truthful reporting of actual bribe payments and to apply these to a representative sample of firms in each country (EBRD, 1999, 2005, 2009a). This type of survey data allowed for more specific and therefore meaningful longitudinal and cross-sectional comparisons of corruption in different countries.

Firms' experience of corruption in Ukraine dropped dramatically between 1999 and 2005, whereas it remained relatively stable between 2005 and 2009 (Figure 5.3). Firms in Ukraine and Russia in Eastern Europe, followed by Kazakhstan in Central Asia, and Romania in South East Europe, report the highest frequency of unofficial payments. These countries were affected by the transition process from communism to the free market in their recent history and their institutional environment and governance lack the maturity of established democracies. Firms in Central European countries, such as Poland, and in Caucasus countries, such as Georgia, report bribing less frequently. The frequency of corruption in Ukraine, as measured in 2009, is the second highest among the comparator transition countries, with Russia being at the top. Georgia has the lowest frequency in unofficial payments, which may be due to the recent anticorruption reforms.

Similarly in Figure 5.4, corruption in courts seems to be particularly preva-

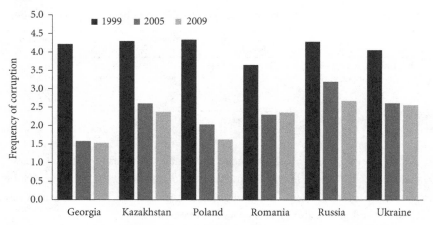

FIG. 5.3: Frequency of Corruption in Ukraine and Comparator Countries. Source: BEEPS surveys 1999, 2005, and 2009.

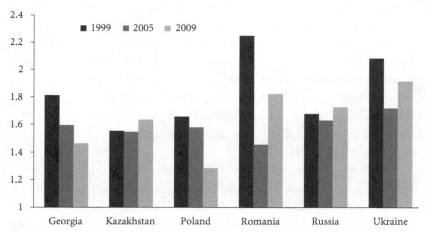

FIG. 5.4: Frequency of Corruption in Courts. Source: BEEPS surveys 1999, 2005, and 2009.

lent in Ukraine. Firms in Ukraine, followed by Romania, Kazakhstan, and Russia, give unofficial payments to "deal" with courts more frequently than firms in Poland and Georgia. It is evident that even though most transition countries displayed high levels of corruption in dealing with courts in 1999, some countries, such as Georgia and Poland, have significantly progressed toward more transparency in the judicial system.

Figure 5.5 shows the frequency of corruption reported by firms across sever-

Fɪɢ. 5.5: Frequency of Corruption in the Capital and Other Cities in 2009. Source: BEEPS surveys 1999, 2005, and 2009.

al postcommunist countries' capital and other cities in 2009. Firms in Ukraine's capital and other cities engage more often in corrupt practices and unofficial payments than in those of other countries. The frequency of corruption in firms based in Kyiv is higher than that in other cities of Ukraine, and it exceeds the level of corruption in the other transition countries. In Russia and Romania there is a similar picture, with high corruption levels and more frequent corrupt payments encountered in the capital. Poland and Georgia appear less corrupt, with less internal country variation.

Rent-seeking Activities across Countries and Firms

Some of the reasons that drive firms to engage in corrupt practices include market expansion and profit maximization ambitions. Firms often engage in illegal practices and bribes to launch their operations and then expand in a country. However Hellman and Kaufmann (Hellman and Kaufmann 2001) have shown that oligarchs in transition countries managed to exert power and use illegal, corrupt practices for their benefit, to ensure their dominance, with important social implications. In this "capture economy" that characterizes the transition, legal and policy conditions are formed to benefit the captor at the expense of the rest of the enterprises. As a result, a few large firms with good political connections may have benefited from corruption.

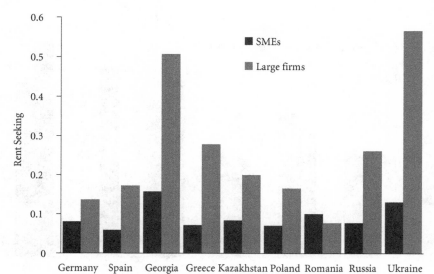

FIG. 5.6: Rent-seeking Behaviors of SMEs and Large Firms in 2005. Note: The sample includes only privately owned establishments. SMEs and large firms are firms with fewer than 250 full-time employees and more than 250 full-time employees, respectively. Source: BEEPS survey 2005.

A question on rent-seeking used (only) in the 2005 BEEPS survey asks if firms initiate payments and gifts to change government decrees, laws, and regulations affecting their business. Firms may try to influence the regulatory environment and to divert government resources in their favor.

Figure 5.6 shows the comparison between Ukraine and the rest of the comparator transition countries with respect to rent-seeking behavior among different types of firms. The results clearly indicate that rent-seeking behavior is widespread in Ukraine, which is particularly observed in large and previously state-owned firms.

Rent-seeking does not display the same pattern across firms. In particular, the managers of small- and medium-size enterprises (SMEs) respond that they are rarely involved in rent seeking practices (Figure 5.6). SMEs may lack the ability to influence high-level public officials, with respect to rules and regulations. On the contrary, rent-seeking is prevalent among the managers of large firms (more than 250 employees), which declare the highest level of rent-seeking. In 2005, firms in Ukraine and Georgia displayed the highest levels of rent-seeking activities, followed by Greece and Russia. Firms in Romania display the lowest levels among the countries of the study.

Severity of Corruption—Regulatory Capture and Rent-seeking as Business Constraints

This section relates the severity of corruption across countries to the overall institutional environment. In particular, it investigates the relationship between the evolution of corruption, competition, and the extent of state capture. Ukraine is particularly hampered by corruption and state capture. The concentration of power in the hands of the oligarchs, who are favored and assisted by public officials, has given rise to business conglomerates able to capture the state and prevent effective political and economic reforms (Orttung 2011).

Figure 5.7 shows that rent-seeking (by sector) is associated with the fact that corruption is perceived as a business obstacle. The diameter of the circles denotes the size of the particular industry, and shows that the trend remains positive all across the range of businesses.

Regulatory capture (by sector) is also associated with the fact that corruption is perceived as a business obstacle (Figure 5.8). Although this correlation shows that regulatory capture is considered a business barrier for all firms, firms are

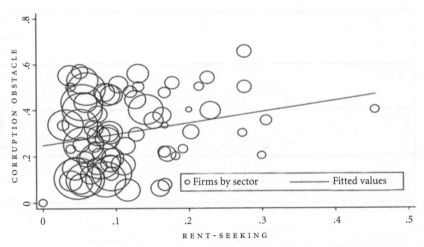

FIG. 5.7: Rent-seeking and the Perception of Corruption as a Business Barrier. Note: The sample includes only privately owned establishments. Observations are one-digit industry by countries. The circles' sizes represent the number of firms interviewed in the BEEPS for each industry-country observation. The y-axis is the share of managers stating that corruption is a moderate or severe problem for their business developments. Source: BEEPS survey 2005.

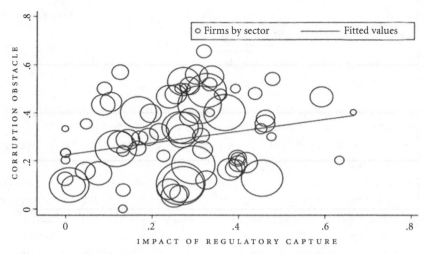

FIG. 5.8: Impact of Regulatory Capture and the Perception of Corruption as a Business Barrier. Note: The sample includes only privately owned establishments. Observations are one-digit industry by countries. The circles' sizes represent the number of firms interviewed in the BEEPS for each industry-country observation. The y-axis is the share of managers stating that corruption is a moderate or severe problem for their business developments. Source: BEEPS survey 2005.

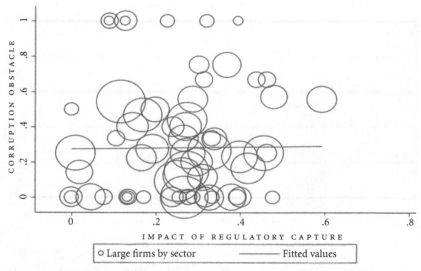

FIG. 5.9: Impact of Regulatory Capture and the Perception of Corruption as a Business Barrier for Large Firms. Note: The sample includes only privately owned establishments. Observations are one-digit industry by countries. The circles' sizes represent the number of firms interviewed in the BEEPS for each industry-country observation. The y-axis is the share of managers stating that corruption is a moderate or severe problem for their business developments. Source: BEEPS survey 2005.

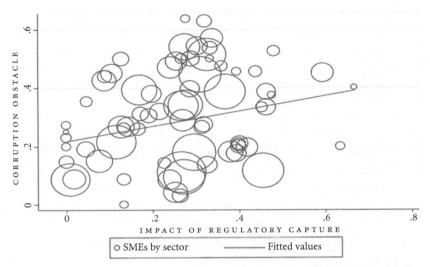

FIG. 5.10: Impact of State Capture and the Perception of Corruption as a Barrier for SMEs. Note: The sample includes only privately owned establishments. Observations are one-digit industry by countries. The circles' sizes represent the number of firms interviewed in the BEEPS for each industry-country observation. The y-axis is the share of managers stating that corruption is a moderate or severe problem for their business developments. Source: BEEPS survey 2005.

differently affected. Large firms do not find the impact of regulatory capture to be a strong corruption obstacle (Figure 5.9). On the other hand, the association between the impact of regulatory capture and the perception of corruption as a barrier in doing business is strongly evident for small firms (Figure 5.10). The findings for SMEs indicate that regulatory capture constitutes a greater obstacle in the operation and growth of their business.

The differences in the perception of regulatory capture as a barrier in doing business for large firms and SMEs could be explained by the possible engagement of firms in bribery and incentives of firms to bribe. It could be expected that firms that can exert influence on legislation and regulations related to their business mainly would be established, well-connected, large firms that aim to gain advantages and maximize their profits in return for a type of unofficial reward. In this respect, some large "insider" firms together with the government officials are "setters" of the institutional environment and seek individual advantages to increase their private gain at the expense of other firms. On the contrary, SMEs usually lack the influence, connections, and the necessary resources to be able to negotiate changes in government decrees and regulations. Therefore most SMEs are "outsider" firms and are primarily "takers" of an institutional environment in which regulations are unevenly or partially enforced across different firms and competitive structures are obstructed.[3]

Rent-seeking and Competition

Widespread corruption may have negative effects on competition and private sector development. It can cause misallocation of resources, notably through changes in the composition of public expenditures (Mauro 1996). A corrupt environment deprives firms of equal market opportunities and increases the cost of doing business. This increase can create obstacles in the market entry of firms (Sullivan and Shkolnikov 2004). Firms that are not involved in practices to capture the state and do not influence government decisions to their benefit will have less access to resources and higher costs, whereas their sales could be hampered by the discrimination and misallocation of resources induced by the bribing firms.

Figure 5.11 shows the relationship between rent-seeking practices and

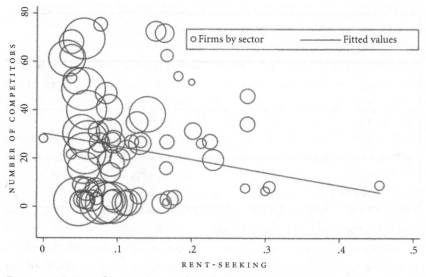

FIG. 5.11: Rent-seeking on the Number of Competitors across Industries. Note: The sample includes only privately owned establishments. Observations are one-digit industry by countries. The circles' sizes represent the number of firms interviewed in the BEEPS for each industry-country observation. Source: BEEPS survey 2005.

the number of competitors in each industry. The correlation indicates that rent-seeking is associated with a smaller number of competitors, thus lower competition and more concentrated, oligopolistic and monopolistic sectors. In turn, the presence of fewer actors within a sector may lead to increased rent-seeking practices and prevent effective and necessary reforms. Indeed, the absence of new entrants (and the absence of a threat of new entrants) lowers pressure for improvements in efficiency and innovation from existing firms and may help inefficient firms to survive.

As a result, progress toward transparency may be severely constrained by the limited competition in some sectors and the concentration of power in the hands of "oligarchs." These findings also indicate the links between rent-seeking, regulatory capture, and low competition in old and large connected firms. The results indicate that in order to support a well-functioning institutional environment, the barriers to competition need to be removed from highly concentrated sectors that attempt to capture the state and prevent reforms and regulations not in line with their vested interests.

Addressing Corruption in Ukraine from a Comparative Perspective

Ukraine's failure to address corruption during the Yanukovych era highlights the increasing importance of institutions for any successful reform. Whereas other transition countries, and particularly Georgia, have taken important steps toward transparency, particularly in terms of petty corruption, in Ukraine both petty and grand forms of corruption display the highest levels among the comparator countries used in the study. While Ukraine did adopt various anticorruption measures, particularly after 2005, the reforms did not prove to be effective. Critics noted that the reforms lacked a comprehensive response toward corruption, instead relying on partial measures that were implemented slowly. Such a noncomprehensive, partial response might obstruct some types of corrupt behavior but does not address corrupt practices as a whole.

The Problem of Partial Reform

This chapter argues that the reforms were not effective because they were only partial and slowly implemented. The partial implementation of anticorruption packages and the speed of reforms toward transparency are affected by the political will of the ruling government and by vested interests that are evident from the analysis of rent-seeking and regulatory capture in Ukraine. High government officials and some usually large, previously state owned, privatized firms have established favor-for-favor transactions in which the state can "exchange" legislation and regulations that apply to businesses for votes, unofficial payments, or other gifts. At the same time, rent-seeking practices can hamper competitive structures and lead to more concentrated sectors that can further increase the influence sphere and power of incumbents. It is evident that progress in transparency and comprehensive, rapid reforms may not have the necessary political support, as government officials gain monetary advantages in their corrupt transactions with some firms, can ensure votes for sustaining their political power, or can acquire other gifts and services that may advance other individual or political objectives.

The partial character and slow speed of anticorruption policies was evident during the 2005–11 period. The anticorruption measures adopted during that period addressed corrupt payments among lower level public officials and prosecutors and resulted in the filing of several cases. However, prosecutions of high-level public officials were much rarer, in part because the requirements exposing political funding were lax. Also, the anticorruption measures criminalized bribery only on the basis of monetary transactions between the individual who offers and the person who receives a bribe, ignoring corruption that included exchanges for votes, other gifts, or services. The slow adoption of partial measures toward transparency results in corrupt activities being covered up, allowing time for the various interest groups to respond and adapt their methods based on each "revised" measure. The Yanukovych era anticorruption actions did not directly challenge the status quo structures and benefits of the political and economic elites. The measures gave a positive signal and may have signified a possible gradual change in the institutional environment in Ukraine. Potentially, the role of citizens could have been particularly important in addressing the weaknesses of the institutional environment by pressuring the government to implement a comprehensive response to corruption and address vested interests, but this did not happen during the Yanukovych era.

Is a Georgian-style Reform Possible in Ukraine?

The rest of this section identifies measures to advance the anticorruption reforms in Ukraine. The existing structures in the political and economic environment can obstruct specific policies and necessary reforms. Limiting the discretion of public officials and holding politicians accountable can address both petty and grand corruption.

Controlling corruption requires strong governance, but unfortunately Ukraine performs poorly on this score. Based on the WGI, Ukraine consistently maintained below-average levels regarding the control of corruption, rule of law, regulatory quality, and government effectiveness indicators from 1996 to 2012. Voice and accountability and political stability showed more variation over time, but also hovered at below-average levels. The only period when Ukraine showed some evidence of progress on most governance indicators was in 2005 and 2006, during the aftermath of the Orange Revolution. Voice and accountability particularly improved in 2005, followed by political stability. However from 2009 onward, following the 2008 financial crisis, the governance indicators again dropped and remained below average through 2012.

In order to determine which factors can drive the institutional development of a country, Principal Component Analysis (PCA) was carried out on the WGI dataset for Ukraine and Georgia for the years between 1996 and 2012 for which data are available. PCA is applied to analyze the level of variation in the measurement of the overall progress in governance based on the variation in each indicator. The findings depict a different story of institutional progress over time between the two transition countries.

In Ukraine, voice and accountability and political stability are the two indicators that seem to vary the most from 1996 to 2012. These two factors account for more than 75 percent of the variation in overall governance. Government effectiveness, regulatory quality, control of corruption, and rule of law stagnated at a below-average level during this period. No significant improvements in the indicators related to the formal public institutions have been made.

By contrast, Georgia has achieved significant progress in the governance indicators from 1996 to 2012. The control of corruption is highly correlated with the rule of law, government effectiveness, and regulatory quality, and is positively correlated with all the governance indicators. The principal component analysis shows that the overall variation in governance is driven mainly by the rule of law and control of corruption, which account for 83 percent of variation in overall governance quality from 1996 to 2012. That said, there was a strong political will to restructure and improve the quality of public services and battle petty corruption. Consequently, the control of corruption, government effectiveness, regulatory quality, and rule of law significantly improved in Georgia, though that country still scores consistently below average on political stability and voice and accountability, with less variation over time.

In Ukraine, progress in these formal and informal institutions would require effective restructuring and strong political will. Voice and account-ability—namely, the ability of citizens to participate in the selection of their government, freedom of the media, and freedom of expression—significant-ly improved after the Orange Revolution in 2004, indicating that there could be similar progress after the Euromaidan led to the removal of Yanukovych in February 2014. These findings suggest that voice and accountability may be a mechanism for reforms in Ukraine. The freedom of media, freedom of expres-sion, and the citizens' ability to hold politicians accountable and participate in the selection of their government can exert pressure for the implementation of comprehensive anticorruption reforms and restructuring of the public ad-ministration and court system, suggesting that a bottom-up approach may be possible.

Post-Euromaidan steps taken in Ukraine on the anticorruption agenda share similarities with the anticorruption reforms in Georgia. As in Georgia, where the elimination of the corrupt traffic police was a major success story, the government in Ukraine is taking steps to combat petty corruption within this law enforcement agency. In July 2015 the entire traffic police force in Kyiv was replaced by new officers who benefited from foreign training. The traffic po-lice had long been long associated with extracting bribes and inefficiency. The replacement of the patrol police seems to have quickly increased citizen satis-faction and trust in daily law enforcement, as in Georgia, with the willingness of citizens to contact the police significantly increasing, based on the number of calls made to them.[4]

Easing the administrative burden remains a major challenge in Ukraine. The facilitation of administrative processes and the reform of the bureaucracy in Georgia brought significant improvements in revenue collection, while the shadow economy shrank (Shelley, Scott, and Latta 2007). In Ukraine, however, reforms are still needed to address excessive bureaucracy and complex adminis-trative procedures. Currently, reforms of the legal framework regarding admin-istrative decisions are ongoing, and the Law on Administrative Procedures is not finalized. The functioning of the state bureaucracy lacks coherence, where-as citizens do not have consistent information on their administrative rights and obligations. The legal framework on administrative decisions needs to be urgently finalized.[5] Further improvements in the area of e-government would also help define clear administrative processes and ease citizens' interactions with public administration (see below).

Beyond the reforms of the traffic police, the clarification of administrative processes would have a further visible impact on the daily life of citizens in Ukraine, as they had in Georgia, and they can ensure public support for further anticorruption reforms, despite the opposition of vested interest groups. The appointment of former Georgian president Mikheil Saakashvili as the new governor of Odessa in May 2015 is a symbol of the Ukrainian government's willingness to follow Georgia's example in tackling petty corruption. Significant progress was made in Ukraine in 2014 with the adoption of the anticorruption package in October and the creation of an independent anticorruption agency.[6] However, some shortcomings need to be addressed in terms of cooperation with civil society, especially regarding the independence of its monitoring. Improving the administrative and judicial system, as well as finalizing partly implemented measures, should be a priority.

Voice and Accountability: E-government and Press Freedom

International organizations have pointed out the importance of e-government for good governance across emerging economies (OECD 2005; World Bank 2009). The recent wave of EU funded projects on e-government has highlighted the importance of web-based institutions for the emergence of sound common legal institutions (European Union 2012). E-government may increase transparency and also lead to higher government effectiveness by rendering the public services to businesses and citizens more efficiently, modernizing public administration, and adapting the information infrastructure. Reducing the time needed to deal with government regulations could foster entrepreneurship (Ciccone and Papaioannou 2007; Torfinn and Javorcik 2011), and increase incentives to move to the formal sector. Therefore, the development of e-government is an important driver for reducing corruption at the country level.

Progress in e-government can decrease corruption, rent-seeking, and regulatory capture in Ukraine by strengthening the accountability of public officials and politicians. The higher level of transparency in public decisions could increase the accountability of governments as well as reduce the costs of monitoring large public administrations in countries with weak institutions (Shleifer and Vishny 1993). The increase in transparency of government decisions, access to information, and the accountability of politicians could in turn influence their incentives to respect their electoral mandates (Treisman 2000; Fan, Lin, and Treisman 2009). Ferraz and Finan (2011, 2008) document that disclosure of information on corrupt activities significantly decreases corruption and that this effect is magnified when local media divulge broadly the information about corrupt practices.

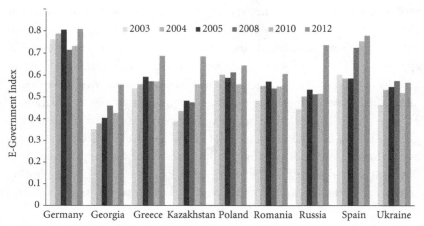

FIG. 5.12: E-Government Index across Countries from 2003 to 2012. Source: UN E-Government Index, 2003–12.

E-government can also reduce the time of interaction with public officials and their discretionary power, thereby reducing administrative corruption. Through e-government, citizens are given more information and access to public services, bypassing lengthy bureaucratic processes and contact with public officials, who are now also more easily monitored. The citizen empowerment and drop in time spent with public officials can reduce the discretionary power of public officials to demand bribes. The development of e-government and provision of more interactive government services is expected to reduce the levels of petty administrative corruption and the amount of bribes paid by firms to facilitate transactions with the public sector.

Figure 5.12 shows a comparison of the E-Government Index in Ukraine and the rest of the comparator countries. The E-Government Index published by the United Nations (UN) is a composite indicator measuring the willingness and capacity of national administrations to use information and communication technologies (ICT) to deliver public services.[7] Although this dataset includes the effects of the 2008 financial crisis and the reduction in government investments resulting from budget constraints, it seems that all countries actively increased the use of e-government for ICT-led development with a strong increase between 2010 and 2012, after the 2010 UN General Assembly and the proposal of an Open Government Partnership. Most countries show a significant improvement, with Russia gaining more than 40 percent. In 2012, Georgia, despite the progress made since 2005, seems to maintain the weakest

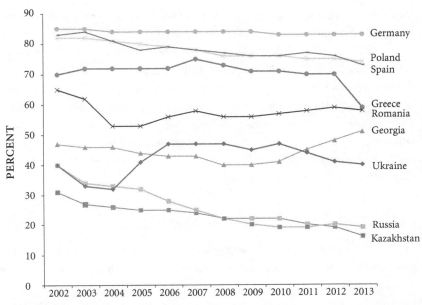

FIG. 5.13: Freedom of the Press from 2002 to 2013. Source: Freedom House Freedom of the Press Index.

e-government presence, followed by Ukraine. Ukraine was lagging behind and, after the drop in 2010 that was driven by the 2009 financial crisis, did not make any significant progress. However, in 2012 Ukraine endorsed a new Open Government Plan (OGP) with the active participation of civil society organizations and the United Nations Development Programme (UNDP) office in Ukraine. The OGP included initiatives to improve the provision of public services to citizens and the introduction of administrative services in digital format by the end of 2014.[8] Many of these reforms were successful.

Figure 5.13 shows the Freedom of the Press index from 2002 to 2013. This measure is an assessment by journalists of the legal, economic, and political environment in which the media operate. Free media can promote democracy and public policy discussion. The figure shows that Germany, Spain, and Poland enjoy a free media. Greece dropped from free to partly free in 2013 because of rising intimidation against journalists, as well as closures and cutbacks of broadcasting stations and print outlets.[9] The media environment in Russia and Kazakhstan is not considered free. Georgia has a partly free status but displays improvements in the environment in which media has operated since 2010. On the other hand, Ukraine had a partly free status, but bordered on being not free. Despite significant progress in the aftermath of the Orange Revolution in 2005 and 2006, with a gain of approximately 20 points between 2004 and 2006, media conditions began to deteriorate beginning in 2010, when Yanukovych assumed the presidency. Prior to the 2012 parliamentary elections, the last national television station that criticized Yanukovych was raided by tax police and prosecutors, who froze its accounts and assets, while after the election an increased number of attacks and threats were observed against journalists. Following the Euromaidan revolution, the media situation improved considerably. However, oligarchs continue to own the main television networks and they determine the content of their broadcasts.

Concluding Remarks and Policy Recommendations

The development of e-government and access to online information about government services help increase accountability and tackle petty corruption by limiting the discretionary power of government officials and public servants. An environment that can also support free media is pivotal for this purpose, since it helps support an anticorruption agenda, expose corrupt practices, and exert pressure on the government for reforms. In order to be able to examine the reasons that corruption levels have remained so high in Ukraine, monitoring the status of anticorruption reforms and current progress is vital. Specific attention should be devoted to online services and support to citizens offered through other anticorruption agencies and civil society organizations working against corruption. Available information on the ways to respond to an incident of corruption should increase, while whistle-blowing and complaints about corrupt acts and practices should be encouraged. There have been some initiatives by independent organizations, such as Transparency International-Ukraine, that have introduced several tools for evaluating corruption levels of various public services, medical establishments, courts, and the public procurement bidding process, while also promoting the Open Government Partnership in Ukraine. These efforts seek to ensure a close partnership between civil society and the government, strengthening citizen participation, and access to information, by improving government services and promoting e-government.[10] Coordinated actions can affect values and beliefs and strengthen anticorruption efforts, and have a bottom-up effect on promoting transparency. Indicators of information on anticorruption progress need to be developed and frequently monitored.

Continually monitoring the government's anticorruption efforts through a free and objective media is particularly important for successful reforms. Such efforts can lead to strong political institutions, strengthen anticorruption efforts, and increase transparency. The citizens and the media can act as monitoring agents against both administrative and grand corruption, promote anticorruption reforms and the work of law enforcement agencies, and increase political accountability by tracking the progress of reforms and exposing mischief or delays in the implementation of specific measures.

The decrease of petty and grand corruption can strengthen regulatory quality and the rule of law, promote private sector development by securing the protection of property and contract rights, reduce the time required to receive public services, and support competitive structures in the market. Corruption and individual benefits to some well-connected firms in exchange for unofficial payments and gifts create barriers to entry, and hinder the survival and the opportunities for growth and expansion of nonbribing firms, particularly SMEs and young firms that often lack informational resources and adequate funding. Economic activity in Ukraine still remains highly concentrated within a small number of firms with strong political links.[11] Although Ukraine sought to cut red tape and reform its public sector to address corruption through the 2011 Anticorruption Act, the Ease of Doing Business Index rank in 2012 was 112 out of 189 economies, whereas for Georgia the same index was 8 out 189, demonstrating the significant progress that Georgia had made in the provision of public services, cutting red tape, and promoting entrepreneurship. Ukraine's adoption of the October 2014 anticorruption package and its creation of an independent anticorruption agency, in combination with the government's efforts to tackle petty corruption in the traffic police and state bureaucracy as in Georgia, are important steps on the road to transparency. They can increase public support and trust in the government, leading the way for further successful reforms. However, implementation risks remain significant, as several anticorruption measures have been only partially implemented.[12]

Notes

1. The author is grateful for comments and suggestions from Antoine Goujard, Henry Hale, Tomasz Mickiewicz, and Robert Orttung, and would also like to thank two anonymous reviewers for their helpful feedback.

2. Transparency International, 2014, "A Year After Maidan Ukraine Is Still the Most Corrupt Country in Europe." See http://www.transparency.org/news/pressrelease/a_year_after_maidan_ukraine_is_still_the_most_corrupt_country_in_europe.

3.   The BEEPS survey does not provide information on the informal sector that could be important.

4.   "Ukraine Replaces Entire Police Force to Beat Corruption," CBS News, July 25, 2015. See http://www.cbsnews.com/news/ukraine-replace-kiev-traffic-police-force-america-trained-officers- bribery/.

5.   GRECO, Joint First and Second Evaluation Round, Fifth Addendum to the Compliance Report on Ukraine, 68th Plenary Meeting, Strasbourg, June 2015. See http://www.coe.int/t/dghl/monitoring/greco/evaluations/round2/GrecoRC1&2(2009)1_FifthAdd_Ukraine_EN.pdf.

6.   GRECO, Joint First and Second Evaluation Round, Fifth Addendum.

7.   The E-Government Index is a weighted average of three normalized scores on the most important dimensions of e-government: scope and quality of online services, development status of telecommunication infrastructure, and inherent human capital (United Nations 2008).

8.   UNDP, Ukraine Open Government Action Plan. See http://www.opengovpartnership.org/country/ukraine/action-plan.

9.   Freedom House, Freedom of the Press. For reports from 2002, see https: //freedomhouse.org/report-types/freedom-press.

10.   Transparency International-Ukraine. See http:www.ti-ukraine.org.

11.   OECD Anticorruption Network for Eastern Europe and Central Asia, Instanbul Anticorruption Action Plan country reports for Ukraine. See http://www.oecd.org/corruption/acn/istanbulactionplancountryreports.htm.

12.   GRECO, Joint First and Second Evaluation Round, Fifth Addendum.

PART IV

Constitution

6 Ukrainian Constitutional Politics: Neopatrimonialism, Rent-seeking, and Regime Change

Oleksandr Fisun

The institutional environment—the set of political interaction rules, established relations, and recurrent practices—is of key importance for the political process. Institutions create incentives for political players, shape how they organize, and influence the "price" of any political action (by reducing or driving up the associated costs). The most fundamental formal institution is the constitution, supported by constitutional law.

The post-Soviet states tend to be characterized by weak constitutions, subject to frequent changes and a continuing process of constitutional engineering and experimentation. Constitutions and constitutional law arise to reflect specific constellations of political forces as political forces strike deals on the distribution of power and patronage. Constitutions and constitutional laws therefore change according to the political climate and the factional interests of certain political players and groups. Such fluid constitutions thus reinforce political arrangements only temporarily. The balance is disturbed when, for some actors, the benefits from changing the rules of the game begin to exceed the costs required for such changes, at which point they begin to manipulate the constitution and laws. Constitutional politics, therefore, is subject to stops, turns, and cycles driven by the current political agendas of those who hold power.

Ukraine is unique among post-Soviet states, however, in its pattern of constitutional dynamics. First, in Ukraine, all attempts to build a superpresidential regime that concentrates formal and informal power in an unified center of authority have failed. All such efforts have ended in political crises that resulted in a radical regime change and brought to power new political groups. This was the case in 1994, 2004, and 2014. Second, constitutional policy in Ukraine is an important and supple element in the bargaining among political elites about the distribution of power and the rules guiding the functioning of the political system. The dominant Ukrainian actors use constitutional policy as an instrument to expand and strengthen their political influence and also as a method to codify compromise agreements (political pacts) for stabilizing their dominance.

What are the sources of these unique dynamics? To a significant degree they result from the "neopatrimonial" structure of the political and economic systems and the prevalence of informal institutions (institutions that are not written down or considered official) over formal institutions (institutions that are officially codified and explicitly recognized) (Helmke and Levitsky 2006). A core feature of "patrimonialism" is that ruling groups regard society as their private domain and think that their public offices are legitimate means for them to enrich themselves. In such systems, the national leader generally controls the political and economic life of the country, and for others in society, personal "client" relationships with the leader play a crucial role in amassing personal wealth, or in the rise and decline of members of the political elite. Accordingly, patron-client bonds, rather than rational-legal relations, play the key role in public sphere power relations, since they regulate access by neopatrimonial players to various resources on the basis of personal loyalty and capital exchanges. What distinguishes "neopatrimonialism" from simple "patrimonialism" (an older concept) is a symbiosis of patrimonial and modern rational-bureaucratic rule, in which the formal institutions of political democracy (for example, the parliament, a multiparty system, and electoral competition) function but yield and adapt to the larger patrimonial logic as to how the political system operates as a whole.

In contrast to Latin America and southern and east central Europe, where democratization took place after a process of nation-building and rational-legal state-building, initial democratization efforts in the post-Soviet states (with the exception of the Baltic region) preceded both nation-building and rational-legal state-building (Kuzio 2001; Grzymala-Busse and Jones Luong 2002; Ekiert and Hanson 2003; Bunce 2003; Kopstein 2003). In this context, neopatrimonial modes of ruler and state-society relations compensated for the unfinished process of modern state-building and nation-building. According to Shmuel Eisenstadt, postcolonial rulers in newly independent states reintroduce patrimonial methods of political relations in the face of increasing problems with state-building and national consolidation during the postindependence period (Eisenstadt 1973, 7–30, 50–68). Applying the neopatrimonial framework to our analysis emphasizes the informal features of Ukrainian constitutional politics and places them in the wider political and historical context of the different trajectories of transition to modernity that have been well studied in western Europe, Asia, Africa, and Latin America.

Why and how have Ukraine's constitutions changed? What are the forces driving these changes? What explains the nature of Ukrainian constitutional policy? Which constitutional configurations facilitate the development of democracy in Ukraine, and which lead to the development of authoritarianism and political crises? What are the prospects for constitutional reforms in Ukraine after the Euromaidan Revolution of 2013–14, and what recommendations can we give Ukrainian reformers? The following pages address these questions.

Patronal Presidents versus Rent-seeking Entrepreneurs

The key players in Ukrainian constitutional policy are the *patronal presidents* and *rent-seeking entrepreneurs*, who support contradictory political-constitutional strategies to strengthen their particular formal and informal influence. Compromise among them (the zone of their mutual interests) is codified in formal constitutional agreements, the main content of which defines the principles for the informal division of resources.

Patronal presidentialism, by definition, involves a president elected by a nationwide popular vote who wields wide formal powers derived from constitutions and informal powers based on patron-client relations and the institutionalization of the link connecting political power with control over economic assets (Hale 2005a, 2006a). Standing at the center of the political system and serving as a focal point for the expectations and orientations of political elites in the post-Soviet states, patronal presidents wield considerable powers but are forced (at least formally) to legitimize their claims to power in the course of periodic nationwide popular elections. Such presidents draw support from their personal patron-client networks, which are composed primarily of economic and regional elites. These networks help the president implement decisions and serve as a "reelection machine"—that is, the elites provide financial and informational support and mobilize votes in the regions in exchange for protection of their property and wide discretion in implementing policies at the regional level. The presidential monopoly on the law enforcement and fiscal sectors of the state, particularly personnel policies and privatization management, ensures that this deal remains in place.

Patronal presidents can maintain control over the party system through the establishment of a dominant party or the creation of a parliamentary majority and local authorities loyal to the president by means of bureaucratic patronage and individual co-option. Similarly, the president must retain wide powers in the executive branch to ensure that the prime minister either remains loyal or has little ability to act independently. He must control coercive and fiscal powers and retain influence over the judicial branch as a basis for monopolizing property rights and protecting the rents of the big political players. Likewise, he must have a system in place to control and punish individuals who breach the established balance, and maintain an ability to fight the opposition (Darden 2008).

In addition to the patronal presidency, the post-Soviet institutional environment contributed to the growth of a new kind of political actor—*rent-seeking entrepreneurs*. The key features of these actors include the neopatrimonial privatization of public offices and associated rents and privileges, devotion to partial reforms (Hellman 1998), and diversification of political risks. Rent-seeking entrepreneurs participate in the state-building process mostly as a potential opposition to the centralizing tendencies of patronal presidentialism. In other words, despite the fact that they tend to participate in the patron-client network of the president, at least theoretically they represent forces that are able to organize and support another polity-building project—parliamentarization, which means power-sharing among party players and their mutual containment. In fact, rent-seeking entrepreneurs encounter the same problems and challenges that various elite groups (aristocracy, oligarchs) historically ran into during the state-building process when they opposed the centralizing and redistributive initiatives of polity leaders (tyrants, absolutist monarchs) (Tilly 1992, 1975; Spruyt 1994; Ertman 1997).

Understanding Ukrainian Constitutional Dynamics

The main focus of Ukrainian constitutional policy is the battle between patronal presidents and their competitors among the rent-seeking entrepreneurs for control over the central office of the constitutional system—the office of president, which sits atop the patronage system pyramid (Hale 2011). Ukraine's political regimes are characterized by a concentration of power in the hands of an individual ruler who maintains control mainly by distributing patronage to a network of various rent-seeking actors such as political entrepreneurs, economic magnates, regional barons, loyal elites, particular societal groups, cronies, and relatives. The neopatrimonial center encourages popular political participation through joining patron-client networks, different corporatist arrangements, or a formal "party of power." Within the "party of power," the core positions belong to the "presidential clan," which holds the key position in the polity and controls profitable industries. The binding element within this clan is a system of personal ties, centered on the president and based primarily on regional or ethnic unity, as well as on present-day rent-seeking interests. The neopatrimonial ruler completely dominates and controls the political and administrative elite around him. The formal constitutions define to what extent the neopatrimonial system is centralized or how much decentralization is possible and what kind of limits can be placed on the president.

Essentially, Ukrainian politics follows the logic of the neopatrimonial political process: it is not a struggle of political alternatives in the context of parliamentary contestation but a struggle carried out by different factions of rent-seeking entrepreneurs to monopolize the main segments of patron-client networks. The neopatrimonial elite in Ukraine is divided, above all, over who has access to patronage and the ruler-controlled clientelistic distribution of "fiefs and benefices." Ukrainian party/elite cleavages may be defined according to who is inside and who is outside the pork-barrel and spoils system (Bratton and van de Walle 1997; Snyder and Mahoney 1999).

The rent-seeking entrepreneurs who emerged in the wake of postcommunist reforms usually do not aspire to engage in autonomous political activity beyond the patronage network set up by the state ruler, rarely support alternative political forces, and, generally, do not show interest in the democratic transformation of the political sphere whereby democratic rules would govern political and economic competition. However, they do maneuver between the costs and benefits of retaining patronal presidentialism, through which they can lobby their particular interests via a single patron-client network, versus parliamentarization, a system that requires them to lobby their interests among several divided patron-client networks.

Accordingly, Ukrainian constitutional policy can be described as a battle between patronal presidents, who fight against attempts to limit their power by rent-seeking entrepreneurs, who tend to support projects to switch to a parliamentary system and increase the role of parliamentary parties in determining the composition of the cabinet of ministers, appointing the heads of state corporations, and naming regional leaders. In the Ukrainian context, parliamentarianism means the creation of a power-sharing system with divided executive rule and the cohabitation of competing patron-client networks and party holdings. Entrepreneurs try to achieve these goals through the support of opposition parties, the establishment of their own party substitutes (Hale 2005b) in the form of party holdings of financial and industrial groups or regional political machines, or the mobilization of grass-root protests, which have proven, as the color revolutions showed, to be a key resource. Successful opposition to the president requires the cooperation of a wide counterelite coalition, whose formation means overcoming a variety of conflicting interests and ideologies, and solving the collective action problem.

In this battle, Ukrainian presidents have employed three strategies:

Building a large presidential party, capable of winning, at a minimum, a relative majority of seats in the parliament by deploying the national and local bureaucracies and representatives of regional patron-client networks;

Strongly controlling the regional elite, much of which views their provinces (*oblasti*) as patrimonial domains (*votchyna*), through appointing regional governors and district (*raion*) heads, as well as the chiefs of local law enforcement, the secret service, judiciary, and prosecutors' offices.

Limiting the influence of powerful rent-seeking entrepreneurs (oligarchs) through blackmail politics (Darden 2001) on the basis of their control over central coercion and fiscal state bodies.

As a rule, attempts to widen the presidential base of support have led to short-term stabilizations of the regime and expanded the influence of the patronal presidents by co-opting many influential competitors into the party of power (Kuchma 1997–99, 2002–4; Yushchenko 2005–6; Yanukovych 2010–12). Efforts to strengthen the influence of the presidential hierarchy rely on successfully incorporating influential representatives of local clans into the president's orbit, both formal (propresidential party) and informal (co-option into patron-client networks through appointments to influential posts). Such outreach to local clans strengthens both the vertical penetration of the presidential hierarchy into the regions and its horizontal expansion by including representatives of local patron-client networks from areas beyond the core regions of the president's base support.

In Ukraine, efforts to build a "party of power" around the president have, as a rule, led only to the short-term consolidation of the propresidential forces and only whetted the appetite of the rent-seeking entrepreneurs, who preferred to unite in battle against the president, mobilizing their supporters in influential regional bases and resolving the collective action problem. This was seen in the standoff between the president and parliament during the 1994–95 crisis, the 2004 Orange Revolution, and the 2013–14 Euromaidan. To prevent antipresidential consolidation among rent-seeking entrepreneurs, Ukrainian presidents have often had to compromise and appoint representatives of competing patron-client networks as prime ministers. Thus Leonid Kuchma tapped Pavlo Lazarenko in 1996–97, Leonid Kuchma appointed Viktor Yushchenko for 1999–2001, and Viktor Yushchenko backed Viktor Yanukovych to serve in 2006–7.

Setting the Rules of Game: The 1996 Constitution and Its Consequences

In contrast to its neighbors, Ukraine suffered through a drawn-out constitution-writing process because of a stalemate that prevailed among various elite political groups, each of which lacked the necessary resources and influence to strengthen and formalize their institutional position in the constitutional rules of the game. Because of this stalemate, with no strong institutional player or dominant political/economic elite group, the adoption of the Constitution in 1996 was preceded by a series of political crises. The chain of crises and subsequent agreements reflected efforts by the various players to overcome the stalemate by changing the political landscape for their own benefit and installing new constitutional arrangements that would guarantee the gains that they had made. Thus, the confrontation between President Leonid Kravchuk, Prime Minister Leonid Kuchma, and the parliament (Verkhovna Rada) in 1993 led to a compromise between the three parties: calling early parliamentary and presidential elections in 1994. The crisis between Kuchma and the Verkhovna Rada of 1994–95 was resolved by adopting a constitutional agreement that was valid for one year. When that agreement expired on June 28, 1996, the Verkhovna Rada adopted a new constitution with considerable presidential powers but also featuring a prime minister as the operational head of government (a system known widely as "semipresidentialism" (Duverger 1980).

The process for adopting the constitution was determined by the existing political situation, in which Kuchma managed to strengthen his own powers and began to build a patron-client network that aimed to turn a formally semipresidential system into what was sometimes called a "superpresidential" one. The process of promoting this superpresidentialism meant a concomitant weakening of the parliament. Witnessing the rise of the president, some members of parliament started participating in the formation and expansion of the president's patron-client network. Nevertheless, the main task of the parliament (and its elite support base) was to retain its status and block the buildup of superpresidential power. In this regard, the Verkhovna Rada hastily tried to anchor the existing political status quo at the constitutional level through various compromises among the parliamentary delegations (for example, through package voting for the status of Crimea and state flag of Ukraine). The president was never able to build up a strong parliamentary base, and his patron-client network unsuccessfully tried to form a formal party of power (the People's Democratic Party) in a situation in which multiple clan networks dominated the Verkhovna Rada.

The functioning of Ukraine's political system under the Constitution of 1996 reflects formal semipresidentialism's institutional proclivity toward permanent internal conflict. The vertical structure of power under semipresidentialism may be built by forming a dominant propresidential political party in legislatures, enhancing the advantages of the presidency and leading to the establishment of strong patronal presidentialism. In attempting to create his own dominant political machine, Kuchma was forced to co-opt politicians trying to build their own parties (for example, the influential Kyiv-based clan of the Social Democratic Party of Ukraine [United] of Viktor Medvedchuk). However, the formation of such a broad propresidential coalition (both by personal co-option and through bureaucratic resources) meant that there was considerable opposition to the president within his own party.

From the early 2000s, the superpresidential vertical informal power hierarchy stopped functioning properly, and a critical mass of opposition-minded groups emerged. This emerging opposition pushed the president to actively co-opt regional elites through personal ties as an alternative to building a dominant party, as reflected in the Zlagoda movement in 1999 and the movement ZaEdU (For a United Ukraine) in 2002. As part of the abortive effort to build a dominant party, in 2000 Kuchma replaced the speaker of the Verkhovna Rada, removing Oleksandr Tkachenko in favor of Ivan Plusch. Nevertheless, within a year, the parliament lacked the votes to implement the results of the 2000 referendum, which had created a potential mechanism for the co-option of the political elite in the form of adding an upper chamber to Ukraine's parliament. The failure of this vote was indicative of the emerging opposition moods within the party of power.

In 2003 Kuchma tried to carry out a constitutional reform, which included establishing a bicameral parliament, institutionalizing a parliamentary majority, and limiting the participation of the president in government formation (on the proposal of the parliament, the president was only to appoint the ministers of emergency affairs, defense, and foreign affairs) while leaving intact the president's influence on key appointments in the security and fiscal areas (appointing the heads of the tax administration, security service, and customs agency) as well as appointments of local authorities. One of the main reasons for this reform was the president's desire, by making a number of significant concessions to the parliament, to create a solid base of support for the president in the form of an upper chamber, to improve presidential levers to counter the parliament (particularly through referendum), and to overcome the "feckless pluralism" (Carothers 2002, 10) in the party system and stabilize the work of the parliament through the institutionalization of a coalition of key propresidential party players.

The 2004 Constitutional Reform
and the Triumph of Neopatrimonial Democracy

By end of his second term, Kuchma had become a lame duck, which caused rent-seeking political entrepreneurs to look for an alternative candidate for the presidency. The search for the right candidate resulted in a split among the members of the patron-client network, which led to a sharp political confrontation during the 2004 presidential campaign. The situation evolved from crisis to deadlock, which could only be broken by an elite settlement to carry out a constitutional reform and turn Ukraine into a "premier-presidential" regime, a form of semipresidentialism with a very strong prime minister (Shugart and Carey 1992). One of the main motivations behind this constitutional reform was an effort to overcome the electoral crisis of 2004 by lowering the value of the presidential prize and to maintain the political influence of the then ruling party of power in case its candidate lost the presidential election.

The 2004 constitutional reform included (1) measures for strengthening the position of the parliament by giving it broad powers to form a government and extending its term to five years; (2) incentives to promote party-building (through a party-list proportional representation electoral system) and party discipline (the imperative mandate, a system whereby a deputy cannot change parties after being elected on a party list); (3) institutionalizing a governing coalition of party delegations (called "factions" in Ukrainian parlance); (4) strengthening the position of the prime minister by expanding that post's appointment power and the power to countersign laws; (5) limiting the role of the president in government formation while leaving intact the office's influence on the defense and foreign affairs ministers as well as the fiscal and coercive power hierarchies (prosecutor general, head of Ukraine's Security Service, the National Bank, and the National Security and Defense Council) and extending the grounds on which the president can dissolve parliament.

For influential political and economic actors on every level (national magnates, regional bosses, and autonomous segments of the bureaucracy), the 2004 constitutional reform and the establishing of a premier-presidential regime became a vehicle for making partial changes to the political rules of the game and minimizing the role of the head of state as the principal veto-player (someone with the formal or informal power to stop any major policy move) and focal point in the neopatrimonial hierarchy. The 2004 constitutional reform made it more difficult to implement any kind of winner-take-all policies and stimulated stakeholder cooperation to jointly distribute political dividends proportionate to voting results. This created the basis for a transition from a monopolistic to a power-sharing distribution of governing benefits.

The post-Orange Ukraine of 2005–9 saw a division of neopatrimonial patron-client networks between two major players—the president and the prime minister—and the formation thereupon of two autonomous competing power centers: Yushchenko's patronal presidentialism and Yulia Tymoshenko's patronal premiership. The two parallel power verticals persisted through the control of different apparatuses of the state machinery, including law enforcement, the security services, and the judiciary. This duality prevented one vertical from strong-arming the other. The fact that the rent-seeking political entrepreneurs from the Orange Bloc failed to establish a broad and unified party of power (that is, to institutionalize and centralize patron-client networks solely around President Yushchenko) meant that a pluralistic political system could take shape in Ukraine, with none of the elite groups or social segments securing a majority stake in power. In the absence of his own strong party and in order to counteract Tymoshenko's influence, Yushchenko was forced to co-opt representatives of Viktor Yanukovych's Party of Regions into governing structures, such as the National Security and Defense Council and even to the premiership (that is, the 2006–7 Yanukovych cabinet).

The Ukrainian political reality after 2004 can best be described as a peculiar hybrid regime of *neopatrimonial democracy*. This regime resulted from the constitutional reform of 2004 that transformed Kuchma's attempt at superpresidentialism into a premier-presidential system. In this context, neopatrimonial democracy is a standard modification of the premier-presidential regime in a clientelistic setting, in which rent seeking is the key motive of politics. Political actors compete through formal electoral mechanisms (for the presidential office and seats in parliament), but their goals still focus on state capture as the primary gain. In fact, the constitutional reform of 2004 secured the coexistence of competing patron-client networks that used their own party machines to derive rents within a pluralistic power-sharing political model. The power balance resulted in permanent conflicts, which ended with crises and new agreements. The state of constant stalemate, defined by the lack of a central political figure and the inability to form an effective pluralistic political model, imposed serious political and economic costs on the rent-seeking political entrepreneurs.

During 2009, Yushchenko initiated a draft law for constitutional reform. This reform envisioned a bicameral legislature (adding a senate), increased presidential influence on local government (the president was to appoint heads of local state administration with no recommendation from the government), national security (broad powers in determining the composition of the National Security and Defense Council), and the process of constitutional change (making the decision to call a referendum on changing the constitution) and would have made former presidents lifetime members of the senate. The idea of dividing parliament into two chambers was an effort by the president to counter the growing influence of the prime minister. According to the reform, the lower house was to provide the support base for the prime minister while the upper chamber would be a base for the president. Similarly, the president would be strengthened relative to the prime minister through the establishment of an alternative center of power (the National Security and Defense Council) and expansion of the president's ability to use referenda as an instrument of presidential power.

This constitutional reform effort reflected the political strategy of Yushchenko, who, unlike Kuchma, Yanukovych, and Tymoshenko, made no serious attempts to build a dominant party. This resulted in the breakup of his party Nasha Ukraina (Our Ukraine) and raised the stakes for individual co-option as an alternative strategy to building a dominant party. Yushchenko's focus on co-opting individuals instead of party-building is one of the main reasons for his defeat in the 2010 presidential election, since he had to compete with the more organized political machines of the Party of Regions and the Bloc of Yulia Tymoshenko, which both had a strong resource base to potentially form a patronal presidential system. During the 2010 presidential campaign, the rent-seeking entrepreneurs ultimately decided in favor of Yanukovych, who seemed more tractable to the various rent-seeking interests than Tymoshenko.

Constitutional Dilemmas of Yanukovych's Presidency, 2010–14

The victory of Yanukovych in Ukraine's February 2010 presidential election launched a new cycle of regime change in Ukraine, marked by movement from a premier-presidential system to a superpresidential system dominated by a single principal. Establishing superpresidentialism was made possible through Yanukovych's success in constructing an effective party machine out of the Party of Regions, which became the dominant political party. Thus the rapid move by Yanukovych toward building a single "power vertical" was conditioned not so much by any inherent authoritarianism per se but by the fact that the president—for the first time—did not have to share power with coalition party partners or appoint a compromise prime minister. Yanukovych made much more progress in constructing a propresidential dominant party than did his predecessors Kuchma and Yushchenko. In fact, the existence of the dominant party broke the premier-presidential logic and made possible the establishment of a superpresidential regime. This process was formalized by the decision of the Constitutional Court, which restored the 1996 Constitution and declared invalid the 2004 amendments when it ruled Law IV-2222 unconstitutional. Restoring the 1996 Constitution returned broad powers to the executive branch, placing personnel policy in the hands of the president while weakening other political centers, such as the parliament and the prime minister, who now played a merely technical role.

Yanukovych's politics during 2010–13 might be understood as a "dual spiral" consisting of an efficient combination of two political strategies. The first was a party-building strategy based on incorporating the remnants of alternative patron-client networks into the dominant party (the Party of Regions). Combined with executive control over parliament, this move prevented the semi-presidential regime from getting caught in a stalemate between two branches of government. The second strategy was to use bureaucratic resources, both sticks and carrots, to expand the executive vertical of power. These efforts allowed for an ever-widening propresidential coalition in both parliament and local government, producing a spiraling growth in presidential power. This strategy chipped away at the regional bases of the Yulia Tymoshenko Bloc and encouraged its investors and influential members to move toward the new party of power. The constitutional rollback gave the president direct control over cabinet formation. This new power strengthened the executive's hand vis-à-vis not only parliament but also his own party coalition and political investors.

From 2011 to 2013, Yanukovych placed his bets on strengthening his own domain and co-opting political actors to enhance his top-down power by utilizing bureaucratic resources. The main beneficiaries were "The Family," which included his sons and some of their friends. Yanukovych's administration forced a redistribution of economic spheres (both legal and shadow) among the different groups involved in the presidential patron-client network. Because of the lack of a real mechanism for developing the economy, which was one of the consequences of the "winner take all" monopolization, no significant new assets appeared; rather, the Yanukovych era witnessed the redistribution of existing assets, while rents were derived by establishing control over the fiscal policy of the state. In this situation, the president and his closest associates became a main beneficiary of the new fiscal policy. The result was that basic resources, previously owned by other elite political-economic groups, were redistributed in favor of the president and his close associates.

This system, however, contained the seeds of its own demise. The situation posed a real danger for some members of the presidential patron-client network: not only was there no longer a balanced allocation of resources, but some members of the elite began to serve as "donors" who were forced to further strengthen the president's family. This presidential strategy caused the emergence and enhancement of opposition groups within the dominant party and among political entrepreneurs associated with the president's patron-client network. Thus, at the end of 2013 patronal presidentialism in Ukraine faced the emergence of a field for confrontation within the party of power and the possibility of supporting opposition party projects. For Yanukovych, the only possibility to retain an elite support base was to carry out a new constitutional reform, which would bring Ukraine back to the premier-presidential form of government that existed in 2004, with possible institutional adaptations and modifications.

After the Euromaidan Revolution:
A New Pendulum Cycle or Breaking the Teeter-totter?

The 2013–14 Euromaidan revolution resulted in the collapse of Yanukovych's superpresidential regime and opened a way for political and economic reforms toward a more pluralistic political system. In February 2014, Ukraine returned to the 2004 premier-presidential constitution that significantly limited presidential powers in favor of the prime minister and members of a parliamentary coalition. In May 2014 early presidential elections were held, and for the first time in Ukrainian political history a new president, Petro Poroshenko, was elected without needing a runoff to gain the necessary majority of votes. Then, in October 2014, early parliamentary elections were held. The majority of the seats were taken by pro-European democratic parties, which formed a new ruling coalition that had around three hundred members (representing two-thirds of the MPs, which is enough to pass constitutional changes).

What changed and what has remained the same in Ukrainian politics after the Euromaidan revolution? Beyond doubt, the political regime became more democratic and open because of enhanced competition between several power centers, the rise of civic sector activism, and the absence of a dominant party of power. On the other hand, the patrimonial nature of the political regime, its organizing principles, and its functioning remained the same. Informal institutions continue to dominate formal institutions. Patron-client ties, personal loyalty, and clan membership (relatives and/or business partners) still persist as organizing principles of the system. These patrimonial principles determine the formation of political parties, define the majority of public office appointments, and structure relations among political actors at national and regional levels.

The new political regime has three key elements. First, right after the Euromaidan revolution in February 2014, the Yatsenyuk-Klitschko-Tyahnybok triumvirate (representing the key Euromaidan parties) supported by Oleksandr Turchynov (then chairman of the Verkhovna Rada and acting president of Ukraine) passed a law re-establishing the 2004 premier-presidential constitution, which renders the concentration of power in the president's hands institutionally impossible. A crucial element on which the new interelite consensus rests is the belief that building a single pyramid of power, vesting the president with wide formal and informal powers, is a threat to the democratic development of Ukraine.

Second, a crucial component of the present premier-presidential system is the informal arrangement between the future president Poroshenko and one of the members of the triumvirate, Klitschko, the leader of the Ukrainian Democratic Alliance for Reform (UDAR) Party. The arrangement aimed to divide spheres of influence between the two politicians: Klitschko became mayor of Ukraine's capital, Kyiv, and his network retained control over some offices in the national executive branch.

The third element of the new power system was the power-sharing arrangement with the second member of the Euromaidan triumvirate, Arseniy Yatsenyuk, who retained the office of prime minister and received control over the major political and economic levers of the executive branch, including the Interior Ministry, tax service, and custom service. This is a "tandemocracy" regime built on the institutional separation of presidential and premier power verticals through the divided government and competition between Poroshenko's and Yatsenyuk's parties (respectively, Solidarity and People's Front), which peaked just before and immediately after the October 2014 parliamentary elections.

Thus, the post-Euromaidan revolutionary restructuring of Yanukovych's superpresidential regime has again led to the formation of a neopatrimonial democracy in 2014–15. The new regime is built on the combination of the formal and informal competition of various patron-client party networks over the control of key positions in generating rents in state administration and key sectors of the economy. Political parties are formed by political investors not to protect the interests of the electorate but to promote quota-based distribution of the rent-seeking positions in the Cabinet of Ministers and the state apparatus. However, what is specific to the post-Euromaidan neopatrimonial democracy is that the winners are determined in highly competitive political struggles and the results are not known in advance.

For the effective implementation of reform policies, President Poroshenko must overcome the main source of gridlock in any premier-presidential system. Effectively, he must at a minimum transform the prime minister from the president's main rival into his ally and ideally make the prime minister his partisan representative. To achieve that goal, Poroshenko has pursued a three-prong strategy since his election in May 2014:

1. *Building a wide presidential party capable of securing at least a relative majority in elections.* The strategy for building a presidential party is based on patronage and clientelism, as well as the inclusion of influential regional businesspeople capable of financing local party organizations, into the president's patron-client network. A crucial element of presidential party formation is the absorption of other parties and the networks behind them (Klitschko's UDAR and others). In many ways, the formation of the presidential party resembles Kuchma's attempts to create the propresidential blocs Zlagoda in 1999 and ZaEdU in 2002, Yushchenko's efforts to unite small political parties around Our Ukraine in 2006 and 2007, and the absorption by the Party of Regions of other parties after the 2012 parliamentary election.

2. *Controlling regional elites, some of whom treat their regions as patrimonial domains* and even have their own paramilitary forces. A key element of the presidential decentralization reform is establishing presidential representatives (prefects) to control local regional barons. The regional elites' integration into the presidential sphere of influence is also envisioned through patronage provided for regional party projects capable of uniting and organizing local government people into party structures allied to the president. These regional parties should have a majority in local councils, nominate their heads, and control their local executive branches after decentralization reform.

3. *Restraining the political influence of the principal rent-seeking entrepreneurs by undermining their economic resource base.* The key drama here belongs to the conflict between Poroshenko and influential Ukrainian oligarch Ihor Kolomoiskiy, who was one of the few oligarchs to support the Euromaidan Revolution. Paradoxically, post-Euromaidan neopatrimonial democracy fosters the creation of both formal (premier-presidential divided rule) and informal (patronage networks' contestation) barriers and limitations to the development of a superpresidential regime and transition to personal rule. On the other hand, the same formal and informal rules hinder state capture by the representatives of one oligarchic group and monopolization of the political space at the national and regional levels by a single political and economic clan.

Conclusion and Implications for Reform

Overall, Ukrainian constitutional dynamics is distinguished so far by four cycles of patronal presidentialism.

During the first cycle, 1994 to 2004, the president secured the formal and informal powers of the head of state in the coercive and fiscal spheres. In the second cycle, 2004 to 2010, the Orange Revolution dismantled the superpresidential version of patronal presidentialism and created a pluralistic power-sharing premier-presidential system, within which the president and prime minister were relatively equal in their political influence. The 2004 constitutional reform limited presidential powers, lowering the value of the presidential prize, and secured "cohabitation" and competition between the presidential and the primeministerial patron-client networks. During the third cycle, 2010 to February 2014, the president enhanced his authority by returning to the head of state significant formal and informal powers and established control over the parliament though the dominant Party of Regions' machine. The restoration of the 1996 Constitution in 2010 placed patronal presidentialism's logic back in the center of Ukrainian politics. The 2010 pendulum swing from premier-presidential to presidential-parliamentary constitutions served Yanukovych's goal of authoritarian power consolidation in his hands while simultaneously reducing the power of the parliament. The Euromaidan Revolution of 2013–14 started the new fourth presidential cycle with the restoration in February 2014 of the premier-presidential constitution. In each of the cycles, the change of constitution meant not just the creation of a new system of checks and balances among public authorities but also the establishment of a new system for distributing power among state officials and the various political forces at the national and regional levels around them (Derluguian and Earle 2010).

In selecting a new constitutional model for Ukraine, the drafters should take into consideration the neopatrimonial features of key political actors. There is some space for the swing of the described pendulum of Ukrainian politics within the framework of the current premier-presidential constitution. The 2014 constitutional reform provided the basis for developing a curious institutional hybrid, capable of functioning in two different modes. The first is a dominant party regime of *managed democracy*, whereby a president has control over both parliament and a prime minister from his or her own party and, hence, can potentially monopolize coercive and fiscal tools. The second is a competitive-democratic regime of *neopatrimonial democracy*, existing against the backdrop of a patron-client network divided between two centers and based upon deficient executive control over parliament, weakness in the president's party structure, and a prime minister co-opted from a nonpresidential party or alternative patron-client network.

The crucial question is, however, what is the basis for curbing competitiveness in the first case and supporting it in the second? The answer appears to be less the formal premier-presidential system than the mode chosen to reproduce patron-client networks. These networks are reproduced through either formal parties or informal personal patronage and co-option. The degree to which the controlled segments of the patron-client networks are institutionalized (by setting up powerful parties) is the key factor. Political parties become decisive factors for success in electoral competition and interelite bargaining for the office of prime minister. Insufficient party institutionalization became a major cause of Kuchma's and Yushchenko's failure to form a government coalition through patron-client networks and limited their abilities to promote a prime minister.

Will Poroshenko continue investing resources in the expansion of the pro-presidential coalition, with a prospect of forming a dominant party of power (a strategy of *dominant-party presidentialism*), or will he try to buttress his position with administrative-bureaucratic resources, in particular the coercive tools of state machinery (a strategy of *patronal-bureaucratic presidentialism*)? Or will he combine the two, as Kuchma and Yanukovych did previously?

At least three potential prospective scenarios exist:

1. *Electoral Bonapartism.* This is a regime of personal rule based on the monopolization of coercive and fiscal state machinery; zigzagging between the interests of major financial-industrial groups; curtailing electoral competition in favor of plebiscites; developing the executive bureaucratic vertical based on personal loyalty, controls over the regional barons by the president's prefects, and resorting to coercive pressures (via law enforcement, the security service, and the judiciary).

2. *Power-sharing oligarchy.* This is a regime based on power division between key players and their resultant control over patronal-social and regional actors in the political (and likely constitutional) realm, which eventually produces a transition to a situation in which parliament elects the president.

3. *Dominant-party managed democracy.* This is a regime in which the president strives to win pluralities within most social segments rather than the single largest group. Under this type of regime, the president can discipline the national bureaucracy and regional elites through their membership in the party of power. This will involve incorporation into the ruling coalition of most of the remaining rent-seeking entrepreneurs from different political camps.

However, the constitutional reform of 2014 can be viewed in the long term as part of a broader pendulum swing from a superpresidential regime to a premier-presidential one. This implies a potential for a new swing back toward restoration of the superpresidential model (in the case of an authoritarian-bureaucratic consolidation of the regime). Ukrainian political developments demonstrate that constitutional rules in the neopatrimonial environment are typically retained only for one electoral cycle. The question of re-election emerges in any neopatrimonial system and is resolved through changes in constitutional rules that can ensure succession in the power and security of elite privileges (as with the constitutional reform projects of Kuchma, Yushchenko, and Yanukovych). Long-term rule depends on the ability of political actors to make the transition from ad hoc personal-patron coalitions to steady institutionalized structures that are capable of surviving several election cycles and insensitive to changes in leadership.

The principal survival strategy of Ukraine's political actors (1994–96, 2002–4, 2012–14) has been to neutralize the negative effects of personal rule and institutionalize formal political competition via the development of party holdings. It is the weakness of their own party structures that has always been the Achilles' heel of Ukrainian presidents, and they have had to compensate for this weakness with strategies of co-option, including the summoning of a prime minister from alternative political camps.

From this point of view, the pendulum of Ukrainian politics can swing without the need to change the constitution and constitutional law in a radical way. At this stage, constitutional and political modernization should focus not so much on the redistribution of powers among the president, prime minister, and parliament but rather on subverting the political capacity of patronal presidents and rent-seeking entrepreneurs to "play with the rules" and conduct frequent constitutional experiments.

7   Constitutional Performance after Communism: Implications for Ukraine

HENRY E. HALE

What kind of constitution would give Ukraine the best prospects for democracy and good governance? This chapter ventures an answer by comparing the experiences of countries that share certain features with Ukraine, in particular high levels of "patronalism" and a legacy of communist rule (Wolczuk 2001). Since constitutions can be expected to have different effects in patronalistic and postcommunist polities than they do in other kinds of settings (especially Western ones), the analysis considers three broad types of constitutions that are especially relevant to such countries: presidentialist, parliamentarist, and divided-executive. An examination of how each type of constitution has influenced politics in patronalistic postcommunist countries leads to the relatively pessimistic conclusion that none can be considered a panacea, each being associated with different sorts of problems. Nevertheless, the balance of evidence suggests a challenge to conventional wisdom: Divided-executive constitutions, often maligned in Ukraine and elsewhere, may in fact be the best of the available bad solutions, giving Ukraine the greatest hope of escaping a syndrome of nondemocratic politics and poor governance in the long run, though at the cost of some short-run dysfunction. This hope is most likely to be realized if other reforms come into place that reinforce constitutional reform.

Criteria for Useful Comparisons:
Legacies of Patronalism and Communism

Many arguments on constitutional reform focus on formal law, tending to assume that the provisions constitutions stipulate will be generally followed (Diamond and Plattner 1996; Shugart and Carey 1992). Other research, however, has found that this assumption is unwarranted in many societies—especially those in which the rule of law is weak and much of politics is about informal understandings rather than formal procedures and institutions (Cheibub 2007; Easter 1997; Levitsky and Way 2010). In addition, a great deal of research has found that the communist past tends to weigh heavily on current patterns of politics (Kitschelt et al. 1999; Tucker and Pop-Eleches 2012). In making constitutional recommendations for Ukraine, therefore, it makes little sense to assume that constitutions will have the same kind of effects in Ukraine that they do in countries in which the tradition of rule of law is strong and where society is not still struggling with decades of totalitarianism that destroyed many pre-existing cleavages and institutions that underpin much of constitutional politics in other countries.

In particular, comparative research has found that constitutions tend to have distinct effects in highly patronalistic societies (Hale 2011). *Patronalism* refers to a social equilibrium in which politics is organized far more around extended networks of actual personal acquaintance than around what Benedict Anderson called "imagined communities" (Anderson 1991), groups of people united not by personal acquaintance but instead by impersonal factors such as shared ideologies (for example, nationalism or positions on a left-right divide) or common stands on key issues (such as gun control or environmental protection) (Hale 2015). Patronalistic societies tend to stand out from others for weak rule of law, high levels of corruption, extensive clientelism, low social capital, and the predominance of (neo-)patrimonial forms of authority (Fisun 2012; Grzymala-Busse 2008; Putnam 1993). In such societies, one clearly cannot expect that constitutional niceties will be observed or enforced with substantial regularity and consistency. But this does not mean that constitutions have no impact upon how politically open a country is or how well it can supply governance. Instead, as the present author has argued elsewhere, constitutions can strongly impact such things by shaping how the country's most important political-economic networks coordinate their activities in vying for power and resources through state structures. In particular, constitutions can strongly impact political outcomes by *shaping formally illegal as well as legal* behavior by providing certain kinds of information regarding who are the most powerful actors and by creating focal points around which elites find it convenient to coordinate *both* their law-disregarding and their law-regarding behavior (Hale 2011).

We are now in position to narrow down the case selection for a useful comparative study. Since there is good reason to believe that constitutions may have distinct effects in countries with legacies of postcommunism and patronalism, it makes sense to focus on those countries that share such legacies with Ukraine because they are particularly likely to have relevant lessons for Ukraine. Choosing which cases to count as postcommunist is relatively straightforward: While some today consider countries like China and Vietnam to be postcommunist (Wang 2002), this chapter focuses primarily on countries in which ruling communist parties have actually fallen from power or at least shed the label "communist." This includes all of the former communist countries of Europe and the USSR, as well as Mongolia.

As for patronalism, all societies feature some elements of it, but clearly some display it in much more comprehensive measure than others. A reading of the specialist literature makes clear that Ukraine quite strongly displays the signs of patronalism mentioned above (D'Anieri 2007b; Fisun 2007; Kudelia 2013; Kuzio 2015b; Matsuzato 2005). But how to identify which other countries share similar levels of patronalism? Here it is useful to draw on a study by Herbert Kitschelt and three colleagues that sorts postcommunist countries by the degree to which they have historically featured "patrimonial" politics, which can be taken as a good indicator of patronalism. Ukraine falls into the most patronalistic category, along with the other non-Baltic post-Soviet countries and Romania, Bulgaria, Macedonia, and Albania.[1] To this set we might usefully add Mongolia, which was not included in the Kitschelt study but which is postcommunist and which few would dispute looks similar to Ukraine on indicators of patronalism noted above. This set of sixteen countries, then, will form the comparison set for our analysis.

Presidentialist, Parliamentarist, and Divided-executive Constitutions

While there are myriad ways that constitutions differ from each other (Shugart and Carey 1992; Elkins, Ginsburg, and Melton 2009), this chapter focuses on three general types that arguably have particularly important implications for how open or closed a patronalistic polity becomes: presidentialist, parliamentarist, and divided-executive constitutions.

Presidentialism

Presidentialist constitutions formally concentrate the lion's share of executive power in the hands of a directly elected president or offices whose holder the president can directly influence by appointment, nomination, or dismissal. In highly patronalistic polities, where elites have strong incentive to seek to be on the winning side of political struggles regardless of ideology, the creation of such an office gives at least a small political advantage to its holder relative to those who do not hold it, ceteris paribus, even if laws governing power relationships are routinely disregarded. This is because a post with such symbolism of power is likely to be desired by those who seek to communicate their power to elites, and a reputation for power is crucial to actually maintaining and exercising power itself. In addition, such a single dominant post can become a kind of focal point for elite coordination: elites that have no other basis for deciding which among multiple competing patrons is likely to be dominant in the future are likely to find the holder of the formal presidency to be a convenient solution to their coordination problem (Hale 2011). One would expect, therefore, to observe a general tendency toward power concentration in the hands of a president under presidentialist constitutions in patronalistic societies. At the same time, we would also expect this tendency toward power concentration to be periodically disrupted when a president is expected to leave office, which can happen for any number of reasons ranging from gross missteps to announced resignation plans. In this situation, elites know that the future president will *not* be the incumbent, removing the tendency of the presidential office to provide direct information and a focal point for elite network coordination. Presidentialist constitutions, therefore, can be expected to facilitate cyclic patterns of power concentration punctuated by major disruptions organized around moments of expected succession (Hale 2005a).

Parliamentarism

A parliamentarist constitution is one by which the parliament fills the most important state executive offices, typically a prime minister but also sometimes a president. Such constitutions are often presented as the democratic alternative to presidentialism, but this is usually based on assumptions about how politics works in the less patronalistic West (Fish 2006). In patronalistic societies, the impact of parliamentarism is likely to vary greatly depending on what kind of parliamentarism we are talking about. If parliamentarism means that a parliamentary majority elects a prime minister who then wields a great formal concentration of executive power, in patronalistic polities the effects are not likely to be very different from presidentialism (Hale 2014). Parliamentarist constitutions can have moderating effects, though, when they create more than one top executive post that a parliament can fill (such as a president along with a prime minister), because this can help anchor coalitional deals among otherwise rival networks, giving each some resources to oppose reneging by the other. But to the extent that any one party (network) can demonstratively defeat the other in a parliamentary system's elections, a single election victory is all that is needed in order for the winning network to capture both top executive posts, setting the stage for a trend to political closure.

Divided-executive Constitutions

A divided-executive constitution is one that stipulates a directly elected president with substantial powers, but that also creates another executive office with roughly counterbalancing formal powers (usually a prime minister) that—crucially—is chosen and removed by parliament autonomously of the president. It is important not to confuse the concept of divided-executive constitution with "semipresidentialism" (Duverger 1980; Roper 2002; Shugart and Carey 1992) (including its "premier-presidentialism" subtype) (Shugart and Carey 1992). Semipresidentialism refers only to the formal division of executive powers between a president and prime minister, but the prime minister can still be appointed, nominated, or removed by the president. This difference may at first seem like a small nuance, but in highly patronalistic societies like Ukraine's, it has major implications: the fact that a president has the right autonomously to appoint, nominate, or remove a prime minister—even if such decisions are still subject to parliamentary approval of some kind—can constitute an important signal of which of the two offices is dominant over the other, triggering the effects of presidentialist constitutions discussed above.

In contrast with presidentialist constitutions, divided-executive constitutions tend to create *two* key focal points for elite network coordination rather than one, disrupting the tendency of presidentialism to encourage coordinated political closure. Individuals or networks that do not like what the president is doing under a divided-executive constitution, therefore, are more likely to see the prime minister as an alternative point of coordination in their search for power, resources, and political protection, just as those who are dissatisfied with the prime minister now have the alternative of orienting themselves to the president with reasonable confidence that others will also be doing so. This tends to complicate the concentration of power in the hands of a single patron that both presidentialist and parliamentarist constitutions can foster. This tendency should not be overestimated; it is entirely possible for a political battle to result in one network gaining control of both posts, negating the interpretation of either one as a real alternative to the other. But the formal independence of each post at least creates some incentive for power networks to divide rather than unite that is not present with presidentialism, tending to preserve political contestation.

Implications for Constitutional Reform

What, then, are the implications of these three varieties of constitution for a country's potential to develop in a democratizing direction and adopt other reforms to improve governance? If the goal is political openness and pluralism, the expectation is that divided-executive constitutions are likely to be best able to facilitate it, since they most complicate the coordination of elite networks around a single source of authority. If the goal is full-fledged democracy, however, we have few grounds for immediate optimism: what is described in the preceding sentence is not a pluralism based on the rule of law, but one that essentially boils down to the unruly competition of political networks that are at least as likely to use the methods of political machines as they are to struggle through legal channels through a competition of ideas (elsewhere I have called this a "competing pyramid system") (Hale 2011). The question, however, is whether the other varieties of constitution can be expected to perform any better in highly patronalistic societies, ceteris paribus, and the answer supplied above is no.

When we turn from democracy promotion to other kinds of reforms for the benefit of the people, however, the costs of the divided-executive constitution come in sharp focus: the risk of policy paralysis or—worse—destructive in-fighting among the different branches of executive power. The question, of course, is whether other available constitutions would have effects that would improve on this situation. Proponents of presidentialism, including many patronal presidents themselves, frequently argue that presidentialist constitutions can underpin stability and the kind of executive unity that can be vital for deciding on and carrying out needed reforms. While the resulting closed political system may look or be authoritarian, in principle the concentration of power can be used for good. And here lies the key difficulty with presidentialist systems: so long as the leadership is providing good governance and necessary reforms, many may think this is worth a loss of pluralism, but when the leadership is not doing this the people get stuck with these bad policies, potentially for a long time as the regime works to prevent possibilities for change. And the sad fate of highly patronalistic countries is that often the leadership has a strong predatory component, or at least that it provides a relatively low ratio of public goods for society to private goods for cronies. And as the concentration of power grows, the rulers are decreasingly likely to feel the need to improve the ratio for the people. When change does come, it is likely to come through highly destabilizing and potentially destructive events like revolutions; indeed, revolutions are quite arguably a regular feature of patronal presidentialist systems. Upon closer examination, then, the advantages of presidentialism in policy-making and stability are not so great in highly patronalistic contexts as widely assumed.

Parliamentarist constitutions may provide a sort of middle ground when they provide for multiple powerful executive posts that can be used to anchor power-sharing deals by networks in which one network has a vested interest in checking any usurpation attempts by the other. One risk of even this form of parliamentarism, however, is that by making both executive posts accountable to the same elected body, parliament, there is a greater risk than under divided-executive constitutions that both posts will be captured by the same network, leading again to political closure. And if the posts are controlled by both networks, you potentially gain the same risk of policy paralysis and destructive in-fighting among branches of executive power that divided-executive constitutions are associated with.

The divided-executive constitution, therefore, starts to look less bad when one considers the available alternatives. And certain other considerations might reduce its unattractiveness a bit further. For one thing, if we turn to the longer run, to the extent that voters in these countries actually oppose corruption in politics and to the extent that genuine public support does in fact constitute at least a somewhat valuable resource in this elite political struggle, rulers have at least some incentive to start actually providing good governance as a way of getting a competitive advantage over their rivals. While this positive effect might be weak and work only in the long run, it is absent in the closed systems that presidentialist and parliamentarist systems are more likely to pro-mote. Moreover, at least in theory, government gridlock and policy failure are not necessary outcomes. It is instead quite possible that different sides could reach an agreement to cooperate and avoid self-destructive elite wars. But even though such an agreement would likely appear as a rent-seeking cartel (Kudelia 2012), the existence of multiple focal points for elite coordination would still likely promote more pluralism and allow for more actual competition for pop-ular support during elections, which supplies at least some greater incentive for enacting reforms that benefit the people. What, then, has been the actual experience with these different constitutional types in patronalistic postcom-munist states?

Empirical Evidence from Patronalistic Postcommunist Countries

Table 7.1 breaks down the set of highly patronalistic post-Soviet countries according to the type of constitution they feature.[2] As one can see, there are far more cases of presidentialism (nine) than any other type of constitution as of 2016, with two featuring parliamentarist constitutions and six holding divided-executive constitutions. We are thus in a stronger position to weigh divided-executive constitutions against presidentialist ones, though the exam-ination of our two parliamentarist cases will also provide at least some leverage on parliamentarism's potential for a country like Ukraine.

TABLE 7.1: Constitution Type in Highly Patronalistic Polities: Overview of Post-Soviet Period

Presidentialism	Divided-Executive	Parliamentarism[a]
Armenia	**Bulgaria**	**Albania**
Azerbaijan	Georgia 2013–	Moldova 2001–16[a]
Belarus	Kyrgyzstan 2010–	
Georgia until 2013	**Mongolia**	
Kazakhstan	**Macedonia**	
Kyrgyzstan until 2010	Ukraine 2006–10	
Moldova until 2000	Ukraine 2014–	
Romania		
Russia		
Tajikistan		
Turkmenistan		
Ukraine until 2006, 2010–14		
Uzbekistan		

[a]Has a president elected by parliament. **Bold-face** type refers to countries outside the former USSR.

HENRY E. HALE

TABLE 7.2: Constitution Type by Freedom House NIT Democracy Score
for the Year 2014

Presidentialism	Divided-Executive	Parliamentarism
5.36 Armenia	**3.29 Bulgaria**	**4.14 Albania**
6.75 Azerbaijan	4.64 Georgia	4.86 Moldova
6.71 Belarus	5.93 Kyrgyzstan	
6.61 Kazakhstan	**n/a Mongolia**	
3.46 Romania	**4.07 Macedonia**	
6.46 Russia		
6.39 Tajikistan		
6.93 Turkmenistan		
4.75 Ukraine		
6.93 Uzbekistan		
6.04	4.48	4.50

Bottom row reports the average for each kind of constitution.

As a starting point, let us consider broad patterns of democracy (and the lack of it) in this set of countries as of 2014, the most recent year for which data are available. Table 7.2 reports overall democracy scores given by the prominent Freedom House *Nations in Transit* project (Freedom House 2015). As can be seen, since higher scores represent more authoritarianism and less democracy, the presidentialist countries are on average significantly less democratic than the others, and among the others, divided-executive countries come out slightly on top. While not presented here, if one looks at different components going into the overall democracy score, one also finds that as expected, the advantage of divided-executive constitutions is greater in the specific sphere of electoral process than with respect to spheres like corruption, which would not be expected to decrease in the short run with a change in constitution. This at least suggests that the analysis presented above is plausible.

Of course, we cannot tell cause from effect by looking at this table alone. Prior research on constitutional politics tells us that countries that are more likely to have problems with democracy may also be more likely to adopt presidentialism (Cheibub 2007), that constitutions tend to reflect perceptions of existing power balances (Frye 1997; Knight 1992; Kudelia 2010), and that authoritarian leaders might attempt to pass presidentialist constitutions to reinforce their own power, all of which might mean presidentialist constitutions are a reflection of preexisting power relationships more than a source of them (Easter 1997). Furthermore, many other factors surely influence democracy scores that may or may not reflect these dynamics, such as the influence of the

European Union or the uninterrupted rule of the Communist Party (mainly just changing its name) in Turkmenistan and Uzbekistan (Kopstein and Reilly 2000; Levitsky and Way 2010; Vachudova 2005). But this does not mean that constitutions have no effect. Even if, say, presidentialism is adopted by leaders because they are planning on consolidating their power, the fact that they consider presidentialism to be their model of choice indicates that they do perceive it as being capable of helping them along their nondemocratic paths. For this reason, it is important to engage in a closer look at actual political processes in these countries as they relate to their constitutions.

The Presidentialist Countries

The overwhelming experience of postcommunist presidentialism has been toward growing political closure, interrupted only by revolutions or other forms of leadership ouster as moments of expected succession arise for leaders who are widely unpopular. The trend is particularly stark for countries in which the leadership has not been ousted by any form of opposition since the initial transition period ended: Turkmenistan, Uzbekistan, and Kazakhstan. Another set of states began the 1990s in considerable political turmoil, ranging from outright civil war in Azerbaijan and Tajikistan to the political turbulence that rocked Russia throughout the decade. But in each case, the president who came to be in charge by the mid-1990s was able to consolidate power or to successfully hand off power to a successor who did so, resulting in a steady decline in political freedoms. Belarus represents a middle pattern, experiencing a peaceful political free-for-all in the early 1990s before Aliaksandr Lukashenka won the presidency and started the process of patronal presidential consolidation there.

The pattern in post-Soviet patronal presidential countries that experienced regime ousters of some kind since 1995 also fits the logic described in this chapter. For one thing, every ouster but one came after a period of growing authoritarianism much as in the countries described in the previous paragraph; the only exception is Moldova, where the president never managed to defeat the parliament, which ultimately converted the country to parliamentarism. Moreover, almost all ousters occurred when the sitting president was both unpopular and expected to leave the presidency either because he was in his final constitutional term in office (Ter-Petrossian in Armenia, Shevardnadze in Georgia, Akaev in Kyrgyzstan, Bakiev in Kyrgyzstan) or because he opted not to run for reelection despite having the right to do so, attempting to hand power off to a successor through the vote (Kuchma in Ukraine); Ukraine's 2014

Euromaidan revolution was the only exception, as President Yanukovych was not in his constitutionally final term when he was overthrown, though he was unpopular. And everywhere a presidentialist constitution was left in place after one of these revolutions, the result was a new rise in political consolidation in the direction of authoritarianism.

How have the presidentialist countries performed in terms of governance? While Belarus, Azerbaijan, Russia, and Kazakhstan have performed reasonably well in economic growth, much of this can be attributed to subsidies from Russia (Belarus) or energy resources (the others), not simply policy-making capacity that might be attributed to presidentialism (Jones Luong and Weinthal 2010). And in any case, in the areas of reform considered in this book (including the economy, judiciary, corruption, and dealing with the past and identity divides), the presidentialist countries have routinely been found wanting, and in any case do not stand out as any better than countries with the other kinds of constitutions (once oil and subsidies are factored in) (Shevel 2011b; White, Sakwa, and Hale 2010). Some are, indeed, among the worst performers, as in Turkmenistan and Tajikistan.

Romania might seem to be an outlier, a presidentialist system (by our definition) that has remained relatively democratic and implemented significant reforms. But here we must consider its position in the 1990s as a serious candidate for joining the EU, widely regarded as having democratizing effects (Levitsky and Way 2010; Vachudova 2005). One also notices that among the new EU states, the vast majority of which have either parliamentarist or divided-executive constitutions, Romania is one of the poorest performers in terms of democracy and governance, even though it looks good in comparison with post-Soviet countries. All this strongly suggests that there is something about the formal presidentialist constitution that tends toward political closure and disruptive, costly regime cycles.

The Parliamentarist Countries

We only have Albania and Moldova to consider in this set, though both countries well illustrate the ambiguities of parliamentarism in highly patronalistic societies that were described above. As noted above, Moldova initially had a presidentialist constitution but wound up being the only such country in which the president lost the struggles of the 1990s to the parliament, which instituted a parliamentarist constitution in 2000 (Popescu 2012; Lucan A. Way 2002). Unexpectedly, the incumbent parliamentary leadership at that time then lost the 2001 parliamentary elections, which instead produced a landslide victory for the Communist Party of the Republic of Moldova (PCRM). The resulting supermajority meant that the PCRM could unilaterally fill all major executive posts by itself, including president, prime minister, and parliamentary chair. A single election for a single organ with a single election system (in this case, proportional representation) had thus handed complete control of all executive offices over to a single network, something much less likely to occur in divided-executive systems where top offices are filled in separate elections.

In keeping with the theory elaborated above, new chief patron Vladimir Voronin then presided over a period of steady political closure during the 2000s until he too fell victim to term limits, when succession politics caused a rupture in his network that culminated in 2009 as key defectors helped an opposition force win (Hale 2013). Analysis of the 2000s in Moldova does indicate, however, that Moldova's parliamentarist system did serve to weaken Voronin in ways that presidents in presidentialist countries are unlikely to experience. In particular, he proved unable to repeat his 2001 supermajority in the 2005 elections, meaning that he now had to cut deals with other major networks in parliament to secure his own and his associates' election to the major executive posts. This encouraged at least some opposition forces to maintain at least some independence from Voronin instead of capitulating to his authority.

The period starting in 2009, however, reflects the promise of parliamentarism: when Voronin left office, he was succeeded not by a single rival network but by a *coalition* of distinct networks (represented by four separate parties). With each winning network now unable to dominate on its own, they had to strike a power-sharing deal that was anchored by dividing up the three major executive posts. While complicated, the bottom line has been that with each main party (or an agreed-upon neutral figure) occupying a significant executive post, each has been in position to block attempts by the others to amass power. Often such blocking has included allying tactically with the communists on particular votes. One result is that while Moldovan politics has remained highly corrupt, it has also remained quite pluralistic (despite some coalition encroachments on communist resources, such as a ban on communist symbolism and the shutting down of a couple media outlets sympathetic to it).

Albania has performed broadly similarly, winning an association agreement with the European Union and successfully implementing reforms required as part of that process, at the same time that, like Moldova, it has not escaped deep problems of corruption and machine politics (Peshkopia 2014). Thus, overall, Moldova and Albania show that parliamentarism has the potential for sustained political pluralism and reform, but that it also comes with a risk of a new phase of political closure should a single political force win decisively in a single election.

Countries with Divided-executive Constitutions

While the divided-executive countries have certainly faced their share of problems and are not known for high policy-making performance, in comparison with the experience of other highly patronalistic societies they come out looking not so bad. For one thing, we notice in Table 7.2 that Bulgaria and Macedonia are the two most democratic countries in the whole postcommunist and highly patronalistic world, except for perhaps Mongolia, for which *Nations in Transit* does not provide a score but which in any case is also a divided-executive country. One might of course explain Bulgaria's relative democracy by citing the European Union, but it is perhaps noteworthy that it scores better on this measure than Romania, which is presidentialist and joined the EU through the same process. Moreover, Mongolia represents a success story in something like the opposite kind of "neighborhood," sandwiched in between a highly authoritarian China and increasingly autocratic Russia, with undemocratic Kazakhstan nearby. Yet Mongolia has sustained political contestation throughout the 1990s, 2000s, and into the 2010s. And the facts that Bulgaria is in the European Union and that Macedonia has been widely considered ready except for its well-known "name dispute" with Greece (which claims sole right to the geographical term "Macedonia" for one of its regions) indicate that their divided-executive constitutions have not prevented them from adopting some serious reform packages required for joining the EU.

To be sure, massive problems remain. Venelin Ganev, for example, uses Bulgaria as a classic case of "reverse Tillyanism" by which "predatory elites" systematically weaken state structures in the absence of an external imperative such as war (Ganev 2007). There and in the other divided-executive countries, elites frequently struggle with each other over power and (at least implicitly) resources, frequently manifested in battles between presidents and prime ministers that appear senseless and hinder policy-making (Sedelius and Mashtaler 2013). But the theory discussed above does not claim that this constitutional type is perfect, capable of completely transforming society and producing altruistic harmony among politicians in power. Indeed, what divided-executive constitutions do is to facilitate the disruption of the tendency associated with other constitutional types of elites tending to coalesce into a single rent-seeking coalition on which there are essentially no meaningful checks and no mechanism for accountability except when the machine starts to near a succession crisis for some reason, in which case the accountability is often exercised through revolution.

Another advantage relative to other constitutional forms is that the elite splits occurring under divided-executive constitutions do not tend to end in highly disruptive revolutions. Instead, these elite splits tend to resolve themselves peacefully through elections since the consequences of losing one office are less likely to be disastrous for incumbents, making them more likely to concede electoral defeat in any given election. That is, authorities from all sides can be expected to cheat and use administrative methods where they can, but once the battle is fought, the losing side tends to concede without major resistance. It is thus noteworthy that all of the major revolutionary regime ousters in the post-Soviet world have taken place either in presidentialist or parliamentarist countries, and not in countries with divided-executive constitutions.

This experience has generally been borne out in the two post-Soviet countries other than Ukraine to adopt a divided-executive constitution. Kyrgyzstan is a particularly interesting case because the deck seemed so stacked against success: the divided-executive constitution was adopted right after the fatally violent April 2010 revolution and the tragically lethal ethnically charged pogrom that followed in Osh in June 2010. Observers widely predicted a failed state. But while the state is still weak, Kyrgyzstan has held together and avoided further large-scale bloodshed despite ongoing political turmoil. Similarly, Georgia's shift to a divided-executive constitution since 2010 has come along with an opening of the country's political space. Bidzina Ivanishvili, who successfully led a coalition effort to replace Saakashvili's network in both the presidential and parliamentary elections in 2012–13, has used the divided-executive constitution to anchor a power-sharing arrangement with his various coalition partners, with different relatively weak figures installed in each major executive post. This division of authority did not hinder Georgia from adopting key reforms necessary for initialing a far-reaching EU Association Agreement at the 2013 Vilnius summit.

It is in this context that one must consider Ukraine's disappointing experience with its 2006–10 divided-executive constitution. To be sure, infighting between President Yushchenko and his prime ministers Tymoshenko and Yanukovych was destructive and even crippling for the country, especially during the

2008–9 financial crisis, when the leadership failed to react adequately. But the question is whether other constitutional forms would have facilitated anything better with any degree of confidence, and whether any improvement from these other forms was likely to be sustained over the longer run. The jury is still out on this question. There is some evidence that the competition may have actually increased corruption in some spheres like the judiciary, since there arose new demands for courts as a weapon in these struggles (Popova 2010b). It may also have contributed to the lack of anticorruption reform, which many had expected the Orange Revolution to bring (Barrowman 2015). And some suggest that such corrupt contestation can taint the whole idea of democracy because competing elites use their own media to expose the corruption of the other side (Sharafutdinova 2010). So perhaps voters are better off saving their democratic ideals for some indeterminate long-run future by living with an authoritarian reality until some other force happens to democratize the country.

On the other hand, if nothing else, Ukraine's divided-executive constitution helped allow voters to peacefully replace Yushchenko and Tymoshenko. This stands in great contrast to the way in which Kuchma and Yanukovych were replaced under a presidentialist system, with the latest presidential ouster resulting in the deaths of more than one hundred people and arguably helping trigger a war and loss of territory by giving an aggressive neighbor an opening. The comparative experience of the postcommunist world thus suggests that in the longer run Ukraine's prospects for democracy and good governance are no better and likely worse with presidentialist or parliamentarist constitutions. Ukraine faces great difficulties for many reasons, and the constitution alone will not solve them. The question is only which form of basic law gives the country its best among unfortunately low prospects.

Conclusions

Constitutions are only one of many influences on democracy and governance in patronal polities, and they can be overpowered by other forces. But since they clearly do constitute one such influence, it is worth trying to get the formal law as right as possible. This must be done by looking at the right sources of experience, which this chapter has argued is the set of postcommunist and highly patronalistic countries that we have now had the opportunity to observe for more than two decades. In highly patronalistic, postcommunist contexts, there are generally no good constitutional solutions. Every form—presidentialist, parliamentarist, and divided-executive—comes with its own set of problems that is in full view after each particular form is adopted. So the question is really which form performs less badly than the others, thereby giving a country its best possible chance to reform and improve its standing in terms of democracy and governance.

This chapter has contended that the evidence now indicates divided-executive constitutions constitute the lesser of basic law evils. Parliamentarist constitutions are a decent second choice. Presidentialism, despite its intuitive attractiveness as a possible source of unified and bold reformist leadership, has routinely disappointed. Moreover, because of its tendency for disruptive revolutionary politics to become "normal" as part of predictable regime cycles, presidentialism may even be worse for stability despite the illusion to the contrary that can appear when presidents are not lame ducks or are performing at least reasonably well. Indeed, one of the most important things that divided-executive constitutions do in the long run for highly patronalistic societies is provide the people with a better chance to be able to remove poor-performing leaders, and to do so without the kind of society-wrenching upheavals like the color revolutions or the bloodier episodes like Kyrgyzstan's 2010 revolution. Over time, the political competition underpinned by a divided-executive constitution supplies a potential engine for real change: at least some incentive to win popular support by actually reducing corruption and promoting economic development. This is more reliable than presidentialism and parliamentarism, whose success in generating prodemocracy and progovernance reform depends more on getting a nearly superhuman leader who happens to eschew short-term self-interest and have the greater good in mind. Alas, such leaders have been few and far between in the post-Soviet space, and even in the world. And while leaders are sometimes in a position to change constitutions to serve their own interests, they cannot always do so, meaning that constitutions can have effects independent of what leaders themselves want.

What might help reinforce the positive and minimize the negative effects of divided-executive constitutions? One helpful reform could be decentralization of power, whether or not one calls it "federalism," since that would complicate the process of consolidating central power around a single patron. Real EU prospects would also be likely to help, since this might create greater reluctance to fall into line with a single patron and raise elite expectations that authoritarian power-grabs are destined to fail, expectations that can become self-fulfilling. The constitutional advice offered here should thus not be considered a cure-all, but the comparative evidence accumulated in the postcommunist world over the last quarter century indicates that the right constitutional design can help promote the cause of democratization and perhaps (in the longer run) good governance.

Notes

1.   Kitschelt et al. 1999, p. 39. Low-patronalism countries by this measure include Croatia, Poland, the Czech Republic, Hungary, and Slovenia. Moderate patronalism countries include the three Baltic states, Serbia, and Slovakia.

2.   This is based on a coding of constitutions conducted by the author with research assistance by Justin Schoville, to whom the author is grateful.

8   Ukraine's Politicized Courts

Maria Popova

The December 3, 2004, Ukrainian Supreme Court decision, canceling the results of the fraudulent presidential runoff, provided a peaceful dénouement to the Orange Revolution. It also seemed like a watershed moment for the emergence of an independent judiciary. It was not.

A closer look at the post-1991 Ukrainian judiciary reveals an institution that has been regularly pressured into subservience by political incumbents despite an institutional setup that meets basic international standards. Both the upper and the lower echelons of the judiciary have consistently delivered decisions in line with the preferences of the powerful of the day. This assessment applies both to headline-grabbing cases, such as former prime minister Yulia Tymoshenko and former interior minister Yuriy Lutsenko's convictions, and to more routine cases in politically salient legal issue areas, such as electoral law, media law, the prosecution of corruption, and the treatment of protestors during the Euromaidan protests. Why has Ukraine failed to establish an independent judiciary that can constrain incumbent politicians and uphold the rule of law?

The Soviet tradition of weak and politically dependent courts has impeded the development of an independent judiciary in Ukraine and this chapter discusses some of the ways in which this institutional legacy affects current outcomes. The legacy obstacle is not insurmountable, however. Some post-Soviet states (the Baltics) overcame it quickly, and others (Georgia and Moldova) have made more recent strides toward better implementation of the rule of law. Ukraine, by contrast, appears to be stuck in a stable, inferior position (World Bank 2013). Even the massive attention to court performance during and after the Euromaidan did not produce any notable gains in judicial independence.

Neither is Ukraine's rule of law problem easily attributable to the poor institutional design of the judiciary during the post-Soviet period. Ukraine's judiciary conforms to the standard continental European civil law tradition's institutional formula. At the same time, there are institutional channels of executive interference in judicial governance or decision-making, and this chapter discusses them as well. But the availability of these institutional opportunities cannot fully account for the pitiful state of the rule of law in Ukraine. Many western European and North American executive incumbents enjoy similar points of access to their countries' judiciaries, yet appear not to use them to impose their preferences on judicial outcomes. Why have Ukrainian executives, in contrast, regularly taken those opportunities?

The main argument advanced in this chapter is that Ukraine's highly competitive, but not fully consolidated, democratic regime provides an environment in which executives face stronger incentives than their counterparts in mature democratic regimes to abrogate judicial independence and use the courts as an instrument for achieving political goals. Specifically, I argue that, in Ukraine, the benefits of dependent courts to political incumbents are particularly high, while the costs of subordinating the courts are quite low. Rational actors in the executive, therefore, engage regularly in pressuring the courts. Judicial corruption and a lingering legal culture of subordination also make judges receptive to political interference, rather than prone to opposing it. The longer the track record of executive interference, the lower the costs of engaging in it. This equilibrium is stable and will persist until some part of the cost-benefit analysis changes significantly.

The State of Judicial Independence in Post-Soviet Ukraine

There are two kinds of judicial independence—*de jure* and *de facto* (Russell and O'Brien 2001). De jure independence refers mainly to the formal institutional autonomy that courts enjoy vis-à-vis other actors. De jure independence—alternatively called institutional independence, structural independence, judicial autonomy, or judicial insulation—is easier to establish. Life tenure for judges, stable salaries, judicial control over judicial careers and the budget are institutional safeguards against interference from extrajudicial actors in judicial self-government and decision-making. The problem is that de jure independence is neither inherently desirable nor directly linked to the rule of law. De jure independence is important only insofar as it may allow judges to deliver impartial decisions, regardless of who the litigants are—that is, to the extent that it may help the courts establish the rule of law (Popova 2012a). What people usually think about when they decry the absence of independent courts in Ukraine, or anywhere else, is de facto judicial independence. De facto judicial independence—alternatively called decisional or behavioral judicial independence, or judicial impartiality—is a tougher nut to crack. It refers to the ability of the courts to consistently deliver rulings in line with the judges' bona fide interpretation of the facts and the laws, regardless of the identity and political (or other) resources of the litigants and free from extrajudicial interference and pressure. De facto judicial independence is at the crux of the rule of law, as it is necessary for the attainment of the doctrine's central ideals of equal responsibility and protection under the law.

There is considerable evidence that de facto judicial independence has been low in Ukraine throughout the post-Soviet period. The courts appear to be biased in favor of politically powerful litigants, and judges are regularly subjected to pressure from extrajudicial actors. There are signs of the politicization of court decisions both in high-profile cases and in routine but politically consequential cases. My earlier research on electoral registration disputes, adjudicated by the district courts during the 2002 Rada campaign, indicated that plaintiffs associated with the Kuchma regime had substantially better chances of winning in court than opposition-affiliated plaintiffs, even when controlling for the viability of candidate and the competitiveness of the district. Specifically, oppositionists had a 37 percent probability of winning in court, while progovernment candidates had a 64 percent chance (Popova 2010b). My analysis of defamation lawsuits against media outlets, decided by the Ukrainian judiciary between 1997 and 2004, painted a similar picture of bias toward plaintiffs with substantial political or financial resources. The average opposition-leaning plaintiff had a 45 percent probability of winning a defamation lawsuit, but the average, progovernment plaintiff had a much higher, 88 percent, probability of success (Popova 2012a). In addition, research by Trochev (2010; 2013, 67) has documented both some of the attacks by political incumbents on the occasional judge who has delivered constraining rulings and some judges' attempts to resist political pressure.

During the Yanukovych era, the main manifestations of low judicial independence were the flurry of corruption prosecutions against Orange-era cabinet ministers (among them Tymoshenko and Lutsenko), and the arbitrary prosecution of Euromaidan and Automaidan activists. The investigation that led to the criminal indictment and conviction of Tymoshenko started on April 28, 2010, when a member of the Rada sent an inquiry to the office of the prosecutor general.[1] The deputy prosecutor general immediately assigned the task of conducting an inspection into the behavior of the former PM during the gas crisis to the head of the prosecution department in charge of overseeing the compliance with laws concerning the rights and freedoms of citizens. A year later, on April 4, 2011, the prosecution finished its inquiry and opened a criminal case against the PM for abuse of office under Article 365, par. 3. On May 24, the prosecution finished its pretrial investigation and filed an indictment in Pechersk District Court and Tymoshenko was detained. In June, Judge Rodion Kireev was selected as the presiding judge.[2] The trial unfolded under increasing domestic and international scrutiny over the rest of the summer. On August 5, Judge Kireev ordered Tymoshenko taken into custody, purportedly to prevent her from impeding the proceedings.[3] On October 11, 2011, Judge Kireev announced his verdict—a seven-year prison sentence, a $190 million fine, and a three-year ban from political activity. After her conviction, Tymoshenko's legal team appealed at the Kyiv Appellate Court and later at the last-instance court for criminal cases—the newly established High Specialized Court for Civil and Criminal Cases. On August 29, 2012, the high court rejected her appeal and upheld the Pechersk District Court verdict.[4]

The first sign of politicization is that politicians, rather than technocrats or the prosecution, initiated the investigation into Tymoshenko's role in the 2009 gas affair. The Pechersk District Court verdict provides considerable suggestive evidence on this point. It pinpoints the start of the case to an inquiry sent by a Rada MP to the prosecutor general's office barely two months after the Yanukovych administration came to power. In addition, Mykola Azarov testified that "after taking the position of prime minister, he individually examined all the documents that dealt with financial and economic relations between NSC 'Naftogaz of Ukraine' and OJSC 'Gazprom' on gas supply and transit for 2009–2019." Three officials from the Ministry of Energy and Mines and the Main Control and Revision Agency of Ukraine also testified at the trial, and Judge Kireev mentions their testimony in the verdict, that in March and April 2011 they were instructed by the prime minister (rather than by the prosecutor's office) to conduct an inspection of the economic and financial activity of Naftogaz of Ukraine and calculate how much the increase in the price of gas between 2008 and 2009 cost the company.[5] This information was then used to prove that the consequences of Tymoshenko's decision were gravely negative. Finally, Tymoshenko's defense team pointed out that an expert report, crucial to the case, was ordered by the prosecution on April 19, 2011, and submitted to the court only a day later, on April 20. Ironically, Judge Kireev states in the verdict that the expert report was "put together as a result of a complex technical and criminological expertise."[6] Since it is hard to conceive of the criminologists putting together this complex technical document in less than a day, the swift response suggests that the report had been prepared much earlier and the prosecution played a reactive, rather than a proactive, role in the investigation.

A second indirect sign of the politicization of Tymoshenko's prosecution is the role of the Yanukovych administration in the assignment of a young judge without life tenure to the case. Judge Kireev (b. 1980) barely had two years of experience and was still in his probationary period (in line with Article 126 of the Constitution of Ukraine) when he was selected to hear the most salient criminal case in the nation. He was transferred to Pechersk District Court from Kyiv Oblast's Berezan City Court by presidential decree on April 20, 2011.[7] During the probationary period, the threshold for removing judges from office is low. In addition, they have to obtain both a recommendation from the High Qualification Commission and the approval of a Rada committee and eventually the president's signature in order to gain life tenure.[8] Thus, probationary-period judges are more vulnerable to pressure both from their judicial superiors and from extrajudicial actors. Barely a year and a half after delivering the Tymoshenko verdict, Judge Kireev was promoted to acting deputy chair of Pechersk District court—an unusually quick move up the judicial ladder.

In addition to Tymoshenko, more than a dozen other Orange era (2005–10) politicians found themselves under criminal prosecution for abuse of office or exceeding authority after Yanukovych's 2010 presidential victory. Eight individuals who previously held important positions in the executive branch stood trial in 2010–12. Only one of the nine criminal trials ended in a dismissal of the charges; six people served prison sentences (Tymoshenko, Lutsenko, Ivashchenko, Sin'kovskii, Volha, and Filipchuk) and three others received suspended sentences. Finally, criminal cases were opened against five others who disappeared or fled the country shortly after becoming the subject of a criminal investigation. Former minister of economy Bohdan Danylishyn received political asylum in the Czech Republic. The former head of the State Committee for Material Reserves, Mikhail Pozhivanov, received asylum in Austria. Italy refused to extradite former Kharkiv governor Arsen Avakov, who hid there for two years. He won a parliamentary seat (and immunity) in October 2012. Former head of the state treasury, Tat'yana Slyuz, also was in hiding and the subject of an international search warrant for two years (2010–12), until entering parliament (and gaining immunity) in the fall of 2012.

Notably, most of the Pechersk Court cases, like Tymoshenko's, were heard by young judges who had been recently appointed and were still within the probationary period at the time of delivering the verdict. Oksana Tzarevich, Anna Medushevska, and Viktor Kyschuk were all in their early thirties and had been appointed to the Pechersk Court between 2010 and 2012. Each has been assigned to *more than one* high-profile prosecution of oppositionists (Lutsenko, Ivashchenko, Tymoshenko, and Kornyichuk). Given that the Pechersk Court has thirty-five judges and that cases are purportedly assigned using a random selection system, it appears that these young judges were entrusted with more than their "fair" share of high-profile cases.[9]

The politicization of justice was also evident during the Euromaidan protests. In the first days of December, 2013, several dozen Euromaidan activists were arrested during clashes with police and faced criminal charges. While some may have indeed committed criminal acts, there are reasons to believe that the judicial process was closely controlled by the executive and that the courts were used as a political instrument, rather than as a criminal justice institution. Initially, all protestors who were arrested were remanded to custody for two months by several district courts around Kyiv. Despite the different circumstances of the arrests and, presumably, the varying skill levels of the defense lawyers, no suspects managed to convince the court to release them on bail or to house arrest. The courts also did not dismiss charges against anyone whom the prosecution wanted to charge. Then on December 10, after a meeting with former president Leonid Kravchuk, Yanukovych publicly commented that many of the protestors would be freed.[10] The promise signaled that the courts would not be taking these decisions themselves. And, indeed, a few days later, the appellate courts started reversing the lower court custody decisions and released activists on bail or to house arrest. The appeal success rate thus came up to an almost perfect 100 percent, when usually only about 5 percent of lower court custody decisions are reversed on appeal. This contrast underscores executive influence over the judicial decision-making process.

In January, the number of detained protestors swelled significantly and virtually all of them were again remanded to custody. In addition, scores of Automaidan activists who had organized trips to Yanukovych's residence in Mezhyhirya had their driver's licenses suspended for three to six months. Others were charged with "extremism" and "organizing mass disturbances" for transporting tires or other supplies to the Maidan. The only district court where four activists were ordered detained under house arrest rather than remanded to custody was the Obolonsky District Court in Kyiv. On January 23, the chairwoman of that court abruptly resigned.[11] A few days later, a judge from Vinnitsya oblast also stepped down and gave a press conference, at which he complained of relentless executive pressure on judges and claimed that any judge who stepped out of line could be fired within four hours.[12]

Why Does Ukraine Lack an Independent Judiciary?

Soviet Legacy?

The Soviet legacy of politically dependent judiciaries is an obvious obstacle to the development of independent courts in post-Soviet Ukraine. Specifically, telephone justice, ex parte communication between judges and other actors interested in individual cases, the dominance of the prosecution over the bench, and the dominance of court chairs over individual judges are, perhaps, the four most problematic aspects of the Soviet legal heritage. Telephone justice refers to the Soviet-era practice of party functionaries directly communicating the "correct" ruling to judges. Studies by Ledeneva (2008) and Hendley (1999; 2006, 347) have discussed the survival of the practice in post-Soviet Russia, and Trochev (2010) and my research have confirmed that continuity exists in Ukraine as well. Ex parte communication is a similar but less sinister practice. It describes the discussion of a concrete case between the judge hearing the case and one or both of the litigants, their lawyers, or any party interested in the outcome of the case outside of the courtroom and the legal process. At its worst ex parte communication may be a conduit for telephone justice. At its most innocuous, the practice resembles informal plea bargaining. The fact that it takes place outside of the courtroom, and thus without the constraint and transparency of public legal procedures, makes it problematic, as it still provides opportunities for extrajudicial actors to unduly influence the decision-making process of the judge. While recent legislative changes have sought to limit the incidence of ex parte communication, it is unlikely that a well-established informal practice can be made obsolete overnight.

During the Soviet era, the prosecution was clearly the more powerful branch of the judiciary, and judges rarely disagreed with the prosecution's take on a case, hence the nearly perfect conviction rate. In addition to having their behavioral independence circumscribed by the prosecutors, Soviet-era judges were also highly dependent on their immediate superior—the court chair. The court chair played an important role in distributing workload, dividing bonuses, and assessing the work of each individual judge. Thus individual judges regularly took "guidance" from the court chair on how to best resolve complicated cases (Berman 1963; Ginsburgs 1993, 233; Mikhailovskaya 1999; Solomon and Foglesong 2000).

As we know from numerous historical institutionalist accounts, institutional legacies are difficult to overcome, but in the context of a civil law judiciary (as opposed to common law), legacies appear to be even stickier because judges in the civil law judiciary are recruited right out of law school and are socialized into their professional roles by judicial superiors. Given the absence of lustration policies vis-à-vis the post-Soviet judiciaries, we should not be surprised that young, post-Soviet judges would be socialized into accepting parts of the Soviet legal legacy from their superiors. Indeed, there is considerable evidence that court chairs continue to hold power over individual judges (Solomon and Foglesong 2000; Solomon Jr. 2005, 325, 2010; Tiede and Rennalls 2012).

The Soviet legacy alone, however, cannot explain Ukraine's problems with low judicial independence. There is significant variation in the level of judicial independence across the post-Soviet region. The Baltic states apparently overcame the inauspicious legacy quite early after independence. Georgia appears to have made a breakthrough after the Rose Revolution, and recent rule of law indices consistently identify the Georgian judiciary as the undisputed leader in the post-Soviet region. The Georgian judiciary enjoys levels of public trust, efficiency, and independence comparable to those in the postcommunist EU members.

Low De Jure Independence?

Could it be that the poor institutional design of the post-Soviet judiciary is compounding the inauspicious Soviet legacy? By poor institutional design, I mean a set of institutions that hinder independent judicial behavior and leave judges vulnerable to outside pressure. The setup of the Ukrainian judiciary provides the basic guarantees for de jure judicial independence. The Ukrainian judiciary has had the main elements of judicial self-government—life tenure, control over judicial careers, and some control over the judicial budget—since the creation of the State Judicial Administration in 2002. If de jure judicial independence were enough to guarantee de facto independent courts, Ukraine would not be facing such a serious rule of law deficit.

Ukrainian judges enter the judicial corps soon after they finish law school and after passing qualifying examinations. Judicial candidates are vetted by the

Qualification Commissions (QCs) and then by the High Council of Justice (HCJ), which submits the roster of candidates proposed for appointment to the president, who ultimately signs appointments and has to be present when new judges take their oaths. The recruitment and appointment process is thus similar to that in many civil law countries that use the judicial council model. New judges serve a five-year probationary term, at the end of which the HCJ can recommend to the legislature that they be appointed for life tenure. Newly appointed judges in many civil law countries (such as Italy, Germany, and France) serve probationary terms. The existence of the five-year probationary term is not a priori problematic, as it aims to allow flexibility in removing judicial recruits who turn out not to be suitable judges. As the prosecutions against Tymoshenko, Lutsenko, and other oppositionists suggest, however, problems with de facto judicial independence arise when probationary-term judges, who should be treated more as trainee-judges who are still learning the ropes of the profession, are assigned to hear high-profile, politically consequential cases. The abuse of the probationary term undermines judicial independence, rather than the idea of forcing judges to serve for five years before they receive life tenure. Likewise, the participation of the president in the appointment process, which is widely practiced in the civil law world, has become problematic in the Ukrainian context. Whereas in consolidated western European democracies (and many of the new postcommunist democracies) the president's participation is entirely ceremonial, in Ukraine it has been used to signal to newly appointed judges that they owe their positions to the president's benevolence. In 2014–15, Poroshenko reportedly delayed the judicial oath ceremony several times, mainly to signal to new judges that they depend on his good will.

To underscore the existence of institutional provisions for independent courts, contrast Ukrainian judicial career organization to that in many mature democracies in western Europe and North America. The United States uses a politicized appointment procedure whereby both branches of government and/or the public have more input in appointing judges than the judiciary. At the state level, the U.S. also has judges fight to remain in office in competitive or uncompetitive elections (Ramseyer 1994; Tolley 2006). In Canada, the prime minister has unchecked power to appoint Supreme Court justices. In many Canadian provinces, the provincial attorney general (that is, a member of the executive) appoints all judges without any input by either the judiciary or by the legislature (Morton 2006, 56–57). In Germany, as in Canada, judges sitting in the ordinary courts in half of the federal regions (*Lander*) are appointed by the regional justice minister, without any input from outside of the executive branch. In the other half, where there is a selection committee that nominates judges (an institution roughly equivalent to the Ukrainian Qualification Commissions), the committee is not dominated by members of the judiciary, as in Ukraine, but displays a power balance between representatives of the legislature, the executive, the bar, and the bench. At the federal level, appointments to Germany's five Supreme Courts take place without any input from the judiciary—the committee advising the executive on appointments and promotions includes only representatives of the executive and the legislative branches (Guarnieri, Pederzoli, and Thomas 2002, 51–52).

Apparently, though, having "mostly good" judicial institutions is woefully insufficient to provide de facto independent courts. De facto judicial independence is compromised through the informal politicization of the judicial self-government bodies (the High Council of Judges, the Qualification Commissions, and the Council of Judges [CJ]). The detrimental effects of this politicization are compounded by frequent targeted institutional reforms, which reconfigure parts of the institutional setup of the judiciary, seemingly, with the primary goal of empowering incumbent-friendly judicial institutions and emasculating opposition-friendly judicial institutions. In other words, formal institutions that generally provide for de jure independence can be easily undermined through informal mechanisms or compromised by existing loopholes. A few recent examples of these long-standing problems follow.

Soon after assuming office in the spring of 2010, the Yanukovych administration and the Party of Regions launched an institutional attack on the Supreme Court that was completed by the fall of 2010. The parliamentary majority adopted major revisions to the Law of Ukraine on the Judiciary and the Status of Judges, which provided for the creation of a new High Specialized Court for Civil and Criminal Cases and drastically reduced the jurisdiction of the Supreme Court. The Supreme Court would no longer be the cassation court (that is, highest court of appeal) for criminal and civil cases, which make up the vast majority of cases heard by the courts. In addition, the Supreme Court would no longer be the institution responsible for supervising the activity of the lower courts and issuing guidelines on how laws should be interpreted and applied. The jurisdictional change meant that the Supreme Court's caseload would decline dramatically, so the law also provided for the institutional shrinkage of the Supreme Court from ninety-four judges to twenty. Since the Ukrainian Constitution provides Supreme Court judges with life tenure guarantees, which means that judges cannot be removed from office, the amendments provided options for voluntary early retirement or for voluntary transfers to other courts, and many judges accepted the offers. The High Specialized Court for Civil and Criminal Cases was established by presidential decree on October 1, 2010.[13] In its advisory opinion on the draft law, the Council of Europe's Venice Commission bluntly stated that it sees the institutional change as an overt attack on the Supreme Court: "It is hard to avoid the conclusion that there is a deliberate intention to reduce the power of the Supreme Court which goes far beyond the desire to create a more efficient judicial system."[14]

The weakening of the Supreme Court had enormous significance for the Tymoshenko prosecution. The redrawing of jurisdictional boundaries meant that the first-instance court's decision on the Tymoshenko case could not be appealed all the way to the Supreme Court but would end up at the newly established High Specialized Court for Civil and Criminal Cases. Now consider the composition and leadership of the two courts. From 2005 to September 2011, the chief justice of the Supreme Court was Vasyl Onopenko, a former MP from the Yulia Tymoshenko Bloc and a close political ally of the former prime minister. Onopenko's son-in-law, Evhen Korniychuk, served as deputy minister of justice in Tymoshenko's cabinet. Onopenko also purportedly enjoyed wide support among his fellow Supreme Court judges. By contrast, the High Specialized Court for Civil and Criminal Cases had been headed since its inception by Leonid Fesenko, a former judge on the Luhansk Court of Appeals and a former MP from the Party of Regions. The rest of the judges on the new court were appointed by the Party of Regions parliamentary majority.[15] Which of the two courts would be more likely to uphold the first-instance court verdict against Tymoshenko? The obvious answer suggests that the attack on the Supreme Court and the establishment of a brand new court might have been part of Yanukovych's strategy of using the courts to sideline his main political opponent.

In addition to gutting the jurisdiction of the Supreme Court, the 2010 Law on the Judiciary and the Status of Judges contained provisions that centralized appointment and disciplinary powers. The High Judicial Qualification Commission (HJQC) in Kyiv, rather than the regional Qualification Commissions, became the administrator of exams that applicants for judicial positions have to take. In addition, all complaints against judges went to the HJQC, which could decide whether to open a disciplinary proceeding. The centralization of appointments and the initiation of disciplinary proceedings made it easier to maximize hierarchical control within the ordinary judiciary.

Finally, the 2010 law transferred important powers from the Council of Judges, controlled by judges close to Supreme Court chairman Onopenko, to the High Council of Justice, controlled by Yanukovych ally Sergei Kivalov and dominated by Party of Regions appointees. The HCJ obtained the power to appoint court chairs, previously within the purview of the Council of Judges. This was a highly consequential change because court chairs hold considerable sway over the individual judges serving on their courts—they determine salary bonuses, affect case allocation, and, informally, are known to advise judges on how to interpret certain legal provisions or judicial practice (Solomon and Foglesong 2000; Popova 2012a).

The post-Maidan period has seen a continuation of the practice of redrawing institutional boundaries in order to sideline or promote political loyalists in the judiciary. During most of 2014, both the High Council of Justice and the High Qualification Commission for Judges became veritable battlegrounds between the old leadership cadre within the judiciary and Yanukovych loyalists on one side, and newcomers backed by Poroshenko and his chosen point person for the judiciary, Aleksei Filatov. By mid-2015, the Presidential Administration (PA) had largely succeeded in establishing control over the crucial judicial self-government institutions.

Strategic Actor Account

De facto judicial independence in Ukraine is undermined not only by the institutional fault lines just discussed, but also by the strategic behavior of self-interested politicians. In Ukraine's hybrid, unconsolidated, competitive regime, the benefits that incumbent politicians can reap from dependent courts are much higher than any potential costs of obtaining judicial subservience. Moreover, the long-term benefits from an independent judiciary, which seem to motivate politicians in mature democracies to refrain from pressuring the courts, are less relevant to Ukraine's politicians. The latter face higher levels of uncertainty than their counterparts in consolidated democracies and therefore care much more about the short-term benefits of dependent courts than about the long-term benefits of independent courts.

There are several benefits of a dependent judiciary for incumbent state officials. First, incumbents can use a dependent judiciary to remove or undermine political competitors. The most obvious examples include the imprisonment of Tymoshenko and Lutsenko, but there are also more subtle ways in which dependent courts have been useful to incumbents. They have acted as gate-keepers at each stage of the electoral representation process—registration as a candidate, taking up office after an electoral victory, and continuing to hold office until the next election. Courts have been routinely used to deny registration to viable opposition candidates in parliamentary and municipal elections (Popova 2010b; 2012a).

Second, pliable courts can be a useful instrument in exercising control over the media. Courts have been employed to keep in line and harass opposition media outlets. In the 1990s and 2000s, the Socialist Party newspaper *Silsky Visti* was effectively brought to bankruptcy by a series of law suits against it for defamation and for inciting religious hatred. In 2012, plans to recriminalize libel appeared to be another attempt to use the judiciary as a tool for regime domination and interference in the media.

Third, courts have been utilized to control economic actors and harass those who oppose the incumbents. During election campaigns, incumbents have regularly threatened entrepreneurs with legal consequences if they do not actively support the campaign effort. Oligarchs who have challenged incumbents have also been targeted with lawsuits.

Fourth, during the Euromaidan protests and previous instances of social mobilization (such as the "Tax Maidan" in 2010 and "Language Maidan" in 2012), the courts were used to harass protestors and activists. The Yanukovych government adopted a strategy of targeted repression. The arrest and prosecution of sometimes random bystanders and charging them with organizing mass disturbances seem to have had the goal of driving home the message that *anyone* can be sued. A reliably dependent judiciary is extremely useful in carrying out this strategy efficiently.

Ironically, de jure independence allows Ukrainian incumbents to use de facto judicial dependence to achieve political goals while hiding behind a facade of court independence. For example, Yanukovych often said he could not release Tymoshenko because the decision was within the purview of the independent judiciary. Putting protestors in jail on extremism charges temporarily allowed the regime to suppress dissent without firing on crowds. Bankrupting opposition media through lawsuits has allowed different presidential administrations to suppress media freedom without having to resort to media closures or official censorship. Keeping property rights insecure, because assets can be expropriated at any time through the courts, allows incumbents to extract, rather than solicit, political support from major asset owners.

The utility of a dependent judiciary as a tool for manipulating electoral competition is heightened by the underinstitutionalization of party systems and the resulting high electoral volatility, which is endemic in hybrid regimes such as Ukraine's. When parties lack well-developed grass-roots organizations, stable financing, and a party label that transcends the name recognition of the leader, a few court decisions can inflict dramatic damage. For example, one court through one single trial at a crucial moment can destroy even major oligarchic structures and thus severely undercut a party's campaign. By contrast, it would be much harder (more costly and more time-consuming) for the courts to systematically persecute the hundreds of individuals and companies who finance established parties in consolidated democracies. Similarly, closing down a party newspaper will have much greater impact on that party's popular approval rating if the newspaper is the only channel for communicating with its supporters. The same court decision will have a smaller effect on established parties that have a dense network of grass-roots organizations through which to energize their base.

At the same time, the costs of pressuring the courts are low. First, the Soviet legacy of judicial subservience means that all actors expect and assume the courts to be vulnerable to political pressure. Therefore, politicians who attempt to interfere in judicial decision-making do not suffer significant reputational costs. In addition, informal mechanisms for exercising pressure on judges are available and facilitate interference by motivated politicians. At the same time, a weak civil society and infrequent investigative journalism mean that societal actors do not monitor the courts consistently and thoroughly, nor do they lobby effectively in support of reform. Finally, judges do not effectively resist pressure, because they face a collective action problem in doing so. Some of them even actively participate in delivering politically biased decisions in exchange for bribes or political protection that allows them to engage in corrupt practices in other cases.

The comparative judicial politics literature identifies a number of long-term benefits for incumbent state officeholders that make independent courts sustainable in some political environments (Landes and Posner 1975; Ramseyer 1994; Stephenson 2003; Ginsburg 2003; Epperly 2013). The most obvious benefit of an independent judiciary is that it gives incumbents some guarantee that they will not be prosecuted unfairly after they leave office, that their policies will not be gutted and reversed without consideration for legal procedure by their successors, and that they will retain some control over future policy processes by having an independent judiciary as a recourse.

In Ukraine's uncertain political environment, however, short-term gains seem to trump long-term benefits. Yanukovych's use of the courts to jail political opponents created a dangerous precedent that further solidified the perception that the judiciary is useful to incumbents only while they are in power to control it. His decision to flee in the middle of the night on February 22, 2014, underscores the inability of anyone to credibly guarantee to him that he would not end up in prison if he left office and remained in Ukraine. In addition, the extralegal change of government in February 2014 has likely only exacerbated the sense among incumbents that they can use institutional levers of influence such as the judiciary only while they are in office. Thus the prospects for the creation of independent courts have become even dimmer over the past two years.

Is the Current State of Affairs a Stable Equilibrium?

We should expect the Ukrainian judiciary to continue to be de facto dependent on politicians for the foreseeable future unless the cost-benefit calculus changes significantly. Such a change could occur if the institutional environment in Ukraine becomes more stable, since that would lengthen the time horizons of incumbent politicians. Stabilization would require fewer constitutional amendments, changes to the electoral system, and reconfigurations of judicial institutions. If they are confident that the institutional environment is likely to last longer than their mandate in office, politicians may start considering the long-term effects of some institutions on their fundamental interests. Thus incumbents may start considering the long-term benefits of an independent judiciary as an impartial arbiter who might be able to protect them once they are out of office.

During the post-Maidan period, however, the institutional environment has become considerably less, rather than more, stable. Both the Presidential Administration and the parliamentary majority have proposed and passed various judicial institutional reforms. The parliamentary judicial reform bill, drafted with extensive input from civil society and championed by the Samopomich Party's deputy speaker of parliament Oksana Syroyid, envisioned a considerable increase in the de jure independence of the judiciary. But after some behind-the-scenes wrangling with the Presidential Administration, the law eventually passed by parliament was significantly watered down and safeguarded the president's institutional levers of influence over the judiciary. Prominent judges have flocked to the Presidential Administration's side by taking part in a consultative council set up by the PA, which suggests that there is no strong constituency within the judiciary pushing for the courts' political emancipation.

Alternatively, an increase in party system institutionalization would also be beneficial for the emergence of an independent judiciary because it would significantly reduce one of the main benefits of a subservient court—the ability to remove individual competitors from the political scene through selective prosecution. The collapse of the Party of Regions, however, does not bode well for party-system institutionalization. No alternative political actors have emerged in the southern and eastern regions, which jeopardizes these regions' continued representation in national politics. The transformation of the governing majority into new parties and coalitions has also increased electoral volatility and further put off party system institutionalization.

Finally, an independent judiciary would become possible if a spirit of democratic competition starts replacing the "pluralism by default" of a competitive authoritarian regime (Levitsky and Way 2010; Way 2015). By contrasting "democratic competition" and "pluralism by default," I highlight the difference between competition that is based on a shared recognition that competition provides political legitimacy and better policy outcomes and competition that results from the simple inability of political adversaries to destroy each other. A shift from the latter to the former would be auspicious for the emergence of an independent judiciary. Recent attempts to marginalize and ban the Communist Party and the Opposition Bloc, however, signal that a shift away from pluralism by default is not forthcoming.

The post-Maidan government received a huge popular mandate to reform the courts and take some small steps that could help Ukraine angle out of the judicial dependence equilibrium. First, the government could work to reduce the power imbalance between the courts and the procuracy. Currently, the procuracy still holds on to its Soviet-era power of general oversight of legality, which allows it to exercise considerable control over the legal process. Removing this power could be a step toward emancipating the judiciary. Second, the new government could adopt reforms that empower younger judges to organize as a professional group outside the framework of existing judicial self-government institutions. Such an organization could help them resist pressure from extrajudicial actors more effectively, raising the costs of pressuring the judiciary. Third, the government could reform judicial salary policy to eliminate the mechanisms for performance-based pay (bonuses and merit exercises) in order to reduce the level of internal dependence of individual judges on their superiors in the judicial hierarchy (court chairs and Qualification Commissions).

There is mixed evidence on whether the new incumbents are committed even to these small incremental changes. On the one hand, the appointment of several Georgian reformers to high positions within the procuracy signals some political will to revamp the relationship between the procuracy and the courts. On the other, rather than doing away with bonuses and merit exercises, the new PA-drafted judicial reform law, adopted on February 12, 2015, introduced additional layers of performance-based pay within the judiciary that are likely to strengthen, rather than weaken, internal dependence.

Does Democracy Complicate Things?

Does political competition boost the chances of establishing an independent judiciary or does it complicate the picture? Some of the literature on the origins of independent courts (Ginsburg 2003) argues that insecure incumbents will rush to create independent judiciaries as a political insurance policy against future persecution or against the abolition of all their policies. The dynamics of incumbent-judiciary interaction in Ukraine during its most recent period of intense political competition does not offer support for this theoretical prediction. At no point during the Euromaidan did the Yanukovych regime seem to be exploring ways of strengthening the independence of the judiciary in order to extract guarantees that any offer of immunity could be credibly enforced by an independent court later. On the contrary, the January 16 legislative initiative that the pro-Yanukovych majority in parliament billed as an attempt to increase judicial independence by guaranteeing judges' personal safety was in fact an attempt to suppress the protests.

Another theoretical strand, known as the strategic defection theory (Helmke 2005), predicts that in hybrid regimes such as Ukraine's, as a turnover in power draws near, the judiciary will gradually abandon the political incumbents and start ruling against them in order to curry favor with potential future incumbents. The last months of the Yanukovych regime do not provide evidence to support a strategic defection prediction either. Rather than abandon the Yanukovych regime or at least attempt to distance itself from the incumbents, the Ukrainian judiciary continued propping up the regime with its decisions until the very end.

This brings me to the last point—namely, that democracy may foster judicial independence, but political competition within the framework of a hybrid regime like Ukraine's exacerbates political pressure on the courts significantly. The more uncertain incumbents in hybrid regimes become about their grip on power, the more motivated they become to use the judiciary as a tool for accomplishing political goals (Popova 2012a). The use of the courts during the stand-off between civil society and the Yanukovych regime underscores this point. The courts refused to issue protest permits; prosecuted the beaten protestors for hooliganism rather than the perpetrators of the beatings from the Berkut for excessive force; issued orders to protestors to vacate occupied government buildings; and prosecuted Automaidan activists. Thus it seems that the intensification of the competitive environment in Ukraine led to more politicized judicial output.

Notes

1. Ukraine v. Tymoshenko. The text of the verdict is available at //www.reyestr.court.gov.ua/Review/18536012.

2. European Parliament Resolution. See http://www.europarl.europa.eu/document/activities/cont/201106/20110620ATT21953/20110620ATT21953EN.pdf.

3. "Protesters Gather as Tymoshenko Trial Resumes in Kiev," BBC, August 9, 2011. See http://www.bbc.co.uk/news/world-europe-14419216.

4. RFE/RL's Ukrainian Service, "Ukrainian High Court Rejects Tymoshenko Appeal," August 29, 2012. See http://www.rferl.org/content/ukrainian-court-to-rule-on-tymoshenko-appeal/24691133.html.

5. Ukraine v. Tymoshenko.

6. Ukraine v. Tymoshenko.

7. The text of the presidential decree is available at http://zakon1.rada.gov.ua/laws/show/489/2011.

8. An English translation of the Law on the Judiciary and the Status of Judges is available at http://www.venice.coe.int/docs/2010/CDL%282010%29084-e.pdf.

9. Halya Coynash, "Political Trials on the Career Trajectory," Kharkiv Human Rights Protection Group, March 4, 2013. See http://khpg.org/index.php?id=1362262090.

10. "Yanukovich poobeshchal osvobodit' vsekh arestovannykh aktivistov—Kravchuk," Censor.net, December 10, 2013. See http://censor.net.ua/news/262876/yanukovich_poobeschal_osvobodit_vseh_arestovannyh_aktivistov_kravchuk.

11. "Predsedatel' Obolonskogo raisuda Kieva uvolilas' posle prigovora studentam universiteta Karpenko-Karogo," January 24, 2014. See http://112.ua/politika/predse-

datel-obolonskogo-raysuda-kieva-uvolilas-posle-prigovora-studentam-universite-ta-karpenko-karogo-13738.html.

12. "V Vinnitskoi oblasti sud'ia napisal zaiavlenie o slozhenii polnomochii," Liga. net, January 16, 2014. See http://m.liga.net/news/politics/169684-v_vinnitskoy_oblas-ti_sudya_napisal_zayavlenie_o_slojenii_polnomochiy.htm.

13. The court's official website describes its history. See http://sc.gov.ua/ua/istori-ja_vssu.html.

14. European Commission for Democracy through Law (Venice Commission), Joint Opinion on the Law on the Judicial System and the Status of Judges of Ukraine, Venice, October 15–16, 2010, p. 9. See http://www.venice.coe.int/webforms/documents/ default.aspx?pdffile=CDL-AD(2010)026-e.

15. "Verkhovnyi sud vozglavit luganskii sud'ia-'regional,'" August 28, 2012. See http://politics.comments.ua/2012/08/28/356900/verhovniy-sud-vozglavit.html.

9   Judicial Reform in Comparative Perspective: Assessing the Prospects for Ukraine

Daniel J. Beers

Introduction

This chapter presents a comparative analysis of postcommunist judicial reform, identifying trends and policy lessons from more than two decades of developments in eastern Europe and the former Soviet Union. The analysis takes a wide-ranging cross-national perspective. Its primary objective is not to scrutinize the reform process in Ukraine but to contextualize it within the broader experience of Ukraine's postcommunist neighbors—with the ultimate goal of identifying possible avenues for the future.

One of the clearest lessons to emerge from this study is that judicial reform is a process fraught with challenges, particularly in the complex transitioning societies of eastern Europe. Even in the best cases, courts are subject to politicization and manipulation by elites, claims of judicial corruption and inefficiency are endemic, and skeptical citizens hold judicial institutions in remarkably low esteem. As one study observes; "It is probably fair to say that less overall progress has been made in judicial reform and strengthening than in almost any other area of policy or institutional reform in transition countries since 1990" (Anderson, Bernstein, and Gray 2005).

Many explanations have been posited for the halting development of the rule of law in postcommunist states. In this chapter, I focus on a few key obstacles that have shaped the reform process in judiciaries across the region. These include under-resourced courts, entrenched corruption and public mistrust, an overemphasis on formal institutional solutions, and elite politicization of the judiciary. Considering each of these obstacles, I argue that Ukraine presents an especially challenging environment for democratic judicial reform.

Nevertheless, comparative analysis can offer some positive lessons about potential pathways to reform in Ukraine. Specifically, I examine the role of the European Union (EU) as a catalyst for change, as well as the impact of international law on domestic court systems in the region. I also explore how forces within the judiciary, including lower court judges and independent professional associations, can aid the reform process even in highly corrupt and politicized environments.

Ultimately, I argue that these pathways constitute viable options for reformers in Ukraine. However, their impact is likely to be limited in the absence of genuine and sustained elite commitment to the cause of democratic judicial reform. With the recent political opening following the 2013–14 Euromaidan protests, Ukraine may well be entering a new phase of democratic transition. In order to capitalize on this unparalleled opportunity, Ukraine's new leaders will need to demonstrate a renewed commitment to partnership with the EU, as well as genuine respect for the rule of law and the independence of the judiciary.

Obstacles to Reform

In the following pages, I outline some of the primary roadblocks to postcommunist judicial reform, including resource scarcity, entrenched corruption, weak institutionalization, and politicization of the judiciary. Viewed from a comparative perspective, Ukraine faces challenges common to many states in the region. However, the scale and severity of the obstacles to reform are especially acute in Ukraine.

Resource Scarcity

For legal professionals in many postcommunist states, practical problems such as long case backlogs, low salaries, and insufficient support staff frequently top the list of grievances about the state of justice. Although notable improvements have been made to update court infrastructures and streamline administrative processes throughout the region, poor working conditions and impossibly long court dockets remain a significant challenge in many under-resourced judicial systems.

According to judges and reform advocates, low salaries compromise the independence of the judiciary by making judges more susceptible to bribery and corruption (ABA/CEELI 2007; Rodriguez and Ehrichs 2007). Scarce or unevenly distributed material resources can foster clientelism within the judiciary—or, in extreme cases, between court officials and external court sponsors (Solomon Jr. 2008). Even among principled and independent legal professionals, dissatisfaction with working conditions may lead to more lenient attitudes about the misconduct of colleagues, contributing to a culture of impunity (Beers 2011).

Further, it is important to recognize that courts are embedded in a complex network of institutions governing the legal process, which includes police, prosecutors, bailiffs, and a host of other bureaucratic organs. If these partner agencies are unable or unwilling to enforce and monitor the implementation of court decisions, the authority and legitimacy of the judicial process may be seriously compromised (Trochev 2012a). Judicial reforms must therefore be accompanied by efforts to strengthen—both institutionally and materially—those complementary bureaucratic institutions necessary for the rule of law.

While problems related to resource scarcity have hampered reform efforts throughout the region, conditions in Ukraine are particularly stark. To help contextualize the challenges facing Ukrainian courts, Tables 9.1 and 9.2 present comparative data on judicial salaries and annual court expenditures. Admittedly, such aggregate-level statistics offer only a crude approximation of conditions on the ground, but the data throw into sharp relief the deficit of resources in the Ukrainian system. Out of twenty-two postcommunist states for which data is available, Ukraine ranks third to last in judicial salaries, following only Moldova and Armenia. With a starting salary for first instance judges of 6,210 euros per annum, Ukrainian judges are paid approximately one-third of the

TABLE 9.1: Gross Annual Salary of First Instance Judge

Country	Annual Salary (€)	Country	Annual Salary (€)
Moldova	3,220	Hungary	18,252
Armenia	5,637	Poland	20,736
Ukraine	6,120	Bosnia and Herzegovina	22,936
Albania	7,350	Montenegro	24,142
Bulgaria	10,230	Czech Republic	24,324
Azerbaijan	11,364	Romania	25,750
Georgia	11,642	Slovakia	28,148
Serbia	13,595	Slovenia	28,968
Latvia	13,798	Croatia	30,396
Russian Federation	15,988	Estonia	31,992
Republic of Macedonia	17,219		
Lithuania	18,072	Regional Average	17,721

SOURCE: European Commission for the Efficiency of Justice (CEPEJ) 2012, 262. Figures based on 2010 data.

TABLE 9.2: Annual Per Capita Judicial Budget Expenditures

Country	Per Capita Expenditures (€)	Country	Per Capita Expenditures (€)
Moldova	2.4	Bosnia and Herzegovina	18.0
Albania	3.3	Estonia	20.0
Armenia	3.5	Russian Federation	20.4
Georgia	3.6	Slovakia	25.5
Azerbaijan	4.5	Hungary	26.0
Ukraine	5.8	Montenegro	32.2
Republic of Macedonia	13.9	Czech Republic	32.9
Serbia	15.2	Poland	35.7
Bulgaria	15.2	Croatia	47.9
Lithuania	15.6	Slovenia	86.9
Latvia	16.6		
Romania	16.6	Regional Average	21.0

SOURCE: European Commission for the Efficiency of Justice (CEPEJ) 2012, 28. Figures based on 2010 data.

average judicial salary for the region. Similarly, Ukraine ranks near the bottom of the region in overall court spending. In real terms, Ukraine annually spends 5.8 euros per capita on courts—roughly one-quarter of the regional average.

Corruption and Public Mistrust

Corruption poses another critical challenge to judicial reformers in post-communist states. Given the prevalence of official corruption during the communist period, allegations of bribery, patronage, and abuse of judicial authority are commonplace. With few exceptions, courts are among the least trusted, least respected institutions among postcommunist citizens across the region.

From the standpoint of democratic reform, the consequences of judicial corruption can be serious and multifaceted. At the most fundamental level, judicial corruption undermines the impartiality of the legal process, making it less efficient and less predictable as a mechanism of dispute resolution. It also erodes public trust in the rule of law. To the extent that citizens question the integrity of judges and the judicial process, perceptions of corruption delegitimize judicial authority and may deter citizens and firms from using the courts to arbitrate disputes. As scholars have noted, the lack of "demand" for law in the postcommunist period owes largely to public perceptions that the judiciary has remained corrupt and politically controlled long after the official end of communist rule (Hendley 1999). Whether deserved or not, this reputation can also be leveraged by unscrupulous elites who use allegations of corruption and clientelism to undermine the legitimacy of court rulings and weaken the oversight authority of the judiciary vis-à-vis other branches of government (Kühn 2012).

The consequences of judicial corruption also reach beyond the legal sector. When corruption permeates the very system charged with adjudicating and punishing illicit behavior, it creates a "re-enforcing inter-relationship" whereby judicial corruption perpetuates corruption in other sectors of society (Herzfeld and Weiss 2003). Put differently, where judicial corruption prevails, "graft effectively becomes the new 'rule of law'" (Rodriguez and Ehrichs 2007, xvi).

While corruption has thwarted judicial reformers throughout the region, research suggests that not all postcommunist societies face the same challenges. Corruption in the legal sector appears most problematic in states in which clientelistic networks from the communist period remain strongest. Qualitative accounts of judicial corruption in Romania (Beers 2011; Parau 2012; Hein 2015; Alistar 2007), Bulgaria (Popova 2012b), Russia (Burger 2004), and Ukraine (Trochev 2010) suggest that judicial corruption often follows a familiar pattern. Endemic corruption persists where elites from the ancien régime have gained a foothold in the new institutional system—that is, where the transition was orchestrated by former communist elites, where old power structures and political networks remain firmly entrenched, or where old regime elites have gained positions of power in the "reformed" institutions of the postcommunist judiciary.

The experience of postcommunist Ukraine has largely followed this pattern, whereby old elite networks and communist-era norms and behaviors have taken root within the new institutional structures of the judiciary. Claims of corruption in the legal sector have been persistent and widespread—from students bribing officials to enter law school, to judges altering the outcomes of politically salient cases. Clientelistic networks are strong, and antireform elites have maintained a firm grasp on the levers of judicial power. As a consequence, survey data have consistently shown that few Ukrainians approve of the judiciary's performance in the postcommunist period (as little as 3 percent in a 2009 poll by the Razumkov Center). Moreover, the data suggest that public trust in the judiciary has been declining in recent years (Trochev 2010). This pattern of official corruption and public mistrust poses a clear threat to the integrity of the judicial process and the success of future reform efforts.

The Limits of Institutional Design

From early in the transition period, much of the focus among judicial reform advocates has been on formal institutional design. Proponents of this approach have argued that by crafting institutional rules that encourage judicial independence and protect against improper influence, policy-makers can lay the groundwork for the democratic rule of law. Jensen and Heller (2003) dub this the "field-of-dreams" approach to democratic legal reform: if you build the legal institutions, the rule of law will come.

The appeal of formal institutional solutions is immediate and obvious. Institutional rules are clear and concrete. They are relatively easy to manipulate. Moreover, institutional rules constitute the formal legal foundation upon which the rule of law is built. They determine who holds authority in the legal system, what kinds of powers they enjoy, how they are selected, trained, and evaluated, and to whom they must answer. In short, they spell out the rules of the game by which participants in the legal process must abide. However, scholarship on the practical application of judicial reform policy suggests that formal institutional solutions have important limitations.

One of the difficulties is that there is no clear prescription for reformers. Given the complex and multifaceted nature of the available options—ranging from rules about asset disclosure and case assignments, to judicial appointment and promotion systems, to court budgets and legislative oversight mechanisms—the effects of the resulting institutional configurations are poorly understood. As scholars have attempted to derive policy lessons about the impact of institutional design on judicial outcomes, their findings converge on the idea that there is no single path to reform. In some cases, differing packages of institutional rules may lead to roughly equivalent outcomes (Jackson 2012). In other cases, the same institutional solutions may produce dramatically different results—depending on the legal, political, and historical context in which they are implemented. Indeed, experts implore policy-makers to "approach with caution efforts to develop 'best practices' guides to judicial independence, at least insofar as those guides are intended to be transformed into rigid constitutional or quasi-constitutional rules" (Jackson 2012, 86). It appears that any attempt to apply a one-size-fits-all model of institutional design is fundamentally misguided.

Complicating matters further, research on the process of institutional design suggests that even if reformers know definitively which institutional choices will produce the optimal results, technocratic prescriptions are no match for the particularized interests of politicians who ultimately dictate the rules of the game. In a seminal study analyzing the correlates of postcommunist legal institutional design, Smithey and Ishiyama (2000) conclude that "political bargaining" is the most important determinant of institutional choice. Specifically, constitution writers in the postcommunist region have tended to favor courts that are nominally powerful but effectively subordinate to the executive or legislative branches—enabling the judiciary to serve an important legitimizing function without fundamentally challenging the authority of political elites.

Even when favorable institutional reforms are adopted, the comparative evidence suggests that they are far from a cure-all. In part, this follows from the simple observation that formal institutional rules are not the only constraints on judicial behavior—or even the most influential ones. Judicial actors are situated in a web of formal and informal rules, with overlapping interests, loyalties, and incentives shaping their behavior. The process of attitudinal and behavioral change that must accompany a change in formal institutional design is thus long and complex—leading to many documented instances in which informal judicial attitudes and behaviors differ significantly from the dictates of formal institutional rules (Burger 2004; Bobek 2008; Beers 2011; Parau 2012; Hein 2015; Schönfelder 2005; Alistar 2007).

In practice, this mismatch between formal and informal rules can have a substantial impact on the role that courts play in transitioning political systems. Comparative research on the application of judicial authority suggests that postcommunist courts with strong formal powers are often constrained by mitigating factors. Focusing on the power of judicial review, Herron and Randazzo (2003) argue that strong presidents and poor economic conditions (which invite corruption and incentivize politicians to restrict potential sources of opposition) systematically undermine the de facto exercise of judicial authority. Bumin, Randazzo, and Walker (2009) offer further evidence that the legal provision of formal institutional powers is only a small part of the process they term "judicial institutionalization." In a comparative study of postcommunist courts, they observe that many judiciaries fail to demonstrate a distinct and persistent record of autonomous action—despite formal institutional rules that give them such powers.

Finally, the evidence suggests that institutional reforms may not only fail to produce the desired outcomes but may actually create new obstacles to the democratic rule of law. In particular, the record suggests that too much judicial independence can backfire if institutional veto players use their authority in ways that undermine the intended objectives of transparency and accountability. For example, Popova (2012a) observes that Bulgaria's powerful and extraordinarily independent judiciary has failed to prosecute high-level corruption within the legal system, arguing that strong institutional provisions intended to protect judicial independence have insulated judicial officials from public and political pressure to act against corrupt judges. In Romania, Parau (2012) notes that the powerful and independent Superior Council of Magistracy (SCM) has been misappropriated by similarly antireformist leaders, many of whom subscribe to a "misrepresented meaning of judicial independence." The results have included a high-profile corruption scandal over judicial entrance exams, the controversial election of a former secret police collaborator as SCM president, and widespread accusations that judicial officials have colluded to undermine the prosecution of high-level corruption cases (Beers 2012; Parau 2012). In a scenario that Parau describes as "vicious judicial supremacism," the very institutional protections that were created to guarantee judicial independence have instead contributed to the ongoing corruption and politicization of the judiciary.

As Popova details in this volume, Ukraine has fallen victim to a similar fate. Despite a relatively strong set of institutional provisions protecting the de jure independence of the judiciary, officials in Ukraine have found ways to use those very institutional rules to undermine de facto independence. Whether by centralizing appointment and disciplinary authority in the hands of the politically loyal High Judicial Qualification Commission, or by assigning probationary-term judges to highly politicized cases like the trial of Yulia Tymoshenko, Ukrainian officials have repeatedly used seemingly democratic institutional means to pursue nondemocratic ends. In short, Ukraine exhibits the hallmarks of a weakly institutionalized judiciary—manipulated and marginalized by political elites, rather than a genuine counterbalance to political power (Bumin, Randazzo, and Walker 2009). In Ukraine, as elsewhere in the region, formal institutional design has been an insufficient guarantor of the rule of law.

Politicization of the Judiciary

A final related obstacle to reform is the politicization of the judiciary. Although the degree of political intrusion into the judicial sphere varies considerably from case to case, politicization of the judiciary is a common problem throughout the region. No postcommunist state has managed a completely clean break from the communist legacy of politically subservient courts. Nevertheless, the literature suggests that political interference in the judiciary is more likely to occur under certain conditions—namely, in hybrid regimes in which genuine political competition is coupled with uncertainty about the durability of the regime, and in transitioning states where judicial authority poses a challenge to the supremacy of ruling elites. As I argue below, both of these scenarios suggest that the well established pattern of judicial politicization in Ukraine is at least partly the result of deep political tensions that have characterized much of the postcommunist period in Ukraine—and that are likely to continue for the foreseeable future.

In established democracies, scholars have long argued that increased political competition increases judicial independence (Stephenson 2003; Magalhaes 1999). Conversely, research on law in authoritarian states suggests that courts are typically less salient actors in political disputes in noncompetitive regimes. Thus, somewhat paradoxically, they are often afforded a good deal of independence in their day-to-day work—except in cases of clear political import, when the government intervenes to ensure a favorable outcome (Solomon Jr. 2012; Moustafa 2008; Balasubramaniam 2009). In hybrid regimes, because incumbents cannot depend on easily winning reelection, they must employ all tools at their disposal to increase their chances of retaining power—including the courts (Popova 2010b; Trochev 2010). Meanwhile, pressuring the judiciary is easier and less risky than in consolidated democracies because elites have access to existing networks and mechanisms of influence inherited from the ancien régime, and because politicians are "less fearful of public backlash" (Popova 2010b, 1208). Further, the logic that independent courts can protect the interests of competing political elites does not obtain in hybrid regimes. In part, the deep mistrust between elite factions that characterizes most hybrid regimes undercuts the possibility of establishing "credible commitments" through the judicial process. Moreover, the inherent instability of many hybrid systems shortens political time horizons, causing elites to value tangible short-term political gains over uncertain long-term guarantees. Therefore hybrid regimes tend to result in greater politicization of the judiciary because of the incentives facing regime elites.

Beyond the nature of the regime itself, Hein (2011) argues that judicial politicization is also related to the level of independent authority afforded to the judiciary. Specifically, he contends that both excessively dependent courts and exceptionally autonomous courts can attract unwanted attention from political elites. Following this logic, comparative evidence suggests that some of the most powerful and independent judiciaries in the postcommunist region—especially those with constitutional courts willing and able to challenge the authority of incumbent political elites—have experienced the most serious political attacks on their independence. Simply put, undemocratic politicians in transitioning states seem to resent the challenge to their authority posed by genuine judicial oversight. As a result, political leaders have sought to curtail the legal authority of powerful and independent judiciaries in a number of prominent examples across the region, including Hungary and Romania.

For Ukraine, the lesson is clear. As a highly contested hybrid regime whose courts have played a decisive role in past political disputes, Ukraine's judiciary has predictably been targeted by regime elites as a key political battleground. During the last major crisis in 2004, both the Supreme Court and the Constitutional Court issued key decisions influencing the outcome of the Orange Revolution, in which Viktor Yanukovych and the Party of Regions lost power (Christensen, Rakhimkulov, and Wise 2005). After clinching control of the government in 2010, the Yanukovych administration launched an "institutional attack" on the Supreme Court and the independent powers of the judicial branch, while simultaneously using the courts to sideline key political adversaries such as Yulia Tymoshenko and Yuriy Lutsenko (see Popova, this volume). Viewed through a comparative lens, the politicization of the Ukrainian judiciary appears not simply a product of the uniquely polemical character of Ukrainian politics. Instead, it offers further confirmation of the challenges posed by powerful and independent courts in highly contested regimes. Moreover, as long as political power in Ukraine remains in dispute, the courts are likely to be one of the battlegrounds on which elites compete for influence.

Pathways to Reform

Surveying the obstacles to judicial reform across the postcommunist region, the preceding discussion highlights the particularly challenging conditions facing democratic reformers in Ukraine. However, a comparative survey also provides perspective on the mechanisms and opportunities that have allowed some postcommunist states to take positive steps toward the rule of law. In this section, I focus on the EU as a driver of democratic reforms in eastern Europe, acknowledging both the positive effects of European intervention and the limitations of EU policies. I also discuss the influence of pan-national European courts on the development of law and legal precedent in postcommunist states. Finally, I examine how internal actors such as lower court judges and professional associations may facilitate the development of independent and impartial courts.

EU as Agenda Setter

One of the most active debates in the literature on postcommunist politics concerns the influence of European integration on political development in eastern Europe. Proponents assert that the attractive pull of EU membership has given European leaders significant leverage over the political agenda in EU candidate states—ensuring that transitioning states set their sights on liberal democracy and market capitalism. With the democratic goal posts firmly in place, the EU has used monitoring and enforcement mechanisms to ensure that reform policies are implemented, requiring candidate states to pass a series of formal evaluations before being granted full membership status. Kopstein (2006) claims that, relying on soft power and systematic incentives and rewards, the EU's use of membership "conditionality" is one of its most important foreign policy accomplishments to date—a position widely shared in policy circles in Europe and North America.

Critics contend that the accession process is deeply flawed, and that EU integration has negatively impacted the quality of democracy and democratic institutions in new member states. The power asymmetry between the EU and candidate states has inhibited public debate and limited policy input from domestic political actors, resulting in policies that are unfair or out of touch with the needs of newly democratizing states (Sissenich 2006; Grabbe 2002). Moreover, the inherently undemocratic nature of the process has undermined the legitimacy of democratic politics and political competition in new member states (Zielonka 2007). As a result, critics question how deeply the policies and principles advocated by the EU have taken root, noting that many of the formal policy provisions adopted by candidate states have been poorly implemented, resulting in "hollow institutions" and large implementation gaps between formal laws and informal practices. Others voice concern about the strength of the underlying commitment to democracy and liberalism in societies in which the transition process was so strongly influenced by outside actors.

What most scholars can agree on is that the EU's negotiation and monitoring process has significantly impacted the reform agenda in candidate states. In postcommunist states where full EU membership was a viable prospect (an important caveat in discussions about Ukraine, where it is not), the accession process set out a clear and detailed policy agenda that candidate states were obliged to follow. In the legal sphere, EU leaders demanded the adoption of a number of formal institutional provisions to protect judicial independence and promote transparency and accountability. Moreover, comparative evidence suggests that the EU's influence on the reform agenda has been most pronounced in cases in which it has exerted the strongest pressure.

For example, the EU placed great emphasis in its accession negotiations with Romania and Bulgaria on the need to secure the independence of the judiciary and strengthen the rule of law. In both cases, concerns about corruption and politicization of the judiciary were among the key sticking points that delayed the states' formal accession to the EU from 2004 to 2007. As a consequence, judicial reform topped the political agendas of both countries for several years in the lead-up to EU accession, and government officials in both states adopted some of the most comprehensive and institutionally sophisticated provisions in Europe aimed at promoting judicial independence and transparency.

Beyond the EU's direct impact on the policy agenda, some scholars argue that the accession process also creates indirect avenues of influence. Piana (2010) identifies several mechanisms through which EU integration has advanced the goal of democratic judicial reform in candidate states. Through twinning projects, international exchange programs, and pan-European professional association meetings, the EU's enlargement to eastern Europe has expanded opportunities for the transfer of professional norms and expertise, and has incorporated legal professionals from candidate states into international networks of "social and professional accountability."

Yet even the most ardent EU supporters recognize that the influence of Brussels has limits. Many question the depth of the EU's impact on democratizing states. Acting primarily as a democratic agenda setter, the EU has a limited set of tools to ensure genuine and lasting reforms. Where the EU has had the strongest influence on institutional reforms in the judicial sector (for example, Romania and Bulgaria), serious questions remain about the legitimacy and efficacy of the resulting institutional provisions, which have been weakly enforced or misappropriated for nondemocratic purposes (Piana 2010; Beers 2011, 2012; Popova 2010a, 2012b). Among the lessons emerging from the Romanian and Bulgarian cases, it is increasingly apparent that who controls these institutions—whether genuine allies of reform or not—is a critical determinant of their impact on the rule of law. Likewise, it is clear that genuine elite commitment to the principles of judicial independence and transparency is a necessary component of the reform process. As in Romania and Bulgaria, pressure from outside actors goes only so far.

The EU's reform agenda is also limited in its breadth—particularly with respect to its finite geographic reach. For Ukraine, a country that has long en-

tertained the prospect of EU candidacy but never moved beyond limited cooperation agreements, this point is especially salient. The EU's ability to influence
reforms in any sector of Ukrainian politics is necessarily bound up with its
perceived commitment to Ukraine as a future EU member state.

European Courts

Even in states beyond the direct reach of the EU's formal accession process, recent research suggests that European courts—especially the European
Court of Human Rights (ECtHR)—have been used by legal actors as a point
of leverage in domestic legal practice. One of the most interesting findings to
emerge from the literature in recent years is that European courts appear to be
influencing legal developments in states outside the EU's immediate sphere of
influence.

In Russia, Trochev (2009) finds that judges "increasingly refer to the juris-
prudence of the ECtHR" in their legal rulings, "despite facing a host of pressures to do otherwise." Although Russian courts typically bend to the will of the
regime in cases of extreme political import, judges frequently refer to ECtHR
precedent in their rulings on routine matters. Moreover, Trochev argues that,
despite its unpopularity with the Putin regime, the international standing of
the ECtHR "protects such judges from being punished by politicians" because
of the potential backlash for persecuting judges following international con-
ventions to which Russia is a signatory.

Similarly, Wilson (2012) finds that judges in Ukraine have also grown accustomed to referencing ECtHR decisions in their rulings on freedom of speech
issues. Focusing mainly on defamation suits during the Kuchma era, she con-
cedes that Ukrainian judges ruled against journalists in an overwhelming majority of cases. However, she observes "a gradual increase in court reliance on
the European Convention and the decisions of the European Court of Human
Rights," citing a host of cases in which Ukrainian judges specifically referenced
the ECtHR and its decisions to justify rulings protecting the rights of journalists.

These findings suggest that even in (semi-)authoritarian regimes beyond
the direct influence of the EU, European law can have an important impact on
the development of domestic law and legal precedent. For Ukraine, the incorporation of the European Convention and ECtHR case law into the domestic
legal arena—a practice that was continued and strengthened after the Orange
Revolution under the Yushchenko administration—suggests a positive path-

way toward improving the rule of law and the protection of Ukrainian citizens' legal rights and freedoms. This pathway is unlikely to bring wide-ranging systemic improvements to the Ukrainian judiciary. However, it does represent an important source of support and leverage for democratic reformers in Ukraine.

Internal Drivers of Reform

Finally, despite the obstacles facing domestic legal actors, comparative evidence suggests that factions within the judiciary—specifically, lower court judges and judicial associations—can serve as advocates for reform. Although lower court judges have little formal power over the reform process, they can play a key role in normalizing and institutionalizing fair and impartial court hearings in politically insignificant cases. They also represent a potentially important proreform constituency within the judiciary, lacking the entrenched interests of their more seasoned superiors. For their part, judicial associations can aid the reform process by strengthening professional norms, and by agitating for democratic reforms on behalf of their members. Ultimately, these internal actors are unlikely to prevent high-level corruption or extreme politicization of the judiciary. However, they can help to establish more regular patterns of impartiality and objectivity in the judicial process, while strengthening the hand of would-be reformers should the opportunity for systemic reform arise.

Admittedly, skepticism about the political efficacy of low-level judicial functionaries is widespread. Among frustrated reform advocates, one often hears claims that judges are little more than unimaginative bureaucrats who routinely bend to the will of their superiors—overworked, underpaid, and easily manipulated. However, lower court judges possess some important qualities that make them natural allies of reform. Their relatively low status means that they are less important to political elites, and therefore less likely to be implicated in clientelistic networks or politicized trials. Left to their own devices, these judges can routinize fair and impartial rulings at lower levels of the court system. Supporting this view, research findings from some of the most highly politicized judicial systems in the region, including Russia, Azerbaijan, Tajikistan, and Ukraine, suggest that lower court judges may, in fact, exercise greater autonomy in their rulings than their high court superiors (Wilson 2012; Trochev 2012b; Hendley 2012).

A second (perhaps more tenuous) characteristic of lower court judges is their relatively shallow integration into entrenched networks of clientelism and corruption. In a post-Soviet context like Ukraine, where corruption is rife, it is important not to overstate the youthful idealism of newly minted judges.

However, by virtue of their relatively short tenure in office and their relatively low status within the judiciary, many lower court judges simply have less of a stake in propagating old systems of patronage and clientelism. As a result, many observers have noted what Mendelski describes as a "generational discrepancy" in postcommunist judiciaries. While "old guard" members of the judicial establishment block substantive reforms and leverage their positions to reap financial rewards, the majority of judges are "reform-minded young magistrates," many of whom are skilled and impartial professionals with little to gain from the status quo of corruption and political servitude (Mendelski 2011, 244). This generational discrepancy does not imply that younger judges are impervious to corruption or political influence. Nor does it mean that they are likely to actively agitate for reforms from below. What it does suggest is that a younger generation of judges may be sympathetic to calls for reform, because they have little to gain from a system that disproportionately benefits their corrupt superiors and damages the reputation of their profession. So while they may not be active agents of change, lower court judges represent an important constituency for those who are.

Beyond the latent proreform orientation of many individual judges, professional associations and judicial unions have openly advocated for reform in many East European states. In part, their influence derives from the agenda-setting power of professional associations that shape the content and tenor of professional discourse through official communications, sponsored events, workshops and training programs, and the like. When associations pursue an agenda of professionalization, increased transparency, and judicial accountability, they facilitate the spread of professional norms that are critical to the development of the rule of law (Piana 2010; Beers 2011; Solomon Jr. 2012). Further, judicial associations may help to establish links with other national or supranational associations across state borders, thereby precipitating the exchange or "diffusion" of democratic norms (Guarnieri 2003; Piana 2010). In addition to professionalization, some of the most active judicial associations in the region have taken a clear position as agents for democratic change. For example, both the Czech Union of Judges (SUČR) and the National Union of Romanian Judges (UNJR) have actively lobbied for democratic reforms on behalf of their constituents.

Of course, it is important not to overstate the impact that judicial associations can have on the reform process. Nor should we understate the obstacles that activist associations would likely face in a rigid and hierarchical political setting like Ukraine. However, it is equally important to acknowledge the potential that reform-minded judges and judicial associations may represent. If nothing else, the comparative evidence suggests that high-level policy reformers are likely to find allies within the lower ranks of the judiciary. In turn, policy-makers should consider strategies to empower lower court judges and embolden autonomous and democratically oriented professional associations as a means of strengthening the reform process from within.

Conclusion

Considering the state of Ukraine's judicial sector in comparative perspective, a few broad lessons emerge. The first is that judicial reformers in Ukraine face an uphill battle. Under-resourced and weakly institutionalized, with deeply imbedded patterns of corruption and politicization, the conditions for judicial reform in Ukraine are less than propitious. However, a cross-national comparison also suggests some potential avenues for change. In particular, both the agenda-setting power of the EU accession process and the increasing influence of European law across the Continent represent important points of leverage for reformers in Ukraine. Further, the comparative record suggests that Ukrainian reformers may well find allies within the judiciary, especially among lower court judges and reform-oriented professional associations.

In the final analysis, it is difficult to escape the conclusion that much rests on the genuine commitment of elites to the project of democratic legal reform. Durable high-level reforms are rare and difficult to achieve, in part because they require respect and self-restraint from political elites, even when it may not serve their immediate self-interest. Where lasting reforms have occurred, they have resulted from consistent and enduring elite support for the principle of judicial independence as a positive political good. In the most successful cases, this has coincided with both external pressure from the European Union and internal elite consensus about the need for independent courts to preserve and mediate democratic political competition. Where such consensus has been absent, the record shows mixed results—most commonly in the form of sweeping de jure reforms that are only partially and halfheartedly translated into everyday practice.

Low-level reforms are more readily achievable, even in the absence of genuine elite support. Examples from the region suggest that reform-oriented judges and well organized professional organizations can act as change agents to improve the quality of justice at lower levels of the court system. They can professionalize the judicial process and make routine legal transactions fairer, more transparent, and more predictable. Moreover, judges and litigants may apply international legal precedents to domestic cases, or appeal cases directly to European courts, thereby circumnavigating politically subservient courts at home. These kinds of reforms may not prevent executive intrusion into the legal sphere, nor can they guarantee fair and equal application of the law to all citizens in all cases. However, they can strengthen the rule of law and improve the fairness and efficacy of the court system, with real and positive social and economic benefits.

For Ukraine, these lessons suggest that a number of formidable obstacles will continue to inhibit comprehensive reform in the judicial sector. However, the successful toppling of the Yanukovych regime appears to have laid the groundwork for an important political opening. If Ukraine's newly elected leaders can demonstrate sincere commitment to the rule of law and the process of democratic legal reform, there is reason to believe that real progress can be made.

PART VI

Patrimonialism and the Oligarchs

10   Oligarchs, the Partial Reform Equilibrium, and the Euromaidan Revolution

TARAS KUZIO

What are oligarchs and who are the oligarchs in Ukraine? The term "oligarch" has been used since the 1990s when referring to big business tycoons and natural gas moguls in Ukraine and other post-Soviet states, frequently without citing an established definition. The key feature of oligarchs in the Ukrainian context is their penchant to become monopolists in every field where they operate: media, economy, and politics. They therefore have an intrinsically negative influence on Ukraine's quadruple transitions of democratization, marketization, state-institution building, and national integration (Kuzio 2001). Oligarchs have benefited from maintaining the country in a "partial reform equilibrium" (Hellman 1998) at the crossroads of Eurasia and Europe. Ukraine's oligarchs are in many ways nationalists, seeing closer ties with both Russia and the EU as leading to a decline in Ukraine's sovereignty and therefore threats to their interests.

Oligarchs prevent the emergence of a level playing field in politics by blocking the entrance of genuine political parties into the political arena. Instead, for each election cycle, they like to support disposable election vehicles, which are dubbed political "projects" by Ukrainian observers. They co-opt opposition political parties and political leaders through political corruption and finance fake candidates and parties with the sole purpose of confusing voters. Oligarchs' control over Ukraine's major television networks distorts the information available to voters during elections while preventing governments from explaining their reforms and policies to the public. Oligarchs typically care more about making money than ideology, and the most successful oligarchic groups are able to work with every incumbent. With no interest in the rule of law, they corrupt the political and economic systems and seek to control law enforcement structures. Oligarch interests rarely coincide with those of the state: they send billions of dollars to tax havens to avoid paying taxes and prefer a weak state they can more readily control. Tax avoidance by Ukraine's wealthiest citizens encourages similar practices at the lower levels of society, generating a stable and large shadow economy. The failure to develop a robust small and medium enterprise sector stymies the growth of Ukraine's middle class, which typically provides the strongest basis for a liberal democracy and market economy.

Orange Revolutionary leaders who came to power in 2005 failed to move Ukraine from the crossroads into Europe. Euromaidan revolutionary leaders are operating in worse domestic and external environments thanks to Ukraine's deep economic and financial crises combined with Russian aggression and the EU's ongoing internal crisis. European integration will be impossible without breaking the power of Ukraine's oligarchs and significantly reducing the close relationship between big business and politics. Anders Aslund believes that "[t]here is too much continuity from the Soviet state. Ukraine needs a clear break from the old system, as Estonia and Georgia did resolutely." In current circumstances, the partial reform equilibrium has led to the "enrichment of a few" because "big businessmen have captured the state in Ukraine, more than any other post-communist country," Aslund writes. "At present, Ukraine stands out as the last post-communist outpost where tycoons wield substantial political power" (Aslund 2015, 29). Therefore, "[t]he power of the oligarchs has to be broken" (Aslund 2015, 12, 8, 18). The jury is still out on whether President Petro Poroshenko's "deoligarchization" will be successful; after all, Ukraine's oligarchs have much to lose if Ukraine were to reform its political and economic system and successfully integrate with Europe.

This chapter examines Ukraine's oligarchs by first laying out the economic context in which they operate. It then lists the four successful oligarchic groups that have emerged since Ukrainian independence. The next section examines the actions of the oligarchs and their relation to reform. Finally, the chapter looks at the impact of the state's deoligarchization campaign. Overall, the chapter argues that without reducing the powers of the oligarchs, Ukraine's reform efforts are doomed to another failure.

Partial Reform Equilibrium

Soviet Legacy of Corruption and Crime

When the Soviet Union disintegrated in December 1991, its fifteen con-stituent republics embarked on a quadruple transition. While state- and na-tion-building continued to be pursued in post-Soviet Eurasia, by the late 1990s democratization had been reversed in a majority of former Soviet republics, while marketization was never completed and most states, including Ukraine, gradually stabilized into partially reformed equilibriums. A nexus of corrupt state elites, officials, and oligarchs hijacked the emerging market economy and established cooperative relations with criminal elements that had grown exten-sively from the late 1980s and unreformed law enforcement structures.

Although there are no longer failed states among the twelve non-Bal-tic former Soviet republics, their state institutions were inevitably shaped by the political, legal, economic, and criminal environments within which they emerged. Research in Russia found that by the mid-1990s, 30 to 50 percent of entrepreneurs cooperated with criminals, criminal groups controlled four hun-dred banks and exchanges, and forty-one thousand enterprises and 80 percent of joint ventures possessed criminal links (Frisby 1998, 35). Ukraine, although with a population a third the size of Russia's, could not escape such develop-ments, and the links between crime, state elites, officials, and the newly emerg-ing private sector developed in a similar manner. As in Russia, certain regions had higher levels of crime and violence; in the Ukrainian case these were the Crimea, Donetsk, and Odessa, according to the number of murders.[1]

Large underground shadow economies emerged throughout the USSR in the 1970s and 1980s and were particularly vibrant in the Crimea, with its large number of tourist resorts; Odessa, which had always been a major hub for ille-gal and untaxed trade; and Donetsk, with its major industrial and raw material resources. Business leaders in the shadow economy (called *akuly* [sharks] by criminals) cooperated with the criminal world in a conspiratorial and hierar-chical double life. Louise Shelley points out that the Soviet shadow economy could only have existed with the participation of government and security force personnel (Shelley 2003, 203). Along with numerous Komsomol (Communist Youth League) leaders, former shadow economy entrepreneurs (*tsekhoviki*) were among the first to "anticipate the coming political changes and act ac-cordingly" during the second half of the 1980s (Frisby 1998, 34).

Impact on Ukraine's Post-Soviet Transition

Since independence, the Ukrainian state has been financially weak and unable to provide social services, education, pensions, decent salaries for state officials, and effective law enforcement and military structures. At critical crisis points, such as 1998, 2008, 2010, and 2014, Ukraine has been forced to turn to international financial institutions for assistance. Although Ukrainian governments have had little choice but to pursue stabilization policies, the second stage of structural reforms demanded by international financial institutions never took place until the Euromaidan, leaving Ukraine in a partial reform equilibrium. Ukraine's state budget has been weak because different socioeconomic groups of Ukrainians have pursued a policy of extensive tax evasion by operating in the shadow economy and/or sending their profits and rents offshore to tax havens. Tax evasion was popular because there were limited criminal consequences and because Ukrainians—like Greeks and Italians—do not trust their state institutions and law enforcement. Weak political will to tackle corruption created a permanent shadow economy, leading to high and numerous taxes on the small official economy.

The shadow economy is roughly equal in size to half of Ukraine's GDP and higher than in all post-Soviet states, except Georgia until the Rose Revolution, where it had accounted for 62 percent of GDP.[2] Ukraine's shadow economy is larger than in energy-rich Russia and Kazakhstan, war-torn and impoverished Tajikistan, Armenia, and two EU members Bulgaria and Romania, where high levels of corruption continue to fester. The share of the shadow economy in Ukraine's GDP has remained constant throughout the transition to a market economy in the 1990s and following the return to economic growth in 2000 under presidents Yushchenko and Yanukovych.

Oligarchic capture of the Ukrainian state has blocked economic development by preventing the growth of the economy overall while blocking new entrants, discouraging foreign investment and making it difficult to expand small and medium business. Ukraine's economic recession following 1989 was one of the deepest in the former USSR and its recovery began only in 2000, the last of the CIS states. Nearly a quarter of a century after the USSR disintegrated, only Ukraine of the fifteen former Soviet republics has not recovered to the level of its Soviet era GDP and the Ukrainian economy remains only three-quarters of the size it had reached in the late Soviet era.

Ukraine's Oligarchs: Komsomol and Gangsters

The imprecise definition of oligarchs in Ukraine is compounded by the lack of clarity as to who they are and where they are based. The term "clans" when used in the context of Ukraine and other post-Soviet states does not convey the traditional sense of kinship and descent, such as, for example, the Scottish Highlanders. Clans, in a nonethnic context, refers to groups of people from regions (such as Donetsk and Dnipropetrovsk) that have a history of social, business, and family ties stretching back into the Soviet era; the term is consequently more akin to "old boy networks." In the Ukrainian case, clans (often said to provide *krysha* [criminal slang for protection, the literal translation being "a roof"]) have been created to lobby big business interests through political parties and, when their leaders are in power, through the president, government, and parliament.

There have been four successful oligarchic clans in Ukraine. First, the only region to successfully unite into one clan was Donetsk, which formed the Party of Regions, now largely defunct but previously constituting what was arguably Ukraine's only true party-based political machine (Kudelia and Kuzio 2015; Kuzio 2015a). The Party of Regions monopolized politics, economy, and the media in the Donbas and spread its branches to eastern and southern Ukraine. The party's attempt to fraudulently elect Yanukovych in 2004 and impose a monopoly of power on the remainder of Ukraine during Yanukovych's presidency provoked the Orange Revolution and Euromaidan respectively.

Second, the gas lobby has no relationship to a region, although many of its leading members are from western Ukraine.[3] It has been the most successful of all clans in surviving Ukraine's political changes and maintaining cordial and close relations with all of Ukraine's presidents, including Poroshenko. While the United States has pursued criminal charges against Dmytro Firtash, seeking to extradite him from Austria, his business allies (Serhiy Lyovochkin and Yuriy Boyko) remain above the law as leaders of parliament's Opposition Bloc, which gives them parliamentary immunity. Other oligarchs have also been heavily involved in the lucrative energy sector. Pavlo Lazarenko and Yulia Tymoshenko cooperated in the mid-1990s through United Energy Systems of Ukraine, but their involvement was destroyed by 1998 when they went into opposition to Kuchma. Dnipropetrovsk Pryvat group oligarchs Ihor Kolomoiskiy and Gennadiy Bogolyubov, who controlled the state companies UkrNafta and

UkrTransNafta, developed a more successful long-term involvement in the oil sector that was partially reduced only in 2015.

A third set of oligarchs remains powerful even though they have never sought to build personally loyal clans or have failed in their attempts; indeed, many more embryo clans and oligarchic virtual political projects have failed than have been successful. Viktor Pinchuk (owner of the Interpipe business group) and Serhiy Tihipko utterly failed to build loyal clans through the political party projects Labor Ukraine, Strong Ukraine, KOP (Winter Crop Generation), and Viche. Kharkiv and Odessa, cities with large student and middle-class populations (rather than working-class, as in Donetsk), did not produce oligarchic clans of nationwide import.

Finally, the Kyiv clan never actually achieved popularity in the capital city, and its political manifestation, the Social Democratic United Party (SDPUo), established temporary bases of support in Trans-Carpathia and more tenuously in western and central Ukraine. SDPUo leader Viktor Medvedchuk's political and business ambitions reached their peak when he was chief of staff to President Kuchma in 2002–4 and went into irreversible decline following his departure from office. Dnipropetrovsk-Kharkiv political party projects, the People's Democratic Party (NDP), and the Inter-Regional Bloc of Reforms (MBR) also proved to be failures—perhaps the reason that they united in 2000 and then disappeared after Kuchma left office.

How Do the Oligarchs Relate to Reform?

Ukraine's oligarchs naturally benefit from the "partial reform equilibrium" status quo and do not support overall structural reforms. However, the removal of Yanukovych from the presidency by Euromaidan revolutionaries led to oligarchs with long-standing ties to the opposition, Kolomoiskiy and Serhiy Taruta (cohead of the Industrial Union of the Donbas), being appointed regional governors. Their assignment was to shore up Ukraine's defenses against a Russian invasion of eastern Ukraine. However, their tenure in office was short. Although successful in blocking a possible Russian advance into Dnipropetrovsk, Kolomoiskiy lost his job after he sent armed guards to block Poroshenko from removing his control over state oil companies as part of the president's deoligarchization campaign. Taruta's task of governing Donetsk, a territory whose separatist insurgents were receiving military supplies from neighboring Russia, proved to be impossible, leading to his removal. His two immediate successors have proven no more effective in the job.

Oligarchs Kolomoiskiy and Taruta have both supported pro-Western political forces; Kolomoiskiy helped finance Viktor Yushchenko's Our Ukraine, Vitaliy Klitschko's Ukrainian Democratic Alliance for Reforms (UDAR), the *Svoboda* (Freedom) nationalist party, and, more recently, Prime Minister Arseniy Yatsenyuk's Popular Front and (together with the gas lobby) Oleh Liashko's populist Radical Party. Taruta supported Tymoshenko. However, their funding of pro-Western political forces should be not misunderstood as backing reforms, fighting corruption, or promoting European integration, but instead understood as opportunism and survival tactics. Jewish-Ukrainian oligarch Kolomoiskiy backed the nationalist Svoboda party not for ideological reasons but because he wished to protect his energy interests in Galicia, where Svoboda was popular.

Ukraine's oligarchs, like British foreign policy, do not have perennial friends and enemies but only permanent interests, and they (particularly the gas lobby) have transferred the corrupt franchise to every new president. Ukraine's oligarchs do not commit to deeply held ideological preferences, and personalities matter more than political party programs. Western Ukrainians have dominated the pro-Russian gas lobby even though the region was always anti-Russian in its national identity.

The gas lobby and SDPUo, although with roots in the west and center of the country, nevertheless were the most pro-Russian oligarchs in Ukraine. Ukraine's gas lobby made huge rents from arbitrage on gas deliveries from Russia and therefore had no interest in Ukraine's achieving even a modicum of energy independence. Supporting close ties to Russia goes against the grain of western Ukrainian foreign preferences, but for the gas lobby business trumps politics. The gas lobby had excellent relations with the anti-Russian president Yushchenko, while simultaneously penetrating the commanding heights of the pro-Russian Party of Regions and holding high-level positions such as chief of staff during the Yanukovych presidency. The pro-Western Yushchenko's financial relationship with Firtash ignored the fact that he was, like Medvedchuk, Moscow's man in Ukraine. Russian President Vladimir Putin is the godfather of Medvedchuk's daughter Darina. While Ukraine was charged the highest gas price in Europe, Ostchem,[4] a company owned by Firtash and investigated by the Ukrainian government, was able to import Russian gas at a fraction of the official government price. The large profits derived from exploiting the price difference gave Firtash capital to purchase strategic areas of the economy on behalf of his Russian backers.[5] After his arrest in Vienna, he "received another loan in order to pay his bail: $155 million from Vasily Anisimov, the billionaire who heads the Russian Judo Federation, the governing body in Russia of Putin's beloved sport."[6] While the US has sought Firtash's deportation to stand trial on corruption charges, Poroshenko, who is commander of Ukrainian armed forces fighting Russia, has protected the interests of the pro-Russian gas lobby in Ukraine. During his presidency, no criminal charges have been brought against the key representatives of this lobby, and they have not been placed on the list of Ukrainians sought by Interpol.

In the 2010 presidential elections, the gas lobby backed Yatsenyuk as a counterweight to Tymoshenko, the only Ukrainian politician with whom they had a poor relationship. In 2012–14, the gas lobby supported President Yanukovych while simultaneously financing Klitschko's UDAR. After the Euromaidan the gas lobby brokered an immunity deal with Klitschko and Poroshenko and backed the latter, whose main opponent in the May 2014 presidential elections was Tymoshenko. Within a span of three months the gas lobby distanced itself from Yanukovych, after Lyovochkin resigned as chief of staff in January 2014, and recaptured the initiative from Euromaidan revolutionaries by successfully promoting Poroshenko for the presidency and Klitschko for mayor of Kyiv. "We got what we wanted—Poroshenko as president and Klitschko as mayor," Firtash bragged to the Viennese court.[7]

After Kuchma left office in 2004, the SDPUo became increasingly pro-Russian as Medvedchuk developed a close personal and family relationship with Putin. Medvedchuk's Ukrainian Way NGO and the free *Vesti* newspaper were part of what Russia viewed as its "soft power" answer to what it claimed were the West's conspiracies behind the Orange and Euromaidan revolutions.

Although it is important to bear in mind that use of labels such as "pro-Western" and "pro-Russian" are nebulous categories when applied to oligarchs, it is nevertheless the case that Russophone eastern Ukraine has produced two distinct types of centrist parties. From 1994 until the 2000–1 Kuchmagate crisis, when secretly recorded conversations with President Leonid Kuchma seemed to implicate him in the murder of journalist Georgi Gongadze, Ukraine was ruled by leaders representing Dnipropetrovsk and Kharkiv, led by former Komsomol leaders (for example, presidential chief of staff and Kharkiv mayor Yevhen Kushnaryov, NDP leader Anatoliy Matviyenko, and MBR leader Volodymyr

Hrynyov) and technocratic nomenklatura (such as President Kuchma and Prime Minister Valeriy Pustovoytenko). The importance of the Komsomol to post-Soviet Ukraine was evident in the 2004 elections when former Komsomol leaders Serhiy Tihipko ran the Yanukovych campaign and Oleksandr Zinchenko headed Yushchenko's campaign. During Kuchma's presidency, therefore, Ukraine's rulers resembled those in the Soviet period, when Dnipropetrovsk and Kharkiv had also dominated Ukraine's ruling elites.

The Kuchmagate crisis changed Ukraine's politics by radicalizing eastern and western Ukraine and breaking the partnership between centrists and national democrats, damaging prospects for national integration and reforms. Centrist liberals became marginalized after Kuchma left office in 2004 and were replaced by the rise of the Donetsk clan's Party of Regions, which, although forced to enter a bloc with four propresidential centrists in 2002, became an independent political actor from 2005. The Donbas had never played an influential political role in Soviet Ukraine.

The former Komsomol centrists, who led political party projects they viewed as "liberal" in ideological orientation, cooperated with the national democratic Rukh (Popular Movement for Restructuring) Party led by Vyacheslav Chornovil and other national democratic parties. Komsomol-led centrist and national democratic parties both viewed the Communist Party of Ukraine (KPU) and Crimean Russian nationalist-separatists as their common enemy. This distancing from the communists and Crimeans made them crucially different from the Donetsk clan and the more leftist-populist Party of Regions, who closely cooperated with the KPU and Crimean Russian nationalists and, like Putin's Russia, disparaged national democrats as "fascists" in the pay of the West.

The Party of Regions received overwhelming support from its home base regions of Donetsk and Luhansk oblasts (which together form the Donbas) and the Crimea. The Donbas has a far stronger regional than Ukrainian identity, embedded Soviet working-class culture, a long tradition of violence stretching back to the late nineteenth century, and, together with the Crimea, a Soviet cultural identity. A political party can become a machine only if it successfully mobilizes a large enough number of voters, both real supporters and voters attracted through patronage, in order for it win elections. The Party of Regions successfully combined populist and neopatrimonial client relations with big business and the working classes, who had earlier voted for the KPU. This strategy was successful because of greater discipline, support for unity of the Donetsk clan from regional governor Yanukovych, the concentration of large numbers of voters in factory towns, and access to huge financial resources provided by oligarchs.

By 2000, then Donetsk governor Yanukovych and his oligarch allies, many of whom had emerged from organized crime and had emerged victorious from the violent civil war that had gripped the Donbas in the late 1980s and 1990s, had successfully established a total monopoly of power in the Donbas years ahead of Putin in Russia and just behind President Aliaksandr Lukashenka in Belarus. Big business was united into a single clan that viewed the Party of Regions as its political *krysha*. Other parties, such as the KPU and smaller leftist and Pan-Slavic groups, were either submerged into the Party of Regions or became satellites. The media environment was totally monopolized. Building on the low election turnouts in the 1990s, the Party of Regions ensured massive majorities, including more than 100 percent participation in select precincts during the 2004 presidential elections for Yanukovych. Law enforcement (Ministry of Interior, Security Service, Prosecutor-General's Office) was infiltrated and co-opted, which became a strategic factor in spring 2014 when they adopted a neutral stance or defected to the separatists (Kuzio 2014). This local influence was coupled with the Donetsk clan's capture of the prosecutor-general's office of Ukraine from 2002 to 2014 and control over financial flows through the State Tax Administration (1996–2002) and Ministry of Finance, National Bank, and Customs (2010–14). During his presidency, Yanukovych's newly emerging "Family" clan privatized law enforcement (Security Service chairman Oleksandr Yakymenko,[8] Minister of Interior Vitaliy Zakharchenko) and financial revenues (head of the State Tax Administration Oleksandr Klymenko, First Deputy Prime Minister Serhiy Arbuzov).[9]

Regional monopolization, first in the Donbas (1997–2000), then in the Crimea (2006), and from then attempted in the remainder of eastern and southern Ukraine, was aided by exceptional discipline and organizational skills. In addition to a desire for Russian-style total monopolization of power, the Donetsk clan and Party of Regions differed from former Komsomol-led centrist parties in their attitudes toward democratization and violence. The Party of Regions was an antidemocratic party that established an authoritarian regime in the Donbas that it sought to expand to the remainder of Ukraine. When led by Mykola Azarov, the State Tax Administration harassed the opposition while President Yanukovych imprisoned his opponents. Journalist and Poroshenko Bloc deputy Serhiy Leshchenko pointed out that Donetsk clan oligarch Rinat Akhmetov controlled fifty deputies in the Party of Regions faction who remained loyal to Yanukovych to the day he fled from Kyiv. None of the deputies loyal to Akhmetov voted for the December 3, 2013, no-confidence motion in the Azarov government, which "proves that Akhmetov, through his deputies as on previous occasions, supports the policies of Yanukovych by remaining silent when the security forces spill blood against demonstrators." Akhmetov's solidarity with Yanukovych was understandable because he, together with Firtash and Oleksandr Yanukovych, the president's eldest son and a dentist by profession, gained the most financially during the Yanukovych presidency. In Akhmetov's case the money flowed from "taking control over whole sectors (of the economy) and also by obtaining shares (in companies) during dubious tenders." For anybody who understands how business is undertaken in Ukraine, Leshchenko pointed out that "it is obvious that to be able to receive such bonuses, Akhmetov could only do so by being Yanukovych's partner, not only in politics, but also in business."[10]

Accusations of corruption and lack of transparency in funding have been leveled against all political parties in Ukraine because their income is provided by big business through the shadow economy and capital held in offshore tax havens. The gas lobby, Party of Regions, and Crimean Russian nationalists have integrated individuals with criminal connections who facilitated grand corruption and encouraged gangland-style violence of the type witnessed during the Euromaidan. The Donetsk clan had extensively drawn upon vigilante sportsmen (Kuzio 2015c) for corporate raiding, election fraud,[11] and the undertaking of violence against journalists, civil society activists, and political opponents.[12] A culture of widespread use of violence and control over law enforcement contributed to the unprecedented use of vigilantes to kidnap, torture, and murder protest leaders and the use of live rounds against unarmed protesters during the Euromaidan. During the Orange Revolution, when Kuchma and former Komsomol-led centrists were in charge, not a single incident of violence, let alone murder, took place. After the Euromaidan, unexplained "suicides" and "accidents" have befallen nine individuals with ties to the Party of Regions,[13] and Kharkiv mayor Hennadiy Kernes survived an April 2014 assassination attempt. High-profile "suicides" and murders were orchestrated by Party of Regions oligarchs and their organized crime allies to remove witnesses, as they also had done in the late 1990s.[14] A smaller number of "suicides" occurred after the Orange Revolution, the most prominent of which was former interior minister Yuriy Kravchenko on the eve of the time when he was due to give testimony to the prosecutor-general's office about the murder of journalist Gongadze.

At a two-and-a-half-hour December 2008 meeting with U.S. ambassador William Taylor, called at Firtash's request, the oligarch revealed his ties to Russian organized crime boss Semyon Mogilevych. Such criminals were permitted by Russian and Ukrainian leaders to take a leading role in energy transportation—the best example of which was Mogilevych. These figures organized gas intermediaries Respublika, Interhaz, Itera, Eural-Trans Gas, RosUkrEnergo (RUE), and Ostchem, which made money by selling subsidized gas at full-market price. Mogilevych's Russian Solntsevo organized crime gang provided the "muscle" for Gazprom's Itera in the 1990s. In October 2007, in the middle of preterm Ukrainian elections, a contract was signed by Vanco International (registered in the Bermuda Islands) with the outgoing Yanukovych government to explore the 13,000-square-kilometer Prykerchenska region of Ukraine's Black Sea shelf, which reportedly held large reserves of oil and gas.[15] The four owners of the Ukrainian arm of Vanco's operation, Vanco Prykerchenska, included DTEK (Donbas Fuel-Energy holding,[16] owned by oligarch Akhmetov),[17] Austrian company Integrum Technologies, linked to Party of Regions parliamentary deputy Vasyl Khmelnytsky, and Shadowlight Investments, owned by Russian oligarch Yevgeniy Novitsky, who controlled the Solntsevo criminal gang.

The FBI placed Mogilevych and his associate Igor Fisherman on their Ten Most Wanted list in the 1990s,[18] and in December 1999 U.S. ambassador to Ukraine Steven Pifer presented a thirty-one-page dossier to the Ukrainian authorities on the FBI's charges against Mogilevych. Military Intelligence chairperson Smeshko, who was unhappy at Kuchma's (and Russia's) willingness to cooperate with Mogilevych, told President Kuchma that the "FBI considers Mogilevych's organization to be under the complete protection of the SBU (Security Service of Ukraine)." SBU chairperson Leonid Derkach did not find this to be a problem, telling Kuchma that "[h]e (Mogilevych) is ours. He is an informer."[19]

Firtash "acknowledged that he needed, and received, permission from Mogilevych when he established various businesses, but he denied any close relationship to him." This account was pure deception, as Mogilevych's involvement in the energy trade continued through to 2008 on the eve of the removal of RUE from the Ukrainian-Russian gas trade.

Firtash also said that he "knows several businessmen who are linked to organized crime, including members of the Solntsevo Brotherhood."[20] Nevertheless, "Firtash's bottom line was that he did not deny having links to those associated with organized crime. Instead, he argued that he was forced into dealing with organized crime members including Mogilevych or he would never have been able to build a business."[21] Firtash was arguing that the chaos and lawlessness widely prevalent in the 1990s meant that new business ventures inevitably rubbed shoulders with criminal figures during that period of time. Nevertheless, after this and other U.S. diplomatic cables became public in Wikileaks, Firtash denied that he had told the U.S. ambassador he had ties to Mogilevych; ultimately Firtash had never expected his candor to the U.S. ambassador to be leaked into the public domain. He also denied having ties to the opaque gas intermediary RUE, which contradicted interviews he had given in 2006 to Western newspapers[22] and information available on the website of the DF Group, his business empire.[23]

Criminality in the Donbas had been high since World War II,[24] and this underworld emerged into the open during the late 1980s and 1990s. In terms of numbers of murders, Donetsk came second to the Crimea in the 1990s, but what is more striking is the degree to which the oblast was so different from neighboring Kharkiv and Dnipropetrovsk, where former Komsomol-led centrist parties dominated and violence was on a far smaller scale. The rampant violence calmed only after Yanukovych became governor in May 1997, after which organized crime allies were integrated into the political system while criminal opponents were destroyed. Yevhen Kushnir, who led an organized crime gang that was behind twenty-seven murders and seventeen attempted murders, saw his group destroyed in 1997–99, when twenty-three members were murdered and eight were criminally sentenced.[25] Governor Yanukovych oversaw the integration of "Red Directors," new younger oligarchs, trade unionists, former criminal authoritative figures, and Russian nationalist and pan-Slavic leaders such as Vadym Kolesnichenko into the Party of Regions. This process was no different from that which took place in other countries, such as Italy: "No matter how he had begun his career, the leader of a mafia group was no longer a bandit, an outlaw. Indeed, he portrayed himself as a man of law and order and paid formal respect to state authority" (Paoli 2003, 33).

Some local leaders such as Akhmetov understood the need to evolve from ties with criminal figures (known as a vor v zakone [thief in law]), such as Akhat Bragin, into legitimate business players, but this never ended their willingness to accept insider deals that increased their business empires. Their rapacious greed was never satisfied. Hans van Zon writes: "Yanukovych, Akhmetov and Kolesnikov (Akhmetov's associate and close friend) put an end to uncontrolled criminal activities and restored order. Restoring order, however, did not mean restoring rule of law; in Donetsk the law of the strongest reigned" (von Zon 2007, 383). Through to the Euromaidan, eighteen parliamentary deputies within the Party of Regions continued to have ties to organized crime.[26]

Allegations about Akhmetov's involvement with criminal groups are to be found in a 1999 Interior Ministry document on organized crime groups in the Donetsk region.[27] Zon writes that in the first half of the 1990s, Bragin, who was a well-known Donetsk businessperson and a criminal "authority," allegedly became Akhmetov's "mentor."[28] Photographic and video footage of Akhmetov and Bragin at the funeral of Oleksandr Krantz, a major Donetsk organized crime boss who was murdered in 1992, and at other events, was published after the Interior Ministry leaked them.[29] In October 1995, Bragin and six of his bodyguards were murdered in Donetsk Shakhtar football stadium by a bomb explosion, and, although Akhmetov usually accompanied Bragin everywhere, on that occasion he arrived suspiciously late, after the explosion, and subsequently inherited all of Bragin's assets.[30] Akhmetov also inherited the business assets of oligarch Yevhen Shcherban, who was assassinated a year later. Over the next two decades following Bragin's murder, Akhmetov became fabulously wealthy when Yanukovych provided political protection as Donetsk governor, prime minister, Party of Regions leader, and president. In Bloomberg's two hundred wealthiest people in the world, on the eve of the Euromaidan Akhmetov was ranked ninety-fifth, with a $11.4 billion net worth.[31]

There were two attempts to destroy ties between organized crime and politics. Crimea Autonomous Republic minister of interior Hennadiy Moskal from 1996 to 2000 undertook the first attempt. In 2005 and 2007–10, when Yuriy Lutsenko led Ukraine's Interior Ministry, similar attempts were made to break up the national nexus between politics and organized crime. When the Party of Regions was in power in 2006–7 and during Yanukovych's presidency, the criminal world felt greater freedom to emerge from the shadows and flex its muscles. In 2006–7, the U.S. embassy reported from Kyiv that "organized crime feels that there will be no follow up from the government."[32] In 2010, soon after Yanukovych came to power, Givi Nemsadze, head of the bloodiest organized crime gang in Ukraine, which was active in the Donetsk region in the 1990s and responsible for fifty-seven murders (including destroying the Kushnir criminal gang), was rehabilitated by the prosecutor-general's office.[33]

In 2006, the new alliance forged between the Party of Regions and Crimean Russian nationalists facilitated the ability of organized crime leaders to emerge from the shadows and their decade-long marginalization and to re-enter local and national politics.[34] In spring 2014, organized crime leaders such as Sergei Aksyonov (criminal name "Goblin") were installed as Russia's puppet leaders in the annexed Crimea. Mark Galeotti noted that "Aksyonov, head of the Russian Unity party, seemed an ideal choice as a Kremlin figurehead. Even though he had been elected to the regional parliament in 2010 with just 4 percent of the vote, he was ambitious, ruthless, and closely connected with Crimean parliament speaker Vladimir Konstantinov, perhaps the pivotal powerbroker on the peninsula then and now."[35] The "unidentified thugs in mismatched fatigues and red armbands" of the so-called Crimean self-defense forces were in fact "the foot soldiers of the peninsula's crime gangs, including Bashmaki and the descendants of Salem, who had temporarily put their rivalries aside to pull Crimea out of Ukraine."[36]

Does Deoligarchization Mean the End for Oligarchs?

Skepticism about deoligarchization rests on past weak presidential and government performance, where rhetoric trumped action and Poroshenko's status as an oligarch himself. His campaign promise to sell his own business has not been fulfilled. Poroshenko has flip-flopped between the Party of Regions, as one of its founding leaders in 2000, and national democratic parties. However, he is clearly more at home with the moderate centrist parties of the 1990s than the authoritarian, kleptocratic, and violent Party of Regions. He has always feared and strongly opposed Tymoshenko. Since September 2003, Poroshenko's Channel 5 has traditionally provided balanced coverage of Ukrainian politics. Nevertheless, the obstacles to deoligarchization are formidable in and of themselves and the chances of its success are made worse by Poroshenko's long-standing ties to oligarchs. The arrest of oligarchs might not be welcomed in the West, as seen in criticism of the imprisonment of Russian oligarch Mikhail Khodorokovsky. The nationalization of oligarch assets, which Prime Minister Tymoshenko backed in 2005, was heavily criticized as "populism" by Yushchenko and Poroshenko, then secretary of the National Security and Defence Council, and in the West. What parameters should therefore deoligarchization consist of if criminal charges against oligarchs and renationalization of their assets are taken off the agenda?

Deoligarchization will be meaningless without challenging the biggest monopolist in Ukraine, Akhmetov. His future following the fall of his long-time business and political ally Yanukovych is unclear, as he entered parliament only when he felt threatened—as in 2006 and 2007—to receive immunity from prosecution and therefore did not stand for parliament in 2012 when his patron, Yanukovych, was president. Political protection by Yanukovych came at a price, and Leshchenko's investigations found that the former president owned approximately half of the enormous assets accumulated by Akhmetov.[37]

The Party of Regions will never be revived in its former form, and the recently formed Opposition Bloc pales in comparison. The end of the Party of Regions and KPU's monopolization of eastern and southern Ukraine has opened up a political vacuum that will, over time, return to the centrist pluralism of the 1990s. In the short term, as illustrated in the October 2015 local elections, the Opposition Bloc will capitalize on local populist discontent over economic dislocation blamed on the government and the Donbas conflict.

With Ukrainian criminal charges against Yanukovych and his entourage and international sanctions against their assets, "The Family" is in retreat, but it also remains unclear how their assets will be recovered. These assets were estimated to be $130 million, ranking them sixty-fourth among Ukraine's one hundred wealthiest Ukrainians and business groups.[38] In 2011, after purchasing the All-Ukrainian Bank for Development, Oleksandr Yanukovych entered the list of the top one hundred wealthiest Ukrainians. In 2012 he doubled his wealth from $99 to $187 million (his company's shares increased from 505.5 million to 970 million hryvnya) and occupied fifty-ninth place in Ukraine's top one hundred wealthiest.[39] Serhiy Kurchenko, who emerged from nowhere in 2011, also began to expand his business empires as a front for "The Family." Criminal charges were instituted (but not completed) against Oleksandr Yanukovych and Kurchenko by the post-Euromaidan government.

Escaping the Partial Reform Equilibrium and the Crossroads

The 2014 parliamentary elections produced for the first time a pro-European constitutional majority that cooperates with President Poroshenko, who was elected on a pro-European platform. Presidential and government policies that will encourage reforms can now operate under the country's natural "pluralism by default" (a product of regional diversity) that existed under Ukraine's first three presidents and clashed with the monopolistic tendencies of the Yanukovych administration and Party of Regions (Levitsky and Way 2002). The key to Ukraine breaking free of the partial reform equilibrium and entering the path of European integration is the political will to demonopolize Ukraine's economy, politics, and media by reducing the power of the oligarchs and separating business and politics. How to reduce the power of the oligarchs remains elusive if imprisonment and renationalization are taken off the table and as long as banks, real estate, think tanks, and political consultants and foundations in Europe and the United States continue to accept funds from oligarchic groups.

Much of the work to take on Ukraine's oligarchs rests at the national level and should be undertaken by President Poroshenko and Prime Minister Yatsenyuk. But an important focus has to be also on reaching out to the population in Ukraine's east and south, where there are two Russian-speaking Ukraines after the Euromaidan and Russia's aggression. The first is a civil society extension of the Euromaidan that has produced volunteer patriots fighting on the front line and volunteer groups providing support to them and internally displaced persons. The majority of the volunteer groups collecting assistance for the military and National Guard are women activists. The growth of civic and military volunteerism is reflected in the eastward spread of the anti-Soviet identity of the Euromaidan; eight hundred monuments to Soviet leader Vladimir Lenin have been removed. A process of de-Sovietization that began with the removal of Lenin monuments in Lviv on the cusp of the disintegration of the USSR has spread to Russophone Ukraine a quarter of a century later.

Supporters of the Party of Regions and KPU who have traditionally prioritized standards of living and "stability" over democratization and Europe also represent a large constituency in Russophone Ukraine. Economic and financial crises will turn many of them away from the government's reforms. These voters represent the constituency of the Opposition Bloc that continues to pursue paternalistic neopatrimonial policies and antireform populism enabling the party to win votes in 2014 and 2015. In big factory towns like Mariupol, large groups of workers can be cajoled into voting for oligarch-controlled counter-revolutionary forces threatened by reforms and Europeanization. Poroshenko's reliance in eastern and southern Ukraine on local political and economic vestiges of the Yanukovych regime will not lead to the changes and reforms demanded on the Euromaidan; the president should be instead supporting reformers and new political leaders who will not continue to pursue established criminalized and corrupt business ways. The importance of change has to mean President Poroshenko demonstratively showing to oligarchs and old cronies from the Yanukovych era that it is no longer "business as usual." If he fails to do this, the policy of "deoligarchization" will be simply empty rhetoric.

A more difficult external environment than that following the Orange Revolution compounds domestic obstacles to reform. Russia, through the use of military, economic, and trade pressure, seeks the failure of Ukraine's European integration. But Russia is not the only obstacle on Ukraine's path to Europe. Unlike postcommunist central Europe, the EU is requiring Ukraine to undertake deep structural reforms within the Association Agreement and DCFTA (Deep and Comprehensive Free Trade Agreement) without the inducement of a membership perspective and with far less financial support.[40] In the short term, Ukraine will have to spend a huge amount of resources to adapt to European standards while losing trade with Russia following that country's annexation of the Crimea and aggression in the Donbas, which accounted for 16 percent of GDP, 25 percent of industrial production, and a quarter of Ukraine's exports in 2013 on the eve of the Ukraine-Russia crisis. In central Europe, populist backlash against reforms led to the election of leftist governments that nevertheless remained in support of NATO and EU membership. Populist backlash in Ukraine would come from anti-European, counter-revolutionary forces ensconced in the east and south who would look to Russia as a savior.

President Poroshenko's deoligarchization campaign will fail if it does not destroy the power of Ukraine's most powerful oligarchs, particularly the two groups (Akhmetov and the gas lobby) that finance the pro-Russian Opposition Bloc. The Yatsenyuk government is moving against Firtash's Ostchem, but this is too little and has received tepid support from Poroshenko. President Poroshenko has two choices that would impact the success of Ukraine's reforms. The first would be to honor the agreement that he and Klitschko reached with Firtash in Vienna, thereby permitting revenge down the road by pro-Russian counter-revolutionary forces. This option would become a replay of Yushchenko's cooperation with the gas lobby in which he sought grand coalitions with the Party of Regions that facilitated Yanukovych's comeback in 2010 and counter-revolution during his presidency. Alternatively, Poroshenko can target Akhmetov and the gas lobby in his deoligarchization campaign and in so doing reduce the power and influence of the most powerful pro-Russian groups in Ukraine. This second scenario would have the added benefit of assisting the United States, Ukraine's most important strategic partner, in its attempt to have Firtash deported from Austria.

Putin was surprised at the toughness and patriotism of Ukraine's soldiers and volunteers who defeated his "Novorossiya" (New Russia) project for eastern and southern Ukraine. It is incumbent upon Poroshenko to show the same determination as his Ukrainian citizens have shown in the Euromaidan and on the front line by defeating the threat posed to Ukraine's European integration by the country's oligarchs. Without the de-monopolization of oligarchic political, media, and economic influence Ukraine will be unable to move from its partial reform equilibrium and enter the path of European integration.

Economic growth can only be unlocked through reforms designed to demonopolize economic life and lessen the stranglehold on the economy by big business through expanding the small and medium business sector and reducing the size of the shadow economy to levels found in southern Europe. At a time of economic and financial near-bankruptcy, the Euromaidan leadership introduced stabilization policies that cannot be avoided, and these will be followed by unpopular structural reforms in pensions, utility prices, and the downsizing of overmanned state institutions that will generate unemployment. Other reforms in human rights, law enforcement, and fighting high-level corruption will be popular. Structural reforms, which have eluded all Ukrainian governments, should move Ukraine beyond the current partial reform equilibrium and toward a consolidated democracy, efficient state institutions with greater public trust, and a market economy not captured by big business tycoons.

If Ukraine fails to break through a second time, the country will remain politically unstable and weak, leaving it at the mercy of an imperialistic Russia. Large segments of the population, particularly active and energized representatives of civil society, the middle class, Ukrainian patriots, and nationalists, carried out two revolutions against oligarchic capture of the state in 2004 and 2013-4. The Orange Revolution failed to change Ukraine, facilitating the rise of a counter-revolution and a second revolution. Only a successful breakout from the partial reform equilibrium that removes oligarchic capture of the state and places Ukraine on the path toward European integration will prevent a third cycle of public disillusionment, stagnation, counter-revolution, and revolution from taking place.

The Association Agreement and DCFTA will promote all-round reforms in Ukraine, but they will be difficult to implement without a membership perspective and large financial resources. A failure to launch breakthrough reforms and deoligarchization would not merely consign Ukraine to remaining stuck at the crossroads, as under Yushchenko, but with Russia seeking the failure of the Euromaidan, would represent an existential threat to the very sovereignty of the Ukrainian state. The stakes are high for Ukraine, and downsizing the ambitions and rapacious greed of Ukraine's oligarchs is central to the success of reforms, European integration, and ending cycles of revolution and counter-revolution.

Notes

1. Interview with Yuriy Lutsenko, Kyiv, November 1, 2013.

2. See the size of the shadow economies in OECD countries at http://www.proget-toitaliafederale.it/docs/ForthcomingPFPC_final_version_08_07.pdf.

3. On Ukraine's gas lobby, see Kuzio 2015b, 394–408.

4. Taras Kuzio, "Dmytro Firtash Launches New Opaque Gas Intermediary," *Eurasia Daily Monitor* 10 (55), March 25, 2013. See http://www.jamestown.org/single/?tx_ttnews%5Btt_news%5D=40641#.VZrc-xNViko.

5. Stephen Grey, Tom Bergin, Sevgil Musaieva, and Roman Anin, "SPECIAL REPORT—Putin's Allies Channeled Billions to Ukraine Oligarch," *Reuters*, November 26, 2014. See http://www.reuters.com/article/2014/11/26/russia-capitalism-gas-special-report-pix-idUSL3N0TF4QD20141126.

6. "SPECIAL REPORT—Putin's Allies Channeled Billions to Ukraine Oligarch."

7. Johannes Wamberg Andersen, "Firtash Claim Kingmaker Role in Ukrainian Politics," *Kyiv Post*, May 7, 2015. See http://www.kyivpost.com/content/ukraine/firtash-claims-kingmaker-role-in-ukrainian-politics-388070.html.

8. "Oleksandr G. Yakimenko." See http://politrada.com/dossier/persone/id/4242.

9. Anders Aslund, "All Power to 'The Family,'" *Kyiv Post*, March 27, 2012. See http://www.kyivpost.com/opinion/op-ed/all-power-to-the-family-124996.html; and Wojciech Kononczuk and Arkadiusz Sarna, "The Presidential 'Family' in Ukraine Is Developing Its Business Base," Centre for Eastern Studies, June 26, 2013. See http://www.osw.waw.pl/en/publikacje/eastweek/2013-06-26/presidential-family-ukraine-developing-its-business-base.

10. S. Leshchenko, "Yakshcho Akhmetov ne zupynyt Yanukovycha, to rozdilyt vidpovidalnist iz nym," *Ukrayinska Pravda blog*, December 3, 2013. See http://blogs.pravda.com.ua/authors/leschenko/529e2f5be32c1/.

11. A detailed review of election fraud methods can be found in the special issue on parliamentary democracy and the 2012 parliamentary elections of *Natsionalna Bezpeka i Oborona*, nos. 7–8, 2012, pp. 76–77. See http://www.razumkov.org.ua/ukr/journal.php?y=2012&cat=177.

12. On corporate raiding, see Valeria Burlakova, "No Holds Barred," *Ukrainian Week*, July 19, 2013. See http://ukrainianweek.com/Society/85012. On earlier uses of violence, see Kuzio 2010, 383–95.

13. The "suicides" and murders were of Oleh Kalashnikov, Oleksandr Bordyukh, Serhiy Melnychuk, Stanislav Melnyk, Oleksandr Peklushenko, Mykhaylo Chechetov, Oleksiy Kolesnik, Mykola Serhiyenko, and Serhiy Valter.

14. Maxim Tucker, "Ukraine's Old Guard and the Mystery of a Series of Unlikely Suicides," *Newsweek*, April 8, 2015. See http://www.newsweek.com/2015/04/17/ukraine-plagued-succession-unlikely-suicides-former-ruling-party-320584.html.

15. "Ukraine: Cabinet of Ministers Approves PSA—Signing to Follow Oct 8," U.S. Embassy Kyiv, October 2, 2007. See http://wikileaks.org/cable/2007/10/07KYIV2505.html#.

16. See http://dtek.com/en/home.

17. "Ukraine: Vanco Case Sent to Constitutional Court, Neither Side Backing Down," U.S. Embassy Kyiv, June 23, 2008. See http://wikileaks.org/cable/2008/06/08KYIV1219.html#.

18. The FBI accused Mogilevych and his associates of laundering $10 billion through the Bank of New York, stealing $1.2 billion in World Bank loans, and being behind a $150 million scam on the Toronto Stock Exchange. See http://www.fbi.gov/wanted/topten/semion-mogilevich/view/; http://www.fbi.gov/wanted/cei/igor-lvovich-fisherman.

19. These quotations are available on the tapes produced by presidential guard Mykola Melnychenko and cited by Koshiw 2013, 62–65.

20. Firtash also recounted how Itera head Igor Makarov invited him to dinner in Kyiv in January 2002, after he established Eural Trans Gas to replace Itera. Makarov attended with his head of security, Mogilevych, Sergei Mikhas from the "*Solnstevo* Brotherhood," and a "Mr. Overin." Cited from "Ukraine: Firtash Makes His Case to the USG," U.S. Embassy Kyiv, December 10, 2008. See http://wikileaks.org/cable/2008/12/08KYIV2414.html.

21. "Ukraine: Firtash Makes His Case to the USG."

22. Steven Wagstyl and Tom Warner, "Firtash Considers LSE Listing for Rosukrenergo," *Financial Times*, April 28, 2006. See http://www.ft.com/intl/cms/s/0/7fcde8b0-d652-11da-8b3a-0000779e2340.html.

23. See interviews with Firtash in *Fokus* and *Vedomosti* at http://www.epravda.com.ua/news/2008/01/28/157119/ and http://focus.ua/politics/159734/. At the same time, Firtash's personal website (http://groupdf.com/en/about/history) writes that in 2002, "Eural TransGas Kft, a company founded by Dmitry Firtash, secured exclusive contracts to supply Turkmen gas to Ukraine," and in 2004, "RosUkrEnergo AG joint company (was) established by Dmitry Firtash and Gazprom (Russia)."

24. In postwar Donetsk, one in ten residents was imprisoned in prisons or colonies, and the region held three times the number of inmates as those institutions had been constructed to hold. The largest numbers of criminal prosecutions in Soviet Ukraine were in Stalino (Donetsk) and Voroshilovohrad (Luhansk) oblasts, accounting for a third of all criminal prosecutions in Soviet Ukraine (Kuromiya 1998).

25. Serhiy Kuzin, "Aktualni spravy mynulykh dniv," *Dzerkalo Tyzhnya*, April 6, 2012. See http://gazeta.dt.ua/POLITICS/aktualni_spravi_minulih_dniv.html. See table with names of the Kushnir gang members in (Koshiw 2013, 208).

26. Interview with first deputy head of the Parliamentary Committee on Fighting Organized Crime and Corruption, Hennadiy Moskal, by *Ukrayinska Pravda*, March 21, 2013. See http://www.pravda.com.ua/articles/2013/03/21/6986155/.

27. A September 1999 report by the Interior Ministry Directorate on Combating Organized Crime entitled "Overview of the Most Dangerous Organized Crime Structures in Ukraine" lists seven groups in Donetsk Oblast. The report alleges that the "Renit" organized group "dealt with money laundering and financial fraud, and controlled a large number of both real and fictitious companies. It goes by the name Lyuksovska hrupa." Underneath the report is written: "The leader is Akhmetov, Rinat Leonidovych born in 1966, who lives at 16 Udarnyy Street, Donetsk." Twice, former interior minister Yuriy Lutsenko confirmed in an interview conducted with this author on November 1, 2013, in Kyiv that the document is authentic. See http://reportingproject.net/new/RE-PORTS/Document%20about%20Donetsk%20crime%20group.pdf.

28. See von Zon 2007, 382. See also Roman Kupchinsky, "The Clan from Donetsk," *RFERL Poland, Belarus and Ukraine Report*, November 26 and December 10, 2002. See http://www.rferl.org/content/article/1344102.html and http://www.rferl.org/content/article/1344104.html.

29. The photograph has been published in many publications, and a copy can be viewed at http://blogs.pravda.com.ua/authors/chornovol/5106584eed6da/. Sławomir Matuszak writes that "[l]inks between Akhmetov and Brahin were documented in the operational evidence of the Ministry of Internal Affairs," and he provides a link to a video at http://www.youtube.com/watch?v=dA29BDRfCEA (Matuszak 2012, 88).

30. Taras Kuzio, "Murder and Selective Use of Justice in Ukraine (Part Two)," *Eurasia Daily Monitor* 10 (44), March 8, 2013. See http://www.jamestown.org/single/?no_cache=1&tx_ttnews[tt_news]=40578#.UoQ4JrT3Opo.

31. See http://www.bloomberg.com/billionaires/2014-03-03/cya. These eighteen deputies included Elbrus Tedeyev, Nurulislam Arkallayev, Yuriy Ivanyushchenko, and Yuriy Chertkov. On their background in the 1990s, see http://censor.net.ua/resonance/203607/vendetta_kto_ubil_scherbanya.

32. "Ukraine: Engaging Yanukovych, the Man of the Moment," U.S. Embassy Kyiv, November 20, 2006. See http://wikileaks.org/cable/2006/11/06KYIV4313.html.

33. See Lutsenko's speech to the court (http://www.unian.ua/politics/605142-lutsenko-moya-sprava-prirechena-na-vipravdalniy-virok-tekst-vistupu-u-sudi.html) and Serhiy Sydorenko and Olha Kurishko, "Vspomnil vse. Yuriy Lutsenko rasskazal sudu o svoyikh delakh," *Komersant Ukraina*, February 7, 2012. See http://kommersant.ua/doc/1867436. Nemsadze was released from criminal liability by First Deputy Prosecutor Rinat Kuzmin, claiming that there was a mix-up because it had been his deceased brother Guram who had led the organized crime gang, not Givi. Investigative journalist and Popular Front deputy Tatyana Chornovol believes that Kuzmin covered up Nemadze's crimes. *Ukrayinska Pravda blog*, August 5, 2013. See http://blogs.pravda.com.ua/authors/chornovol/51ff5c67acbaa/.

34. On this question, see T. Kuzio, "Yanukovych Provides a Krysha for Organized

Crime," *Eurasia Daily Monitor* 9 (34), February 17, 2012. See http://www.jamestown.org/single/?no_cache=1&tx_ttnews[tt_news]=39024#.UoQ7EbT3Opo.

35. Mark Galeotti, "Crime and Crimea: Criminals as Allies and Agents," *RFERL*, November 3, 2014. See http://www.rferl.org/content/crimea-crime-criminals-as-agents-allies/26671923.html.

36. Galeotti, "Crime and Crimea."

37. Oleksandr Kurilenko, "'Akhmetov otrimav naibil'she koristi vid rephimu Yanukovicha' Leshchenko," gazeta.ua, February 23, 2014. See http://gazeta.ua/articles/politics/_ahmetov-otrimav-najbilshe-koristi-vid-rezhimu-anukovicha-leschenko/543759.

38. *Korrespondent*, November 11, 2011.

39. "Kholding sina Yaukovicha zbil'shiv aktivi maizhe vdvichi," July 9, 2013. See http://www.pravda.com.ua/news/2013/07/9/6993901/.

40. "Slipping away from the West," *Economist*, May 21, 2015. See http://www.economist.com/blogs/freeexchange/2015/05/ukraine.

11

Missing the China Exit:
A World-systems Perspective
on the Ukrainian State

Georgi Derluguian

An accountable understanding of Ukraine's present travails and prospects must combine detailed country expertise with the larger geopolitical and geo-economic context. Let us sharpen our analysis by asking why the postcommunist Ukraine did not follow the Chinese path to export-oriented market success? The question is far from merely a mental exercise in paradoxes. Ukraine is obviously not China, yet social philosophers warn us that "obvious" typically serves to conceal something important from our gaze. The People's Republic of China since 1989 subverts the cliché of communist collapse (Dimitrov 2013; Saxonberg 2013). An economically ascendant path from communism was also possible. The human rights record of the Chinese authorities and their notorious corruption did not abort such a different outcome. Moreover, if science and education were really the driving force of twenty-first century economic growth, then who should be surging ahead, China or Ukraine?

The unsurprising answers can be identified at the outset. Institutions, of course, make China a successful developmental state (Heilmann and Perry 2011). A different set of institutions rendered post-Soviet Ukraine a poorly consolidated or competitive authoritarian state incapable of fostering economic growth and remarkably susceptible to revolutions (Levitsky and Way 2010). Comparative institutional morphology, however, operates with static "skeletal" descriptions, only peeling away one layer of causality while leaving many more unaddressed. A better explanation has to be simultaneously evolutionary and environmental. Put differently, who fashioned the institutions and on what motivations or constraints did they act? This perspective reveals how Ukraine's problems of predatory elites and frustrated economic development are in fact symptoms of forces that are much larger than Ukraine itself, forces that can be overcome but only by determined elite cooperation that is historically rare. The events of 2014, as traumatic as they have been, could perhaps provide Ukrainian elites with the incentive they need to forge a more China-like developmental state, though it is far from clear now that such an outcome is emerging.

How World-systems Theory Predicted Ukraine's Predicament

We might mesh two kinds of theoretical insight. In the new generation of macrohistorical sociologists, Richard Lachmann achieved a nuanced theory of the original capitalist breakthroughs in the early modern West (Lachmann 2000). It allows tracing in detail how, across the entire European continent during the pivotal "long sixteenth century" (ca 1450 to 1650), a variety of institutional taxonomies had emerged from the contingent conflicts and alliances among elite fractions populating the upper echelons in the overlapping yet noncongruous networks of social power (economic, ideological, military, and political). This theory fills important gaps in the original formulations of Immanuel Wallerstein (2011 [1974]) by explaining which areas of Early Modern Europe became core in the nascent capitalist world economy and which areas drifted into its periphery. Lachmann builds directly on the Marxian and Weberian traditions and the theoretical breakthroughs made during the 1970s in the understanding of historical transitions from feudalism to capitalism (Mann 1993; Collins 1999). Importantly for our concerns, Lachmann's theory finds independent validation in the growing body of research on the contemporary developmental states in the former Third World (Chibber 2003; Evans 1995; Kohli 2004). Studying the postcolonial states in Southeast Asia, the political scientist Dan Slater arrives at a remarkably similar conclusion: the differential in state power directly relates to the institutionalization of the collective action problem among elites (Slater 2010).

The second insight only slightly paraphrases the famous aphorism of Karl Marx from the *Eighteenth Brumaire*: elites make their own history, but they do not make it as they please. In the modern world system elites are found at different tiers in the global division of labor. Capitalism introduced an unprecedented degree of dynamism, and yet its global economic hierarchy has remained astonishingly stable for more than two centuries after the Industrial Revolution in the West (Allen 2011). All countries in the original core remain at the top while the dependent countries stayed in the world's periphery. This situation began visibly changing in the 1970s with the tremendous economic ascendancy of East Asia. The advance of more than a billion people from impoverished periphery presented a major challenge to the world-systems school. The challenge was taken by Giovanni Arrighi, whose formulations regarding communist China could be extended also to explain the counterexample of post-Soviet Ukraine (Arrighi 2007). The ultimate test of theory explaining postcommunism must be its ability to explain with the same set of theoretical propositions the divergent trajectories of former Soviet Bloc countries *and* China after 1989.

Two striking predictions were made at the time when Ukraine was still a Soviet republic. In July 1991 Arrighi, Terence Hopkins, and Wallerstein warned that the "improbable embrace of market economization by the revolutionaries in Eastern Europe would surely bring their region closer to America, though not the promised shores of North America but rather to the harsher realities of South America" (Arrighi, Hopkins, and Wallerstein 1992). The three founders of the world-systems school, however, did not detail in their polemic the social mechanisms and forces bound to result in such misdirection of the political compass. An elaboration might be gleaned in another prediction made by Peter Evans. Writing still earlier in 1988, Evans was not discussing the "second world," which had yet to become postcommunist. He was rather contrasting the extremes of Mobutu's predatory regime in Zaïre to the paragon of the developmental state found in Japan, South Korea, and Taiwan, with Brazil posited as intermediate example. Yet in retrospect Evans's warning sounds almost prophetic: "Intermediate state apparatuses are most vulnerable to the negative consequences of neoutilitarian policies. Stringent cuts in real wages and the reduction of resources for training of personnel will undermine the 'islands of efficiency' that still exist in these bureaucracies, undercutting any possibility of moving in the direction of becoming developmental states and pushing those who remain trapped in bureaucracy to become predators" (Evans 1989, 583).

Let us see how these predictions may relate to the political economy of independent Ukraine. We should be especially puzzled by the simultaneously liberal and nationalist conversions of Ukrainian politicians in 1989, both the incumbent nomenklatura and their social movement challengers. It is not so wonderful that former communists suddenly woke up to the calls of Free Ukraine and free markets; it should look far more puzzling that the former totalitarian bureaucrats could at all suddenly adopt the neoutilitarian policies of shrinking their own superpower state and breaking it along the nationalist lines, too. But what exactly drove Deng Xiao-ping in Beijing and his comrades in Kyiv to such different ends in their pursuits of political survival? Contrasting the chaotic post-Soviet transitions to the market prowess of East Asian communists could be analytically more useful than the standard comparisons of Ukraine with a highly stylized example of the West.

The Soviet Origins of Ukrainian State Institutions

Ukraine achieved the status of nation-state in 1991 much like the majority of new nation-states over the last two centuries: by upgrading from the previous status of imperial province (Roeder 2007). Different regions of Ukraine, however, had been historically provinces of quite different empires. The Ottoman Muslim legacy endures mainly in the Crimean Tatar population despite the recurrent waves of deportations since the Russian annexation in the eighteenth century. The Austrian imperial state left a deeper and larger imprint in the western regions of Ukraine (Darden and Grzymala-Busse 2006; Peisakhin 2012). In the wake of the twentieth century's world wars this area experienced one of the last great peasant revolts on the European continent. As in many such eruptions of popular furies and eschatological expectations, the revolt of the western Ukrainian peasantry and their largely rural intelligentsia fused the social and ethnic targets to produce a militant variety of nationalism that even Soviet totalitarianism could not eradicate (Wolf 1999 [ca.1969]). Yet for the same reason of being deeply rooted in informal institutions and families, western Ukrainian nationalism remained largely limited to its regional and diaspora bases.

The present-day Ukrainian state is entirely a legacy of Russian and Soviet empires. The Russian empire in the twentieth century experienced two cataclysmic bouts of state building directly associated with world wars. The historian Peter Holquist documented how the period between 1914 and 1921 generated state institutions, organizational ideologies and practices, as well as the very personnel for total mobilization (Holquist 2002). The new revolutionary state expelled or violently obliterated the old regime elites and instead imposed in the 1920s a new vanguard for the transformative project of high modernism (Scott 1998). As we know, the Bolsheviks failed to stop there. Their postrevolutionary factionalism in the face of mounting domestic dilemmas and the typically revolutionary scare/expectation of external attack drew the Bolsheviks into a second mad bout of state building. The Bolsheviks have by far surpassed their French Jacobin forerunners (Goldstone 2014). The decade of the 1930s witnessed in the USSR both human miseries and material growth on scales unseen in the previous Western industrializations (Allen 2003). It also produced a revolutionary imperialism and ideological cult surpassing Napoleon Bonaparte himself (Derluguian 2013).

In the seminal phrase of Stephen Hanson, the Soviet state became a charismatic bureaucracy (Hanson 1997). But what does this mean in the more mundane terms of organizational sociology? And how would such a "charismatic bureaucracy" fare in successor generations? The fundamental reality of the Soviet state was that its planning apparatus modeled on the German war economy became deliberately fused with the ideological apparatus transmitting commands and exerting top-down pressures to violate routine planning for the sake of impossible extra-achievements (Woodruff 1999). A typical bureaucratic counterstrategy, amply apparent already in the 1930s, was dissimulation and evasion through the patronage networks of *kumovstvo* (mutual obligations) and *mestnichestvo* (office patriotism) (Kotkin 1995; Rigby 1990; Urban 1989). Moscow countered these tendencies with ideological campaigns and revolutionary terror whose apparatus and personnel had originated in the 1914–21 warfare. Earlier in the French Revolution, as well as in many later revolutions, terror tended to assume a self-propellant and rather chaotic dynamic. What seems now the empirically established ability of Stalin to unleash, direct, and eventually end his terror campaigns must also be recognized as a sign of remarkable state strength rarely seen in revolutionary dictatorships (Khlevniuk 2008). Or, as the Russian sociologist of religion Dmitry Furman put it, beginning as catacomb Christian, Stalin lived to become Great Inquisitor and then his own Renaissance Pope, too (Furman 1989). Once again, this is a powerfully evocative metaphor. What forces drove the evolution of Stalinism?

In 1941 this unprecedented state survived, if very clumsily, the horrific shock of Nazi invasion still reliant on totalitarian means. Yet later in 1942 Stalin had to begin relaxing and dismantling his own totalitarian controls. The protracted industrial warfare on a massive scale required a degree of self-organizing across the state structures of command (Tooze 2007). In the process Soviet military commanders and economic managers inevitably acquired the skills and taste for more autonomy to act and enjoy their newly accrued power along with its privileges. After 1945 Stalin would try to take back the powers given to his elites in the moment of existential emergency. His lashing out at elite individuals and networks could be still murderous, yet it was ultimately futile. The long historical transition to the present had started perhaps as early as the 1940s.

In 1953, with the death of the revolutionary emperor, the Soviet nomenklatura rushed to dismantle totalitarianism because it represented a direct physical threat to their own lives and because it became too much of a burden. But what would now stiffen the huge centralized state and drive it toward the new historical goals? And what now were these goals anyway? The answers were never found. In the 1964 elite coup toppling the rambunctious Nikita Khrushchev, sealed after the great scare of the 1968 popular democratic revolts (the Prague Spring above all), the Soviet regime chose the comforts of bureaucratic inertia devoid of any charisma. Bureaucratic pathologies bloomed though still checked by the requirements of superpower confrontation and the deeply felt fear of popular uprisings, a suppressed yet ever-present reality of life in the Soviet Bloc.

The Soviet empire became essentially rudderless. A command economy must have its supreme commander. Yet the elite compact of the Brezhnev decades was based on no longer having a supremo of any sort. The Soviet power dissipated into the bureaucratic oligarchies embedded in powerful territorial offices (national republics and key provinces) dating back to the 1920s and the gigantic economic ministries inherited from the 1930s (Bunce 1998). This institutional configuration was disastrously unsettled by the desperate improvisations of Gorbachev's perestroika (Zubok 2007). The central fact of national republics and giant economic ministries in the main shaped the pattern of Soviet collapse along the nomenklatura lines of national and industrial jurisdictions (Derluguian 2005).

How Ukrainian Institutions Came into the Service of Neoliberal Ideas

Peter Evans perhaps never intended to explain the USSR, yet his dynamic theory of the life cycle of developmental states seems eminently applicable here (Evans 1995). The USSR, after all, was the original and longest-lasting developmental state of the twentieth century. According to Evans, mature developmental states acquire three distinct pressures toward dismantling their dictatorial political economies:

> Big economic interests whose bosses seek to free themselves from central
> dictates, normalize their elite status and property rights down to fam-

ily inheritance, and cash in on their oligarchic positions. Privatization would be their main agenda.

Workers who find themselves in a better position for collective bargaining, whether through labor unions or forging informal shopfloor mutual understandings, especially once the demographic pools of rural labor and women become scarce. The worker agenda is typically trade-unionist.

Educated specialists and professionals demanding to transform political structures to reflect their increased importance in running the industrial economy and society. The typical demands of specialists and intelligentsia are cosmopolitan and democratic.

We can see all three forces coalescing across the Soviet Bloc countries, especially those that had been most affected by industrial modernization during the impressively activist and generally optimistic period between 1956 and 1968. In the following two decades of "stagnation," Soviet political leaders sought to keep in check the three subversive vectors. The renewed stability everywhere, even in post-1968 Czechoslovakia, relied on only some degree of repression that looked very restrained by the totalitarian measure of the 1930s or even the 1950s. The main supports of post-1968 stabilization were détente in the Cold War and the steadily increasing popular consumption subsidized by the Soviet windfall of petrodollars after 1973 (Suri 2007). The balancing act of Brezhnev's reign, logically, had to pursue the triple goal of restraining the self-serving tendencies within the nomenklatura while preventing the "liberal-labor coalition" of intelligentsia and workers. In the medium run the strategy of avoiding democratization proved successful. Its longer-term costs, however, proved horrendous in terms of state finances, effectiveness, and work ethics. The official ideology of the geopolitical superpower, along with the daily-life embrace of Philistinism, completely replaced the original Bolshevik eschatology of world revolution and even the goals of modernization. The stalemated arms race against the much wealthier America and the upkeep of a growing circle of "Third World" clients then added another unbearable cost to the dilemma of late Soviet power.

Perestroika in this perspective appears as a bold, but also quite conservative, attempt to shed geopolitical and ideological burdens while preserving at least the more "progressive" junior nomenklatura as a power elite by recasting them as state capitalist technocrats. This is what Isaac Deutcher had predicted decades earlier (Deutscher 1953). (In world history, good predictions might wait that long to be realized.) Essentially, Gorbachev gambled on trading the Soviet superpower position for honorable inclusion in the West European capitalist networks. Until 1989 Gorbachev's new agenda of building a "common European home" could be judged remarkably successful. The Soviet leader seemed then on his way to becoming also a world capitalist leader and leaving behind the excessively ideological Chinese comrades. The downfall of the last general secretary came from where few observers could have expected it—namely, the failure of central control over elites and domestic institutions in an ostensibly totalitarian state.

The nascent "civil societies" of dissidents and intelligentsias in the republic capitals did not destroy the USSR, and this was because they could not, at least not on their own (Kotkin 2008). Nor could the cause be the much celebrated yet nebulous "power of ideas" on its own. Nevertheless we must take seriously the political opportunities created by shifts in ideological fields. The rapid conversion of the 1989 East European revolutions to neoliberal and nationalist creeds followed a historically familiar pattern of ideological polarization at peak moments in revolutionary sequences. As in all such historical moments fraught with tensions, uncertainty, and emotional energy, new ideas can quickly gain mass followings, especially if presented in a drastically stripped down form and in the moralistic tenor of absolute good versus absolute evil. The ideological message of neoliberal economic theory came loaded with moralistic connotations right at its source in the political struggles gripping the West in the wake of the 1968 moralistic challenges of the New Left variety. Seen from this angle, the prodemocracy revolts of 1989 in the communist countries—and here we must always include China—were a continuation of global 1968. The question is, what social forces were involved in the 1989 wave of contention, and what social structures channeled the outcomes in such divergent directions?

Why China, Unlike Ukraine, Bucked Neoliberalism and Became a Developmental State

China baffles outsiders. It looks so ancient, big, and complex. And yet the Chinese communist state was in fact much simpler than the Soviet Union, and its economic miracle is not difficult to explain as a continental extension of what Bruce Cumings called the East Asian "capitalist archipelago" of Japan, Taiwan, South Korea, Hong Kong, and Singapore (Cumings 2005). Drawing from the specialist literatures on China, let us briefly reconstruct what seems the emerging scholarly consensus regarding the economic resurgence of East Asia (Wong 2000; Goldstone 2008; Allen 2011).

In spring 1989, a factional split at the top of the Chinese Communist Party provoked a student revolt in Beijing's Tiananmen Square (Calhoun 1997). The Tiananmen movement displayed the same strengths and weaknesses as contemporary antiauthoritarian movements in the Soviet Union or, for that matter, the Western New Left in 1968 and the Arab Spring of 2011. The protest delivered a huge charge of youthful emotional energy directed primarily at the senior conservatives in the country's leadership, who were in a rather generic manner presented as hypocritical and self-serving. The movement, however, lacked an extensive organization, short- and medium-run political goals, and robust connections to provincial towns, let alone the countryside. Still, Chinese party cadres had good reasons to close their ranks against the movement because the previous episode of upper-echelon factionalism provoking student militancy, the disastrous Cultural Revolution of the late 1960s, was very much in their memory. Perhaps more important, senior Chinese cadres at the time still belonged to the founding generations of armed struggle—much unlike Gorbachev and his comrades, who were three generations removed from the revolution and civil war. For leaders like Deng Xiaoping, the notion of power growing from a gun barrel evidently was not merely a metaphor (MacFarquhar 1997).

The suppression of the Tiananmen protests, however, came at a steep ideological cost. The activist students laid claim to the same ideals that legitimated the Communist Party itself. The leftist attack on a leftist regime produced a turn to the right even if nobody from the top ever dared to officially acknowledge it. In effect, 1989 marked the end of Chinese communism, too. The ruling CCP quietly put aside its dangerously double-sided ideology and shifted instead to what might be called performance-based legitimacy. It was, in fact, a well-known move in the repertoire of ruling communist regimes. As early as in 1921 the Russian Bolsheviks, ever mindful of past revolutionary precedents, had been coyly admitting that their market-driven New Economic Policy (NEP) meant, in the words of Nikolai Bukharin, the unavoidable phase of "self-Thermidorean" restoration. Or recall the once famous examples of the Titoist Yugoslavia and Kadarist Hungary in the 1960s and the 1970s that combined various market experiments with judiciously limited political repression. The uneventful reign of Leonid Brezhnev in the Soviet Union, in retrospect nostalgically remembered as the "good decades," in fact meant a conservative reaction to the boisterous and unsettling period of Khrushchev's Thaw. In the 1970s Soviet leaders, however, ended any talk of "market socialism" because the export earnings from oil and natural gas afforded them the transient luxury of a risk-free bureaucratic inertia.

Post-Maoist China, of course, had no oil to export. Instead, the CCP could base its latter-day NEP on the human ocean of poor but industrious peasants; provincial artisans with their centuries-long traditions of family and community enterprise; and, not least, on the market knowledge of the diaspora Chinese (Arrighi and Hamashita 2003). The political rationale for admitting market forces into the Chinese countryside and export zones seemed straightforward: to let the peasants feed themselves and the towns in order to drive a wedge between the urban educated liberalizers and common "people." By making this first defensive step, the Chinese communists stumbled onto the road that eventually led them to become the political-administrative intermediaries between global capital and the productive reserves of Chinese labor and local entrepreneurship. Unlike in the former Soviet Bloc, the political crisis of 1989 produced in China essentially the new edition of a developmental state. After 1989 the nominally communist China became politically conservative and institutionally repressive though no longer economically autarchic. The outcome, at a vastly greater scale, reproduced the earlier pattern of anticommunist developmental states in East Asia such as South Korea and Taiwan (Wade 2003).

Why Ukraine Reaped Elite Predation Rather than Elite Cooperation for Development

The economic miracle of the Chinese exit from communism was a contingency waiting to happen. The Chinese communist cadres proved capable of holding together in the face of a moralistic challenge from leftist students. Next, the Chinese communists stumbled into the broader East Asian path of economic growth predicated on the region's deeply historical foundations and the contemporary search of global capitalist groups for outsourcing destinations. Hypothetically, the Soviet Union or Ukraine alone could have plugged into the same shifting patterns of global capitalism, exploiting as initial advantage its industrial bases, natural resources, large domestic markets, and the still relatively cheap labor. But such a counterfactual would be possible only if the Soviet elites could somehow solve the problem of their collective action. This problem was easier to solve for the Chinese cadres, with their relatively simple and underdeveloped state. The USSR, along with its peoples and elites, fell victim to the institutional complexity inherited from the Bolsheviks' improbable success, first in refounding the multiethnic state as a federation of republics in the 1920s, and then industrializing and militarizing the USSR during the 1930s and 1940s. Superpowers, like supertankers, come with an enormous inertial drag.

By default rather than anyone's plot, the USSR was disassembled and torn apart along the lines of the nomenklatura jurisdictions in the national republics and the prime economic sectors, which also happened to be the easily marketable assets such as finance, commodities, or real estate (Solnick 1998). The driving force was the onset of panic among the nomenklatura embedded in the different segments of the Soviet state and economy. In the fall of 1989 they rightly sensed grave peril in Gorbachev's wanton sacrifice of their counterparts in Central Europe for the sake of his muddled foreign goals.

The fleeing nomenklatura logically, if unexpectedly, found salvation in hijacking the slogans of their rising critics and opponents: national sovereignty, privatizations, and competitive elections. The nomenklatura incumbents, finding themselves between the mercurial Gorbachev in Moscow and the emboldened opponents in the streets of their own capitals, bet on preemptively moving their old patronage networks into the three new institutions: national sovereignty separating them from Moscow; quickly organized presidential elections providing the incumbents a critical edge over the upstart competition; and the private ownership of economic assets, ensuring both the personal wealth and political resources of the newly sovereign presidents.

The chaotic process also created openings for the various enablers and interlopers, either invited or forcing their way into the scramble for Soviet spoils. They could range from the new business "oligarchs" politically appointed to skim the rents (in the contemporary parlance, "seated on the financial flows") from the choicest economic sectors to the downright "violent entrepreneurs" of the mafia variety (Volkov 2002).

The resulting institutional configurations might look like the American "political machines" of yesteryear (Hale 2006b). Yet world-systemic positioning makes all the difference. A century ago America was a dynamic capitalist state emerging from the crucial Civil War and ascending to the core zone in the world economy. Its entrepreneurial elites possessed both mighty reasons and resources to impose a respect for property rights and the rule of law. Meanwhile, America's numerous politically engaged and idealistic farmers, workers, and independent middle classes could force from below quite effective restraints on the corruption of city bosses and business monopolists (Bensel 1991). A closer analogy might be the Arab presidential dictatorships. Yet the countries like Syria, Egypt, Iraq, or Algeria had all been dominated by the populist military strongmen reliant on the extensive and rightly feared security forces (Owen 2012). The post-Soviet states, with the exception of Putin's Russia and, in a different vein, Georgia under Mikheil Saakashvili, tended not to acquire ideologically activist and corporatist-militarized regimes of the kind previously seen across the Middle East, Latin America, East Asia, or, for that matter, the interwar Central Europe. Instead, the prevalent pattern has been either purely personalistic state patronage or the combination of several patronage networks within a looser state competing for power with its rents and protections in an irregular political cycle occasionally producing revolutions in the main squares (Hale 2012).

Ukrainian Oligarchs and Bosses as Symptoms of World-system Periphery

Ukraine, because of its considerable size and regional diversity, offers grotesquely rich examples of the nomenklatura escape strategies and their further results. Very fortunately, these results prior to 2014 have involved remarkably little armed violence. Warfare in postcommunist countries had two main dimensions—mafia and ethnic conflict—intersecting in empirical reality even though we tend to keep them in separate analytical and discursive boxes. Both were scrambles for the expropriation and privatization (writ large) of formerly Soviet territories and their resources, material or politically symbolic. These were essentially guerrilla wars fought by the relatively small groups of violent volunteers whom we define as purely criminal when the assets at stake were local and purely economic—or ethnic warlords when at stake were pieces of state territories (Marten 2012).

Remarkably, the majority of Ukraine's regions during the 1990s seemed to remain, by and large, under the control of local police and politicians rather than warlords and gangsters. In fact, this attests to the continuity of political control that dropped from the summits of Moscow and Kiev to the level of regional former bureaucratic oligarchies (Darden 2008). No less this attests to the sudden weakness of social movements, both intelligentsia and worker, who after 1991 found themselves possessing neither a voice nor moral cause (Crowley and Ost 2001). Ukrainian politics could afford to become brutally cynical because the polity in effect had shrunk to the insider circle of elite intrigues safely insulated from popular demands and pressures.

Perhaps even more remarkably, until the Russian annexation of the Crimea in spring 2014, no foreign power had moved to claim Ukraine's borderlands in Odessa, Bukovina, Trans-Carpathia, or Lviv/Lwow/Lemberg. As recently as between 1914 and 1945, weaker and disorderly states could rarely survive intact in the jungle of imperial geopolitics. The answer is, of course, the American hegemony and the kind of geopolitical structures it had installed after 1945 in order to safeguard the existing states and capitalist markets. Wars still could be fought, but only farther away, on the periphery where warfare (and dictatorship) still remained in the repertoire of domestic and international politics. Ukraine was decidedly European thanks to its geography and Soviet legacies. Yet Ukraine was no longer part of a superpower and therefore not a strong collective bargainer in European geopolitics and markets. Economically and, at a frightening rate socially, postcommunist Ukraine bounced into the world's periphery. The old practice of imperialism and colonization seemed too costly and simply unwarranted in a globalized world with a clearly established hegemon. Ukraine could be kept reasonably stable, if not prosperous, by its own elites in exchange for external protection. In the short run, this arrangement could work as an unspoken bargain.

In the longer run, however, uneasy compromises tend to acquire destructive effects. The post-Soviet Ukrainian state and the elites populating its various echelons and segments were just strong enough to maintain a minimal degree of order. The elite survivors of the Soviet collapse found their place under the global protection of American hegemony. Ironically enough, the loss of the Cold War superpower pretensions removed from the agenda of the formerly Soviet politicians two major concerns—external war and taxpayer compliance—that historically drove the growth of all effective states (Tilly 1992). In other words, postcommunist states could afford to behave irresponsibly because in their "postmodernist" historical context the classical model of state development was set in reverse: no need for real armies and armaments industries, and no need for effective administration and therefore little need for domestic political bargaining over taxation and personnel recruitment, the classical triggers of rebellions and revolutions (Ganev 2007).

This is why and when the behavior of Ukrainian elites becomes rent-seeking and downright predatory. Here the neoutilitarian theories of public choice provide a brutally compelling explanation (Buchanan, Tullock, and Tollison 1980). Ukraine is a large and historically composite state in which elites must compete in domestic politics by forging patronage networks and political "machines" that, in turn, must be empowered and rewarded with the continuous and inevitably contentious redistribution of rents. Such configurations of power generate the trap of involution where existing resources are exploited beyond the limit. This is a recipe for Zaïrean-type dynamics of competitive cannibalizing of the state—until the eroded state breaks down amid warlordism (Reno 2011).

Conclusion: What Could Compel Ukraine's Oligarchs to Cooperate for Development?

In 2014 Ukraine experienced its third revolution since becoming independent in 1991. Its enabling conditions were served by the aggravation of chronic splits among the Ukrainian oligarchic elites when President Yanukovych attempted to consolidate his rule through the brazen imposition of sultanism. The oligarchic resistance to sultanistic menace, however, provoked a popular revolution that was able to focus and mobilize, for months in a row, the diffuse yet pervasive energies of social discontent. The months-long street confrontations culminating in the days of bloodshed had radicalized popular contention, which merged social and nationalist demands. In turn, the radicalizing contention in Kyiv produced countermobilizations leading to the institutionalization and arming of radical fringes in the western and eastern outliers of Ukraine (Ishchenko 2014). Such dynamics are commonly observed in revolutions. This also suggests that the latest Ukrainian revolution might be far from over.

Revolutions, according to Arthur Stinchcombe, come to an end when political uncertainty is reduced by building enough bargains into the structure that can maintain those bargains (Stinchcombe 1999). Thus far it is not clear what could provide such structure in a future Ukraine, what could be the bargains, or even who will be, in the end, the bargaining sides. Some indications emerged, however, after the Russian annexation of the Crimea in March 2014. Foreign geopolitical interventions both against and in support of revolutions have been part and parcel of revolutionary sequences since the American and French revolutions of the late eighteenth century. Oftentimes the unintended effect of hostile interventions has been to stiffen patriotic resolve and internal solidarity among the revolutionaries facing an external enemy. Eventually the result could be the consolidation of stronger postrevolutionary states (Skocpol 1979).

In 2014 Ukraine came to face existential perils. In the longer run, however, this pointed to the possible coalescing of the two key conditions, internal and geopolitical, for the formation of a developmental state not unlike those previously seen in East Asia. All successful examples originated in civil wars (South Korea, Taiwan, and, later, the People's Republic of China) or the threat of ethnic annihilation (Singapore) that had wiped out local potentates and forced the surviving oligarchic families to pass on to central governments significant shares of their powers. A crucial external condition emerged from the geopolitical and ideological rifts of the Cold War. The fledgling developmental states of East Asia were purposefully hitched to the industrial conglomerates of Japan, and their exports obtained privileged access to the American consumer market.

This analysis is reinforced by the two counterexamples from the same world region, South Vietnam and the Philippines, that may also apply to Ukraine as warnings. In the Philippines, U.S. political and social controls, as in much of Latin America, since the beginning of the twentieth century had been vested in the agrarian oligarchies that endure to this day. In South Vietnam the massive dispatch of American aid and combat troops during the 1960s had unwittingly lessened the incentives for the "puppet" regime in Saigon to build its own state and economic structures, in effect leaving the native oligarchic factions to wrangle over the fleeting spoils of dependency (Slater 2010). In a different region and more recent times, one could add here the tragic examples of Iraq and Afghanistan under American occupation.

It is too early to tell which route Ukraine might be taking now. Ironically, Putin's regime in Moscow might not prove lasting enough to allow for the defensive consolidation of the Ukrainian state and the export reorientation of its economy. More important, the global agenda has also shifted from the post-1945 promotion of developmentalist industrialization to neoliberal reforms ensuring the repayment of debts through government austerity. Yet historical outcomes are never fully preordained, and there is considerable space for political action on the emerging opportunities and constraints. This is what social science could at least clarify.

12

Stuck in Transition: Successes and Failures of Economic Reform in Ukraine

ALEXANDER PIVOVARSKY

Following the recessions of the 1990s, most transition countries experienced fast growth as their economies responded to the liberalization of prices and foreign exchange markets, reorientation of trade, and, in some cases, improved terms of trade. However, the impact of such one-off factors receded over time. Capital inflows to emerging market economies led to another growth spurt in the run-up to the 2008 global financial crisis, but they too proved unsustainable in the longer run (EBRD 2009b). The process of transition economies' convergence with those of more advanced countries has stalled since the crisis. Among the transition countries, Ukraine stands out. Its economy has not yet recovered from the initial transition recession (Figure 12.1). Its per capita income has been stuck at around one-quarter of that of the EU15 countries, and the economy has suffered from unsustainable growth accelerations and significant macroeconomic volatility (Table 12.1).

The key reasons for Ukraine's difficult predicament are its institutional environment and lack of reforms. Good quality institutions are critical for countries' economic development (North 1990). The experience of postcommunist transition has demonstrated that countries that reformed their economic systems and established institutions supportive of private sector development experienced more rapid economic growth and convergence with income levels in the more developed market economies (Campos and Coricelli 2002; Falcetti, Lysenko, and Sanfey 2006). Recent research suggests that, with the initial productivity catch-up completed and cross-border capital inflows receding, to restart economic growth and the process of economic convergence in the tran-

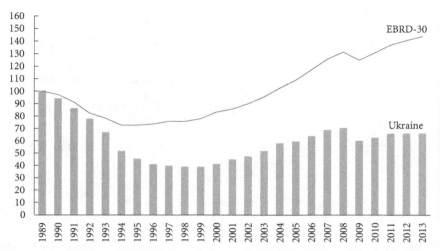

FIG. 12.1: Ukraine—Real GDP Growth. Source: EBRD. Note: EBRD-30 includes all countries of operations of the EBRD that are in transition to market system.

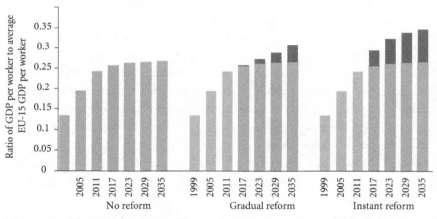

FIG. 12.2: Ukraine—Scenarios of Economic Convergence. Source: Calculations by Jonathan Lehne and the author based on 2013 Transition Report.

sition region, it will be necessary to reinvigorate economic and institutional reforms (EBRD 2013).

An acceleration of reforms is particularly important for Ukraine because its economic institutions are far behind their global frontiers. With population aging and human capital already reasonably strong, standard factors are unlikely to contribute significantly to future economic growth. A forecast by the European Bank for Reconstruction and Development (EBRD) of long-

TABLE 12.1: Ukraine: Macroeconomic Indicators

		2009	2010	2011	2012	2013	2014	2015	2016 Proj.
GDP growth	percent, y-o-y	−15.1	0.3	5.5	0.2	0.0	−6.8	-9.0	2.0
CPI inflation	percent, average	15.9	9.4	8.0	0.6	−0.3	12.1	50.0	14.2
Government balance[a]	percent of GDP	−8.7	−7.4	−4.3	−6.6	−6.7	−10.1	-7.3	-3.9
Current account balance	percent of GDP	−1.4	−2.2	−6.3	−8.1	−9.2	−3.5	-0.2	-1.7
Net FDI	percent of GDP	3.8	4.2	4.3	4.1	2.3	0.2	3.3	...
External debt	percent of GDP	85.1	86.3	77.4	76.6	79.1	96.7	131.7	...
Gross reserves	percent of GDP	21.8	25.4	19.5	14.0	11.4	5.8	14.8	...
Private sector credit	percent of GDP	70.8	62.6	56.6	53.8	58.7	59.8	47.2	...
Nominal GDP	US$ bn	121.6	136.0	163.2	175.7	179.6	130.7	90.1	93.8

SOURCES: IMF and Ukrainian government.
[a]Including Naftogaz operational deficit, IMF calculations.

term growth trends suggests that, without fundamental institutional reforms, Ukraine's relative income is likely to remain at the current level for the foreseeable future. Should deep and comprehensive reforms be introduced, bringing the level of institutional quality close to that of significantly more advanced transition countries, per capita output would begin to converge toward the EU level, albeit gradually (see Figure 12.2).

This chapter describes Ukraine's experience with economic and institutional reforms, analyzes potential causes for their delays, and considers how they can be accelerated. Before proceeding, it is important to clarify what is meant by reform in the transition context. The literature on postcommunist economic transition has focused on a range of indicators of economic reform and institutional development (Hare and Turley 2013). The most long-standing group of indicators measures progress toward basic structural changes essential for transition from a command to a market system (sometimes referred to as "first generation reforms"). The choice of measures in this area is based on what was and remains the prevailing understanding of the main differences between the two systems at the onset of transition. The command economies were dominated by state firms, administered by state bureaucracy through central planning, and subject to administratively determined prices and soft budget constraints (Kornai 1992). In the market system, prices are determined by the market, and firms are administered in a decentralized fashion and subject to hard budget constraints (including exit through bankruptcy). The EBRD has been tracking the indicators of macro- and microeconomic liberalization and privatization in transition countries since the beginning of transition in 1989.

Over the past decade, the literature on transition has also focused on measures of governance, which reflect the quality of institutions and business regulations, as perceived by market participants. This focus underscores the growing appreciation by the economics profession of the critical role of institutions for economic development (Johnson, Acemoglu, and Robinson 2002). There is a large range of sources tracking the economic institutions, many of them available for most countries. As these measures tend to be highly correlated, this chapter will rely only on the World Bank's Worldwide Governance Indicators (WGI), the EBRD's Business Environment and Enterprise Performance Survey (BEEPS), the EBRD/World Bank Life in Transition Survey (LiTS), and the World Economic Forum's Global Competitiveness Index to assess the perceived quality of institutions. It will draw on the World Bank's Doing Business reports to capture regulatory requirements for business.

In addition to the analyses that look at institutions broadly defined, since 2010 the EBRD has been publishing sector-based indicators of transition that aim to capture reforms of sector-specific institutions, as well as broader market structures. For each transition country, sector scores identify the size of transition gaps vis-à-vis their equivalents in advanced market economies.

The remainder of this chapter is organized as follows. The next section describes Ukraine's reform experience to date. Section 3 identifies factors that explain the state of economic reforms before the Euromaidan and the apparent failure of the Orange Revolution to bring about further reforms. Section 4 explores how the Euromaidan movement and subsequent developments might change the environment for reform in Ukraine. Section 5 identifies policy options and presents recommendations. Section 6 concludes.

Ukraine's Reform Experience

The initial conditions for reform in newly independent Ukraine were not favorable. The industrial policy inherited from the Soviet Union was biased toward the production of basic industrial goods and military equipment. With only one-fifth of its population, Ukraine produced more than half of the USSR's iron ore and more than 40 percent of its pig iron and steel. The production of consumer goods and services was underdeveloped. At the onset of transition, external shocks and the loss of regional trade linkages caused serious output collapse. At the same time, the old Soviet elites supported the independence aspirations of the previously repressed national movement only if their social

and economic status quo remained protected in the newly independent country (Plokhy 2014).

It took the government half a decade to stabilize the economy. For a number
of years, it attempted to halt the sharp decline in industrial production through
extensive subsidies and a monetized fiscal deficit, which led to bursts of hyper-
inflation. The loose monetary policy of the early 1990s undermined society's
confidence in state institutions and policy-making. After the population all but
abandoned the local currency, the central bank was given a mandate to focus
on maintaining price stability in 1995. Between 1996, when the hryvnya was
introduced, and 2014 the central bank relied on an exchange rate anchor to
maintain stability. Prices were also liberalized progressively, and at the end of
2013 the share of administered prices in the consumer price index was estimated to be less than 10 percent (primarily for household utility tariffs and natural
gas). Fiscal discipline took longer to establish, fostering a culture of tax and
spending arrears, high quasi-fiscal deficits, and offsets that undermined overall
governance in the economy.

The mass privatization program, which led to dispersed ownership, may
have also contributed to the protracted output decline. Small-scale businesses were privatized relatively early, with thousands of enterprises transferred
to managers and employees who had controlled or leased them since the late
1980s. Shares in many medium and large enterprises were distributed to the
population during the mass privatization stage. In an environment that did not
protect minority shareholders, enterprises were often stripped of assets by their
managers, and large ownership stakes were ultimately concentrated in a few
large holdings (Pivovarsky 2003).

The energy sector became a major source of unofficial rents. Throughout
the first decade of transition, state-owned energy companies failed to establish
hard budget constraints for consumers. Arrears accumulated, which enterprises started to use in barter schemes involving payments to the state, often on
terms that disadvantaged the public sector. On several occasions the government transformed arrears into external public debt owed to the country's main
foreign energy suppliers, Russia and Turkmenistan.

Despite first generation transition advances, successive Ukrainian governments failed to create an institutional environment conducive to private sector development and growth. At the same time, no powerful proreform lobby
emerged after mass privatization, as had been expected by some of its proponents. Throughout the 1990s, surveys revealed unprecedented levels of cor-

ruption in the public and private sectors and a heavy regulatory burden on the economy. The combination of high marginal tax rates on newly created enterprises, overregulation, and rent-seeking pushed approximately half of Ukraine's economic activities into the shadow economy. By 1998, the official economy had lost almost two-thirds of output compared with the pretransition level.

The first growth acceleration happened following the emerging markets crisis of 1998. Rising external demand for steel and chemicals, significant terms of trade improvement following the crisis, exchange rate devaluation, and the end of reallocation of ownership rights after mass privatization combined with extensive unutilized capacity in the economy stimulated output growth. This acceleration was combined with a few reforms, introduced by the government of then-prime minister Viktor Yushchenko in 1999–2000, which included a requirement to settle energy and tax arrears in cash only, reduction of subsidies to the agricultural sector, and introduction of timely social and pension payments by the government. At the same time, the government's access to the international capital market was limited, thus setting a hard constraint on the fiscal deficit. However, as before, there was little focus on broader institutional reforms. In 2004 Ukraine still ranked 122nd of 146 countries in the corruption perception index compiled by Transparency International. Interest among foreign investors in Ukraine remained minimal.

A window of opportunity to proceed with reforms appeared following the Orange Revolution. From November 2004 to January 2005, Ukraine witnessed an unprecedented period of mass civil disobedience following the second round of the 2004 presidential elections, which suffered from reported tampering with the electoral process. Thousands of people gathered in Kyiv's central square for a number of days, and the international community was mobilized to intervene to prevent the use of violence against the crowd. The revolution culminated in a third round of presidential elections, viewed as free and fair by international and domestic observers, and the inauguration of Yushchenko as president. Following the Orange Revolution, for five years Freedom House, an NGO that conducts regular assessments of political rights and civil liberties, classified Ukraine as the only "free" democracy in the post-Soviet space (excluding the Baltic states).

Despite the temporary improvement in the country's "democracy" score and the apparent readiness of a significant share of society to move the country forward, the much-needed institutional reforms did not materialize. In fact, in some areas Ukraine experienced reform reversals. Liberalization of trade was probably the only achievement of the period following the Orange Revolution, culminating in Ukraine joining the World Trade Organization (WTO) in 2008. At the time of entry into the WTO, Ukraine was ranked by the EBRD alongside the new EU member countries in this area. The government was also able to conduct transparent privatization of several leading enterprises. However, despite slow reform progress, following the Orange Revolution Ukraine's economy was able to attract significant direct and portfolio investments. Combined with procyclical macroeconomic policy in Ukraine, the inflows amplified the country's economic vulnerabilities before the 2008 crisis.

In 2008–9, Ukraine's economy underwent a sharp adjustment. A collapse in demand for metals and chemicals together with a rise in gas import prices diminished the contribution of net exports to growth. Domestic demand suffered from the reversal of external capital flows as well as banking sector instability and deleveraging. As a result, total output contracted by 14.8 percent in 2009. After losing almost half of its value, in 2009 the hryvnia was de facto repegged to the U.S. dollar and was supported through the crisis by central bank interventions and exchange control measures. Some of the reforms in the trade and currency markets were reversed. The public sector balance sheet deteriorated rapidly as the authorities increased spending to cushion the impact of the crisis. The overall deficit of the general government, including recapitalization of nationalized and state-owned banks and national gas monopoly Naftogaz, reached 11.3 percent of GDP in 2009 and around 10 percent of GDP in 2010.

After the crisis of 2008, the government took some steps to improve the business environment and committed publicly to increasing Ukraine's ranking in international business surveys. Accordingly, President Yanukovych signed decrees on measures to achieve this goal (including easing company registration procedures and introducing electronic tax filings). In 2013, the parliament adopted several anticorruption measures, aiming to increase the transparency of income and wealth disclosure for public officials. This effort helped the country to climb by a remarkable 28 spots in the World Bank 2014 Doing Business report, making it the fastest improving country during the preceding year. However, despite the improvement, Ukraine's global ranking languished in the bottom third of the distribution. Ukraine also continued to rank in the bottom quartile of the global distribution in the World Bank's measures of rule of law and control of corruption and only slightly better on the measures of government effectiveness and regulatory quality. The 2010 Life in Transition Survey, conducted jointly by the World Bank and the EBRD, revealed that only one-fifth of Ukrainians trusted courts (compared with one-half of people surveyed in western Europe). An evaluation of judicial decisions made by commercial courts, conducted by the EBRD for a number of transition economies between 2010 and 2012 (EBRD, 2012a), revealed that few surveyed believed in the impartiality of Ukrainian courts, and most thought that court decisions were poorly enforced. Application of various rules was not perceived as fair, often reflected in Ukraine's poor scores in measures of corruption.

At the same time, implementation of many declared reforms suffered from delays and poor enforcement, and fiscal and administrative pressures on business increased as the government sought ways to raise tax revenues. Companies often reported incidents of illegal corporate raiding and delays in the payment of VAT refunds to which they were legally entitled. Small businesses were deregistering in large numbers as pressures on them remained high. Enforcement of bankruptcy legislation remained weak, and little action was taken to strengthen corporate governance. In the area of competition policy, there was weak enforcement of laws related to reducing the abuse of market power and promoting a competitive environment, including breakups of dominant conglomerates. While the Antimonopoly Committee was granted wide-reaching investigative powers, including to take enforcement actions similar to those of the EU counterpart bodies, actual practices in this area were viewed to be insufficient.

A summary of the evolution of EBRD transition indicators over time is included in Figure 12.3, and the status of key institutional and governance indicators is included in Figure 12.4.

In the 2013 EBRD assessment of sector-level reforms and market structures, Ukraine continued to lag behind not only best practice countries and the new EU member countries in all sectors but also the EU candidate countries of southeast Europe in most sectors (Figure 12.5). On the positive side, gaps had been narrowed in the power and road sectors that were subject to reform efforts, including with the support of international financial institutions, but also in the capital markets, a sector that had emerged only recently and was not subject to the influence of vested interests. Several sectors, including agribusiness, municipal infrastructure, and banking, were as developed as their equivalents in the EU candidate countries. The natural resources sector stood out, lagging far behind its peers in the more advanced transition countries, as it continued to serve as a source of rents for the country's elites.

The lack of reforms was not due to a lack of understanding about what they would mean. Each of independent Ukraine's governments associated itself directly or indirectly with an economic reform program, often produced by a

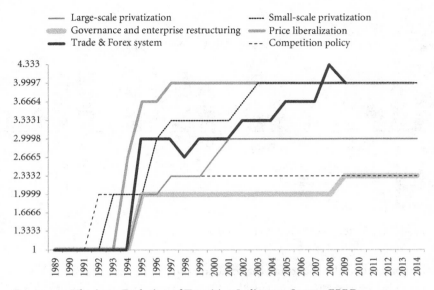

FIG. 12.3: Ukraine—Evolution of Transition Indicators. Source: EBRD.

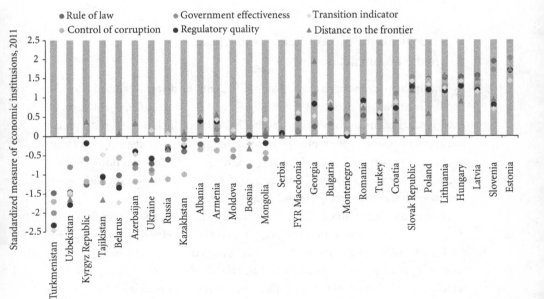

FIG. 12.4: Measures of Economic Institutions. Source: 2013 Transition Report.

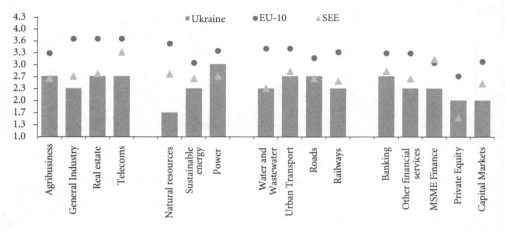

FIG. 12.5: Sector-level Transition Indicators. Source: EBRD.

combination of local and international advisors. Such reform proposals were made by the UN-EU supported Blue Ribbon Analytical and Advisory Center in 2009 and an independent international expert commission in 2010 and were reflected in President Yanukovych's program of economic reforms for 2010–14.

What Explains the State of Reforms in Ukraine before the Euromaidan?

The literature provides a range of hypotheses on the determinants of reforms and institutional development that may help explain Ukraine's difficult reform experience. Factors influencing economic institutions include countries' political systems, history, geographic position, level of economic development and openness to trade and financial flows, political and ethnic fractionalization, natural resource endowments, and degree of economic integration with other countries that benefit from stronger institutions.

If one considers some of the factors on a stand-alone basis, Ukraine's failure to build better institutions before the Maidan is somewhat puzzling. The quality of institutions is lower than would be predicted on the basis of measures of democracy, per capita income, and the degree of resource dependence, which tend to explain why many other post-Soviet countries lag behind more advanced transition economies (Figures 12.6–12.8). When included as variables in a cross-country regression examining determinants of economic institutions, together these three factors tend to explain less than a quarter of the gap between

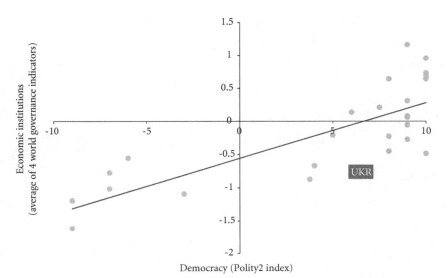

FIG. 12.6: Economic Institutions and Democracy. Source: EBRD.

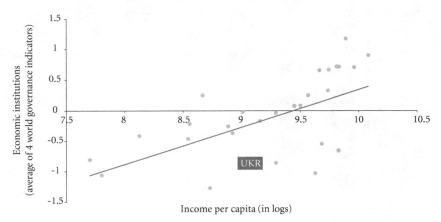

FIG. 12.7: Economic Institutions and Income Levels. Source: EBRD.

the level of Ukraine's institutions and that of the ten new EU member countries (Figure 12.9). The lack of EU membership is one of the leading factors explaining Ukraine's experience, which is not surprising as institutional reforms and adoption of the EU acquis are the sine qua non of EU membership. The still relatively low degree of the country's trade openness is another important factor. Some of the difference is explained by historical factors and Ukraine's geographic location, which cannot be changed. At the same time, a large proportion of the difference remains unexplained.

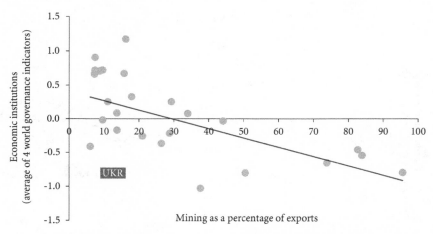

FIG. 12.8: Economic Institutions and Natural Resource Dependence. Source: EBRD.

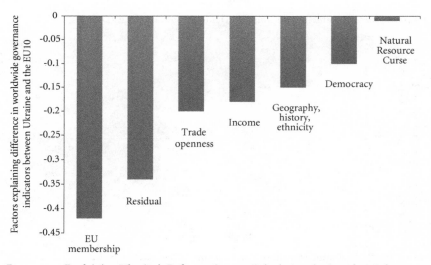

FIG. 12.9: Explaining Ukraine's Reforms. Source: Calculations by Jonathan Lehne and the author based on background research included in the 2013 Transition Report.

Another puzzling feature of Ukraine's recent history is the apparent failure of the Orange Revolution of 2004–5 to serve as a "critical juncture" for reforms. The literature (Collier and Collier 1991) and experience of other countries in the transition region (for example, Georgia and the Slovak Republic) demonstrate that countries sometimes benefit from critical junctures when they can catch up with reforms.

What Explains Ukraine's Poor Economic Reform Track Record?

Early transition history and vested interests. A small class of individuals (today commonly known as "oligarchs"), most of them close to the state at the beginning of the market liberalization process or engaged in criminal activities, were able to accumulate significant wealth quickly, which later allowed them effectively to privatize some functions of the state or to sponsor elected representatives in the parliament and government officials. The initial sources of rents included arbitrage on domestic and international commodity prices, access to subsidized credit, and budget subsidies (Aslund, Boone, and Johnson 2001). Later on, the oligarchs also benefited from privatization through methods that initially dispersed ownership among many individuals and financial intermediaries. As a result, distribution of wealth and income in the country became highly unequal. The leaders of the Orange Revolution sought to tap some of the oligarchs' resources in order to contest the elections, and the price was quite likely an agreement to respect the status quo in terms of the business environment, ownership, and business practices.

Political polarization. Between 1990 and 2004, Ukraine was among the three or four countries in the transition region with the highest degree of political polarization (Frye 2010). Furthermore, Ukraine gained independence as a linguistically divided country, with the predominantly Russian-speaking eastern and southern and the Ukrainian-speaking central and western parts of the country, a feature discussed in Chapters 2 and 3 of this volume. As a result, for a number of years the noncommunist elites were primarily preoccupied with the nation-building project and preserving their own political position and less focused on the institutional foundations for economic development. It may be more costly and riskier for reformers to take on vested interests in such a polarized environment.

Poor leadership. The winners of the Orange Revolution were trained and made their careers exclusively in Ukraine during the Soviet and immediate post-Soviet eras, when they worked in government and industry. Institutional reforms were not their main preoccupation, and that would probably have remained the case even in the absence of opposition from vested interests. The reasons for this may have included a limited understanding of the importance of institutions for well-functioning market economies, but also their pursuit of other legitimate priorities, such as completing nation-building. The post–Orange Revolution call to bring Western-trained Ukrainians to the government, which received a massive response among young Ukrainian professionals around the world, led to no discernible increase in their presence in the government. While society froze in suspended animation, expecting significant changes in the behavior of courts, police, and other law enforcement agencies, nepotism and corruption among the new authorities took hold soon after the elections, thus undermining their credibility.

Economic structure. Although Ukraine is not generally considered a natural resource–based economy, the structure of its industrial sector inherited from the socialist system may have led to challenges similar to those facing natural resource–rich countries. Industrial assets that survived the transition recession of the early 1990s, based predominantly in the steel-producing East, depended on access to cheap natural resources and energy, tax preferences, and protection of the domestic market. This structure gave strong incentives for owners of industrial enterprises to capture the policy-making process with a view to ensuring access to relatively inexpensive energy. For a long time the country's role in transit of natural gas from Russia and Central Asia to Europe offered opportunities for political incumbents to access energy rents. Tellingly, the natural resource sector remained the least reformed and commercialized of all the main sectors of the economy.

Social preferences. Ukrainian society's commitment to democracy and the market system is still shaky. In the 2010 EBRD Life in Transition Survey, only about one-quarter of surveyed individuals supported a combination of a market system and democracy as their preferred social model, compared with a western European average of over 40 percent. About 15 percent of respondents favored a planned economic system and authoritarianism under some circumstances, and a significant proportion of respondents were willing to exchange some political liberties for faster economic growth. A large share of the population depended on public pensions and other social transfers and, thus, preferred the status quo to disruptive change.

External environment. The external environment for Ukraine improved significantly after 2004 as the world economy entered a period of rapid growth. Partly benefiting from the publicity provided by the Orange Revolution, the Ukrainian economy was able to attract significant FDI inflows and gain access to international financial markets, both directly and through European banking groups. Real estate values boomed, and many households and enterprises gained access to relatively cheap finance for the first time. This influx of money likely reduced demand for economic reforms. Rapid growth came to a sudden stop in 2008 as the world entered a new financial crisis. As output declined precipitously, the government rapidly expanded the budget deficit and tapped financing from international financial institutions (IFIs) that was provided with few strings attached. As the strongly contested elections of 2010 approached, reform became even less of a policy priority.

Lack of a credible external anchor and limited external support. Just at the time of the Orange Revolution, the European Union entered a period of expansion fatigue. Therefore, the calls of the revolutionary leaders to gain candidate status for Ukraine received a lukewarm response. The possibility of NATO membership, which seemed more realistic than EU membership in 2004, could have provided some limited impetus for institutional reforms, but prospects fizzled in response to the negative reaction of neighboring Russia and low levels of support within Ukraine. Finally, Western financial support after the Orange Revolution was rather limited. Following the Rose Revolution in Georgia, financial support provided to that country by the United States and other partners ranged between 4.5 percent and 8.4 percent of Georgia's GDP per year in 2005–9, compared with 0.3–0.6 percent of GDP for Ukraine.

Will This Time Be Different?

In 2014, Ukrainian society found itself once again at a potential "critical juncture." After weeks of protests and violent clashes with the police, which followed the government's November 2013 decision to abandon the long-planned signing of Ukraine's Association Agreement with the EU, the Yanukovych regime collapsed, ushering in a new window of opportunity for change but also a period of unprecedented geopolitical turbulence. As demonstrated by the experience of other countries, such as Georgia, it is essential to maintain strong political will to implement change and maintain the realignment of political forces achieved post-Euromaidan (World Bank 2012). Will the historic developments of 2014 lead to a definitive breakthrough in Ukraine's economic and institutional reforms? Several factors weigh in favor of reforms this time around, although some others that have constrained reforms in the past appear to be still firmly in place.

The key difference compared with the post–Orange Revolution period is the strong pressure exerted by civil society on the political class following the regime change. Various nonprofit groups, many of them represented in the parliament, are today engaged in analysis and discussions of policy reform proposals and creating pressures on the government to focus on anticorruption activities, including investigating politicians' sources of income and wealth. Many of these groups are organized around various Internet-based platforms and utilize modern communication technologies to reach broad social groups. Freedom House upgraded Ukraine's political rights rating in recognition of greater political pluralism and government transparency following the departure of Yanukovych and the 2014 parliamentary elections.

Today there is a greater appreciation than ten years ago, among reform-minded political leaders and society at large, for the critical role of institutions. The media covering the Maidan movement were full of interviews and discussions of the need to "reboot" the whole economic system. Sociological surveys reveal that the generation that has grown up in the post-Soviet period associates European integration with a fairer society and greater economic opportunities for all. The reform-minded elements in the political establishment appear to have gained an upper hand in the new post-Maidan parliament and have begun to pursue legislation introducing various outstanding reforms and to set up mechanisms for effective social control over courts and regulators. A number of post-Maidan senior government officials are Western-trained and have lived and worked in countries with strong institutions. The government includes several expatriate ministers and other officials.

The annexation of Crimea and military conflict in Eastern Ukraine have helped to unify Ukrainian society around a vision of the country's future and accelerated the process of nation-building. The significant proportion of population that was still longing for the old socialist system has been marginalized, at least temporarily, in the political process, thereby strengthening support in that process for reforms.

The post-Maidan authorities have much more limited room for maneuver in the economic policy area than the post–Orange Revolution government. The Ukrainian economy continues to suffer from macroeconomic imbalances, including a high current account deficit, low international reserves, a large public sector deficit, and significant public and private debt rollover needs. As long as the global macroeconomic environment remains unfavorable for emerging markets, international investors will continue to shy away from emerging market countries with weak macroeconomic and institutional fundamentals, like Ukraine. The government reached out to foreign bondholders to reduce the stock of public debt and lengthen its maturity. However, even if these negotiations are successful, given the uncertain security situation and the loss of industrial assets in the East, it is unlikely that markets would be willing to offer new loans to the government for some time, thus ensuring strong leverage for international financial institutions. More than in the past, the international institutions are focusing on institutional reforms as part of their lending programs in Ukraine.

Owners of major financial and industrial groups have suffered in recent years from economic and financial instability as well as illegal corporate raiding, rising taxes, and regulatory pressures. Some of them appear to be leaning toward a more balanced political and economic system supported by the rule of law, which would strengthen protection of property rights. Some others have lost their influence as a result of the perception of the public that they supported the Yanukovych regime. In addition, during the worst period of the crisis in January 2014, Western governments sent a strong signal that should oligarchs support the roll-back of democracy in Ukraine, their Western-based financial assets would suffer and they and their families might lose the freedom to travel to the West. The recent deep recession caused by Ukraine's political and military crisis has affected disproportionately the sectors that until recently have relied on subsidized energy and the coal sector. This situation should make it easier to complete the process of commercialization of the gas sector and eliminate untargeted subsidies.

The Association Agreement with the European Union, which was signed by Ukraine's postrevolution leadership and includes commitments on deep and comprehensive reforms, should also help support Ukraine's transformation over the medium term. First of all, it has offered access for Ukrainian enterprises to the enormous European market and increased the potential for growth of investment by European companies in Ukraine over time. Second, it envisions mechanisms for implementing specific institutional arrangements that have been honed throughout Europe and institutional partnerships that should help smooth their transplantation to Ukraine. Third, it is accompanied by the process of liberalization of the visa regime for Ukrainian citizens traveling in the European Union, which should further increase the exposure of Ukraine's people to European values. Finally, it offers some financial assistance, admittedly limited at the initial stage. The United States has also provided financial assistance by guaranteeing some of Ukraine's new government borrowing from markets.

At the same time, some factors are likely to complicate reforms. The distribution of wealth is highly unequal, and the class of small business owners has dwindled since the 2008 financial crisis. Many Ukrainian companies lost access to the Russian market starting in 2014 without gaining access to (or becoming competitive in) the EU market. The collapse of the economy and dislocation of populations affected by the conflict have strengthened the potential electoral base for populist forces. The need to enhance Ukraine's security is draining the public budget, constraining further the already limited resources needed for targeted social assistance and improving public infrastructure. Courts and law enforcement agencies remain highly politicized and subject to corruption. Sources of funding for political campaigns remain nontransparent and income levels of government officials and parliamentarians low, with reported dependence of many on informal financial support by vested interests, making corruption more likely. The large class of midlevel civil servants accustomed to the patronage system of the previous regime is still in place, making implementation of well-intentioned reforms highly uncertain. New paramilitary groups, which emerged initially to support Ukraine's military weakened by years of neglect, are becoming a source of political instability.

What Can Be Done to Exploit the Window of Opportunity?

The remainder of this chapter considers priority measures that could be implemented by reform-oriented policy-makers as well as longer term reforms that would make the institutional changes self-sustaining. It also considers what the international community can do to support the reforms.

Immediate Reforms

Given the country's history of partial reforms, reformers should focus on implementing hard-to-reverse, creative reform solutions. At the initial stage, they should focus on eliminating natural resource rents, strengthening economic (and political) competition and rule of law, and reducing corruption.

Specific measures could include:

Activating in full the Association Agreement with the European Union;
Replacing the entire public prosecutor's office, akin to what is being done with the police;
Reintroducing the simplified registration and taxation regime for small businesses;
Raising natural gas tariffs to the import parity level and providing targeted support to vulnerable target groups;
Allowing extraterritorial jurisdiction for commercial contracts;

Allowing goods (including medicines) certified for consumption in the EU
and other developed markets to be automatically certified in Ukraine;

Eliminating customs control on goods inspected in the EU and subcontract-
ing customs services to reliable international providers;

Requiring all government contractors to disclose the identities of their and
their sub-contractors' beneficiary owners;

Privatizing most remaining state enterprises;

Introducing strict measures to strengthen transparency of political campaign and party finance.

In addition, it will be important to introduce some growth-enhancing and
equality-restoring policy measures to mitigate the effects of crisis on the population and limit the appeal of populist forces.

A Comprehensive Anticorruption Program

Implementation of anticorruption efforts is the single most important and
overarching reform area. As the experience of Georgia suggests, radical measures that clearly break with past governance practices are needed. As a part of
its anticorruption efforts, the Georgian government fired most traffic police
staff and created a new Western-style police patrol, and established a trans-
parently administered national university entrance exam system that decreased
corruption and bribery (Papava 2006). The Ukrainian government has made a
step in this direction by introducing a new police force in the capital and several
other cities and has been using, with mixed success, a national entrance exam
system to reduce corruption in university admissions.

In addition to measures tested by other countries, the government could explore other solutions, such as publishing a list of the largest taxpayers, mandating that public enterprises above a certain size are automatically subject to standards applied to listed companies (or other similar practices advocated by the
OECD), and encouraging the creation of independent watchdogs that would
monitor operations of public companies. Independent boards should be established along with competitive, market-based selection for top management
roles, and oligarchs and political parties should be removed from influencing
activity of state-owned enterprises.

The government should maintain public sector procurement procedures
based on the EU or other international best practices. Significant reforms in this
area, introduced after the 2008 financial crisis, were reversed in the subsequent
years, and some public sector entities were exempted from the procurement rules.

These anticorruption measures should be accompanied by policies making it difficult for the government to constrain access to information. Research demonstrates that in countries with undemocratic governments and a lack of independent traditional news sources, social media could serve as an alternative mechanism for strengthening the accountability of public officials and private companies (Enikolopov, Petrova, and Sonin 2016). Therefore, protecting public access to such news sources may be critical for improving public and corporate governance over time. Nonprofit institutions and international donors may wish to consider investing resources in setting up free Internet access networks throughout the country.

At the same time, reformers and the international community could encourage the creation of transparent mechanisms for bringing the grievances of domestic and international investors to the attention of the government. One such mechanism, an ombudsman institution for businesses, has already been established. In addition, international financial institutions working with the corporate sector could encourage the emergence of anticorruption compacts that would involve checks by third parties of the fulfillment of commitments by the participating companies.

The authorities in countries in which Ukrainians hold their savings could require that owners of significant assets controlled from Ukraine disclose the sources of their funds as well as their political activities. Similar or even more stringent standards could apply when companies of politically exposed persons tap resources in the international markets. The central bank has already adopted steps to make public the information on owners of commercial banks.

Strengthening Accountability of Local Government

Beyond the quick liberalization measures, reforms at the central government level may be complicated by vested interests, corrupt officials, and parliamentary opposition. Therefore, advancing governance reforms at the local government level may prove politically more palatable. Reforming local institutions would benefit, in particular, owners of small- and medium-size enterprises, who tend to suffer most from inspections and regulation by local governments.

Recent research suggests that some of the variation in the quality of local institutions is due to lack of transparency at the local government level. Anecdotal evidence likewise indicates that application of regulatory policies varies across Ukraine. By introducing policies that would make local governments more transparent and publicizing precise regulatory requirements, central government may be able to achieve further de facto liberalization and improved governance at the local level. Research also shows that there are significant regional variations in rule of law and the business environment within most countries (EBRD 2013). Some of the factors that explain cross-country variation in institutional quality (for example, history, geography, and natural resource dependence) may also explain the regional variation. An assessment at the regional level revealed significant variation in institutional quality in Ukraine (Foundation for Effective Governance 2012). To exploit this variation, the central government could establish financial incentives for improving governance at the local level by, for example, offering targeted grants for regions that are able to demonstrate improvements and maintain gains in the quality of institutions, based on the results of independently administered quality surveys. The authorities could also allow businesses to register and report compliance with various regulations anywhere in the country and enter into agreements to settle disputes in their courts of choice.

Strengthening the EU's Offer to Ukraine

As the experience of other transition countries suggests, the process of accession to the EU provides a strong stimulus for economic and institutional reforms, which tend to peak two to three years before accession. Clarifying the conditions under which Ukraine would be able to begin negotiations on EU accession would likely increase support for reforms. At the same time, European institutions may want to consider establishing mechanisms that would mirror the EU integration process, for example, by ensuring that financial resources offered to Ukraine are administered under the same rules as the EU's structural funds.

In parallel, the European Union may need to consider measures that would slow and eventually reverse Ukraine's disengagement from the European financial markets. Before the financial crisis of 2008–9, European banking groups controlled close to one-half of all assets in Ukraine's banking system. In recent years, as the European Union has focused on establishing a banking union, the European banking groups have been withdrawing from Ukraine, thus reversing gains in the improved corporate governance and making the financial system more prone to future volatility. Once Ukrainian authorities make a credible commitment to properly coordinate their financial sector policies with those of the European Union, the EU might want to ensure that European banking groups are not discouraged from maintaining operations in Ukraine.

To facilitate the exchange of values and ideas, the EU could reconfirm its commitment to introducing a visa-free regime for Ukrainians and increase Ukrainian students' access to European scholarship programs. Such programs could target students from southern and eastern parts of the country in particular.

Focusing IFIs' Conditionality on Institutional Development and Governance

In addition to re-establishing basic macroeconomic sustainability by devaluing the hryvnya, tightening fiscal policy, and increasing energy tariffs, any international programs of macrofinancial support would need to contain ambitious conditionality in the area of institutional reforms at the national, sector, and project levels. Examples of specific areas of conditionality include consistent application of public procurement legislation in line with best international practices; reforming the national gas company and subjecting it, along with other large public enterprises, to transparency standards developed for publicly listed companies; transferring expenditure functions to local governments that meet clearly specified standards of governance transparency; revising double taxation treaties with offshore jurisdictions; and reintroducing a simplified regime of taxation for small enterprises.

Any projects in the public sector should focus on sectorwide conditionality. For example, initially, IFIs could ensure that procurement standards applied to IFI-supported portions of investment projects are extended to whole projects no matter what the source of funding for other portions. Over time, such conditionality could be extended to all projects implemented by relevant government agencies. This would ensure that not just parts of projects implemented by IFIs are subject to transparency and good governance standards but entire projects and, eventually, whole sectors are subject to the same standards as those required by IFIs. Furthermore, sovereign loan agreements could include clauses that would ensure that subsequent disbursements are conditional on progress with agreed reforms and contain triggers of automatic loan repayments if the authorities were to later reverse institutional reforms on which the loans were conditional.

International development banks could consider targeting programs for small and medium enterprises, including by offering risk-sharing or risk insurance products, and support local infrastructure projects in regions with better institutional environments, thus helping support private sector development and growth in such regions and also to help maintain demand for improving and maintaining supportive economic institutions in the competing regions. They may also consider varying pricing of loans offered within Ukraine depending on the quality of local government and requiring partner banks to agree to settle disputes in courts with judges vetted by international professional bodies. Company-level conditionality should continue to focus on corporate governance, including transparency regarding the political engagement of key shareholders and the use of offshore jurisdictions.

Increasing Political Competition and Reducing Polarization

Some steps toward increasing political competition and reducing polarization could be made in the economic policy sphere. Specific measures would target rebalancing the tax system in favor of the middle class, including by simplifying the regulatory regime for small entrepreneurs and transferring revenues and expenditure mandates to the local governments. They should also ensure that enterprises still owned by the state are not transferred to politically exposed persons, and that agricultural land distributed to small plot holders does not get concentrated in few hands. Finally, both the government and international financial institutions should support the entry of foreign investors committed to good governance, thus helping to increase competition in the economy and demand for good governance and to reduce the role of vested interests.

Conclusions

Ukraine has been stuck in its transition to a market economy, and, like many developing countries, without comprehensive reforms and an improved institutional environment, it is unlikely to catch up with the world's more advanced economies. The recent historic events suggest that the country's very existence depends on whether it is able to create a social model that its population would wish to defend. As the experiences of other countries demonstrate, Europe's offer of integration will be critical for encouraging reforms. This chapter has outlined some ideas for what reformers and the international community could do to support transition and ensure continued demand for and supply of good economic institutions.

Note

The author is grateful for comments and suggestions from Ihor Burakovsky, Jonathan Charles, Olivier Descamps, Volodymyr Dubrovsky, Dimitri Gvindadze, Jessica Hobart, Jonathan Lehne, Francis Malige, Mykola Miagkyi, Tymofiy Mylovanov, Nienke Oomes, Oleksandr Pavlyuk, Alexander Plekhanov, Franklin Steves, and Jeromin Zettelmeyer. Views represented in this paper are of the author and not necessarily of the EBRD. Elements of this paper appeared in the 2005 assessment by the IMF of long-term program engagement in Ukraine as well as the 2013 Transition Report and other EBRD publications to which the author contributed.

13   Economic Reforms in Ukraine in Comparative Perspective: Formal and Informal Dimensions

ALEXANDER LIBMAN AND

ANASTASSIA OBYDENKOVA

This chapter analyzes the outcome of the economic reforms in Ukraine in comparative perspective with other postcommunist states during the period 1991–2013 (that is, up to the eve of the Euromaidan revolution). Postcommunist countries followed a variety of economic reform paths (Myant and Drahokoupil 2010; Ahrens and Hoen 2013). In this chapter we use an empirical approach to answer our main research question: What were the outcomes of economic reforms in Ukraine compared with those of other countries, and why did similar reforms not always have these effects in other countries? Instead of starting with a predetermined typology of countries and trying to fit Ukraine into one of the groups defined ex ante, we consider the existing quantitative indicators measuring the quality of economic institutions and let the results of the data analysis speak for themselves. To do this we apply hierarchical cluster analysis to identify the countries that are most similar to Ukraine in terms of economic institutions. We also attempt to understand which factors account for the similarities across these countries and Ukraine.

In our analysis, we explicitly concentrate on comparing *formal* and *informal* economic institutions. The difficulty of transplanting formal institutions from advanced economies and the incongruence between formal rules and informal practices has been one of the major topics in the research on postcommunist reforms (Herrmann-Pillath 1993; Leipold 2006; Zweynert and Goldschmied 2006; Hale 2011). In many cases, formal reforms resulted in outcomes very different from the intent of original designers: institutions had a different effect than that they had in the countries from which they were transplanted (Polishchuk 2008). Frequently, the effect of formal reforms turned out to be limited because of the persistence of informal bureaucratic practices (Helmke and Levitsky 2004).

However, even if that is the case (and if formal institutions are primarily "ink-on-paper" and have only a limited effect on actual behavior), we still believe it is necessary to investigate both types of institutions and to understand how Ukraine has performed in comparison with other postcommunist countries in this respect. This is important for three reasons:

First, for a government to implement any reform, it must either change formal institutions or change the personnel (for example, replace the bureaucrats). There is no direct way a government can change informal practices of behavior: the best it can do is to manipulate the formal rules and the staff in such a way that informal institutions adjust, at least in the long run (Nickerson and Zenger 2002).

Second, different types of formal institutions may require different informal practices to function optimally. For example, if a country has a highly nontransparent bureaucracy with complex decision-making patterns, some level of corruption may be preferable to having an extremely honest bureaucracy complying with all the complex norms (Meon and Weill 2010).

Third, looking at the difference between formal and informal institutions is important from the conceptual point of view. Institutions are often defined as rules constraining human behavior (North 1990), but most proxies for informal institutions capture practices of bureaucrats and other actors (such as bribe-taking, compliance with the law, and the like). Glaeser et al. (2004) argue that these informal practices are actually *behavior within the rules* and not *rules or constraints themselves*; therefore the proxies of informal institutions do not actually measure institutions. While the last point has been subject to intensive debate (Voigt 2013), and the definition of "institutions-as-constraints" is not the only one acceptable,[1] we cannot limit our analysis to informal institutions if we intend to take this argument into account.

The chapter proceeds as follows. The second section describes our methodology. The third section looks at the descriptive statistics of the main reform indicators. The fourth section reports the results. The fifth section discusses possible factors influencing the commonality of countries in terms of economic institutions. The sixth section presents an alternative interpretation of one of the proxies we use. The last section concludes.

Approach and Data

A problem one encounters while attempting to compare Ukraine's economic reforms progress with that of other postcommunist countries is that it is impossible to capture the variety of reforms using merely one indicator. Ukraine may be closer to some countries in terms of particular aspects of reforms, but more dissimilar in terms of other aspects. Thus, we need an approach allowing us to compare Ukraine with other countries using all the information on institutional quality available. Hierarchical cluster analysis (HCA) is appropriate for this purpose. This method groups objects (in our case, countries) into hierarchically set clusters based on a particular measure of dissimilarity ("distance") and a rule of separating one cluster from another. In a nutshell, HCA represents each object as a vector in a multidimensional space, where each dimension stands for one of the characteristics of the object. Then it estimates (given the chosen definition of the distance) how far individual objects are from each other. On the basis of these estimates, it groups most proximate objects into clusters (thus, these objects are most similar to each other according to the characteristics chosen), which in turn are grouped into further clusters, now containing more dissimilar objects. Therefore, one obtains a "hierarchy" of clusters, starting from the narrow, containing only objects similar to each other, up to broad clusters containing multiple objects.

In order to measure the quality of economic institutions and the progress of economic reforms, we use two sets of indicators. The first—measuring *formal institutions*—is derived from the Doing Business (DB) report, a large-scale World Bank survey implemented in almost all countries of the world aiming to measure the institutional environment for business activity. A particular feature of the DB is that it tries to rely on objective measures rather than the perceptions of businesses. We, specifically, use the so-called Distance to Frontier (DTF) score of the DB; it shows how far a particular country is from the best performance observed by any economy in this particular measure since the establishment of the DB. A score of 100 indicates that the country is at the frontier, a score of 0 is the lowest performance possible. We use the data from the 2014 report, which measures the quality of institutions as of the end of 2013.

The second set of indicators is derived from the Business Environment and Enterprise Performance Survey (BEEPS), a large enterprise survey by the European Bank for Reconstruction and Development (EBRD) covering all countries we are interested in and containing, among others, questions about institutional quality. Unlike the DB, the BEEPS data we use explicitly aim to capture subjective perceptions of institutional quality by respondents and thus reflect *informal institutions*. We start with individual-level data and compute country-level aggregates, taking into account all respondents who answered the question. Our baseline analysis is based on BEEPS 2009.

For the two sets of indicators (DB and BEEPS) we perform two separate cluster analyses, giving us insight into where Ukraine is located among other transition economies.[2] The set of countries includes all Central and Eastern European (CEE) and South-Eastern European (SEE) countries, as well as former Soviet Union (FSU) states; we also included Turkey, which may be another interesting case for comparison (note that the HCA results are not affected by whether Turkey is included or excluded). We determine the group of countries that have the formal and informal institutions most similar to Ukraine. Specifically, we look at the smallest possible cluster containing only Ukraine and at least four other countries, and concentrate our analysis on the members of this cluster.

Preliminary Discussion

Before we proceed to the actual HCA analysis, it seems prudent to provide a number of descriptive observations regarding Ukraine's position among other transition economies. Table 13.1 reports the DB indicators for Ukraine from the 2014 and 2006 reports (that is, capturing late 2013 and late 2005). To simplify comparison, we provide two indicators: the ratio of the Distance to Frontier of Ukraine to the DTF of the best performing country in the region, and the ratio of the DTF of Ukraine to the average of the region. According to the 2006 report, Ukraine clearly looked like a country with a low quality business environment; it was substantially below the level of the best performing country and mostly below the average level (with the only exceptions being getting credit and enforcing contracts, where Ukraine was roughly at the level of the average postcommunist country).

The 2014 report shows a massive improvement. At this moment, Ukraine still was worse than the best performing postcommunist economy; however, for almost all indicators (with the only exception of resolving insolvency) it was close to the postcommunist region's average. Furthermore, Ukraine seemed to have improved relative to the best performing country and to the region's average in almost every dimension. If we look at the dynamics of the respective

TABLE 13.1: Ukraine's Performance in Terms of Doing Business Indicators versus Other Regional Countries

	2006		2014	
	% of the best	% of average	% of the best	% of average
Starting a business	64	80	89	97
Dealing with construction permits	29	47	92	129
Registering property	52	72	69	86
Getting credit	69	104	93	119
Protecting investors	53	72	59	76
Paying taxes	19	32	59	76
Trading across borders	36	67	61	92
Enforcing contracts	82	105	85	105
Resolving insolvency	17	28	13	21

SOURCE: World Bank's Doing Business.

TABLE 13.2: Ukraine's Performance in Terms of BEEPS Indicators versus Other Regional Countries

Obstacle	% of the best	% of average
Business inspections	174	124
Certification procedures	149	117
Access to land	222	122
Crime	174	117
Tax rates	177	117
Tax administration	153	112
Business licensing	146	116
Political instability	165	120
Corruption	175	115
Courts	184	116
Labor regulation	141	101
Frequency of bribe payments	152	115

SOURCE: EBRD BEEPS.

indicators over time, this improvement trend does not appear to be so straightforward. Rather, we see a substantial jump in the quality of formal economic regulation in some areas since 2012, replacing a small decline in the middle of the first decade of the 2000s. This is an important feature, which we will return to in the next section while explaining our main results.

For the BEEPS indicators, as Table 13.2 shows, Ukraine performed substantially worse than most other postcommunist economies (in this case, a lower value indicator corresponds to better performance) as of 2009. In each dimension, Ukraine was worse than average, and the distance to the average is substantial. Thus, the Ukrainian businesses were substantially more skeptical of the quality of the business environment than one would conjecture looking at the formal regulation. This discrepancy could be explained by the poor quality of informal institutions and poor performance of the bureaucracy, which was likely to disregard formal regulation and abuse its power.

Another important difference between Ukraine's performance in terms of the DB and the BEEPS is that the latter seemed to be much more homogenous: Ukraine's distance from the average and from the best performing country was roughly the same, while in the case of the DB Ukraine performed excellently in some dimensions but poorly in others. The incongruence of different formal institutions may itself have constituted a problem for the business environment and contributed to the poor perception of the quality of the environment by businesses; it also can be interpreted as sign of manipulation: since the DB data are popular (including among international donors), governments seeking legitimacy and support abroad often focus on achieving high scores in this rating rather than on implementing reforms important for the country, or merely improve some dimensions included in the rating but worsen in other dimensions (Davis and Kruse 2007; Arrunada 2007, 2009). Additionally, we observe evidence of inconsistent economic policies plagued by lobbying.

Cluster Analysis

Let us now proceed to the HCA and report the results in the form of dendrograms—that is, graphical representations of distances between individual objects and clusters obtained in the HCA. In our case, dendrograms should be read from the left to the right. On the left-hand side of the dendrogram is each country. Then the countries most proximate to each other are connected into individual clusters (nodes). These nodes, in turn, are connected to other nodes based on their similarity. If a country has no close neighbors, it can be immediately connected to a node already containing multiple smaller clusters. On the x-axis, the graphs represent the dissimilarity measure: if one looks at the length of the branches of the dendrogram until the closest node, one can see the dissimilarity of two countries.

Figures 13.1 and 13.2 report the dendrograms for the cluster analysis for DB and BEEPS data, respectively. The results seem to be strikingly dissimilar. The DB data generally split the transition countries into two large clusters.

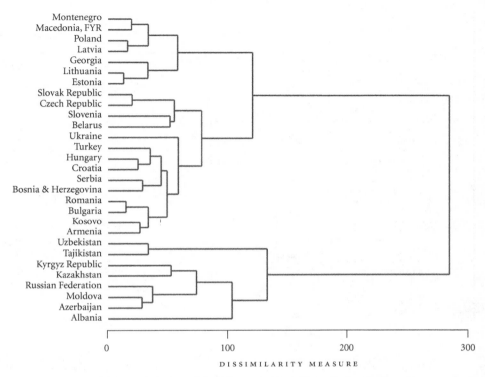

FIG. 13.1: Dendrogram for Hierarchical Cluster Analysis Using Doing Business Data, 2014.

The first included most FSU states:[3] Azerbaijan, Moldova, Kazakhstan, Kyrgyzstan, Tajikistan, Uzbekistan, and Russia, as well as Albania, one of the least advanced countries of the SEE region in terms of economic reforms. Four FSU countries (Armenia, Georgia, Belarus, and Ukraine), however, ended up in a different cluster, which also contained the SEE and the CEE countries. Using our approach, we identified the following countries as having the most similar institutions to Ukraine, according to the DB 2014 data: Armenia, Romania, Bulgaria, Kosovo, Bosnia and Herzegovina, Serbia, Croatia, Hungary, and Turkey (we will refer to them as DB cluster countries). Thus, Ukraine appeared to be closer to the SEE countries than to the majority of the FSU states as of late 2013.

This is not the case if we look at the BEEPS 2009 data. In this case, the analysis shows that there existed a clear separate cluster of post-Soviet countries that contained all FSU states except Azerbaijan and Uzbekistan. Ukraine

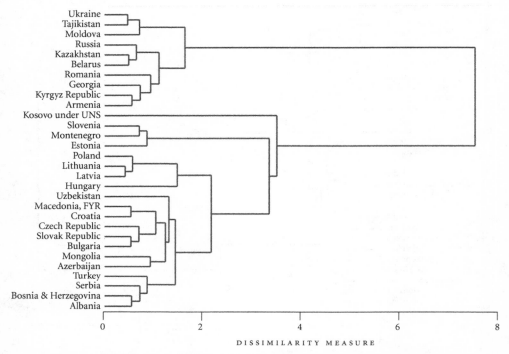

FIG. 13.2: Dendrogram for Hierarchical Cluster Analysis Using BEEPS Data, 2009.

clearly belonged to this cluster, with Tajikistan being the most similar country and Moldova the second closest one: the set of countries with the most similar institutions also contained Russia, Belarus, Kazakhstan, Georgia, Romania, Kyrgyzstan, and Armenia (we refer to this group as BEEPS cluster countries). Somewhat simplified, during the period of our investigation, Ukraine was a SEE country in terms of formal institutions and an FSU country in terms of informal practices.

Our results suggest that there is indeed a gap between formal rules and the informal implementation and enforcement of these rules. Ukraine, although possibly successful in "importing" institutions, had bigger problems with implementing them—either because of the predominance of a "manipulative" approach to changing formal institutions just to improve the country's position in the DB rating, or because of the resilience of informal practices, which substantially limited the effectiveness of reforms.

Why Are They Similar?

After having identified the set of countries having economic institutions particularly similar to Ukraine and other postcommunist states during the period of our investigation, the next task is to analyze what are the potential driving factors behind these similarities. To start with, we have to distinguish between the country-specific conditions, potentially producing similar policy outcomes, and the influence of external factors or common ties.

From the point of view of country-specific conditions, two explanations stand out as potentially important. First, commonality can be based on common history; the most straightforward factor in this respect is the common Soviet legacy, given the large difference between the FSU countries, on the one hand, and the CEE and SEE, on the other (Dabrowski and Gortat 2002). In addition to the simple division, a helpful approach is offered by Kitschelt et al. (1999), who distinguished between three models of communist rule existing in different countries of the former Soviet bloc: patrimonial, national-accommodative, and bureaucratic-authoritarian. Second, commonality in terms of economic reforms could be driven by the political regime transition and its impact on economic reforms in the postcommunist world (Fidrmuc 2003; Giuliano, Mishra, and Spilimbergo 2013).

The influence of external factors can be associated with a multitude of mechanisms (Holzinger and Knill 2005; Obydenkova and Libman 2015a). Empirically, we should expect the influence of the external factor to be especially pronounced if either countries of a cluster are strongly connected to each other (economically, socially or politically), or there is a substantial external influence affecting all countries of the cluster. In the context of this study, this external influence is likely to be associated either with the EU or with Russia.

We will consider these alternative explanations, looking at the results from the DB dataset and from the BEEPS data. Table 13.3 provides a summary of the main arguments in the subsequent section.

Doing Business

If we look at country-specific conditions, one argument seems to be straightforward: the commonality of countries in the group of Ukraine according to the DB data is unlikely to be driven by historical legacies.[4] The FSU states constituted a minority of the DB cluster countries, as they were identified by the 2014 report.

TABLE 13.3: Determinants of Similarity among the DB and BEEPS Cluster Countries

	DB cluster	BEEPS cluster
Communist legacy:		
CEE/SEE vs. FSU	No	Yes
Model of communist rule	No	Yes
Political transition	Yes (mostly weak democracies)	Possible (mostly non-democracies), though heterogeneity is larger than in the DB cluster
External Influence:		
The EU	Yes	No
Russia	No	Yes

In terms of the Kitschelt et al. (1999) typology, half of the DB cluster countries belonged to the group of patrimonial states (Romania, Armenia, Bulgaria, and Ukraine), but the cluster also contained countries that had experienced national-accommodative regimes (Croatia, Hungary) and countries that had lived through a mixed model of patrimonial and national-accommodative elements (Serbia). Only the bureaucratic-authoritarian group was absent (Czech Republic, GDR, and Poland). Furthermore, since Ukraine shifted in the group of DB cluster countries only starting with 2012 (as we will show in what follows), it would be strange to expect the similarities to be based on a common historical past.

In terms of political regimes, the DB cluster countries indeed were more similar to each other. On the one hand, the DB cluster countries' group did not contain any consolidated autocracies similar to those one finds in many post-Soviet countries (Collins 2009; Furman 2010); only the Armenian political regime bears a resemblance to this form of electoral authoritarianism. On the other hand, the cluster consisted of countries that faced a relatively more difficult path to democracy than other states of Central and Eastern Europe. All of them had experienced, at least temporarily, certain autocratic tendencies over the last decades. The turbulent path to democracy—even if successful—could have left an imprint on the quality of economic institutions. A large recent literature has pointed out that weak hybrid regimes and nascent democracies are particularly problematic in terms of economic policies—and face problems different from those of authoritarian regimes (Hellman 1998; Acemoglu and Robinson 2006; Keefer 2007; Darden 2008; Collier and Hoeffler 2009).

In terms of cross-country ties between countries of the same cluster, our hypothesis can be rejected immediately: the extent of economic ties between other countries of the group and Ukraine was negligible. In terms of foreign trade, as of 2012 the country of the group with the highest extent of economic ties to Ukraine, Hungary, accounted only for 2 percent of Ukrainian exports and 1 percent of imports; all other countries played a negligibly small role. They also did not seem to attract Ukrainian labor migrants: the labor migration survey carried out by the Ukrainian statistical agency in 2012 indicated that Hungary—again, the country with the largest inflow of Ukrainian migrants among all other countries of the group—attracted only 1.9 percent of the total labor migration outflow from Ukraine—much less than other countries, to which Ukraine, according to the DB data, was less similar.

Probably, the most obvious common feature of almost all countries in the group was associated with another international influence—the role of the European Union. Of nine countries in the group, three (Romania, Bulgaria, and Croatia) joined the EU during the most recent enlargements; two (Turkey and Serbia) were official candidates, and others (Kosovo and Bosnia and Herzegovina) were considered potential candidates and were actively cooperating with the EU. The only exceptions from this pattern were Hungary (which had already become part of the EU during the 2004 Eastern enlargement) and Armenia (though neither an EU member nor a candidate but an active participant of the European Neighborhood Policy [ENP]—until 2013, when it decided to join the Russia-led Customs Union/Eurasian Economic Union;[5] the country, however, still attempts to maintain effective cooperation with the EU under the external framework it committed to). Therefore, it is compelling to explain the commonality in their reform paths by the influence of EU conditionality, resulting in the adoption of similar reforms.

This interpretation is particularly interesting for us. While the fact that there was an improvement in terms of quality of governance in the SEE member and candidate states and in Turkey, which could have been at least stabilized by EU influence, is well acknowledged in the literature, the impact of the EU on the ENP countries like Ukraine or Moldova is more debatable. Many studies have actually concluded that EU influence in the region was inconsistent and did not necessarily create incentives for implementing economic reforms (Gawrich, Melnykovska, and Schweickert 2010; Börzel and Hüllen 2011; Langbein 2014). Our results imply that at least in terms of formal rules (as measured by the DB indicators), the EU's impact was partially successful.

This positive assessment, however, becomes more questionable if we take into account that the cluster to which Ukraine belonged in 2013 emerged only in 2012. Using 2006 DB data, we obtain a very different picture than the one reported above: at this moment there was a clear cluster of FSU countries according to the DB indicator, as well, including all of them except Moldova and Armenia; Ukraine belonged to this cluster, and Belarus had the most similar institutions to those of Ukraine (other countries in order of decreasing proximity to Ukraine were Uzbekistan, Kyrgyzstan, Georgia, and Azerbaijan). This cluster survived as late as 2012, when it contained all FSU states (except Armenia and Georgia), as well as Albania and Kosovo. The quick change of formal institutions makes it more likely that we are observing an outcome of manipulation. Dimitrova and Dragneva (2013) suggest that the effectiveness of EU influence during the period in question was strongly constrained by domestic interests—in the Ukrainian case, wealthy oligarchs (Melnykovska and Schweickert 2008; Obydenkova and Libman 2014). Certain groups in the Ukrainian business elite had a strong interest in obtaining access to the EU markets, but these interests were at odds with their low readiness to accept transparent EU regulations in practice.[6] DB indicators may have been an "easy" way out: they documented reform progress, but not in the areas painful or costly for oligarchs.

TABLE 13.4: Trade of Ukraine, BEEPS Cluster Countries, and DB Cluster Countries with Russia, percentage of Exports and Imports

	Export	Import
DB cluster countries, 2012		
Armenia	19	25
Bosnia and Herzegovina	1	10
Bulgaria	3	20
Croatia	3	8
Hungary	3	9
Moldova	30	16
Romania	2	4
Serbia	8	11
Turkey	4	11
Ukraine	26	32
BEEPS cluster countries, 2009		
Armenia	16	25
Belarus	32	59
Georgia	2	7
Kazakhstan	8	31
Kyrgyzstan	16	37
Moldova	22	11
Romania	2	4
Tajikistan	nd	nd
Ukraine	21	29

SOURCE: Comtrade.

In terms of Russian influence, the countries of the group we consider were highly heterogeneous. The only country actively participating in the main Russia-led regional economic and political organizations was Armenia. Armenia and Ukraine were the only two countries of the group with substantial trade ties to Russia (see Table 13.4), although Russia was a major energy supplier for most of the countries of the cluster. However, from the DB data it follows that Russia (which also improved substantially in terms of DB indicators in 2013) outperformed Ukraine in almost every DB indicator (except getting credit and trading across borders); Russia was above the average quality of business environment in six of nine indicators. Thus it seems unlikely that one can explain the deficits of formal institutions in Ukraine by direct Russian influence.

BEEPS

The situation looks very different if we consider the results of the BEEPS. To start with, the Soviet legacy seems to be a decisive factor determining inclusion in the BEEPS countries cluster: it contained the majority of FSU countries, and particularly countries as heterogeneous as Georgia (with relatively more advanced market reforms), Belarus (where no systematic economic reforms have been implemented in the last decades), and Tajikistan (with limited basic state capacity). The list was even more homogenous in terms of the Kitschelt et al. (1999) typology, as all countries in the group were former patrimonial communist regimes. This grouping allows us to speculate about one of the possible causes for the persistence of this legacy: the quality of bureaucracy. Ukraine, as well as most other FSU states, took over the Soviet bureaucracy existing on its territory. In the patrimonial communist regimes, with the predominance of clientelism and informal connections, bureaucracy is likely to be particularly inclined to corruption and abuse of norms—much more so than in the two other models of communism. This is indeed what the Ukrainian bureaucracy of the early 2010s, prior to the Euromaidan, looked like (Condrey et al. 2013). At the same time, overcoming informal practices in the bureaucracy is a particularly challenging task. Simply changing the personnel within the civil service is insufficient, as socialization within the old bureaucracy makes its new members accept the same informal rules of the game, and is not feasible because of the lack of alternative staff. In fact, Ukraine never attempted this type of reform until 2014. Therefore, bureaucratic inertia could have contributed to the survival of informal practices and norms.

In terms of political regimes, most of the BEEPS cluster countries were classified as "partly free" or "not free" by Freedom House. Ukraine, in fact, was the most democratic country except Romania in this group in 2009, when the data were collected. However, while none of the countries in the group (except Romania) could have been classified as full-fledged democracies, the differences between countries of this cluster in terms of political regimes were in fact larger than those between the DB cluster countries. The group included both consolidated autocracies (Russia, Kazakhstan, Belarus, or Tajikistan) and countries with more competitive regimes (Moldova or Georgia). While it is possible that the political regimes did affect the problems of economic reforms in these countries, it is also likely that both economic and political institutions were to some extent driven by the persistence of Soviet bureaucracy, which has been shown to be a major obstacle for democratization (Obydenkova and Libman 2015b).

In terms of external factors, the situation is entirely different than what the countries we discussed in the previous subsection faced: as of 2009, the FSU countries were still strongly connected to each other (and especially to Russia) through trade linkages (see Table 13.4) and common infrastructure (these connections persist to this day). In addition, during the last decade there was a growing inflow of Russian foreign direct investment in the FSU (particularly Ukraine) and a growing flow of labor migrants from the FSU countries to Russia (for Ukraine, 43.2 percent of labor migrants in 2012 were working in Russia, 14.3 percent of migrants from Ukraine were working in Poland, and 13.2 percent in Italy). There also existed substantial cultural and social ties. A survey implemented by the Eurasian Development Bank in 2013 (EDB 2013) reported that 50 percent of Ukrainians had relatives, friends, or colleagues in other FSU countries, with whom they kept permanent contacts; 22 percent of Ukrainians had visited an FSU country in the previous five years (compared with only 8 percent having visited an EU country).

The contribution of these ties to the survival of informal practices in the bureaucracy could be non-negligible, although the empirical evidence in this respect is limited. The informal communication could have contributed to the spread of inefficient bureaucratic practices (for example, associated with the ways corruption and graft are used) through mutual learning; it could have been reinforced by strong business ties between countries, with companies using the same practices in dealing with governmental officials at home and abroad. However, again, if we look at the average BEEPS scores in the subset of the FSU countries included in the same cluster as Ukraine, it was slightly lower than that of Ukraine in every single dimension (except access to land), meaning that Ukrainian business perceived its environment as worse than in other FSU countries in terms of informal practices. Russia outperformed Ukraine in terms of almost all BEEPS indicators (except business licensing). Therefore, while cross-border ties could have contributed to the persistence of the problem, they were unlikely to have caused it.

Unlike the DB cluster countries, the BEEPS cluster countries were heterogeneous in terms of how their relations to the EU look. The impact of the EU on the Central Asian countries (Kazakhstan, Tajikistan, and Kyrgyzstan) was definitively much lower than for the SEE states; Belarus exhibited little cooperation with the EU because of the nature of the Lukashenka regime; Moldova, Georgia, and Armenia embraced cooperation with the EU, and Romania became an EU member. It also means that different levels of EU impact led to similar outcomes in terms of informal institutions, again stressing that changing bureaucratic practices is a much more difficult task than changing formal law.

The main part of the analysis of this paper was completed in 2013; at that moment the most recent BEEPS dataset published by the World Bank was for 2009. By 2015, when the final version of this chapter was written, the World Bank had released a more recent dataset based on a survey implemented in 2012–14. We thus updated the results of our baseline analysis using these data. Of the eleven questions in the 2009 questionnaire, two (regarding business inspections and certification procedures) were no longer used by the World Bank, and we had to drop them. But the bank had added a useful new question, asking whether corruption was considered a major obstacle for business (measured on a 0–4 scale). In 2012–14, Ukraine was still in a cluster consisting of the FSU countries: Russia (which became the closest neighbor), as well as Tajikistan and Armenia. However, the post-Soviet countries became more dissimilar in 2012–14 than they had been in 2009 (in particular, Belarus and Kazakhstan were further from Russia and Ukraine than each of these pairs was to some of the CEE/SEE countries). One explanation is that the timing of country surveys in 2012–14 was more different than in 2009. Another is that during this period, because of political turbulence in some of the countries and the stabilization of regimes in others, there was a divergence of expectations—a topic we discuss in the next section.

Alternative Interpretation: The Role of Perceptions

So far, we have interpreted the BEEPS data as proxies for informal institutions. However, these numbers could also be interpreted as perceptions of existing bureaucratic practices and behavior by private businesses (respondents of the survey). Accordingly, the difference between the BEEPS and the DB may reflect a wide gap between actual institutional quality and what businesses have expected. Ukrainian businesses by the end of the first decade of the 2000s could have had particularly high expectations relative to their environment (for example, even although the bureaucracy in, say, Tajikistan was more predatory than in Ukraine, the expectations of businessmen there were lower, reducing the skepticism toward the bureaucracy), creating a large gap between the objective DB and the subjective BEEPS data. Unfortunately, clearly distinguishing this interpretation from that used in the previous part of the chapter is hard, as is generally the case in studying institutions (Green 2011). Hence, we need to discuss the implications of this alternative interpretation.

There are two possible consequences of the gap between expectations and rules. On the one hand, it is possible that what we observe reflects the omnipresent skepticism toward the government in general that dominated during the period we study—whatever rules government created, business was generally likely to interpret them as predatory (given widespread evidence of predatory behavior by the Ukrainian government, this interpretation was not unfounded). Oleinik (2003, 2005) generally describes post-Soviet markets as based on a "pessimistic consensus"—that is, a low level of trust among all participants toward each other and the government. This dominance of pessimism is likely to reduce the willingness of private business to support the demand for institutional reforms and better practices, which can be seen as unachievable in the domestic context. This low level of activism among private business may lead to a further reduction in the quality of the bureaucracy, reinforcing pessimistic expectations.[7]

However, the Ukrainian experience over the last decade refutes the perception of business as inherently pessimistic. What one could see during both the Orange Revolution (Aslund 2009) and the Euromaidan movement in 2013–14 was a divided business community, which partly offered support to the opposition and partly kept strong ties with the regime. After 2014, at least part of the business community embraced the opportunity for reforms. Thus one could hypothesize that the gap we observe in Ukraine was driven by particularly strong and high expectations among businesses as to how bureaucracies should work—at least, relative to other countries of the former Soviet Union. In this case expectations could increase the willingness of private business to proactively support reforms, at least when the respective opportunity arises from the political point of view—a factor important for contemporary Ukraine.

Conclusion and a Look Ahead

The aim of this chapter has been to compare Ukraine with other postcommunist countries in terms of economic reforms in recent years. We looked at two different sets of indicators: the DB measures, which captured formal institutional change, and the BEEPS survey, which looked at informal practices and came to strikingly different conclusions. In terms of formal institutions, Ukraine seemed to have been more similar to the SEE countries (including new EU members and some of the western Balkans countries); the commonality of institutions in this cluster was driven primarily by the external influence of the EU. Ukraine became part of this more reformist DB cluster group only in 2012–13, and while according to some reforms it was among the most successful countries in the group; in other dimensions it clearly underperformed most of the other DB cluster countries. The word "success" should be interpreted with caution: one could see Ukraine's policy of the era as that of manipulating ratings and leaving significant "blind spots" where reforms were lagging behind. In terms of informal institutions, Ukraine, as of 2009, belonged to a cluster composed mainly of post-Soviet countries. In this case, the commonality was driven, evidently, by the Soviet legacy; specifically, one could hypothesize that it is linked to the substantial bureaucratic continuity present in most FSU countries. Furthermore, the existing intensive economic ties were likely to reinforce the existing informal patterns.

The tectonic changes of 2014–15 had a massive influence on factors determining the position of Ukraine in the clusters we discuss. However, making predictions about the direction of this change is not trivial. On the one hand, the new Ukrainian government appears to be firmly committed to implementing economic reforms and to combating corruption. It is willing to do so by both changing formal institutions (in line with the guidelines of the IMF and the EU) and improving the quality of the bureaucracy. Some measures of the new government (such as the lustration laws or experiments similar to appointing Mikheil Saakashvili governor of Odessa) explicitly aim at breaking the continuity with the old bureaucracy. However, there are two major obstacles for the Ukrainian government in terms of achieving this goal. To start with, the necessity of reforms (for example, reduction of taxes and liberalization of regulation) contradicts the imperatives of the war (the need to raise public revenue and to maintain control over the economy). This contradiction is exacerbated by the willingness of numerous Ukrainian politicians to use the war as an excuse for the lack of reforms. The unfortunate experience of Moldova, where the focus of the entire political class on Transnistria distracted it from any serious reforms for almost two decades, could repeat itself in Ukraine.

Furthermore, post-Yanukovych Ukraine faces a trade-off between the need to radically reform the bureaucracy and the costs that such reforms could mean in terms of state capacity. Major changes in public agencies, even if beneficial in the long run, reduce these organs' ability to exercise their functions in the short run, and contemporary Ukraine can hardly afford that. Civil activism at the local level could become one of the tools allowing Ukraine to overcome this dilemma. Indeed, recent years have seen substantial citizen initiatives (backed by private business) to eradicate corruption and to improve the quality of public administration (Pishchikova and Ogryzko 2014). But it is not clear whether this activism will persist in the long term: it can disappear over time if the reforms remain unsuccessful. Furthermore, civil activism could at some point be abused or captured by populists—with disruptive effects for the future of the Ukrainian economy and society.

In terms of external influences, Ukraine's situation has also entirely changed. The country's economic ties to Russia declined dramatically. According to the official statistics, in 2014, as opposed to 2013, Ukraine's exports to Russia dropped by 33.7 percent, and imports from Russia by 45 percent. In January–April 2015, exports declined by 60.6 percent and imports by 64.2 percent. While some of these lost trade flows were probably rerouted through other countries (such as Belarus), the weakening of economic ties to Russia is undisputable, and Russian external influence on economic reforms in Ukraine (other than through Russia's role as a combatant in the Donbas, affecting the entire Ukrainian political situation) became negligible. The EU, on the other hand, emerged as an important donor for the Ukrainian economy, which is also backed by the IMF. Paradoxically, this does not automatically mean that the EU will have a larger impact on Ukrainian reforms. An external donor can exercise influence only if it insists on strict conditionality for aid provision. The EU's involvement in Ukraine is now to some extent driven by geopolitical concerns—the ongoing confrontation with Russia. From this point of view, Ukraine could continue receiving aid for political reasons, even if reforms are not implemented.

Summing up, although the Euromaidan created a window of opportunity for reforms, whether this window will actually be used remains highly uncertain. Both domestic and external factors exercise an ambiguous impact on how the Ukrainian economy will evolve in the years to come.

Notes

1. An alternative is, for example, to use the "institutions-as-equilibria" approach elaborated by (Crawford and Ostrom 1995).

2. We use the most common Euclidean distance measure and perform Ward's linkage clustering.

3. Throughout the paper, FSU explicitly excludes the Baltic states, which are classified as CEE countries.

4. Also, the pre-Soviet legacies of these countries were different: the DB cluster included countries with Habsburg, Ottoman, Russian imperial, and mixed historical legacies.

5. Armenia became a member of this organization in 2015.

6. See the chapter on oligarchs and clans in Ukraine by Taras Kuzio in this volume.

7. This result is consistent with the similarity of BEEPS scores for most post-Soviet countries, which in this case should be interpreted as perceptional similarity, based on the common Soviet legacy.

PART VIII

Conclusion

14 Conclusion: The Comparative Politics of Reform and Lessons for Ukraine

HENRY E. HALE AND ROBERT ORTTUNG

If the Ukrainian state is being founded anew, as Paul D'Anieri notes in his introduction, what have we learned from this volume about how this foundation should be laid, and what lessons does this hold for countries other than Ukraine seeking to reform polity, society, and economy? All together, the chapters in this volume have confirmed that Ukraine faces a wide variety of challenges, some quite fundamental (such as historical legacies of communism and patrimonialism and a peripheral position in the world economy) and some quite contingent (such as decisions that were made on exactly how privatization should be conducted and choices of particular institutions). The chapters also find no "magic bullet" capable of eliminating all of these obstacles and placing Ukraine on a clear path to democracy, prosperity, and good governance.

By digging so deeply in several areas of reform, however, we do find some common threads that offer a forward strategy, and one that might be relevant not only to Ukraine. A good starting point for this strategy is to avoid the assumption that formal institutions will work the same way in Ukraine as they do in countries of the developed West, from which some of the most prominent reform recommendations come. Second, we should distinguish between obstacles that are deeply embedded in society and thus very hard to change dramatically in a single generation and those obstacles that are more contingent. Third, we should focus reform efforts not only on the low-hanging fruit in the latter category but also on the longer-term process of addressing the more fundamental obstacles—first by adopting reforms that make the best of the bad situation posed by these deeper problems, and second by making changes that will facilitate the long-run transformation of society. Fourth, we must think carefully about how realistic each reform is given the interests and incentives of the political actors that have the power to enact them. This means not only recommending reforms but also taking action to alter leadership incentives where possible, or at least identifying and anticipating possible moments where problem incentives can change, moments that the political science literature sometimes calls "critical junctures" (Collier and Collier 1991). And finally, we find that many of these reforms have the potential to reinforce each other, arguing for implementing as many as possible together rather than waiting to carry out any of them out according to a preconceived sequence. Given all these considerations, perhaps the most powerful single driver for reform we find is the European Union, though there are plenty of other institutional and economic changes that Ukrainians themselves can make and push for that hold out the hope for eventually bringing positive reform to Ukraine.

Why Reform Failure in Ukraine?

In his opening essay, D'Anieri outlined seemingly myriad theories that experts have developed over the years to explain why countries may fail to reform for the sake of economy and democracy. These include perverse incentives facing leaders, poor institutional design, historical path-dependence that makes it hard to reform old institutions, state weakness, civil society weakness, patrimonial legacies, identity divides, and external actors that often complicate the reform process as much as help it along. Taken together, our volume's chapters find at least some role for each of these factors in the case of Ukraine. What also comes out, however, is that some of these factors play a more fundamental role than others. That is, some of these challenges reflect deeper social contexts that tend to make other reforms more difficult, whereas some of Ukraine's problems arise from highly contingent choices that could have been made differently along the way and that could, in principle, be undone (or redone) in fairly short order.

What are the most fundamental reform challenges facing Ukraine that come out in the research conducted by our chapter authors? Four such challenges clearly fall into this category. One of the most obvious is the complex of problems known widely as Ukraine's "communist legacy." For example, the chapters by Daniel Beers and Maria Popova observe that judges who received their primary training in the Soviet period, when courts were explicitly politicized, are less likely to be fully and natively independent from powerful political or corporate interests when rendering important rulings. Similarly, the chapter by Alexander Pivovarsky makes clear that the communists' radical construction of a command economy continues to leave Ukraine without the infrastructure and instincts necessary for a market economy to function well for the sake of the broader populace.

Some problem legacies, however, clearly predate the Soviet period, though USSR rule often exacerbated them. One of these is Ukraine's much talked about identity divide, with a western population strongly oriented to the European Union and Western values and an eastern population that is more trusting of deep ties with Russia (Darden and Grzymala-Busse 2006). This divide, reinforced by very different narratives regarding Ukraine's history and natural place in world geopolitics, is argued by Lucan Way and Oxana Shevel to have made it much harder for Ukrainians to work together to solve common problems, hindering governance. Ironically, however, the fact that the events of 2014 have largely brought most Ukrainians together may actually pose new challenges for Ukraine, potentially facilitating long-run authoritarian tendencies and encouraging a tyranny of the majority on issues of culture and memory.

A third fundamental obstacle to reform in Ukraine, which also predates the Soviet period, is its legacy of patrimonialism, or what the chapter by Henry Hale calls "patronalism" and Oleksandr Fisun's contribution to the book calls "neopatrimonialism." While some link this phenomenon to the communist period (Kitschelt et al. 1999), it far predates 1917 throughout this region and, indeed, the greater part of the globe. A deeply embedded social equilibrium, it has been quite stubborn and only escaped by a handful of societies in recent centuries, mostly in the developed West (Hale 2015; North, Wallis, and Weingast 2009). In patrimonial societies, state and economic activity are largely fused, which inherently gives rise to the massive problem of corruption that Serhiy Kudelia's chapter so powerfully shows is pervasive in Ukraine. Patrimonialism is also clearly linked to the phenomenon of weak statehood that D'Anieri's introductory chapter discusses and that Derluguian's and Way's contributions argue has also hindered reform in Ukraine.

In addressing weak statehood, however, Derluguian suggests that a fourth fundamental obstacle to reform may have been at work in Ukraine prior to 2014, though some might consider this obstacle actually to have been a blessing: the absence of an urgent foreign threat. Extensive research beginning with the great sociologist Charles Tilly has found that the strong states of Europe largely arose out of the need to mobilize resources for war in the eighteenth and nineteenth centuries, forcing elites to work together to promote development as opposed to breaking down into ravenously predatory factions. One must consider, therefore, that a silver lining to Ukraine's ongoing military clash with Russia could be a newly serious impetus to building up a strong state, though in the short run Russia has also catalyzed a great deal of internal turmoil in Ukraine, and the chapters in this volume indicate that reforms since 2014 have been far from thoroughgoing. Indeed, for the European cases Tilly studied, this was a process that took generations rather than years.

The comparative research reflected in this book makes clear that these fundamental obstacles are by no means insurmountable. Some postcommunist cases have been success stories in just about every area we have studied, ranging from economic reform (for example, Poland, as the chapter by Alexander Libman and Anastassia Obydenkova notes) to judicial professionalism (for example, the Czech Republic, as Beers shows) to democracy (such as Mongolia, as Hale observes). Likewise, some countries with deep divides over historical memory and identity have managed them relatively well over the years, as Shevel reports is the case in Spain. Similarly, some countries have functioned relatively well in highly patrimonial contexts, as Derluguian argues has been the case with Chinese economic growth.

One conclusion is thus that certain other, more contingent and changeable factors can exacerbate the fundamental problems, accentuating the problems they generate rather than making the best of the situation. Chapters by Taras Kuzio and Pivovarsky demonstrate that Ukraine's poorly designed privatization process did create a form of market economy in Ukraine, but one that tended to feature prominent monopolies and huge holding companies. These contributed not only to a lack of economic competition and to economic inequality and the associated popular discontent, but also to the rise of a class of "oligarchs," hyper-rich businessmen and women who have largely dominated party politics in Ukraine and done much to undermine the rule of law and other democratizing reform. Hale's chapter shows how Ukraine also opted for a presidentialist constitution in the 1990s, interacting with Ukraine's "highly patronalistic" social context to put it on a path toward rising authoritarianism punctuated by revolution. And during the periods when Ukraine did adopt the more promising "divided-executive" type of constitution, its leaders failed to take advantage of it to work together, instead descending into intense political in-fighting that paralyzed the country in the wake of the terrible 2008–9 global financial crisis. This paved the way for a nostalgia for authoritarian practices that in fact helped lead to their return (along with restoration of the old presidentialist constitution) under President Viktor Yanukovych, only for him to be overthrown again in 2014. Fisun has called this a phenomenon of "constitutional cycles." While young judges educated in the postcommunist era could potentially have been a resource for expanding judicial autonomy in Ukraine, Popova shows that Ukraine's leaders actually chose to use their inexperience against them, appointing junior judges to major political cases where they were in over their heads and could be manipulated and, accordingly, "baptized by fire" into the corrupt, patrimonial judicial system.

Indeed, this discussion reveals how these different unfortunate choices and the fundamental contextual obstacles to reform have tended to reinforce each other. With patrimonialism deeply embedded and people seeing little likelihood of this changing, judges and other officials have tended to assume that this is "just the way it is" and to therefore accommodate themselves to it, even when it goes against their own principles. And with nearly every judge doing this, as Beers's comparative research shows and as Popova finds in Ukraine, they thereby *make* this true in a kind of self-fulfilling prophecy. And dishonest, unreliable courts tend to facilitate all kinds of other forms of corruption and wrongdoing. Leaders who rise up in a highly corrupt system with the aid of oligarchs are quite unlikely to work to undermine the very system in which they have proven to be champion manipulators, as Kuzio's chapter brilliantly shows. Accordingly, Kudelia's and Fisun's research finds that changes in state institutional structure tend mainly to rearrange patterns of corruption rather than working against corruption. The interactions are also clearly in play even in the realm of identity and memory politics. Leaders who are facing a lack of public support because of corruption can seek to strategically "play the identity card," deliberately provoking conflicts, as a way of distracting the citizenry from the corruption in their regimes, and leaders seeking to mobilize support on the basis of identity can still find it useful to enlist the aid of powerful oligarchs. True economic reform, the kind capable of generating breakthroughs in foreign investment and economic growth, would mean government officials from the top down would have to pass up lucrative opportunities for rent-seeking and asset-grabbing, opportunities that officials in highly patrimonial contexts are strongly tempted to forgo—especially if they expect the system to continue regardless of the specific choices they themselves make. This corruption tends to squelch economic competition, and the lack of competition tends to facilitate corruption.

One "nonfinding" is worth mentioning in light of the list of factors that D'Anieri outlined in his introduction. Perhaps it will surprise some readers, but interestingly, our chapter authors have reported very little role for Russia as a negative influence on reform in Ukraine. While it appears from time to time largely in passing, our experts tend to find the causes of Ukraine's problems to be largely domestic in nature. While Russia might not be helping, it would appear not to be the main obstacle in Ukraine. It does, however, strongly exploit Ukraine's ongoing problems. And in the long run, there is even the possibility that Russia's intervention will backfire, uniting Ukrainian elites and society more generally around European-oriented reforms.

What Is to Be Done?

D'Anieri's leadoff chapter cites prior research to show that those reform successes that Ukraine has experienced have tended to have two things in common: starkly self-evident negative consequences should reform fail, and powerful positive incentives provided by the international community to encourage reform. The key domestic agents of these reforms have tended to be state officials. Potentially, civil society could drive reform in Ukraine as well, but D'Anieri, citing some of his own previous work, finds that for the most part Ukrainian civil society has not been capable of much more than episodic outbursts, not sustained and institutionalized in ways that could have driven reform home (D'Anieri 2010). The chapters that follow his opening salvo now put us in position to move beyond these previous findings. We certainly find confirmation of the idea that the international community can play a key role, though comparative experience gives many other causes for optimism should Ukraine's leaders have the will or be compelled to act differently.

Let us focus first on what our chapters' analysis of the cases other than Ukraine has to say. Research by Shevel finds that identity divides can be productively incorporated into the political system through conscious state efforts not to legislate a single version of history, behaving in what Shevel, following prior research, terms "mnemonic pluralists" rather than "mnemonic warriors." If elites can be made to understand the destructiveness of such debates, the major players can conclude formal or informal pacts to support such state policies. The European Union, Shevel reports, actually provides a set of principles that can be employed by states like Ukraine to teach history in ways that will be productive rather than destructive for the country in the long run. These findings can be usefully combined with Way's conclusion that Ukraine's identity divide has been an important barrier to rising authoritarianism, so perhaps identity stalemate and experiences of repeated identity-charged revolution and even bloodshed can help convince elites eventually to conclude the kind of pacts and adopt the sort of state policies that can ultimately make memory and identity a productive rather than destructive force with respect to reform. A risk Ukraine now faces, therefore, is that too much "identity rallying" in the face of Russia's military intervention in Ukraine could remove some incentive for elites to make the kinds of compromises necessary for a society to be truly democratic and free.

Turning to the need for anticorruption reforms, our chapters have drawn attention to some cases in which states have made progress. One of these, highlighted in Daphne Athanasouli's chapter, is the post-Soviet case of Georgia. There, while some areas of what Kudelia calls grand corruption continued, the Rose Revolution put in motion a set of reforms that made real progress in eliminating important forms of petty corruption that had plagued ordinary life in Georgia for generations. Important for this and other success stories, Athanasouli finds, have been strong political will, relatively free media that can create opportunities to expose corruption, economic competition, and institutions, especially those providing for transparency, raising the risks and costs of being caught, and facilitating monitoring by groups likely genuinely to be opposed to corruption (for example, firms, households, and civil servants). In particular, technical solutions such as e-government have proven effective as a way to reduce bureaucratic corruption by making it more costly and difficult.

Hale finds that much can also depend on constitutional design even when the rule of law is quite weak in a country. In particular, despite legacies of patronalism and corruption, divided-executive constitutions (and to a slightly lesser extent some kinds of parliamentarist constitutions) can tend to promote political pluralism and thwart tendencies for corrupt networks to become organized into a single political machine dominated by a president. While incumbent rulers tend to favor presidentialist constitutions since they can reinforce their power, there are plenty of historical examples of countries adopting constitutional designs that tend to involve checks and balances. In the postcommunist world, these include Macedonia, Bulgaria, Ukraine, Georgia, Kyrgyzstan, and Mongolia. While some of these countries have had such a constitution since the early 1990s, others adopted them later for various reasons, including political stalemate among rival forces (Ukraine, 2004), a desire by revolutionaries not to repeat mistakes of the past (Ukraine, 2014, and Kyrgyz-stan, 2010), and an effort by an outgoing president to hem in his successors (Georgia, 2010–13). Such constitutional change, then, can be a viable path for supporting political opening. Hale's chapter also suggests that over the long run, divided-executive constitutions might eventually work against corruption by providing greater incentives for politicians to reap public benefits from eliminating such unpopular practices. Other chapters, however, warn against too much optimism that "all good things go together." For example, Popova's chapter finds that democracy in what Hale calls highly patronalistic societies can actually increase incentives for politicians to corrupt the courts and other institutions in an effort to gain a short-run edge over competitors (Hale 2015; Popova 2010b). If voters become too discouraged by an increase in corruption at the outset of democratization, therefore, the risk rises of sentiment for a new authoritarian turn that could undermine long-term progress; this is arguably what happened with the 2010 election of Yanukovych after five years of highly corrupt democracy after the Orange Revolution.

This volume's research on the judiciary, which must be the backbone of any effort to establish the rule of law and end corruption, also points to some paths forward for countries burdened with legacies of communism. Some of these involve formal institutional change that can facilitate transparency and monitoring. Beers, based on his comparative analysis of the Czech Republic (a more successful judicial reformer) and Romania (a less successful one), also points to the strong role that independent professional associations for judges can play in reinforcing instincts that many—especially junior ones—have to practice their trade honestly without the interference of politicians or oligarchs. The European Union has also played a positive role incentivizing judicial reform in its new member states, and international law can also support efforts to promote judicial independence, as when domestic cases can be appealed to, for example, the European Court of Human Rights. Providing judges with a decent living wage also works against the rationale that some judges might have that corruption is a necessary evil for feeding their families.

In the realm of economic reform, success stories range from Poland, which adopted a series of liberalizing "shock therapy" reforms widely recommended by Western economists in the early 1990s, to China, which adopted a very different set of measures (creating a developmental state) that rejected the striving for pure free markets but nevertheless spurred rapid economic growth (though for now without democracy). The chapters by Pivovarsky and Derluguian indicate that both of these options are in principle still open for Ukraine if its elites can unify and adopt the right policies and institutions. The international community has been one important driver for reform, especially through the conditionality that institutions like the International Monetary Fund can impose for badly needed credits, to more positive incentives such as the prospect for membership in the European Union. Libman and Obydenkova's research also reveals that while Ukraine's business practices remain highly corrupt and unfriendly to open competition, Ukrainian practitioners nevertheless appear to have rather strong ideals regarding how an economy *should* function. Their findings indicate that such beliefs could themselves be an engine for change in the future, nudging governments eventually to clean up their acts and implement needed reforms.

While the problem of patrimonialism is generally not overcome rapidly in any society, some of its traits that are most harmful to democracy and society can be overcome through a series of reforms, our chapters find. Efforts to break up monopoly holdings in the economy constitute one such measure that can be taken, along with vigorous law enforcement aimed at rooting out the corrupt deals big business can make with elements of the state, supported by etransparency and similar reforms mandating openness. The European Union has also been held out as a spur for such moves, especially with so many Ukrainians in favor of further integration with the EU. The EU can also conceivably give a country's oligarchs an "outlet" for their economic activity that can help "socialize" Ukraine's various economic and political actors. One hopes that a continued state of war will not be necessary for Ukraine to root this problem out, as Derluguian's sweeping historical analysis suggests could be the case.

Conclusion to Our Conclusion

What, then, might a concrete but realistic platform of reform for Ukraine look like? First, our authors highlight a series of reforms that can essentially help Ukraine make the best of a bad situation, helping make a highly patronalistic society rife with corruption and embroiled in identity-charged political turmoil work more rather than less effectively. These include maintaining (but perfecting) its current divided-executive constitution, moving toward an open-list proportional representation election mechanism for parliament, adopting far-reaching decentralization that can further check central power while taking some of the steam out of identity and memory disputes, pressing ahead with demonopolization of the economy, cleaning up predatory corrupt agencies like the traffic police, and adopting thoroughgoing e-government reforms. These reforms have been shown in other countries to produce improvement even when levels of corruption and patrimonialism remain high, where society remains rent by divides in identity and memory, and where communism still leaves a deep, dark shadow over society.

At the same time, our chapters also urge persistence in pushing for a series of other reforms that may not have immediate effect, but that comparative experience indicates can eventually help solve some of the most fundamental contextual challenges that Ukraine faces, including patrimonialism, postcommunism, and a deep identity-memory divide. These include making mnemonic and identity pluralism central to the Ukrainian state while retaining Ukrainian as the sole official statewide language, adopting laws that mandate transparency and thereby enhance the ability of watchdogs to call attention to areas where such transparency is denied, promoting strong professional organizations for judges and other key civil servants, and empowering small and medium businesses that evidence suggests may yet have a strong vision as to what a functional economy should look like but see themselves as hopelessly trapped in a patrimonial equilibrium.

Perhaps even more important in effecting these more fundamental changes, however, are pressures from outside, including incentives for moving closer to the European Union. The EU's positive effects, however, are likely to be stronger the more realistic such aspirations appear to be. There is an irony here. EU officials have tended to write off Ukraine as too corrupt and dysfunctional to have any real prospect of membership in the foreseeable future. But by writing Ukraine off in this way, the EU is in fact making it more likely that Ukraine will fail. Conversely, holding out genuine hope for accession could in fact bring about the very reforms Ukraine needs to be considered a plausible member. In that sense, then, the EU's attitude about Ukraine is likely to be something of a self-fulfilling prophecy: by stretching out its hand to Ukraine the EU can actually make Ukraine more likely to be a worthy partner, just as withdrawing the hand can discourage Ukrainians and reinforce its negative equilibrium of expectations that nothing will change, in fact making it likely that nothing will in fact change. Most of our chapters have demonstrated that there are positive forces for reform in Ukraine that can be mobilized, and that it primarily needs a major push of some kind to help it break out of the multidimensional self-reinforcing dysfunction in which it finds itself. One fascinating insight that emerges from our study, then, is that EU expansion is not merely about whether countries meet or even appear now to be close to meeting EU accession criteria, the famous acquis, but about patterns of expectations that the EU can set and that can become—crucially—self-fulfilling. The EU can be an equilibrium-changer. To be sure, this is not without risks for the EU. Romania and Bulgaria highlight some of these, states that were reforming with the EU in mind but that have slowed to a near halt far short of expectations after being admitted. Nevertheless, it remains clear that Ukraine is more likely to get out of its morass if EU leaders hold out some real hope that it could one day join, and support it along the way. It is also possible that the ongoing war with Russia could help Ukrainians break out of their negative equilibrium and achieve many of the same reforms, but surely the result will be more positive for all Ukrainians, eastern and western, if the incentive comes from a peace-building EU than from a territorially expansionist and interventionist Russia.

Contributors

DAPHNE ATHANASOULI is a Lecturer on Emerging Market Economies and Political Economy of International Business at University College London, School of Slavonic and East European Studies. She has worked extensively on issues related to corruption, and the results have been published by the *Journal of Comparative Economics*. She is currently focusing on the development of an e-transparency index to evaluate public anticorruption initiatives.

DANIEL J. BEERS is Assistant Professor of Political Science and International Relations at Knox College. He served for three years as a research associate with the Parliamentary Development Project for Ukraine at Indiana University, where he authored numerous technical papers and reports for members of the Verkhovna Rada. He is the recipient of several research and teaching awards, including a Fulbright-Hays doctoral dissertation research fellowship. His work has appeared in peer-reviewed publications including *Problems of Post-Communism, Demokratizatsiya, The Journal of Legislative Studies*, and *International Studies Perspectives*.

PAUL D'ANIERI is Provost and Professor of Political Science and Public Policy at the University of California, Riverside. He previously served on the faculty and in administration at the University of Kansas and the University of Florida. His research focuses on politics and foreign policy in Ukraine and the post-Soviet region. Among his books are *Economic Interdependence in Ukrainian Russian-Relations* (SUNY, 1999) and *Understanding Ukrainian Politics: Power, Politics, and Institutional Design* (M. E. Sharpe, 2007).

GEORGI DERLUGUIAN studies macrohistorical change, preferably through the concatenations of empirical microevents, as shown in his study of Soviet collapse *Bourdieu's Secret Admirer in the Caucasus: A World-Systems Biography* (University of Chicago Press, 2005). His most recent book, *Does Capitalism Have a Future?* (Oxford University Press, 2013), coauthored with Immanuel Wallerstein, Randall Collins, Michael Mann, and Craig Calhoun, has been translated into fifteen languages. Presently Derluguian is Professor of Social Research at New York University Abu Dhabi.

Contributors

OLEKSANDR FISUN is Professor and Chair of Political Science at Kharkiv National University (Ukraine). His primary research interests are comparative politics and democratic theory. He has held visiting fellowships at the Woodrow Wilson Center's Kennan Institute (2001, 2007), the International Forum for Democratic Studies at the National Endowment for Democracy (2004), and the Ellison Center for Russian, East European and Central Asian Studies at the University of Washington (2015). His publications include *Democracy, Neopatrimonialism, and Global Transformations* (Kharkiv, 2006), as well as numerous book chapters and articles on comparative democratization, neopatrimonialism, regime change in post-Soviet Eurasia, and Ukrainian politics.

HENRY E. HALE is Professor of Political Science and International Affairs at George Washington University (GW) and most recently the author of *Patronal Politics: Eurasian Regime Dynamics in Comparative Perspective* (2015). His previous work has won two awards from the American Political Science Association, the Leon D. Epstein Outstanding Book Award for *Why Not Parties in Russia* (2006), and the Alexander L. George Award for his article "Divided We Stand" (*World Politics*, 2005). He is also the author of *The Foundations of Ethnic Politics* (2008) and a wide range of journal articles. During 2009–12, he served as director of the Institute for European, Russian, and Eurasian Studies (IERES) at GW's Elliott School of International Affairs, and he is currently editorial board chair of *Demokratizatsiya: The Journal of Post-Soviet Democratization*.

SERHIY KUDELIA is Assistant Professor of Political Science at Baylor University. Earlier he held teaching and research positions at Johns Hopkins University, George Washington University, University of Toronto, University of Greifswald (Germany), and National University "Kyiv-Mohyla Academy" (Ukraine). Kudelia also worked as an advisor to the deputy prime minister of Ukraine in 2008–9. His articles appeared in various peer-reviewed journals including *Post-Soviet Affairs, Problems of Post-Communism, East European Politics and Societies, Journal of Communist Studies and Transition Politics, Communist and Post-Communist Studies, Demokratizatsiya,* and in an edited volume *Orange Revolution and Aftermath: Mobilization, Apathy and the State in Ukraine* (2010). Additionally, he coauthored *The Strategy of Campaigning: Lessons from Ronald Reagan and Boris Yeltsin* (2007) with Kiron Skinner, Bruce Bueno de Mesquita, and Condoleezza Rice.

TARAS KUZIO is Senior Fellow at the Canadian Institute of Ukrainian Studies, University of Alberta, with previous positions at the University of Hokkaido, Johns Hopkins University-SAIS, Institute for European, Russian and Eurasian Studies at George Washington University, and the University of Toronto. He is the author and editor of fifteen books and monographs, including *Ukraine: Democratization, Corruption and the New Russian Imperialism* (2015), guest editor of eleven special issues of academic journals, and has authored eighty-eight scholarly articles and thirty-seven book chapters on postcommunist and Ukrainian politics.

ALEXANDER LIBMAN is Associate at the German Institute for International and Security Affairs (SWP) in Berlin, Germany. His most recent books include *Causes and Consequences of Democratization: The Regions of Russia* (2015, with Anastassia Obydenkova), and *Autocratic and Democratic External Influences in Post-Soviet Eurasia* (2015, coedited with Anastassia Obydenkova). He also published *Holding-Together Regionalism: Twenty Years of Post-Soviet Integration* and *Eurasian Integration: Challenges of Transcontinental Regionalism* (both 2012, with Evgeny Vinokurov), as well as articles in *World Politics, Review of International Political Economy, Journal of Common Market Studies, Studies in Comparative International Development, Publius: The Journal of Federalism, Public Choice,* and *Political Studies,* among others.

ANASTASSIA V. OBYDENKOVA is a Regional Fellow at the Davis Center for Russian and Eurasian Studies, Harvard University and a Senior Researcher at the Institute for Institutional Studies at the National Research University Higher School of Economics, Moscow. Her research examines comparative politics, international relations, and nondemocracies. She has published three books on these topics as well as numerous chapters and articles in *World Politics, Post-Soviet Affairs, Review of International Organizations, Publius: The Journal of Federalism, European Journal of Political Research, Studies in Comparative International Development, Political Studies,* and other journals.

ROBERT ORTTUNG is Assistant Director of the Institute for European, Russian, and Eurasian Studies and an Associate Research Professor of International Affairs at George Washington University's Elliott School of International Affairs. His research interests include democratization, corruption, energy, and sustainability. He has published numerous works about political and economic developments in Eurasia. For the last ten years, he has written Freedom House reports analyzing the level of democracy and corruption in Ukraine and Russia. Additionally, he is the managing editor of *Demokratizatsiya: The Journal of Post-Soviet Democratization* and coeditor of the *Russian Analytical Digest* and the *Caucasus Analytical Digest,* biweekly electronic newsletters that examine regional political and economic developments.

ALEXANDER PIVOVARSKY is a Deputy Director in the President's Office at the European Bank for Reconstruction and Development (EBRD). He previously was Lead Economist for Eastern Europe and the Caucasus at the EBRD and Senior Economist at the International Monetary Fund for various countries in Eastern Europe, Latin America, Africa, and Central Asia. He coauthored the EBRD's 2009 Transition Report: Transition in Crisis?, the 2010 Transition Report: From Crisis to Reform, and is the author, together with Jeffrey Sachs, of "Economics of Transition: Lessons for Ukraine." His past research has focused on institutional development, privatization, fiscal policy, and the 2008–9 financial crisis in Eastern Europe.

MARIA POPOVA is an Associate Professor in the Department of Political Science, McGill University. Her research examines the rule of law, corruption, and good governance in the postcommunist region. Popova's book on the political (in)dependence of the Russian and Ukrainian judiciaries from the 1990s to the mid-2000s, *Politicized Justice in Emerging Democracies* (Cambridge University Press, 2012) received the American Association for Ukrainian Studies 2012–13 award for best book on Ukrainian history, politics, language, literature, and culture. Her work has also appeared in *Comparative Political Studies, Electoral Studies, Europe-Asia Studies, Problems of Post-Communism, Demokratizatsiya*, and edited volumes. She is currently working on a book project on the prosecution of political corruption in seven postcommunist EU members.

OXANA SHEVEL is an Associate Professor of Political Science at Tufts University, an Associate at the Davis Center for Russian and Eurasian Studies and the Ukrainian Research Institute at Harvard University, a member of the EUDO Citizenship expert group as a country expert on Ukraine, and a member of the Program on New Approaches to Research and Security in Eurasia (PONARS Eurasia) scholarly network. Her research and teaching focus on the postcommunist region surrounding Russia and issues such as nation- and state-building, the politics of citizenship and migration, memory politics, and the influence of international institutions on democratization. She is the author of an award-winning book *Migration, Refugee Policy, and State Building in Postcommunist Europe* (Cambridge 2011), and an award-winning article, "The Politics of Memory in a Divided Society: A Comparison of Post-Franco Spain and Post-Soviet Ukraine." Her research was also published in *Comparative Politics, Post-Soviet Affairs, East European Politics and Societies, Europe-Asia Studies, Nationality Papers, Electoral Studies*, and in edited volumes.

LUCAN A. WAY is Associate Professor of Political Science at the University of Toronto. His research focuses on democratic transitions and the evolution of authoritarian rule in the former Soviet Union and in cross-regional perspective. He is the author of *Pluralism by Default: Weak Autocrats and the Rise of Competitive Politics* (Johns Hopkins University Press, 2015) and *Competitive Authoritarianism: Hybrid Regimes after the Cold War* (with Steven Levitsky) (Cambridge University Press, 2010).

Works Cited

ABA/CEELI. 2007. *Judicial Integrity Roundtable, October 4–6, 2007: Final Report.* Prague: American Bar Association/Central European and Eurasian Law Initiative (ABA/CEELI).

Abdelal, Rawi. 2001. *National Purpose in the World Economy: Post-Soviet States in Comparative Perspective.* Ithaca, NY: Cornell University Press.

Acemoglu, Daron, and James Robinson. 2006. "Economic Backwardness in Political Perspective." *American Political Science Review* 100 (1): 115–31.

Acemoglu, Daron, and James A. Robinson. 2012. *Why Nations Fail: The Origins of Power, Prosperity, and Poverty.* New York: Crown.

Aguilar Fernández, P. 2002. *Memory and Amnesia: The Role of the Spanish Civil War in the Transition to Democracy.* New York: Berghahn Books.

Aguilar, P. 2001. "Justice, Politics, and Memory in the Spanish Transition." In *The Politics of Memory: Transitional Justice in Democratizing Societies,* edited by A. B. d. Brito, C. González Enríquez, and P. Aguilar Fernández, 92–118. New York: Oxford University Press.

Ahmed, Nizam. 2011. "Critical Elections and Democratic Consolidation: The 2008 Parliamentary Elections in Bangladesh." *Contemporary South Asia* 19 (2): 137–52.

Ahrens, Joachim, and Hermann W. Hoen, eds. 2013. *Institutional Reform in Central Asia: Politico-Economic Challenges.* Abingdon: Routledge.

Alamgir, Jalal. 2009. "Bangladesh's Fresh Start." *Journal of Democracy* 20 (3): 41–55.

Alistar, Victor. 2007. "Corruption and Deficiencies in the Romanian Justice System." In *Global Corruption Report 2007: Corruption in Judicial Systems,* edited by Diana Rodriguez and Linda Ehrichs. New York: Cambridge University Press.

Allen, Robert C. 2003. *Farm to Factory: A Reinterpretation of the Soviet Industrial Revolution.* Princeton: Princeton University Press.

Allen, Robert C. 2011. *Global Economic History: A Very Short Introduction.* New York: Oxford University Press.

Amar, Tarik Cyril, Ihor Balyns'kyi, and Iaroslav Hrytsak. 2011. *Strasti za Banderoiu.* Kyïv: Hrani-T.

283

Aminzade, Ronald, and Doug McAdam. 2001. "Emotions and Contentious Politics." In *Silence and Voice in the Study of Contentious Politics,* edited by Ronald Aminzade. New York: Cambridge University Press.

Anderson, Benedict. 1991. *Imagined Communities.* New York: Verso.

Anderson, James H., David S. Bernstein, and Cheryl W. Gray. 2005. *Judicial Systems in Transition Economies: Assessing the Past, Looking to the Future.* Washington, DC: World Bank.

Anderson, John. 1999. *Kyrgyzstan: Central Asia's Island of Democracy?* Amsterdam: Harwood Academic.

Arel, Dominique. 2006. "The Hidden Face of the Orange Revolution: Ukraine in Denial towards Its Regional Problem, translation of La face cachée de la Révolution Orange: l'Ukraine en négation face à son problème régional." *Revue d'études comparatives Est-Ouest* 37 (4): 11–48.

Arrighi, Giovanni. 2007. *Adam Smith in Beijing: Lineages of the Twenty-first Century.* London: Verso.

Arrighi, Giovanni, and Takeshi Hamashita, eds. 2003. *The Resurgence of East Asia: 500, 150 and 50 Year Perspectives.* New York: Routledge.

Arrighi, Giovanni, Terence K. Hopkins, and Immanuel Wallerstein. 1992. "1989, the Continuation of 1968." *REVIEW* 15 (2): 221–42.

Arrunada, Benito. 2007. "Pitfalls to Avoid When Measuring Institutions: Is Doing Business Damaging Business?" *Journal of Comparative Economics* 35 (4): 729–47.

Arrunada, Benito. 2009. "How Doing Business Jeopardizes Institutional Reform." *European Business Operation Law Review* 10 (4): 555–74.

Aslund, Anders. 2009. *How Ukraine Became a Market Economy and Democracy.* Washington, DC: Petersen Institute of International Economics.

Aslund, Anders. 2015. *Ukraine. What Went Wrong and How to Fix It.* Washington, DC: Peterson Institute of International Economics.

Aslund, Anders, Peter Boone, and Simon Johnson. 2001. "Escaping the Under-reform Trap." *IMF Staff Papers* 48 (4): 88–108.

Athanasouli, Daphne, and Antoine Goujard. 2015. "Corruption and Management Practices, Firm-Level Evidence." *Journal of Comparative Economics* 43 (4).

Balasubramaniam, Ratna Rueban. 2009. "Judicial Politics in Authoritarian Regimes." *University of Toronto Law Journal* 59 (3): 405–15.

Barany, Zoltan. 2002. "Ethnic Mobilization without Prerequisites: The East European Gypsies." *World Politics* 54 (3): 277–307.

Barrington, Lowell W., and Erik S. Herron. 2004. "One Ukraine or Many? Regionalism in Ukraine and Its Political Consequences." *Nationalities Papers* 32 (2): 53–86.

Barrowman, Bret T. 2015. "The Reformer's Dilemmas: The Politics of Public Sector Reform in Clientelistic Political Systems." George Washington University: Ph.D. Dissertation.

Beers, Daniel J. 2011. *Building Democratic Courts from the Inside Out: Judicial Culture and the Rule of Law in Postcommunist Eastern Europe*. Indiana University: Ph.D. Dissertation.

Beers, Daniel J. 2012. "Judicial Self-Governance and the Rule of Law: Evidence from Romania and the Czech Republic." *Problems of Post-Communism* 59 (5): 50–67.

Beissinger, Mark R. 2002. *Nationalist Mobilization and the Collapse of the Soviet State*. New York: Cambridge University Press.

Beissinger, Mark R. 2007. "Structure and Example in Modular Political Phenomena: The Diffusion of Bulldozer/Rose/Orange/Tulip Revolutions." *Perspectives on Politics* 5 (2): 259–76.

Beissinger, Mark R. 2013. "The Semblance of Democratic Revolution: Coalitions in Ukraine's Orange Revolution." *American Political Science Review* 107 (3): 574–92.

Bensel, Richard. 1991. *Yankee Leviathan: The Origins of Central State Authority in America, 1859–1877*. New York: Cambridge University Press.

Berezin, Mabel. 2001. "Emotions and Political Identity: Mobilizing Affection for the Polity." In *Passionate Politics: Emotions and Social Movements*, edited by J. Goodwin, J. Jasper, and F. Polletta. Chicago: University of Chicago Press.

Berman, Harold Joseph. 1963. *Justice in the USSR: An Interpretation of Soviet Law*. Vol. 3. Cambridge, MA: Harvard University Press.

Biberaj, Elez. 1998. *Albania in Transition: The Rocky Road to Democracy*. Boulder, CO: Westview Press.

Birch, Sarah. 2000. "Interpreting the Regional Effect in Ukrainian Politics." *Europe-Asia Studies* 52 (6): 1017–41.

Bobek, Michael. 2008. "The Fortress of Judicial Independence and the Mental Transitions of the Central European Judiciaries." *European Public Law* 14 (1): 99–123.

Börzel, Tanja A., and Vera van Hüllen. 2011. "Good Governance and Bad Neighbors? The Limits of the Transformative Power of Europe." In KFG Working Paper No. 35. http://userpage.fu-berlin.de/kfgeu/kfgwp/wpseries/WorkingPaperKFG_35.pdf.

Boyd, C. 2008. "The Politics of History and Memory in Democratic Spain." *Annals of the American Academy of Political and Social Science* 617: 133–48.

Bratton, Michael, and Nicholas van de Walle. 1997. *Democratic Experiments in Africa: Regime Transitions in a Comparative Perspective*. Cambridge: Cambridge University Press.

Brudny, Yitzhak, and Yevgeny Finkel. 2011. "Why Ukraine Is Not Russia. Hegemonic National Identity and Democracy in Russia and Ukraine." *East European Politics and Societies* 25 (4): 813–33.

Buchanan, James M., Gordon Tullock, and Robert Tollison, eds. 1980. *Toward a Theory of the Rent-Seeking Society*. College Station: Texas A&M University Press.

Bueno de Mesquita, Bruce, and Alastair Smith. 2011. *The Dictator's Handbook: Why Bad Behavior Is Almost Always Good Politics*. New York: Public Affairs.

Bueno de Mesquita, Bruce, Alastair Smith, Randolph Siverson, and James Morrow. 2003. *The Logic of Political Survival*. Cambridge, MA: MIT Press.

Bumin, Kirill M., Kirk A. Randazzo, and Lee D. Walker. 2009. "Institutional Viability and High Courts: A Comparative Analysis of Post-Communist States." *Australian Journal of Political Science* 44 (1): 127–53.

Bunce, Valerie. 1995. "Sequencing of Political and Economic Reforms." In *East-Central European Economies in Transition*, edited by John P. Hardt and Richard F. Kaufman. Armonk, NY: M. E. Sharpe.

Bunce, Valerie. 1998. *Subversive Institutions: The Design and the Destruction of Socialism and the State*. New York: Cambridge University Press.

Bunce, Valerie. 1999. "The Political Economy of Post-Socialism." *Slavic Review* 58 (4): 756–93.

Bunce, Valerie. 2003. "Rethinking Recent Democratization: Lessons from the Postcommunist Experience." *World Politics* 55 (2): 167–92.

Bunce, Valerie J., and Sharon L. Wolchik. 2006. "International Diffusion and Postcommunist Electoral Revolutions." *Communist and Post-Communist Studies* 39 (3): 283–304.

Burger, Ethan S. 2004. "Corruption in the Russian Arbitrazh Courts: Will There Be Significant Progress in the Near Term?" *International Lawyer* 38 (1): 15–34.

Calhoun, Craig. 1997. *Neither Gods nor Emperors: Students and the Struggle for Democracy in China*. Berkeley: University of California Press.

Campos, N., and Fabrizio Coricelli. 2002. "Growth in Transition: What We Know, What We Don't Know and What We Should." *Journal of Economic Literature* 40 (3): 793–836.

Carothers, Thomas. 2002. "The End of the Transition Paradigm." *Journal of Democracy* 13 (1): 5–21.

Cheibub, Jose Antonio. 2007. *Presidentialism, Parliamentarism, and Democracy*. New York: Cambridge University Press.

Cheloukhine, Serguei, and Joseph King. 2007. "Corruption Networks as a Sphere of Investment Activities in Modern Russia." *Communist and Post-Communist Studies* 40 (1): 107–22.

Chibber, Vivek. 2003. *Locked in Place: State Building and Late Industrialization in India*. Princeton: Princeton University Press.

Christensen, Robert K., Edward R. Rakhimkulov, and Charles R. Wise. 2005. "The Ukrainian Orange Revolution Brought More than a New President: What Kind of Democracy Will the Institutional Changes Bring?" *Communist and Post-Communist Studies* 38 (2): 207–30.

Ciccone, Antonio, and Elias Papaioannou. 2007. "Red Tape and Delayed Entry." *Journal of the European Economic Association* 5: 444–58.

Collier, Paul, and Anke Hoeffler. 2009. "Testing the Neocon Agenda: Democracy in Resource-Rich Countries." *European Economic Review* 53: 293–308.

Collier, Ruth Berins, and David Collier. 1991. *Shaping the Political Arena: Critical Junctures, the Labor Movement and Regime Dynamics in Latin America*. Princeton: Princeton University Press.

Collins, Kathleen. 2009. *Clan Politics and Regime Transition in Central Asia*. New York: Cambridge University Press.

Collins, Randall. 1999. *Macrohistory: Essays in Sociology of the Long Run*. Stanford: Stanford University Press.

Condrey, Stephen E., Svitlana Slava-Prodan, R. Paul Battaglio, and Mykola Palinchak. 2013. "Ukrainian Public Management: Top-Down or Bottom-Up Reform?" In *Public Administration in Post-Communist Countries*, edited by Saltanat Liebert, Stephen E. Condrey, and Dmitry Goncharov, 7–22. New York: CRC Press.

Crawford, Sue E. S., and Elinor Ostrom. 1995. "A Grammar of Institutions." *American Political Science Review* 89 (3): 582–600.

Crowley, Stephen, and David Ost, eds. 2001. *Workers after Workers' States: Labor and Politics in Postcommunist Eastern Europe*. Lanham, MD: Rowman and Littlefield.

Cuervo-Cazurra, Alvaro. 2006. "Who Cares about Corruption?" *Journal of International Business Studies* 37 (6): 807–22.

Cumings, Bruce. 2005. *Korea's Place in the Sun*. Rev. ed. New York: Norton.

D'Anieri, Paul. 1999. *Economic Interdependence in Ukrainian-Russian Relations*. Albany: SUNY Press.

D'Anieri, Paul. 2007a. "Ethnic Tensions and State Strategies: Understanding the Survival of the Ukrainian State." *Journal of Communist Studies and Transition Politics* 23 (1): 4–29.

D'Anieri, Paul. 2007b. *Understanding Ukrainian Politics: Power, Politics, and Institutional Design*. Armonk, NY: M. E. Sharpe.

D'Anieri, Paul. 2010. *Orange Revolution and Aftermath: Mobilization, Apathy, and the State in Ukraine*. Baltimore, MD: Johns Hopkins University Press.

D'Anieri, Paul. 2014 "Autocratic Diffusion and the Pluralization of Democracy." In *Power in a Complex Global System*, edited by Bruce Jentleson and Louis Pauly. London: Routledge.

Dabrowski, Marek, and Radzislava Gortat. 2002. "Political Determinants of Economic Reforms in Former Communist Countries." In CASE Studies and Analysis No. 24 http://www.case-research.eu/sites/default/files/publications/sa242_0.pdf

Daci, Halic. 1998. *Albanian Military and Regime Changes*. Amsterdam: Centre for European Security Studies.

Dahl, Robert. 1971. *Polyarchy: Participation and Opposition*. New Haven: Yale University Press.

Darden, Keith A. 2001. "Blackmail as a Tool of State Domination: Ukraine under Kuchma." *East European Constitutional Review* 10 (2/3): 67–71.

Darden, Keith. 2008. "The Integrity of Corrupt States: Graft as an Informal Political Institution." *Politics and Society* 36 (1): 35–59.

Darden, Keith, and Anna Grzymala-Busse. 2006. "The Great Divide: Literacy, Nationalism, and the Communist Collapse." *World Politics* 59 (1): 83–115.

Davis, Kevin E., and Michael B. Kruse. 2007. "Taking the Measure of Law: The Case of the Doing Business Project." *Law and Social Inquiry* 32 (4): 1095–1119.

Davis, M. 2008. "Is Spain Recovering Its Memory? Breaking the Pacto del Olvido." *Human Rights Quarterly* 27 (3): 858–80.

Derluguian, Georgi. 2005. *Bourdieu's Secret Admirer in the Caucasus: A World-System Biography*. Chicago: University of Chicago Press.

Derluguian, Georgi. 2013. "What Communism Was." In *Does Capitalism Have a Future?*, edited by Immanuel Wallerstein, Randall Collins, Michael Mann, Georgi Derluguian, and Craig Calhoun. New York: Oxford University Press.

Derluguian, Georgi, and Timothy Earle. 2010. "Strong Chieftaincies out of Weak States, or Elemental Power Unbound." In *Troubled Regions and Failing States: The Clustering and Contagion of Armed Conflict*, edited by Kristian Berg Harpviken, 51–76. Bingley: Emerald Group Publishing Limited.

Deutscher, Isaac. 1953. *Russia: What Next?* New York: Oxford University Press.

Diamond, Larry, and Marc Plattner. 1996. *The Global Resurgence of Democracy*. Baltimore, MD: Johns Hopkins University Press.

Dimitrov, Martin K., ed. 2013. *Why Communism Did Not Collapse: Understanding Authoritarian Regime Resilience in Asia and Europe*. New York: Cambridge University Press.

Dimitrova, Antoaneta, and Rilka Dragneva. 2013. "Shaping Convergence with the EU in Foreign Policy and State Aid in Post-Orange Ukraine: Weak External Incentives, Powerful Veto Players." *Europe-Asia Studies* 65 (4): 658–81.

Duverger, Maurice. 1980. "A New Political System Model: Semi-presidential Government." *European Journal of Political Research* 8 (2): 165–87.

Easter, Gerald M. 1997. "Preference for Presidentialism: Postcommunist Regime Change in Russia and the NIS." *World Politics* 49 (2): 184–211.

Easterly, William. 2006. *The White Man's Burden: Why the West's Efforts to Aid the Rest Have Done So Much Ill and So Little Good*. New York: Penguin.

EBRD. 1999. "The Business Environment and Enterprise Performance Survey (BEEPS) 1999." London: EBRD.

EBRD. 2005. "The Business Environment and Enterprise Performance Survey (BEEPS) 2005." London: EBRD.

EBRD. 2009a. "The Business Environment and Enterprise Performance Survey (BEEPS) 2009." London: EBRD.

EBRD. 2009b. *Transition Report 2009: Transition in Crisis?* London: EBRD.

EBRD. 2010. "The Business Environment and Enterprise Performance Survey (BEEPS) 2008– 2009: A Report on Methodology and Observations," mimeo. London: EBRD.

EBRD. 2012a. *Transition Report 2012: Integration Across Borders*. London: EBRD.

EBRD. 2012b. *Diversifying Russia: Harnessing Regional Diversity.* London: EBRD.

EBRD. 2013. *Transition Report 2013: Stuck in Transition?* London: EBRD.

EDB. 2013. *Integratsionnyi Barometr EABR—2013.* St. Petersburg: Center for Integration Studies of the Eurasian Development Bank.

Eisenstadt, Shmuel. 1973. *Traditional Patrimonialism and Modern Neopatrimonialism.* London: Sage.

Ekiert, Grzegorz, and Stephen E. Hanson, eds. 2003. *Capitalism and Democracy in Central and Eastern Europe: Assessing the Legacy of Communist Rule.* Cambridge: Cambridge University Press.

Elkins, Zachary, Tom Ginsburg, and James Melton. 2009. *The Endurance of National Constitutions.* New York: Cambridge University Press.

Encarnación, O. 2008. "Reconciliation after Democratization. Coping with the Past in Spain." *Political Science Quarterly* 123 (3): 435–59.

Enikolopov, Ruben, Maria Petrova, and Konstantin Sonin. 2016. "Social Media and Corruption." Available at SSRN: http://ssrn.com/abstract=2153378 or http://dx.doi.org/10.2139/ssrn.2153378.

Epperly, Brad. 2013. "The Provision of Insurance?" *Journal of Law and Courts* 1 (2): 247–78.

Ertman, Thomas. 1997. *Birth of the Leviathan: Building States and Regimes in Medieval and Early Modern Europe.* Cambridge: Cambridge University Press.

European Commission for the Efficiency of Justice (CEPEJ). 2012. *European Judicial Systems: Efficiency and Quality of Justice (Edition 2012) CEPEJ Studies* No. 18. Strasbourg: Council of Europe Publishing.

European Union. 2012. *Digital Agenda for Europe, Public Services.* Brussels: European Union.

Evans, Peter B. 1989. "Predatory, Developmental, and Other Apparatuses: A Comparative Political Economy on the Third World States." *Sociological Forum* 4 (4): 561–87.

Evans, Peter. 1995. *Embedded Autonomy: States and Industrial Transformation.* Princeton: Princeton University Press.

Faber, Sebastiaan. 2005. "The Price of Peace: Historical Memory in Post-Franco Spain. A Review Article." *Revista Hispanica Moderna* 58 (1/2): 205–19.

Falcetti, Elisabetta, Tatiana Lysenko, and Peter Sanfey. 2006. "Reforms and Growth in Transition: Re-examining the Evidence." *Journal of Comparative Economics* 34 (3): 421–45.

Fan, C. Simon, Chen Lin, and Daniel Treisman. 2009. "Political Decentralization and Corruption: Evidence from Around the World." *Journal of Public Economics* 93 (1–2): 14–34.

Ferraz, Claudio, and Frederico Finan. 2008. "Exposing Corrupt Politicians: The Effects of Brazil's Publicly Released Audits on Electoral Outcomes." *Quarterly Journal of Economics* 123 (2): 703–45.

Ferraz, Claudio, and Frederico Finan. 2011. "Electoral Accountability and Corruption: Evidence from the Audits of Local Governments." *American Economic Review* 101 (4): 1274–1311.

Fidrmuc, Jan. 2003. "Economic Reform, Democracy and Growth during Post-Communist Transition." *European Journal of Political Economy* 19: 583–604.

Fish, M. Steven. 2006. "Stronger Legislatures, Stronger Democracy." *Journal of Democracy* 17 (1): 5–20.

Fisun, Aleksandr A. 2007. *Demokratiia, neopatrimonializm i global'nye transformatsii.* Kharkiv, Ukraine: Konstanta.

Fisun, Oleksandr. 2012. "Rethinking Post-Soviet Politics from a Neopatrimonial Perspective." *Demokratizatsiya: The Journal of Post-Soviet Democratization* 20 (2): 87–96.

Fisun, Oleksandr, and Oleksandr Polishuk. 2012. "Ukrainian Neopatrimonial Democracy: Dominant Party-Building and Inter-Elite Settlement in the Semi-Presidential System," paper presented at PONARS Eurasia Workshop, Kyiv, November 3–5.

Foundation for Effective Governance. 2012. *Ukrainian National Competitiveness Report 2012: Towards Sustained Growth and Prosperity.* Kyiv: Foundation for Effective Governance.

Freedom House. 2015. *Nations in Transit 2015.* New York: Freedom House.

Frisby, Tanya. 1998. "The Rise of Organised Crime in Russia: Its Roots and Social Significance." *Europe-Asia Studies* 50 (1): 27–49.

Frye, Timothy J. 1997. "A Politics of Institutional Choice: Post-Communist Presidencies." *Comparative Political Studies* 30 (5): 523–52.

Frye, Timothy. 2010. *Building States and Markets after Communism: The Perils of Polarized Democracy.* Cambridge: Cambridge University Press.

Fukuyama, Francis. 2013. "Democracy and the Quality of the State." *Journal of Democracy* 24 (4): 5–16.

Furman, D. E. 1989. "Stalin i my s religioznoi tochki zreniia." In *Osmyslit' kul't Stalina,* edited by D. E. Furman. Moscow: Progress.

Furman, Dmitriy. 2010. *Dvizhenie po Spirali: Politicheskaya Sistema Rossii v Ryadu Drugigkh Sistem.* Moscow: Ves Mir.

Ganev, Venelin. 2007. *Preying on the State: The Transformation of Bulgaria after 1989.* Ithaca, NY: Cornell University Press.

Gardner, Hall, Elinore Schaffer, and Oleg Kobtzeff. 2000. *Central and Southeastern Europe in Transition: Perspectives on Success and Failure since 1989.* Santa Barbara, CA: Praeger.

Gawrich, Andrea, Inna Melnykovska, and Rainer Schweickert. 2010. "Neighborhood Europeanization through ENP: The Case of Ukraine." *Journal of Common Market Studies* 48 (5): 1209–35.

Ginsburg, Tom. 2003. *Judicial Review in New Democracies: Constitutional Courts in Asian Cases.* New York: Cambridge University Press.

Ginsburgs, George. 1993. "From the 1990 Law on the Citizenship of the USSR to the

Citizenship Laws of the Successor Republics (Part II)." *Review of Central and East European Law* 19.

Giuliano, Paola, Prachi Mishra, and Antonio Spilimbergo. 2013. "Democracy and Reforms: Evidence from a New Dataset." *American Economic Journal: Macroeconomics* 5 (4): 179–204.

Glaeser, Edward L., Rafael La Porta, Florencio Lopez-de-Silanes, and Andrei Shleifer. 2004. "Do Institutions Cause Growth?" *Journal of Economic Growth* 9 (3): 271–303.

Goldstone, Jack. 2008. *Why Europe? The Rise of the West in World History 1500–1850.* New York: McGraw-Hill.

Goldstone, Jack. 2014. *Revolutions: A Very Short Introduction.* New York: Oxford University Press.

Grabbe, Heather. 2002. "European Union Conditionality and the Acquis Communautaire." *International Political Science Review* 23 (3): 249–68.

Green, Alan. 2011. "Institutions Matter, but in Surprising Ways: New Evidence on Institutions in Africa." *Kyklos* 64 (1): 87–105.

Gross, Irena. 1998. "When Pyramids Collapse." *East European Constitutional Review* 7 (1) (http://www3.law.nyu.edu/eecr/).

Grzymala-Busse, Anna. 2008. "Beyond Clientelism: Incumbent State Capture and State Formation." *Comparative Political Studies* 41 (4–5): 638–73.

Grzymala-Busse, Anna, and Pauline Jones Luong. 2002. "Reconceptualizing the State: Lessons from Post-Communism." *Politics and Society* 30 (4): 529–54.

Guarnieri, Carlo. 2003. "Courts as an Instrument of Horizontal Accountability: The Case of Latin Europe." In *Democracy and the Rule of Law*, edited by José María Maravall and Adam Przeworski. Cambridge: Cambridge University Press.

Guarnieri, Carlo, Patrizia Pederzoli, and Cheryl A. Thomas. 2002. *The Power of Judges.* New York: Oxford University Press.

Hale, Henry E. 2005a. "Regime Cycles: Democracy, Autocracy, and Revolution in Post-Soviet Eurasia." *World Politics* 58 (1): 133–65.

Hale, Henry E. 2005b. "Why Not Parties? Electoral Markets, Party Substitutes, and Stalled Democratization in Russia." *Comparative Politics* 37 (2): 147–66.

Hale, Henry E. 2006a. "Democracy or Autocracy on the March? The Colored Revolutions as Normal Dynamics of Patronal Presidentialism." *Communist and Post-Communist Studies* 39 (3): 305–29.

Hale, Henry E. 2006b. *Why Not Parties in Russia? Democracy, Federalism, and the State.* Cambridge: Cambridge University Press.

Hale, Henry E. 2011. "Formal Constitutions in Informal Politics: Institutions and Democratization in Eurasia." *World Politics* 63 (4): 581–617.

Hale, Henry E. 2012. "Two Decades of Post-Soviet Regime Dynamics." *Demokratizatsiya: The Journal of Post-Soviet Democratization* 20 (2): 71–78.

Hale, Henry E. 2013. "Did the Internet Break the Political Machine? Moldova's 2009

Twitter Revolution That Wasn't." *Demokratizatsiya: The Journal of Post-Soviet Democratization* 21 (3): 481–505.

Hale, Henry E. 2014. "The Informal Politics of Formal Constitutions: Rethinking the Effects of 'Presidentialism' and 'Parliamentarism' in the Cases of Kyrgyzstan, Moldova, and Ukraine." In *Constitutions in Authoritarian Regimes*, edited by Tom Ginsburg. New York: Cambridge University Press.

Hale, Henry E. 2015. *Patronal Politics: Eurasian Regime Dynamics in Comparative Perspective*. New York: Cambridge University Press.

Hanson, Stephen. 1997. *Time and Revolution: Marxism and the Design of Soviet Institutions*. Chapel Hill: University of North Carolina Press.

Hare, Paul, and Gerard Turley. 2013. *Handbook of the Economics and Political Economy of Transition*. London: Routledge.

Havrylyshyn, Oleh. 2000. "The Political Economy of Delayed Reform in Ukraine." In *Ukraine: The Search for a National Identity*, edited by Sharon Wolchik and Volodymyr Zviglyanich, 49–68. Lanham, MD: Rowman and Littlefield.

Heilmann, Sebastian, and Elizabeth J. Perry, eds. 2011. *Mao's Invisible Hand: The Political Foundations of Adaptive Governance in China*. Cambridge, MA: Harvard Contemporary China Series.

Hein, Michael. 2011. "Constitutional Conflicts between Politics and Law in Transition Societies: A Systems-Theoretical Approach." *Studies of Transition States and Societies* 3 (1): 3–23.

Hein, Michael. 2015. "The Fight against Government Corruption in Romania: Irreversible Results or Sisyphean Challenge?" *Europe-Asia Studies* 67 (5): 747–76.

Hellman, Joel S. 1998. "Winners Take All: The Politics of Partial Reform in Postcommunist Transitions." *World Politics* 50 (2): 203–34.

Hellman, Joel, and Daniel Kaufmann. 2001. *Confronting the Challenges of State Capture in Transition Economies*. Washington, DC: International Monetary Fund.

Helmke, Gretchen. 2005. *Courts under Constraints: Judges, Generals, and Presidents in Argentina*. New York: Cambridge University Press.

Helmke, Gretchen, and Steven Levitsky. 2004. "Informal Institutions and Comparative Politics: A Reform Agenda." *Perspectives on Politics* 2: 725–40.

Helmke, Gretchen, and Steven Levitsky. 2006. "Introduction." In *Informal Institutions and Democracy: Lessons from Latin America*, edited by Gretchen Helmke and Steven Levitsky, 1–30. Baltimore, MD: Johns Hopkins University Press.

Hendley, Kathryn. 1999. "Rewriting the Rules of the Game in Russia: The Neglected Issue of the Demand for Law." *East European Constitutional Review* 8 (4): 89–95.

Hendley, Kathryn. 2006. "Assessing the Rule of Law in Russia." *Cardozo Journal of International and Comparative Law* 14 (2): 347–91.

Hendley, Kathryn. 2012. "The Unsung Heros of the Russian Judicial System: The Justice-of-the-Peace Courts." *Journal of Eurasian Law* 5 (3): 337–66.

Herrmann-Pillath, Carsten. 1993. "Informal Constraints, Culture and Incremental Transition from Plan to Market." In *On the Theory and Policy of Systemic Change*, edited by Hans-Juergen Wagener. Heidelberg: Physica-Verlag.

Herron, Erik S., and Kirk A. Randazzo. 2003. "The Relationship between Independence and Judicial Review in Post-Communist Courts." *Journal of Politics* 65 (2): 422–38.

Herzfeld, Thomas, and Christoph Weiss. 2003. "Corruption and Legal (In)effectiveness: An Empirical Investigation." *European Journal of Political Economy* 19 (3): 621–32.

Holmes, Leslie. 1997. "Corruption and the Crisis of the Post-Communist State." *Crime, Law and Social Change* 27 (3): 275–97.

Holquist, Peter. 2002. *Making War, Forging Revolution: Russia's Continuum of Crisis, 1914–1921*. Cambridge, MA: Harvard University Press.

Holzinger, Katharina, and Christoph Knill. 2005. "Causes and Conditions of Cross-National Policy Convergence." *Journal of European Public Policy* 12: 775–96.

Howard, Marc. 2003. *The Weakness of Civil Society in Post-Communist Europe*. New York: Cambridge University Press.

Hrytsak, Yaroslav. 2004. "Dvadtsiat' dvi Ukrainy." In *Strasti za natsionalizmom*, edited by Yaroslav Hrytsak, 216–28. Kyiv: Krytyka.

Huntington, Samuel. 1968. *Political Order in Changing Societies*. New Haven: Yale University Press.

Huskey, Eugene. 1997. "The Fate of Political Liberalization in Kyrgyzstan." In *Conflict, Cleavage, and Change in Central Asia and the Caucasus*, edited by Karen Dawisha and Bruce Parrott. New York: Cambridge University Press.

Iakoveno, N. 2008. "'Obraz sebe'—'obraz inshoho' u shkilnykah istorii. Shkil'na istoria ochyma istorykiv-naukovtsiv." In *Materialy Robochoii narady z monitoringu shkil'nykh pidruchnyniv istorii Ukrainy*, edited by N. Iakovenko, 113–21. Kyiv: Ukrains'kyi instytut natsionalnoi pamiati.

Ishchenko, Volodymyr. 2014. "Ukraine's Fractures." *New Left Review* 87: 7–33.

Jackson, Vicki C. 2012. "Judicial Independence: Structure, Context, Attitude." In *Judicial Independence in Transition*, edited by Anja Seibert-Fohr. Heidelberg: Springer.

Jacoby, Wade. 2006. "Inspiration, Coalition, and Substitution: External Influences on Postcommunist Transformations." *World Politics* 58 (2): 623–51.

Jensen, Erik G., and Thomas C. Heller, eds. 2003. *Beyond Common Knowledge: Empirical Approaches to the Rule of Law*. Stanford: Stanford University Press.

Johnson, Simon, Daron Acemoglu, and Jim Robinson. 2002. "Reversal of Fortune: Geography and Institutions in the Making of the Modern World Income Distribution." *Quarterly Journal of Economics* 117 (4): 1231–94.

Jones Luong, Pauline. 2002. *Institutional Change and Political Continuity in Post-Soviet Central Asia: Power, Perceptions and Pacts*. New York: Cambridge University Press.

Jones Luong, Pauline, and Erika Weinthal. 2010. *Oil Is Not a Curse: Ownership Structure and Institutions in Soviet Successor States*. New York: Cambridge University Press.

Karklins, Rasma. 2005. *The System Made Me Do It: Corruption in Post-Communist Society*. Armonk, NY: M. E. Sharpe.

Katchanovski, Ivan. 2006. "Regional Political Divisions in Ukraine in 1991–2006." *Nationalities Papers* 34 (5): 507–32.

Katz, Richard, and Peter Mair. 2009. "The Cartel Party Thesis: A Restatement." *Perspectives on Politics* 7 (4): 753–66.

Kaufmann, D., A. Kraay, and M. Mastruzzi. 2010. *The Worldwide Governance Indicators: A Summary of Methodology. Data and Analytical Issues, World Bank Policy Research Working Paper (5430)*. Washington, DC: World Bank.

Keefer, Philip. 2007. "Clientelism, Credibility, and the Policy Choices of Young Democracies." *American Journal of Political Science* 51 (4): 805–21.

Keene, J. 2007. "Turning Memories into History in the Spanish Year of Historical Memory. A Review Article." *Journal of Contemporary History* 42 (4): 661–71.

Khlevniuk, Oleg V. 2008. *Master of the House: Stalin and His Inner Circle*. Translated by Nora Seligman Favorov. New Haven: Yale University Press.

Kitschelt, Herbert, Zdenka Mansfeldova, Radoslaw Markowski, and Gabor Toka, eds. 1999. *Post-Communist Party Systems: Competition, Representation, and Inter-Party Cooperation*. New York: Cambridge University Press.

Knight, Jack. 1992. *Institutions and Social Conflict*. New York: Cambridge University Press.

Kochanek, Stanley A. 1997. "Bangladesh in 1996: The 25th Year of Independence." *Asian Survey* 37 (2): 136–42.

Kohli, Atul. 2004. *State-Directed Development: Political Power and Industrialization in the Global Periphery*. New York: Cambridge University Press.

Kopstein, Jeffrey. 2003. "Post-Communist Democracy: Legacies and Outcomes." *Comparative Politics* 35 (1): 231–50.

Kopstein, Jeffrey. 2006. "The Transatlantic Divide over Democracy Promotion." *Washington Quarterly* 29 (2): 85–98.

Kopstein, Jeffrey S., and D. A. Reilly. 2000. "Geographic Diffusion and the Transformation of the Postcommunist World." *World Politics* 53 (1): 1–37.

Kornai, János. 1992. *The Socialist System: The Political Economy of Communism*. Princeton: Princeton University Press.

Koshiw, J. V. 2013. *Abuse of Power*. Artemia Press.

Kotkin, Stephen. 1995. *Magnetic Mountain: Stalinism as a Civilization*. Berkeley: University of California Press.

Kotkin, Stephen. 2008. *Armageddon Averted: The Soviet Collapse, 1970–2000*. New York: Oxford University Press.

Kubicek, Paul. 1999. "What Happened to the Nationalists in Ukraine?" *Nationalism and Ethnic Politics* 5 (1): 29–45.

Kubik, Jan, and Michael Bernhard. 2014. "A Theory of the Politics of Memory." In *Twenty*

Years after Communism: The Politics of Memory and Commemoration, edited by Jan Kubik and Michael Bernhard, 7–36. Oxford: Oxford University Press.

Kudelia, Serhiy. 2010. "Betting on Society: Power Perceptions and Elite Games in Ukraine." In *Orange Revolution and Aftermath: Mobilization, Apathy, and the State in Ukraine*, edited by Paul D'Anieri. Washington, DC: Woodrow Wilson Center Press.

Kudelia, Serhiy. 2012. "Institutional Design and Elite Interests: The Case of Ukraine." DC Area Postcommunist Politics Social Science Workshop, George Washington University.

Kudelia, Serhiy. 2013. "If Tomorrow Comes: Power Balance and Time Horizons in Ukraine's Constitutional Politics." *Demokratizatsiya: The Journal of Post-Soviet Democratization* 21 (2): 151–78.

Kudelia, Serhiy. 2014. "The House that Yanukovych Built." *Journal of Democracy* 25 (3): 19–34.

Kudelia, Serhiy, and Taras Kuzio. 2015. "Nothing Personal: Explaining the Rise and Decline of Political Machines in Ukraine." *Post-Soviet Affairs* 31 (3): 250–78.

Kühn, Zdeněk. 2012. "Judicial Administration Reforms in Central-Eastern Europe: Lessons to Be Learned." In *Judicial Independence in Transition*, edited by Anja Seibert-Fohr. Heidelberg: Springer.

Kulyk, Volodymyr. 1999. *Ukrains'kyi natsionalizm u nezalezhnii Ukraini*. Kyiv: Tsentr doslidzhen' natsional'noi bezpeky pry Natsional'nomu universyteti "Kyievo-Mohylians'ka akademiia."

Kulyk, Volodymyr. 2013. "War of Memories in the Ukrainian Media. Diversity of Identities, Political Confrontation, and Production Technologies." In *Memory, Conflict, and New Media: Web Wars in Post-Socialist States*, edited by Julie Fedor and Vera Zvereva Ellen Rutten, 63–81. London: Routledge.

Kunicovà, Jana. 2006. "Democratic Institutions and Corruption: Incentives and Constraints in Politics." In *International Handbook on the Economics of Corruption*, edited by Susan Rose-Ackerman, 140–60. Cheltenham: Edward Elgar.

Kuromiya, Hiroaki. 1998. *Freedom and Terror in the Donbas*. Cambridge: Cambridge University Press.

Kuzio, Taras. 1998. *Ukraine: State and Nation Building*. New York: Routledge.

Kuzio, Taras. 2001. "Transition in Post-Communist States: Triple or Quadruple?" *Politics* 21 (3): 169–78.

Kuzio, Taras. 2010. "State-Led Violence in Ukraine's 2004 Elections and Orange Revolution." *Communist and Post-Communist Studies* 43 (4): 383–95.

Kuzio, Taras. 2014. "Crime, Politics and Business in 1990s Ukraine." *Communist and Post-Communist Politics* 47 (2): 195–210.

Kuzio, Taras. 2015a. "The Rise and Fall of the Party of Regions Political Machine." *Problems of Post-Communism* 62 (3): 174–86.

Kuzio, Taras. 2015b. *Ukraine: Democratization, Corruption and the New Russian Imperialism*. Santa Barbara, CA: Praeger.

Kuzio, Taras. 2015c. "Vigilantes, Organized Crime and Russian and Eurasian Nationalism: The Case of Ukraine." In *Ukraine's Euromaidan: Analyses of a Civil Revolution*, edited by David Marples and Frederick V. Mills, 57–76. Stuttgart: Ibidem Verlag and Columbia University Press.

Kuzio, Taras, Robert Kravchuk, and Paul D'Anieri. 1999. *State and Institution Building in Ukraine*. New York: St. Martin's Press.

Kwok, Chuck, and Solomon Tadesse. 2006. "The MNC as an Agent of Change for Host-Country Institutions: FDI and Corruption." *Journal of International Business Studies* 37: 767–85.

Lachmann, Richard. 2000. *Capitalists in Spite of Themselves: Elite Conflicts and Economic Transitions in Early Modern Europe*. New York: Oxford University Press.

Landes, William M., and Richard A. Posner. 1975. "The Independent Judiciary in an Interest-Group Perspective." *Journal of Law and Economics* 18 (3): 875–901.

Langbein, Julia. 2014. "European Union Governance towards the Eastern Neighborhood: Transcending or Redrawing Europe's East-West Divide?" *Journal of Common Market Studies* 52: 157–74.

LeBas, Adrienne. 2011. *From Protest to Parties: Party-Building and Democratization in Africa*. New York: Oxford University Press.

Ledeneva, Alena. 2008. "Telephone Justice in Russia." *Post-Soviet Affairs* 24 (4): 324–50.

Leipold, Helmut. 2006. *Kulturvergleichende Institutionenoekonomik*. Stuttgart: Lucius and Lucius.

Leshchenko, Serhiy. 2013. *Amerykans'ka saga Pavla Lazarenka*. Lviv: Krytyka.

Levitsky, Steven, and Lucan Way. 2002. "The Rise of Competitive Authoritarianism." *Journal of Democracy* 13 (2): 51–65.

Levitsky, Steven, and Lucan A. Way. 2006. "Linkage and Leverage: How Do International Factors Change Domestic Balances of Power?" In *Electoral Authoritarianism: The Dynamics of Unfree Competition*, edited by Andreas Schedler. Boulder, CO: Lynne Reinner.

Levitsky, Steven, and Lucan A. Way. 2010. *Competitive Authoritarianism: Hybrid Regimes after the Cold War*. Cambridge: Cambridge University Press.

Lijphart, Arend. 1977. *Democracy in Plural Societies*. New Haven: Yale University Press.

Linz, Juan, and Alfred Stepan. 1996. *Problems of Democratic Transition and Consolidation: Southern Europe, South America, and Post-Communist Europe*. Baltimore, MD: Johns Hopkins University Press.

Lipset, Seymour Martin, and Stein Rokkan. 1990 [1967]. "Cleavage Structures, Party Systems, and Voter Alignments." In *The West European Party System*, edited by Peter Mair. New York: Oxford University Press.

MacFarquhar, Roderick, ed. 1997. *The Politics of China: The Eras of Mao and Deng*. Cambridge: Cambridge University Press.

Magalhaes, Pedro. 1999. "The Politics of Judicial Reform in Eastern Europe." *Comparative Politics* 32 (1): 43–62.

Mann, Michael. 1993. *The Sources of Social Power. Vol. 2: The Rise of Classes and Nation-States, 1760–1914*. Cambridge: Cambridge University Press.

Marples, David. 2007. *Heroes and Villains: Creating National History in Contemporary Ukraine*. Budapest: Central European University Press.

Marten, Kimberly. 2012. *Warlords: Strong-arm Brokers in Weak States*. Ithaca, NY: Cornell University Press.

Matsuzato, Kimitaka. 2005. "Semi-presidentialism in Ukraine: Institutionalist Centrism in Rampant Clan Politics." *Demokratizatsiya: The Journal of Post-Soviet Democratization* 13 (1): 45–58.

Matuszak, S. 2012. *The Oligarchic Democracy: The Influence of Business Groups on Ukrainian Politics OSW Studies, no.42*. Warsaw: Centre for Eastern Studies.

Mauro, Paolo. 1996. *The Effects of Corruption on Growth, Investment, and Government Expenditure*. Washington, DC: International Monetary Fund.

Melnykovska, Inna, and Rainer Schweickert. 2008. "Who You Gonna Call? Oligarchic Clans as a Bottom-Up Force of Neighborhood Europeanization in Ukraine." In Working Papers of the Eastern Europe Institute No. 67. http://www.oei.fu-berlin.de/politik/publikationen/AP_67.pdf.

Mendelski, Martin. 2011. "Rule of Law Reforms in the Shadow of Clientelism: The Limits of the EU's Transformative Power in Romania." *Polish Sociological Review* 2 (174): 235–53.

Meon, Pierre-Guillaume, and Laurent Weill. 2010. "Is Corruption an Efficient Grease?" *World Development* 38 (3): 244–59.

Migdal, Joel. 1988. *Strong Societies and Weak States: State-Society Relations and State Capabilities in the Third World*. Princeton: Princeton University Press.

Mikhailovskaya, Inga. 1999. "Russia, The Procuracy and Its Problems." *East European Constitutional Review* 8 (1/2): 98–99.

Milam, William B. 2007. "Bangladesh and the Burdens of History." *Current History* 106 (699): 153–60.

Morton, F. L. 2006. "Judicial Appointments in Post-Charter Canada: A System in Transition." In *Appointing Judges in an Age of Judicial Power: Critical Perspectives from Around the World*, edited by Kate Malleson and Peter H. Russell, 56–79. Toronto: University of Toronto Press.

Moshin, Amena. 2013. "The Two Meanings of 'Bangladeshi.'" In *The Bangladesh Reader: History, Culture, Politics*, edited by Meghna Guhatharka and Willem van Schendel. Durham, NC: Duke University Press.

Motyl, Alexander. 1993. *Dilemmas of Independence: Ukraine after Totalitarianism*. New York: Council on Foreign Relations Press.

Moustafa, Tamir. 2008. "Law and Resistance in Authoritarian States: The Judicialization of Politics in Egypt." In *Rule by Law: The Politics of Courts in Authoritarian Regimes*, edited by Tom Ginsburg and Tamir Moustafa. Cambridge: Cambridge University Press.

Mudryi, Mari'an. 2008. "Tema 'Kolonial'nogo Statusu' Ukrainy U Pidruchnykah Z Is-torii." In *Shkil'na Istoria Ochyma Istorykiv-Naukovtsiv. Materialy Robochoii Narady Z Monitoringu Shkil'nykh Pidruchnyniv Istorii Ukrainy*, edited by Natalia Iakovenko, 86–102. Kyiv: Ukrains'kyi instytut natsionalnoi pamiati.

Myant, Martin, and Jan Drahokoupil. 2010. *Transition Economies: Political Economy in Russia, Eastern Europe and Central Asia*. Hoboken: Willey-Blackwell.

Ngo, Tak-Wing. 2008. "Rent-Seeking and Economic Governance in the Structural Nex-us of Corruption in China." *Crime, Law, Social Change* 49: 27–44.

Nickerson, Jack A., and Todd R. Zenger. 2002. "Being Efficiency Fickle: A Dynamic The-ory of Organizational Choice." *Organization Science* 13: 547–66.

North, Douglass C. 1990. *Institutions, Institutional Change and Economic Performance*. New York: Cambridge University Press.

North, Douglass C., John Joseph Wallis, and Barry R. Weingast. 2009. *Violence and Social Orders: A Conceptual Framework for Interpreting Recorded Human History*. New York: Cambridge *University* Press.

Obydenkova, Anastassia, and Alexander Libman. 2014. "Understanding the Foreign Pol-icy of Autocratic Actors: Ideology or Pragmatism? Russia and the Tymoshenko Trial as a Case Study." *Contemporary Politics* 20 (3): 347–64.

Obydenkova, Anastassia, and Alexander Libman. 2015a. *Autocratic and Democratic Ex-ternal Influences in Post-Soviet Eurasia*. Surrey and Burlington: Ashgate.

Obydenkova, Anastassia, and Alexander Libman. 2015b. *Causes and Consequences of De-mocratization: The Regions of Russia*. London and New York: Routledge.

OECD. 2005. *E-Government for Better Government*. Paris: OECD Publishing.

Offe, Claus. 1991. "Capitalism by Democratic Design? Democratic Theory Facing the Triple Transition in East Central Europe." *Social Research* 58 (4): 865–902.

Oleinik, Anton. 2003. "Konstitutsiya Rossiyskogo Rynka: Soglasie na Osnove Pessimiz-ma." *SotsIs* 9: 30–41.

Oleinik, Anton. 2005. "A Distrustful Economy: An Inquiry into Foundations of the Rus-sian Market." *Journal of Economic Issues* 39 (1): 53–74.

Orttung, Robert W. 2011. *What Hinders Reform in Ukraine?* Washington, DC: PONARS Eurasia Memo 166.

Osipian, Ararat, and Alexandr Osipian. 2012. "Regional Diversity and Divided Memory in Ukraine: Contested Past as Electoral Resource, 2004–2010." *East European Politics and Societies* 26 (3): 616–42.

Ostrow, Joel. 2000. *Comparing Post-Soviet Legislatures: A Theory of Institutional Design and Political Conflict*. Columbus: Ohio State University Press.

Owen, Roger. 2012. *The Rise and Fall of Arab Presidents for Life*. Cambridge, MA: Harvard University Press.

Paoli, Letizia. 2003. "Broken Bonds: Mafia and Politics in Sicily." In *Menace to Society: Political-Criminal Collaboration around the World,* edited by Roy Godson. London: Transaction.

Papava, Vladimir. 2006. "The Political Economy of Georgia's Rose Revolution." *Orbis* 50 (4): 657–67.

Parau, Cristina. 2012. "The Drive for Judicial Supremacy." In *Judicial Independence in Transition*, edited by Anja Seibert-Fohr. Heidelberg: Springer.

Peisakhin, Leonid. 2012. *In History's Shadow: Persistence of Identities and Contemporary Political Behavior. Working Paper 272.* Madrid: Instituto Juan March de Estúdios e Investigaciones.

Peshkopia, Ridvan. 2014. *Conditioning Democratization: Institutional Reforms and EU Membership Conditionality in Albania and Macedonia.* London: Anthem.

Peters, Stephen. 1975. "Ingredients of the Communist Takeover in Albania." In *Anatomy of Communist Takeovers*, edited by Thomas Taylor Hammond. New Haven: Yale University Press.

Piana, Daniela. 2010. *Judicial Accountabilities in New Europe: From Rule of Law to Quality of Justice.* Burlington, VT: Ashgate Publishing.

Pishchikova, Kateryna, and Olesia Ogryzko. 2014. *Civic Awakening: The Impact of Euromaidan on Ukraine's Policy and Society.* Madrid: FRIDE.

Pivovarsky, Alexander. 2003. "Ownership Concentration and Performance in Ukraine's Privatized Enterprises." *IMF Staff Papers* 50 (1): 10–42.

Plokhy, Serhii. 2014. *The Last Empire. The Final Days of the Soviet Union.* New York: Basic Books.

Polishchuk, Leonid. 2008. "Misuse of Institutions: Patterns and Causes." *Journal of Comparative Economic Studies* 4: 57–80.

Pop-Eleches, Grigore. 2008. *From Economic Crisis to Reform: IMF Programs in Latin America and Eastern Europe.* Princeton: Princeton University Press.

Pop-Eleches, Grigore, and Graeme Robertson. 2014. "After the Revolution." *Problems of Post-Communism* 61 (4): 3–22.

Popescu, Nicu. 2012. "Moldova's Fragile Pluralism." *Russian Politics and Law* 50 (4): 37–50.

Popova, Maria. 2010a. "Be Careful What You Wish For: A Cautionary Tale of Post-Communist Judicial Empowerment." *Demokratizatsiya: The Journal of Post-Soviet Democratization* 18 (1): 56–73.

Popova, Maria. 2010b. "Political Competition as an Obstacle to Judicial Independence: Evidence from Russia and Ukraine." *Comparative Political Studies* 43 (10): 1202–29.

Popova, Maria. 2012a. *Politicized Justice in Emerging Democracies: A Study of Courts in Russia and Ukraine.* Cambridge: Cambridge University Press.

Popova, Maria. 2012b. "Why Doesn't the Bulgarian Judiciary Prosecute Corruption?" *Problems of Post-Communism* 59 (5): 35–49.

Portnov, Andrij. 2010. *Uprazhneniia s istoriei po-ukrainski.* Moscow: Memorial.

Putnam, Robert. 1993. *Making Democracy Work.* Princeton: Princeton University Press.

Radnitz, Scott. 2010. *Weapons of the Wealthy: Predatory Regimes and Elite-Led Protests in Central Asia.* Ithaca, NY: Cornell University Press.

Ramseyer, J. Mark. 1994. "The Puzzling (In)dependence of Courts: A Comparative Approach." *Journal of Legal Studies* 23 (2): 721–47.

Reno, William. 2011. *Warfare in Independent Africa*. New York: Cambridge University Press.

Riabchuk, Mykola. 2012. "Ukraine's 'Muddling Through': National Identity and Postcommunist Transition." *Communist and Post-Communist Studies* 45 (3–4): 439–46.

Richardson, Tanya. 2004. "Disciplining the Past in Post-Soviet Ukraine: Memory and History in Schools and Families." In *Politics, Religion and Memory: The Past Meets the Present in Contemporary Europe*, edited by Frances Pine, Deema Kaneff, and Haldis Haukanes, 109–35. Munster: Lit Verlag.

Rigby, T. H. 1990. *Political Elites in the USSR: Central Leaders and Local Cadres from Lenin to Gorbachev*. Aldershot: Edward Elgar.

Rodgers, Peter. 2008. *Nation, Region and History in Post-Communist Transitions: Identity Politics in Ukraine, 1991–2006*. Stuttgart: Ibidem-Verlag.

Rodriguez, Diana, and Linda Ehrichs, eds. 2007. *Global Corruption Report 2007: Corruption in Judicial Systems*. Cambridge: Cambridge University Press.

Roeder, Philip. 2007. *Where Nation-States Come From: Institutional Change in the Age of Nationalism*. Princeton: Princeton University Press.

Roper, Steven D. 2002. "Are All Semipresidential Regimes the Same? A Comparison of Premier-Presidential Regimes." *Comparative Politics* 34 (3): 253–72.

Rothschild, Joseph. 1981. *Ethnopolitics: A Conceptual Framework*. New York: Columbia University Press.

Rouso, Alan, and Franklin Steves. 2006. "The Effectiveness of Anti-Corruption Programs: Preliminary Evidence from the Post-Communist Transition Countries." In *International Handbook on the Economics of Corruption*, edited by Susan Rose-Ackerman. Cheltenham: Edward Elgar.

Russell, Peter H., and David M. O'Brien. 2001. *Judicial Independence in the Age of Democracy: Critical Perspectives from around the World*. Charlottesville: University of Virginia Press.

Saxonberg, Steven. 2013. *Transitions and Non-Transitions from Communism: Regime Survival in China, Cuba, North Korea, and Vietnam*. New York: Cambridge University Press.

Schaffer, Howard B. 2002. "Back and Forth in Bangladesh." *Journal of Democracy* 13 (1): 77–83.

Schönfelder, Bruno. 2005. "Judicial Independence in Bulgaria: A Tale of Splendour and Misery." *Europe-Asia Studies* 57 (1): 61–92.

Scott, James C. 1972. *Comparative Political Corruption*. Upper Saddle River, NJ: Prentice-Hall.

Scott, James C. 1998. *Seeing Like a State: How Certain Schemes to Improve the Human Condition Have Failed*. New Haven: Yale University Press.

Sedelius, Thomas, and Olga Mashtaler. 2013. "Two Decades of Semi-Presidentialism: Issues of Intra-Executive Conflict in Central and Eastern Europe 1991–2011." *East European Politics* 29 (2): 109–34.

Sharafutdinova, Gulnaz. 2010. *Political Consequences of Crony Capitalism inside Russia.* South Bend, IN: Notre Dame University Press.

Shefter, Martin. 1993. *Political Parties and the State.* Princeton: Princeton University Press.

Shelley, Louise I. 2003. "Russia and Ukraine: Transition or Tragedy?" In *Menace to Society: Political-Criminal Collaboration around the World,* edited by Roy Godson. London: Transaction Books.

Shelley, Louise, Erik R. Scott, and Anthony Latta. 2007. *Organized Crime and Corruption in Georgia.* London: Routledge.

Shevel, Oxana. 2011a. "The Politics of Memory in a Divided Society. A Comparison of Post-Franco Spain and Post-Soviet Ukraine." *Slavic Review* 70 (1): 137–64.

Shevel, Oxana. 2011b. "Russian Nation-Building from Yeltsin to Medvedev: Ethnic, Civic, or Purposefully Ambiguous?" *Europe-Asia Studies* 63 (2): 179–202.

Shkandrij, Myroslav. 2015. *Ukrainian Nationalism: Politics, Ideology, and Literature, 1929–1956.* New Haven: Yale University Press.

Shleifer, Andrei, and Robert Vishny. 1993. "Corruption." *Quarterly Journal of Economics* 108 (3): 599–617.

Shugart, Matthew Soberg, and John M. Carey. 1992. *Presidents and Assemblies: Constitutional Design and Electoral Dynamics* New York: Cambridge University Press.

Silitski, Vitali. 2010. "Contagion Deterred: Preemptive Authoritarianism in the Former Soviet Union (the Case of Belarus)." In *Democracy and Authoritarianism in the Post-Communist World.*, edited by Valerie J. Bunce, Michael McFaul, and Kathryn Stoner-Weiss, 274–99. New York: Cambridge University Press.

Sissenich, Beate. 2006. "European Union Policies toward Accession Countries." In *Public Opinion, Party Competition, and the European Union in Post-Communist Europe,* edited by Robert Rohrschneider and Stephen Whitefield. New York: Palgrave Macmillan.

Skocpol, Theda. 1979. *States and Social Revolutions: A Comparative Analysis of France, Russia, and China.* Cambridge: Cambridge University Press.

Slater, Dan. 2010. *Ordering Power: Contentious Politics and Authoritarian Leviathans in Southeast Asia.* Cambridge: Cambridge University Press.

Smith, Steven S., and Thomas F. Remington. 2001. *The Politics of Institutional Choice: The Formation of the Russian State Duma.* Princeton: Princeton University Press.

Smithey, Shannon Ishiyama, and John Ishiyama. 2000. "Judicious Choices: Designing Courts in Post-Communist Politics." *Communist and Post-Communist Studies* 33 (2): 163–82.

Snyder, Richard, and James Mahoney. 1999. "The Missing Variable: Institutions and the Study of Regime Change." *Comparative Politics* 32 (1): 103–22.

Snyder, Timothy. 2010. *Bloodlands: Europe between Hitler and Stalin*. New York: Basic Books.

Sobhan, Salma. 2013. "Perceptions of Cultural Identity." In *The Bangladesh Reader: History, Culture, Politics*, edited by Meghna Guhatharka and Willem van Schendel. Durham, NC: Duke University Press.

Solnick, Steven L. 1998. *Stealing the State: Control and Collapse in Soviet Institutions*. Cambridge, MA: Harvard University Press.

Solomon Jr., Peter H. 2005. "Threats of Judicial Counterreform in Putin's Russia." *Demokratizatsiya: The Journal of Post-Soviet Democratization* 13 (3): 325–45.

Solomon Jr., Peter H. 2008. "Assessing the Courts in Russia: Parameters of Progress under Putin." *Demokratizatsiya: The Journal of Post-Soviet Democratization* 16 (1): 63–74.

Solomon Jr., Peter H. 2010. "Authoritarian Legality and Informal Practices: Judges, Lawyers and the State in Russia and China." *Communist and Post-Communist Studies* 43 (4): 351–62.

Solomon Jr., Peter H. 2012. "The Accountability of Judges in Post Communist States: From Bureaucratic to Professional Accountability." In *Judicial Independence in Transition*, edited by Anja Seibert-Fohr. Heidelberg: Springer.

Solomon, Peter H., and Todd S. Foglesong. 2000. *Courts and Transition in Russia: The Challenge of Judicial Reform*. Boulder, CO: Westview Press.

Spruyt, Hendrik. 1994. *The Sovereign State and Its Competitors*. Princeton: Princeton University Press.

Stephenson, Matthew C. 2003. "When the Devil Turns . . . : The Political Foundations of Independent Judicial Review." *Journal of Legal Studies* 32 (1): 59–89.

Stinchcombe, Arthur. 1999. "Ending Revolutions and Building New Governments." *Annual Review of Political Science* 2: 49–73.

Sullivan, John D., and Aleksandr Shkolnikov. 2004. *Combating Corruption: Private Sector Perspectives and Solutions*. Washington, DC: Center for International Private Enterprise.

Suny, Ronald. 1999/2000. "Provisional Stabilities: The Politics of Identities in Post-Soviet Eurasia." *International Security* 24 (3): 139–78.

Suri, Jeremi. 2007. *The Global Revolutions of 1968*. New York: Norton.

Szajkowski, B. 1994. "Albania." In *Political Parties of Eastern Europe, Russia, and the Successor States*, edited by B. Szajkowski. London: Longman.

Tiede, Wolfgang, and Oscar Rennalls. 2012. "Recent Developments in the Ukrainian Judicial System and the Impact of International and European Law." *East European Politics and Societies* 26 (1): 93–114.

Tilly, Charles, ed. 1975. *The Formation of National States in Western Europe*. Princeton: Princeton University Press.

Tilly, Charles. 1992. *Coercion, Capital, and European States, AD 990–1992*. Oxford: Blackwell.

Tolley, Michael C. 2006. "Legal Controversies over Federal Judicial Selection in the United States: Breaking the Cycle of Obstruction and Retribution over Judicial Appointments." In *Appointing Judges in an Age of Judicial Power: Critical Perspectives from Around the World*, edited by Kate Malleson and Peter H. Russell, 80–102. Toronto: University of Toronto Press.

Tooze, Adam. 2007. *Wages of Destruction: The Making and Breaking of the Nazi Economy*. New York: Viking.

Torbakov, Igor. 2011. "History, Memory, and National Identity." *Demokratizatsiya: The Journal of Post-Soviet Democratization* 19 (3): 209–32.

Torfinn, Harding, and Beata S. Javorcik. 2011. "Roll Out the Red Carpet and They Will Come: Investment Promotion and FDI Inflows." *Economic Journal* 121 (557): 1445–76.

Treisman, Daniel. 2000. "The Causes of Corruption: A Cross-National Study." *Journal of Public Economics* 76: 399–457.

Treisman, Daniel. 2007. "What Have We Learned about the Causes of Corruption from Ten Years of Cross-National Empirical Research?" *Annual Review of Political Science* 10: 211–44.

Trochev, Alexei. 2009. "All Appeals Lead to Strasbourg? Unpacking the Impact of the European Court of Human Rights on Russia." *Demokratizatsiya: The Journal of Post-Soviet Democratization* 17 (2): 145–78.

Trochev, Alexei. 2010. "Meddling with Justice: Competitive Politics, Impunity, and Distrusted Courts in Post-Orange Ukraine." *Demokratizatsiya: The Journal of Post-Soviet Democratization* 18 (2): 122–47.

Trochev, Alexei. 2012a. "Can Weak States Have Strong Courts? Evidence from Russia." In *Legitimacy, Legal Development and Change: Law and Modernization Reconsidered*, edited by David Linnan. Burlington, VT: Ashgate Publishing.

Trochev, Alexei. 2012b. "Suing Russia at Home." *Problems of Post-Communism* 59 (5): 18–34.

Trochev, Alexei. 2013. "Fragmentation? Defection? Legitimacy? Explaining Judicial Roles in Post-Communist 'Colored Revolutions'." In *Consequential Courts: Judicial Roles in Global Perspective*, edited by Diana Kapiszewski, Gordon Silverstein, and Robert A. Kagan. Cambridge: Cambridge University Press.

Tucker, Joshua A., and Grigore Pop-Eleches. 2012. "Post-Communist Legacies and Political Behavior and Attitudes." *Demokratizatsiya: The Journal of Post-Soviet Democratization* 20 (2): 157–66.

Ukrains'kyi instytut natsional'noi pamiati. 2009. *Kontseptsiia ta prohramy vykladannia istorii Ukrainy v shkoli (proekt)*. Kyiv: Stylos.

United Nations. 2008. *United Nations e-Government Survey 2008: From e-Government to Connected Governance*. New York: United Nations.

Urban, Michael. 1989. *An Algebra of Soviet Power: Elite Circulation in the Belorussian Republic, 1966–86*. New York: Cambridge University Press.

Vachudova, Milada. 2005. *Europe Undivided: Democracy, Leverage and Integration after Communism*. Oxford: Oxford University Press.

Valls-Montes, Raffel. 2007. "The Spanish Civil War and the Franco Dictatorship: The Challenge of Representing a Conflictive Past in Secondary Schools." In *Teaching the Violent Past: History Education and Reconciliation*, edited by Elizabeth A. Cole, 155–74. Lanham: Rowman and Littlefield.

Vickers, Miranda. 2006. *The Albanians: A Modern History*. London: I. B. Taurus.

Vickers, Miranda, and James Pettifer. 2000. *Albania: From Anarchy to a Balkan Identity*. New York: NYU Press.

Voigt, Stefan. 2013. "How (Not) to Measure Institutions." *Journal of Institutional Economics* 9 (1): 1–26.

Volkov, Vadim. 2002. *Violent Entrepreneurs: The Use of Force in the Making of Russian Capitalism*. Ithaca, NY: Cornell University Press.

von Zon, Hans. 2007. "The Rise of Conglomerates in Ukraine: The Donetsk Case." In *Big Business and Economic Development: Conglomerates and Economic Groups in Developing Countries and Transition Economies under Globalization*, edited by Alex E. Fernandez Jilberto and Barbara Hogenboom. London: Routledge.

Wade, Robert. 2003. *Governing the Market: Economic Theory and the Role of Government in East Asian Industrialization*. Princeton: Princeton University Press.

Wallerstein, Immanuel. 2011 [1974]. *The Modern World-System. Volume I: Capitalist Agriculture and the Origins of the European World-Economy in the Sixteenth Century*. Berkeley: University of California Press.

Wang, Xiaoying. 2002. "The Post-Communist Personality: The Spectre of China's Capitalist Market Reforms." *China Journal* 47: 1–17.

Warner, Carolyn. 2001. "Mass Clientelism and Parties in France and Italy." In *Clientelism, Interests, and Representation: The European Experience in Comparative Perspective*, edited by Simona Piattoni. Cambridge: Cambridge University Press.

Way, Lucan A. 2002. "Pluralism by Default in Moldova." *Journal of Democracy* 13 (4): 127–41.

Way, Lucan. 2005. "Rapacious Individualism and Political Competition in Ukraine, 1992–2004." *Communist and Post-Communist Studies* 38 (2): 191–205.

Way, Lucan. 2011. "National Identity and Authoritarianism: Belarus and Ukraine Compared." In *Social Mobilization in Ukraine*, edited by Paul D'Anieri. Washington, DC: Woodrow Wilson Center Press.

Way, Lucan. 2012. "The Sources of Authoritarian Control after the Cold War: East Africa and the Former Soviet Union." *Post-Soviet Affairs* 28 (4): 424–48.

Way, Lucan. 2015. *Pluralism by Default: Weak Autocrats and the Rise of Competitive Politics*. Baltimore, MD: Johns Hopkins University Press.

White, Stephen, Richard Sakwa, and Henry E. Hale, eds. 2010. *Developments in Russian Politics 7*. Durham, NC: Duke University Press.

Wilson, Andrew. 2000. *The Ukrainians. Unexpected Nation.* New Haven: Yale University Press.

Wilson, Andrew. 2005. *Virtual Politics: Faking Democracy in the Post-Soviet World.* New Haven: Yale University Press.

Wilson, Sophia. 2012. "Courts, Police, and Journalists." *Problems of Post-Communism* 59 (5): 6–17.

Wolczuk, Kateryna. 2001. *The Moulding of Ukraine: The Constitutional Politics of State Formation.* Budapest: Central European Press.

Wolf, Eric. 1999 (ca.1969). *Peasant Wars of the Twentieth Century.* Norman: University of Oklahoma Press.

Wong, R. Bin. 2000. *China Transformed: Historical Change and the Limits of European Experience.* Ithaca, NY: Cornell University Press.

Woodruff, David. 1999. *Money Unmade: Barter and the Fate of Russian Capitalism.* Ithaca, NY: Cornell University Press.

World Bank. 2009. *Information and Communications for Development 2009: Extending Reach and Increasing Impact.* Washington, DC: World Bank.

World Bank. 2012. *Fighting Corruption in Public Services: Chronicling Georgia's Reforms.* Washington, DC: World Bank.

World Bank. 2013. "Worldwide Governance Indicators."

Zakharchenko, Tanya. 2013. "Polyphonic Dichotomies: Memory and Identity in Today's Ukraine." *Demokratizatsiya: The Journal of Post-Soviet Democratization* 21 (2): 241–69.

Zhurzhenko, Tatiana. 2014. "A Divided Nation? Reconsidering the Role of Identity Politics in the Ukraine Crisis." *Die Friedens-Warte* 89 (1/2): 249–67.

Zielonka, Jan. 2007. "The Quality of Democracy after Joining the European Union." *East European Politics and Societies* 21 (1): 162–80.

Zubok, Vladislav. 2007. *A Failed Empire: The Soviet Union in Cold War from Stalin to Gorbachev.* Chapel Hill: University of North Carolina Press.

Zweynert, Joachim, and Nils Goldschmied. 2006. "The Two Transitions in Central and Eastern Europe as Processes of Institutional Transplantation." *Journal of Economic Issues* 40: 895–918.

Index

Bat'kivshchyna (Fatherland), 70, 71, 75
BEEPS, *see* Business Environment and
Enterprise Performance Survey
Beissinger, Mark R., 43, 53
Beknazarov, Azimbek, 49
Belarus: corruption in, 259; patronal
presidentialism, 133; Slavic unity narrative,
29, 33. *See also* Lukashenka, Aliaksandr
Berisha, Sali, 48
Bernhard, Michael, 23, 24–26, 29
Blue Ribbon Analytical and Advisory Center,
230
Bogolyubov, Gennadiy, 69, 185–86
Boyko, Yuriy, 185
Bragin, Akhat, 193, 194
Brezhnev, Leonid, 209, 210, 212
Bribery, 62, 65, 81, 85–86, 94. *See also*
Corruption
Bukharin, Nikolai, 212
Bulgaria: corruption, 166, 168–69;
democratic transition, 136; divided-
executive system, 136; EU membership,
136, 173, 255; judicial system, 166, 168–69,
173; patronalism, 126
Bumin, Kirill M., 168
Bunce, Valerie, 7
Bureaucrats, *see* Civil service
Business Environment and Enterprise
Performance Survey (BEEPS): cluster
analysis using, 249–50, 251–52, 257–59;
corruption as business barrier, 89 (fig.),
90 (fig.), 91 (fig.); corruption perceptions,
85–87, 86 (fig.), 87 (fig.), 88, 88 (fig.), 259;
datasets, 259; institutional quality, 224,
247–48, 249 (table)
Businesses: corporate governance, 81, 228,
240, 241, 243; corruption effects on, 92
(fig.), 92–93, 101; corrupt practices, 81,
85–87, 86 (fig.), 88 (fig.), 275; economic
reforms supported by, 260–61; external
environment, 81; internal structure, 81;
large, 88, 88 (fig.), 89–91, 90 (fig.), 101,
225, 275; ombudsman institution, 240;
shadow economy, 182, 183, 184, 199, 226;
state-owned, 69, 227, 239; support of EU

membership, 256. *See also* Privatizations;
Small- and medium-sized enterprises

Campaign finance laws, 73–74, 75–76, 238. *See
also* Elections; Political parties
Canada, judicial appointments, 151
Capital cities, corruption in, 86–87, 87 (fig.).
See also Kyiv
Capitalism, *see* Developmental states; World-
systems theory
CCP, *see* Chinese Communist Party
Central bank, Ukrainian, 114, 225, 227, 240
Chernovets'kyi, Leonid, 75
China: comparison to Ukraine, 204, 207;
as developmental state, 204, 213, 274;
economic development, 204, 207, 211–12,
213; Tiananmen movement, 211, 212, 213
Chinese Communist Party (CCP), 212, 213
Chirac, Jacques, 61
Chornovil, Vyacheslav, 189
Civil service: anticorruption efforts,
76–77, 96–97, 98, 239, 262, 273; corruption
in, 65, 66, 68, 81, 238, 257; informal
practices, 246, 257; patronage in, 72, 238;
procurement procedures, 100, 239, 242;
professionalization, 76–77; quality of,
83–85, 85 (table); reforms in Georgia,
96–97; salaries, 238. *See also* E-government;
Regulatory capture
Civil society: anticorruption efforts,
77, 97, 100, 236, 262; as constraint on
authoritarianism, 43, 44; freedom of
expression, 96; Orange Revolution and,
7–8, 12; protests, 155; role in reform, 12–13,
235–36, 272; in Soviet period, 211; volunteer
groups supporting military, 197; weakness,
7–8, 156. *See also* Euromaidan revolution
Clans: clientelist networks, 110–11, 185; gas
industry, 185; in Kyrgyzstan, 49; members
of parliament, 185; under patronal
presidentialism, 110–11; persistence after
Euromaidan protests, 118; traditional,
8; in Ukraine, xi–xii, 185–86; violence,
191; of Yanukovych, 117, 190, 196. *See also*
Clientelism; Donetsk clan; Oligarchs